EARLY CHILDHOOD EDUCATION

SECOND EDITION

Edited by
Barry Persky
Leonard H. Golubchick

UNIVERSITY
PRESS OF
AMERICA

Lanham • New York • London

The Doctorate Association
of New York Educators, Inc.

Copyright © 1991 by
University Press of America®, Inc.
4720 Boston Way
Lanham, Maryland 20706

3 Henrietta Street
London WC2E 8LU England

Co-published by arrangement with
The Doctorate Association of New York Educators, Inc.

Library of Congress Cataloging-in-Publication Data

Early childhood education / edited by Barry Persky,
Leonard H. Golubchick.—2nd ed.
p.   cm.
1. Early childhood education—United States.
2. Day care centers—United States.
I. Golubchick, Leonard H.   II. Persky, Barry.
LB1139.25.E25   1991   372.21'0973—dc20   91-13097 CIP

ISBN 0–8191–8296–6 (pbk. : alk. paper)

 ™ The paper used in this publication meets the minimum requirements of
American National Standard for Information Sciences—Permanence
of Paper for Printed Library Materials, ANSI Z39.48–1984.

Table of Contents

Acknowledgement

Chapter 1 "The Case for Public School Sponsorship of Early Childhood Education Revisited." Reprinted by Permission: *Early Schooling: The National Debate* ed. Sharon L. Kagan and Edward Zigler. Yale University Press, 1987, pp. 45–64.

Chapter 2 "Policy Options for Preschool Children." Reprinted by Permission: *Phi Delta Kappan,* March 1987, 68, pp. 524–529.

Chapter 3 "Early Care and Education: Beyond the Schoolhouse Doors." Reprinted by Permission: *Phi Delta Kappan,* October, 1989, pp. 107–112.

Chapter 4 "How Best to Protect Children from Inappropriate School Expectations, Practices, and Policies." Reprinted by Permission: *Young Children,* March, 1989, pp. 14–24.

Chapter 5 "The Impact of Policies for Handicapped Children on Future Early Education Policy." Reprinted by Permission: *Phi Delta Kappan,* October, 1989, pp. 121–124.

Chapter 7 "Origins of Early Childhood Education." Reprinted by Permission: *Early Childhood Education* eds. Barry Persky and Leonard Golubchick. New Jersey: Avery Publishing, 1977, pp. 58–62.

Chapter 8 "Developmentally Appropriate Practice: Philosophical and Practical Implications." Reprinted by Permission: *Phi Delta Kappan,* October, 1989, pp. 113–117.

Chapter 9 "Day Care and Public Schools—Natural Allies, Natural Enemies." Reprinted by Permission: *Educational Leadership,* February, 1986, 43, 5, pp. 34–39.

Chapter 10 "Uses and Abuses of Developmental Screening and School Readiness Testing." Reprinted by Permission: Young Children, January, 1987, pp. 4–6, 68–73.

Chapter 19 "Flunking Kindergarten: Escalating Curriculum leaves Many Behind." Reprinted by Permission: *American Education,* Summer, 1988, pp. 34–39.

Chapter 20 " 'Behind' Before They Start? Deciding How to Deal With the Risk of Kindergarten Failure." Reprinted by Permission: *Young Children,* March, 1988, 44, 3, pp. 5–12.

Chapter 21 "Educating Language—Minority Children: Challenges and Opportunities." Reprinted by Permission: *Phi Delta Kappan,* October, 1989, 71, 2, pp. 118–120.

Chapter 23   "Bringing The 'Moral' Back In." Reprinted by Permission: *NEA Today,* January, 1989, 7, 6, pp. 54–59.

Chapter 30   "Reading and Early Childhood Education: The Critical Issues." Reprinted by Permission: *Principal,* May, 1987, 66, 5, pp. 6–9. (Copyright 1987, National Association of Elementary School Principals. See rights reserved.)

Chapter 31   "Emergent Literacy: How Young Children Learn to Read." Reprinted by Permission: *Educational Leadership,* March, 1990, pp. 18–23.

Chapter 34   "Theoretical Framework for Preschool Science Experiences." Reprinted by Permission: *Young Children,* January, 1987, pp. 34–40.

Chapter 37   "History is for Children." Reprinted by Permission: *American Education,* Winter, 1989, 13, 4, pp. 34–39.

Preface

Early childhood education and child care are now widely perceived to be among the central social needs of the nation. The ever-growing number of working mothers, the proven value of early childhood training to intellectual development, and the scandelous conditions in profit-making day-care operations provide evidence that this perception is well founded. Unfortunately, attempts since 1970 to enact major federal legislation which would establish a coordinated system of early childhood and family services have been unsuccessful, and the United States is still without a comprehensive program for very young children.

The need for child-care facilities and early childhood education programs now far outdistances their unavailability. Limited numbers of children, usually those of welfare mothers or from otherwise impoverished backgrounds, have access to federally-sponsored child-care programs. The large majority of children of the working poor and those of middle-class parents do not. The federal government spends over 1 billion dollars a year in direct funds for child-care related services administrated by at least 60 different federal agencies. The result is a confusing maze of services, which are fragmented and all too often overlapping. In many instances, even federally funded child-care programs fail to meet minimal federal standards and almost all are purely custodial in nature. Consequently many eligible people are reluctant to place their children in such facilities. The present federal expenditure is too much to waste as we are now doing, but not enough to meet the actual need.

There are few affordable alternatives to quality care. Currently, the most frequently used type of child-care is in-home with a relative, sibling, or "baby-sitter" providing the care. Following this in frequency of usage are family day-care homes, of which only five percent are licensed. Although most day-care centers are licensed, licensing standards are minimal and enforcement of regulations is almost non-existent.

We face a critical situation. With rapidly increasing numbers of working mothers and single-parent families, expansion of early childhood services becomes a necessity.

To cite just one example of need, there are almost seven million children under the age of six whose mothers work. Yet, the Child Welfare League of America estimates that there are only 4.3 million spaces available in child-care facilities and of these, some 77 percent are of such inferior quality they should not be used. In too many cases, personnel are untrained and transient; safety and health are neglected; and little attention, if any, is given to children's development. This situation is inevitable as long as the welfare of children remains a low priority. Quality programs naturally cost a great deal more than custodial care.

In addition to the problems faced by working parents in finding adequate child-care, we must take into consideration the needs of the children themselves. Many parents, working and non-working alike, would like to give their children the advantage of developmental early childhood education programs, but are unable to find or afford them. Numerous research studies in the United States and abroad have concluded that the first six years of a child's life are crucial in determining the nature of future development. Harvard researcher Burton White, for example, believes that a child's learning patterns are developing as early as ten months of age. Others, like J. McVicker Hunt, tell us that early experience may be even more important for perceptual, cognitive, and intellectual functions than for emotional functions. And research leaves little doubt about the importance of social, emotional and physical development during these years.

Without parent education programs and comprehensive early childhood services, deficiencies in children's social, emotional, physical and intellectual growth often go undetected and untreated. With each day and year of delay, the problem becomes more and more difficult to correct.

Because of this, the American Federation of Teachers and the Doctorate Association of New York Educators believe that we need comprehensive early childhood services, which would be universally accessible on a voluntary basis, regardless of social or economic status. To achieve this goal, the AFT supports federal legislation which would fund coordinated services for very young children, administered by the public schools, provided they are willing and able to do so. Existing programs which meet appropriate standards probably would continue, but under the administration of the local education agency. The rationale for this position is included in articles within the text.

It should be emphasized, however, that although this book focuses on the role of the public schools and professional personnel in early childhood education, alternative viewpoints are also offered.

The Doctorate Association of New York Educators, in cooperation with the AFT, carefully chose the articles in this book to give the reader a broad comprehensive overview of the issues surrounding early childhood education. These include discussions of the current debate over what constitutes appropriate services, the past history of early childhood programs, classroom theory and techniques, approaches to meeting special needs, and more. The book is divided into five sections: 1. National & Historical Perspectives; 2. Philosophical & Theoretical Issues; 3. Critical Issues; 4. Exceptional Children; 5. Curriculum.

Special thanks to all the members of the DANYE Editorial Review Board for their efforts in preparing this anthology. We extend special thanks also to Maria Elrose and Mary Ann Zadubara for their technical and editorial assistance, as well as to Judith Golubchick, Elaine Morenberg, and Regina Persky for their editorial comments. It is the belief of all of us that *Early Childhood Education* will be a valuable tool to students at the undergraduate and graduate levels and all others concerned with meeting the developmental needs of young children.

Barry S. Persky
Leonard H. Golubchick
EDITORS

Barbara Ruth Peltzman
CHAIR—EDITORIAL BOARD

SECTION 1

National and Historical Perspectives

Introduction

If piety is to take root in any man's heart, it must be engrafted while he is still young; if we wish any one to be virtuous we must train him in early youth; if we wish him to make great progress in the pursuit of wisdom, we must direct his faculties towards it in infancy, when desire burns, when thought is swift, and when memory is tenacious.

The words of John Amos Comenius, a seventeenth century Moravian bishop, are as timely today as they were when Comenius articulated his thoughts. Currently, throughout our nation, there is a demand for quality early childhood education as a sound basis for improving all our educational systems, thus ensuring that our youth is prepared to compete and meet the challenges of the twenty-first century.

Resurgence of interest in early childhood education can be partially attributed to the findings of the long term benefits of quality programming in the High Scope Educational Research Foundation's Perry Preschool Program which encouraged the development of preschool programs across the country. The Perry Preschool results validated years of work and advocacy for many early childhood educators. In New York City, Project Giant Step became an initiative in 1986 which expanded the existing prekindergarten programs provided by the State.

Child care issues are the subject of debate in Congress. The ever increasing number of mothers entering the work force has increased concerns regarding early childhood education. However, there is no debate with regard to the benefits to children who have participated in quality early childhood programs. The research in this area is sound.

The proven effectiveness of quality early schooling challenges the public schools to meet the needs of families by improving and expanding quality early childhood programs and by providing continuity of these programs throughout the early grades and beyond. Public schools must meet this challenge in a time of great social, economic, and environmental stress which include factors such as: substance abuse, inadequate prenatal care, homelessness, the breakdown of public infrastructures, and revenue decline.

The challenge of providing educational services to our young children can and will be met by our public schools. However, success depends on the collaborative efforts of many people sharing in the decisions that formulate policy, and working together to implement these policies in an effective way. My proposal of School-Based Management/Shared-Decision Making is a vehicle which will help address these very issues.

Among the conditions that must exist in order to ensure that all efforts are concentrated and focused to improve early childhood education are:

- Parents, staff and community must unite at the school level to determine the program needs and services of their school/community.
- The school/community must share an early childhood philosophy which permeates all activities. The philosophy should reflect research-based, developmentally appropriate practices and reflect the cultural diversity of the students.
- Practitioners, educators, and researchers in the area of early childhood must support local school efforts.
- Programs must provide children with opportunities to experience daily success.
- Children whose home language is other than English must be provided with opportunities to learn in their first language while they acquire the English language.
- A multi-cultural orientation must be infused into all aspects of the school program in order to share and maintain the rich cultural diversity of our school populations.
- Opportunities must be provided for on-going staff training.
- Community health and social services must be enlisted to ensure comprehensive services to children.
- Resources and training must be provided to ensure continuity of quality programs throughout the grades.

Quality early childhood programs offer our students the opportunities to succeed throughout their school careers. These programs provide the foundation for dropout prevention. It is our responsibility as educators to take the leadership in ensuring that early childhood education becomes a national priority. We can do no less than serve as informed advocates for our children.

Joseph A. Fernandez
Chancellor
New York City Public Schools

CHAPTER 1

The Case for Public School Sponsorship of Early Childhood Education Revisited

Early childhood education has had a long and bumpy history in the United States, much of it spent debating whether it would undermine the "natural" order of mothers' staying at home to care for their young children. The idea that early childhood education is unnatural or un-American has not entirely died, but reality has overtaken ideology. Now that the majority of American mothers of preschool children work outside the home, it has become harder for policymakers to be indifferent to the lack of affordable, quality child care available to families. It is therefore not surprising that early childhood education is making a comeback as a national issue.

Early childhood education is also enjoying a new responsibility. The idea that the early childhood years have a profound impact on human development is an ancient one, but modern social science findings have confirmed that young children who are deliberately exposed to stimulating experiences fare better than children who are not. Although many still would prefer that these experiences take place at home under the loving tutelage of a mother, the accumulating research findings about the positive effects of educationally sound preschool programs have dissipated much of the fear of institutional child care. The latest and most dramatic evidence of the benefits of such programs, particularly for disadvantaged youngsters, comes from the Perry Preschool Project. Not only has this news heartened child advocates, it also has broadened the potential constituency for early childhood education. Usually identified only with the needs of working mothers and the interests of educators, early childhood education now also engages policymakers and citizens concerned about the costs and consequences of the large numbers of disadvantaged children who grow up to become liabilities to themselves and to society.

Early childhood education ought, therefore, to be a political winner. It bridges the interests of parents from all economic levels, of married and single mothers, of mothers who work and those who need or want to work. It has implications for non-parents and for the elderly who also bear the costs if other people's children grow up to become dependent or deviant adults. It obviously touches education, welfare, health, and other social service professionals. Slowly but steadily, and with a recent push

5

from the National Governors' Association, the political community is indeed rousing itself to the issue of early childhood education. Not since the 1960s has the potential for developing a coherent and caring policy toward preschoolers seemed so bright.

Yet despite the signs of popular and political support for early childhood education, it is not at all clear that a consensus surrounds the issue. What exactly do we mean by early childhood education? The dominant image now comes from the Perry Preschool Project, a high-quality, high-cost educational program for disadvantaged youngsters in a public school setting. But the more usual model of early childhood education is a low-quality, low-cost proprietary program. Similarly, the rhetoric of some policymakers focuses on the custodial needs of working parents, which implies full-day, year-round child-care programs. Yet the rhetoric of others concerns the developmental needs of youngsters, which denotes pre-school programs of half a school day or less. Some conceptualize early childhood education as an academic readiness program. Others prefer a whole-child approach that involves attending to the social, emotional, cognitive, and health needs of preschoolers and often includes a parent education component. Differences of opinion (and cost) also exist over whether programs should be compulsory, universally available, or targeted only to the poor and disadvantaged.

Less philosophically complex, but even more controversial than questions about the nature and purpose of early childhood education, is the issue of sponsorship. Historically, the battles over turf have been between the public schools and community-based organizations, between elementary educators and early childhood educators. The transcendent interest in restoring early childhood education to the national agenda has submerged these differences, but the attacks on public schools heard at the 1986 annual meeting of the National Association for the Education of Young Children suggested that a renewal of old antagonisms is not out of the question.

Some of these differences over early childhood education may not be as intractable as they appear or as they once seemed. Ignoring them, however, or acting as if all early childhood education programs or sponsorship arrangements are equal surely will do nothing to reconcile these differences. Indeed, the failure to revisit these issues may mean that in the name of developing a coherent and caring policy toward young children and promoting equity, policymakers will instead be further institutionalizing our present patchwork of policy and exacerbating inequalities. The challenge we now face is to expand both the quantity and the quality of early childhood education. That means insisting on standards while avoiding standardization. It involves promoting flexibility while ending fragmentation. And it means equalizing the opportunity for disadvantaged youngsters to be integrated into the mainstream of American life without further segregating them in poverty programs.

The Sources of Demand and
The Failure of Supply

Recent arguments on behalf of expanding early childhood education are fueled by a number of sources, but chief among them is the influx of mothers of preschoolage children into the labor force. In 1975, 38.8 percent of mothers with children under the age of six were employed. Five years later, the proportion had climbed to 46.8 percent. In the early 1980s, the 50 percent mark was reached, and by 1986 it was 54.4 percent. Almost 60 percent of women with children between the ages of three and five are now in the labor force (U.S. Bureau of Labor Statistics, 1986; Grubb, 1986).

The rise in the proportion of working mothers cannot be explained solely by the increase in single mothers. In fact, whether because of women's liberation or, more demonstrably, the need for a second income, the increase in labor force participation of married mothers of pre-schoolers has been particularly dramatic. In 1948, the proportion of married mothers who worked outside the home was 13 percent. By 1965, the figure had almost doubled to 23 percent, reaching 37 percent a decade later. In 1986, it was 54 percent, with no sign of abating (U.S. Bureau of Labor Statistics, 1986; Grubb, 1986).

Not surprisingly, the proportion of young children enrolled in child-care programs has also increased. Although it is difficult to sort out participation by type of program, we know that between 1970 and 1983, the enrollment rate of three- and four-year-olds in some kind of program increased from 21 to 38 percent. Seven out of ten children of working mothers are cared for in their own homes or in the homes of others. Two out of five children are minded by relatives. Fifteen percent are in day-care centers, and nearly one out of ten accompanies the mother to work (Hechinger, 1986).

Although what falls under the category of preschool education varies from study to study, it is clear that preschool attendance is highly associated with family income. The preschool enrollment rate for families earning below twenty thousand dollars a year is 46 percent and drops to 29 percent for families with annual incomes below ten thousand dollars. In sharp contrast, the preschool enrollment rate for families earning over twenty thousand dollars annually is 64 percent. Viewed from the perspective of parents' educational attainment, the unequal access to preschool is also apparent. Whereas the enrollment rate for three- and four-year-old children of elementary school dropouts was 23 percent, it was 58 percent for children of college graduates (Hechinger, 1986; Schweinhart & Koshel, 1986).

Not only is the supply of child care inadequate and strongly associated with ability to pay, but the quality of many programs fails to live up to the rhetoric about our devotion to children. Many experts have warned about the detrimental effects of substandard child care. Mere custodial care, even in well-maintained facilities, does not provide a child with the experiences necessary for sound cognitive, social, and emotional development. As suggested by a recent headline "Fatal Fire Renews Debate on Child Care Standards" (Education Week, Dec. 3, 1986), when facilities and staffing quality or ratios do not meet even minimal standards, the problem may go beyond the quality of life to life itself. As late as 1986, child advocates were still pressing not only for the enforcement of the Federal Interagency Day Care Requirements but also for a more adequate set of standards.

The low quality custodial model of early childhood "education" owes its existence in no small part to the ill-repute with which the very people child care was supposed to help were regarded for much of American history: working mothers. Although women's participation in the labor force has been steadily increasing since the turn of the century, it was not until recently, when the proportion of mothers who worked outside the home approached 50 percent, that this condition was viewed as something other than a symptom of pathology. To be sure, concern for the welfare of poor children of working mothers was certainly evident from the beginning of American history. But compassion could not overcome the prejudices against these children's poverty-stricken families nor the prevailing view that women, no matter how desperate their circumstances, ought not to put paid work over their child-rearing responsibilities. As a result, the few model programs earlier in this century that accounted for both a child's developmental and custodial needs either disappeared or degenerated into solely custodial programs branded by the perceived deficits of working mothers.

While mothers working and therefore institutional child care were viewed as a perversion of a healthy mother-child relationship, the obverse situation also came to be regarded as true. If the mother-child relationship was "abnormal" for reasons either of poverty or of family breakdown, then institutional child care could be an antidote to "bad" mothers; it could even be a means of allowing poor mothers to get out of the house and work. But whether mothers were damned if they worked or damned if they didn't work, the legacy of child-care programs as essentially babysitting operations remained the same. Only twice, during the Great Depression and during World War II, was the stigma attached to most working mothers lifted and an effort made, at the federal level, to provide educationally sound care for their children. The effort was feeble indeed. At the end of each crisis, the scales again tilted toward mere custodianship.

The custodial model was next elaborated as part of the War on Poverty during the 1960s. Child care again became a part of federal policy, but as a provision of welfare legislation it was again primarily intended to enable poor mothers to receive training or get work, not to provide for the educational needs of their youngsters. The Federal Interagency Day Care Requirements that regulated the policy did mandate an educational component to the programs but this was honored more in the breach than in the promise.

Throughout the 1960s, federal spending for children increased significantly. Yet, with the exception of Head Start, federal policy reinforced a by-then unequal system of services in which the poor received low-cost, low quality custodial day care, the affluent patronized private nursery schools, and those families who fell in neither category were left to fend for themselves. There is no evidence to suggest that this pattern has changed (Grubb, 1986).

In contrast to the traditional custodial model of early childhood programs is the educational or developmental model most commonly associated with good preschools but also characteristic of good day care.[1] Indeed, if the major demographic influence on the revival of interest in early childhood education has been the increased labor force participation of mothers of young children, then another significant influence has been the steadily accumulating research findings about the benefits of educationally sound preschool programs.

The notion that the preschool years are crucial to a child's emotional and intellectual development is, of course not novel. Even before the research confirming this perception was available, and as early as the 1920s, some middle-class and affluent families availed their children of the enriching experiences offered by nursery schools. Initially open only part time, nursery schools steadily increased their hours of operations as even their clientele began to work outside the home. Although they became more similar to custodial child-care programs in hours of operation, however, nursery schools' affluent clientele and quality programs meant that they escaped the stigma attached to day care (Grubb, 1986).

1. Although my characterization of the custodial model of early childhood education is clearly prejorative, it should in no way be construed to denigrate either the function of custodianship or day-care programs in a generic sense. Clearly, meeting a child's custodial needs is very important. Equally clearly, many day-care programs offer developmentally sound activities, while many preschools do not. But although the difference between day-care and preschool programs is frequently only nominal, the distinction between the custodial and developmental models is historical

and real. By custodial model, then, I mean low-quality programs that are no more and sometimes less than mere baby-sitting operations, indifferent to or ignorant of the unique developmental needs of preschoolers.

Researchers confirmed what nursery school advocates and wise mothers involved in full-time child rearing already knew. Within the last thirty years, the work of educators like Jean Piaget and Benjamin Bloom supported the idea that young children should have available to them a variety of guided, stimulating experiences and that such early learning was implicated in children's subsequent development.

Although this line of thinking did not generally produce a reexamination of the traditional custodial model of child care, it did shape Head Start, one of the major programs of the War on Poverty in the 1960s. The inauguration of Head Start with the passage of the Economic Opportunity Act of 1964 marked the beginning of a federal recognition that child-care services for poor children, like those for the more affluent, should have educational content.

Over the past two decades, the primary source of governmental support of early childhood programs has been federal, with Head Start the flagship of this effort. Much research has been devoted to Head Start, and most of it has confirmed the expectations of the program's supporters. Yet despite the largely positive research findings about the effects of Head Start, the political shifts and budgetary vicissitudes afflicting identifiable poverty programs have meant that Head Start now serves a mere 24 percent (and probably less) of the three- and four-year-olds living in poverty (Schweinhart & Koshel, 1986).

The success of Head Start spurted a number of other experiments offering disadvantaged youngsters educationally sound preschool programs. The results thus far have been encouraging, some of them even electrifying. For example, a 1985 study of 175 disadvantaged children conducted by the University of North Carolina concluded that good preschools can raise IQs by as much as 15 points and significantly improve school achievement in later grades. Other studies also confirm that the educational model of preschool programs can help boost children's intellectual and social development (for reviews, see Berrueta-Clement, Schweinhart, Barnett, Epstein & Weikart, 1986, pp. 30–36, Schweinhart & Koshel, 1986, pp. 6–7).

Many of the preschool programs represented by these studies have had their day in the sun. None, however, has captured as much political attention as the High/Scope Educational Research Foundation's Perry Preschool Program study (Berrueta-Clement et al., 1986).

Although a few studies have analyzed the long-term results of early childhood education programs, the Perry Preschool study is the first longitudinal cost-benefit analysis of such a program. It is in no small part due to the stunningly positive outcomes of the Perry Preschool Program that there has been a growing receptivity to expanding early childhood education.

Initiated in 1962, the study examined the long-term effects of participation and nonparticipation in a developmentally based preschool program on 123 disadvantaged black youths who were at risk of school failure. Researchers collected in-depth information about the children starting at age three up to age nineteen. Of prime concern were the children's attitudes and academic and vocational accomplishments.

According to the researchers, preschool attendance altered performance by nearly a factor of two on our major variables at age nineteen. The preschoolers' subsequent rates of employment and participation in college or vocational training were nearly double those of the group without preschool. Moreover, for those who attended preschool, the rate of teenage pregnancy (including live births) and the percentage of years spent in special education classes were about half of what they were for those who did not attend preschool. Preschool attendance was associated with a reduction of twenty percentage points in the detention and arrest rate and nearly that much in the high school drop-out rate. Scores on a test of functional competence were also superior for those who attended preschool (Berrueta-Clement et al., 1986).

Considered in terms of their economic value, these benefits make the preschool program a worthwhile investment for society. Indeed, over the lifetimes of the participants, preschool is estimated to yield economic benefits with a percentage value that is over seven times the cost of one year of the program (Berrueta-Clement et al., 1986).

The key to the extraordinary individual and social benefits of the Perry Preschool Program—in fact, of all the preschool programs that have received similar evaluations—is quality. The Perry program was based on solid principles abut the cognitive and social development of young children. Teachers were intensively trained, and child-staff ratios were no more than 6:1. Weekly home visits also were a part of the program. On the one hand, the program was expensive: $4,818. per child a year in 1981 dollars. On the other hand, the lifetime benefit was about $29,000 per participant. Extraordinarily, just the savings realized from the program participants' reduced need for special education placements in school were sufficient to reimburse taxpayers for the cost of running the program for one year.

Still, the short-term costs of the Perry Preschool Program have had an astringent effect on some of the enthusiasm initially expressed about its results. This is not entirely surprising. Americans are becoming habituated to looking to the immediate bottom line and ignoring the future. The question is, in being penny-wise are we becoming pound-foolish? Do we prefer to be niggardly when it comes to expenditures on young children and instead incur the high economic, social, and, potentially, political costs associated with our high rates of school failure and dropouts, teenage pregnancy, youth unemployment or underemployment, delinquency and criminal behavior, and welfare dependency?

Society's answer thus far is that we do. High quality preschool programs are not the magic bullets that will wipe out poverty. But the evidence is powerful indeed that they can significantly and even permanently revise the grim life sentence stamped on so many children of poverty.

Contradictions and Inequalities

On the face of it, the two major reasons for the resurgence of interest in early childhood education—the fact that a majority of mothers of young children work and the growing body of research about the short- and long-term benefits of good preschools—should be compatible. After all, parents who have to find child care want the best possible arrangements for their youngsters; serving the interests of children through the availability of quality child care serves the interests of their parents. Surely, no one wants public policy to pit the economic needs of young children against their developmental needs.

Unfortunately, although there is not theoretical or moral contradiction between serving the needs of working mothers and those of their young children, practically speaking there is. The legacy of our hostile or ambivalent attitudes toward mothers who work is the persistence of low-quality child-care programs that do not benefit youngsters and can do harm to them: the purely custodial model. Some of these so-called programs are a product of public policy. Many others are private and owe their existence to the failure of public policy to respond to the growing need for quality child care—and to the opportunities for greed and hucksterism this vacuum abets. Whatever their sponsorship, purely custodial early childhood programs do not serve the interests of children.

At the opposite extreme is the legacy of high-quality programs initially associated with nonworking middle-class or affluent mothers and more recently extended to a limited degree to disadvantaged youngsters: the educational model, the only one with demonstrable benefits to children. Some of these high-quality preschool programs are also a product of public policy. Head Start being the major example. Most others are private and owe their existence in part to an implicit public policy that states that the ability to offer one's child quality preschool experiences should be conditioned on one's ability to pay for it.

One result of both the overt and implicit public policies on early childhood education is that the supply of neither public nor private programs of high quality is adequate to the demand. The other related result is a series of inequalities: access to good programs depends on the size of a family's income: and, within the category of quality programs, there is a dual system, one for the rich, the other for the poor—and catch-as-catch-can for those who fall in neither category. Clearly, too, the wealthier a mother is, the greater her opportunity to avoid the wrenching choice between meeting the need or desire to work outside the home and meeting the needs of her youngsters; both interests can be accommodated.

As a matter of public policy, the contradiction between enabling mothers to work and enabling children to thrive can, of course, be reconciled. It is, after all, a product of history and public policy, and both are shaped by human decisions. Although history cannot be undone, public policies can be. In this sense, recent initiatives concerning early childhood education are both encouraging and discouraging. The good news is that no policymaker seems to seek the continuation of the legacy of low-quality custodial chlid-care programs for the poor. The discouraging news is that many of them do not recognize the difference between low-quality and high-quality programs. Indeed, in the name of exemplary programs, some states have enacted and others are in danger of enacting poor programs, in large part because they have failed to recognize and reconcile the different purposes of childhood programs (Grubb, 1986).

The dilemmas are complex but clear. To meet the custodial needs of mothers who work full time is to enact a program that operates for eight or nine hours a day throughout the working year. Such programs typically do not provide the rich, carefully designed developmental experiences associated with the preschool programs cited by the research and touted by policymakers. On the other hand, the Perry Preschool Program and others demonstrating benefits to children usually operate for only about three hours a day and only during the school year, not the regular year. These brief hours obviously leave the child-care needs of a large chunk of families only partially resolved.

In addition to differences in hours of operation, the custodial and educational models are associated with very different staffing patterns. The custodial model may have high child-adult ratios, whereas the educational model supports no more than ten children for every adult; many quality programs have even fewer children per adult. Custodial programs are also generally indifferent to the qualifications of the staff, whereas educational programs insist on teachers with a solid education in child development principles and practices and even a trained support staff. Clearly, too, custodial programs can be run on the cheap; educational programs cannot.

That there has been a failure to recognize different purposes of early childhood education—indeed, even the differences between good and bad or indifferent programs—is best exemplified by the recent experience in Texas. In 1984, the Texas legislature enacted a preschool program as part of its education reform package. Citing the needs of working mothers and at-risk youngsters and aware of the positive findings from Head Start and the Perry Preschool Program, the legislature provided for half-day programs in which child-adult ratios of 22:1—almost three times the ratio of Head Start programs and almost four times that of the Perry Preschool Program—were permitted. The Texas Department of Education had no staff members who were experts in early childhood education and it provided little or no guidance to the many districts that were also unfamiliar with such programs. Not surprisingly, although the legislation noted the desirability of employing teachers with credentials in early childhood, this has been ignored because of the shortage of teachers (Grubb, 1986).

There is no question that the provisions of early childhood education by the state of Texas is a landmark event. A long-shut door has been opened in Texas, and the move is creditable. Whether any future evaluation will bring the program closer to its aim or lead to its abandonment because it failed to produce "Perry-like" results is an open question. As currently implemented, however, the program, at a half day, falls short of meeting custodial needs and, with its 22:1 child-adult ratio and few qualified teachers available, falls short of meeting children's developmental or educational needs.

Finally, it is important to note that research has validated the lasting benefits of good early childhood education programs primarily for disadvantaged youngsters. This is not to say that more privileged children do not benefit from such programs but, rather, that the research has concentrated on economically disadvantaged youngsters. The available evidence that preschools produce greater positive results for disadvantaged children than for more affluent children does, however, raise tough cost-benefit issues for public policy. On the one hand, it is more equitable to concentrate resources on those who most need and can least afford high-quality preschools. The fact that the benefits to this group (and to society) far outweigh the costs of such programs further underscores the prudence of this course. On the other hand, such a policy typically has meant deliberately segregating disadvantaged children in their own programs, a policy that is hardly consistent with our egalitarian principles and ideals. History also teaches us that public programs that are targeted exclusively to the poor—a narrow and powerless constituency—suffer the most from the vicissitudes of politics and budgets.

Contradictions and conflicts therefore abound in this area. For policymakers to persist in acting as if early childhood education were a unified concept, as if all programs going by that name were equal and equally beneficial for children—and as if stating that a program has a variety of purposes obviates the need for carefully designing the program to meet those goals—is to risk exacerbating and extending the worst features of early childhood programs. The opportunity to meet a growing demand for a serivce that at its best is manifestly beneficial will have been squandered.

Although some could argue that something poor is better than nothing, there is an alternative to this fatalism. It involves recognizing that there are historic contradictions and conflicts permeating the early childhood education issue, but that they are neither inherent nor inevitable. The reason is simple, the historical distinctions between custodial and developmental childhood programs do not square with children's needs nor do they reflect current reality. Similarly, the legacy of negative attitudes that forced many mothers to compromise the best interests of their children because of their need to work should be, and is being, broken.

As Norton Grubb has eloquently stated:

> Above all, the idea that early childhood programs should be either "developmental" or "custodial" can only limit these programs. The schools, after all, are rich, multi-purpose institutions, with economic, political, moral, and vocational purposes coexisting. Early childhood programs at their best are similarly rich and multi-faceted, providing cognitive, physical, social, and emotional development for children, security and full-time care for working parents, substantial cooperation between parents and caregivers, and parent education for parents seeking different ways of interacting with their children . . . To search for a single purpose for early childhood programs is to destroy this vision of what early childhood programs could be. (Grubb, 1986, p. 17).

Although this vision has been made manifest in a number of programs in local school districts, most of the initiatives in the states since 1979 have perpetuated the historic distinctions between the custodial and developmental models or have created new hybrids that fulfull neither purpose well (Grubb, 1986). Nonetheless, the recent report devoted to the early childhood education issue by the National Governors' Association (NGA) is cause for optimism. Some of the right questions are now being asked. "In developing early childhood programs, one of the first issues to be raised is the purpose of such programs. Will state-sponsored programs be aimed at children whose families fall within a particular income range? Will the programs include only educational or developmental components, or will they include a daycare component as well?" (National Governors' Association, 1986, p. 105).

The NGA Task Force on Readiness does not offer answers to these questions. Instead, it urges each state to study its existing early childhood programs and demographic factors to determine which programs should be given the highest priority. Given the diversity of the states, this reticence concerning answers is understandable, but, it also means a missed opportunity to publicize and reform the pattern of confusion and fragmentation now afflicting early childhood education. Moreover, although states do indeed face tough decisions about where to put their resources for maximum benefits, the danger continues to exist that they will fail to consider the choice of not choosing a single purpose for early childhhood programs.

Put another way, we should not again miss the opportunity to meet both the custodial and developmental needs of preschoolers, to combine or coordinate day care and preschool education and make them universally available to all children. The American Federation of Teachers (AFT) has sounded that call before, in the 1970s. There is nothing that has transpired to suggest that it was mistaken. Quite the contrary; the demand, the desperation for child care has increased; the incidences of children harmed by substandard programs have increased; the body of evidence about the benefits of quality preschools has increased; and the inequality of access to early childhood education has increased. Now, as then, the arguments on behalf of making public education the prime sponsor—although not necessarily the only site—for multipurpose early childhood education programs are the most compelling.

Public School Sponsorship of
Early Childhood Education

The first advantage of this proposal is that the public education system already has in place organizations experienced in administering large and complex programs. Many state and local education agencies have child development experts on staff. Those that do not would have to hire such people to ensure that programs are age- and need-appropriate or utilize the expertise of such staff in other agencies through interagency agreements. The experience of states such as California and Connecticut suggests that education departments that use an advisory group composed of educators, child development experts, representatives from welfare departments, and other groups whose activities touch the lives of young children are particularly successful at mounting appropriate and flexible programs.

Under the sponsorship of public education and with the formal cooperation of other relevant agencies and groups, order can be brought out of the chaos and fragmentation now characterizing early childhood policies, and the divorce between day-care programs and developmental programs can be reconciled. For example, a public school can run both a preschool program, with its approximately three hours of a deliberately developmental "curriculum," and a quality day-care program whose hours account for the remainder of the working day. Parents would be free to choose whether their child attended only the preschool portion or remained throughout the working day. In some localities, this would involve a new willingness to be flexible about the hours during which school buildings are open. Although costs might increase, new efficiencies and a more rational use of school facilities would be realized.

The school system also can work with other agencies to ensure that plans for preschools are coordinated with existing or anticipated day-care programs. The point is that public school sponsorship of early childhood education does not require uniformity or rigidity. School districts would be free to expand and vary their services to meet local needs or fund other agencies or even non-profit organizations that were providing high-quality services. There is no reason why, at the state or local level, the decision could not be made to provide incentives for home care or extended maternity leaves. The goal is quality, flexibility, and coordination.

A second advantage of this proposal is that public schools are universally available. They exist in urban, suburban, small-town and rural areas. This means that early childhood education could be universally available, although it should not be compulsory. Ideally, of course, programs would be free of cost to all who desired to attend. Short of this ideal, it may be necessary to design a plan that is based on the ability to pay. Such a plan must enable poor children to attend free, permit the majority of families to take advantage of early childhood education services without unnecessary hardship and be sensitive to the need for confidentiality in order to avoid stigmatizing anyone. Since a number of school districts currently charge some sliding scale fees for child-care services, thoughtful models already exist.

Third, the public education system is best equipped to offer or coordinate the variety of services, such as health and nutrition, that support a child's development. The safety and health record of public schools is also superlative, especially in light of the millions of children they serve every day. Moreover, public schools are more ready (and willing) than other providers to respond to the special needs of handicapped and non-English-speaking children, both in the mainstream and through special services.

The public education system is also in a better position to address the problems of staffing that have characterized many programs and undercut confidence in early childhood education. For one, the licensing or credential-checking systems in place in state and local departments of education could help ensure that quality standards for early childhood education staff are both promulgated and monitored. Of course, the existence of such a machinery for enforcing standards does not necessarily mean that it will be used to that end, as the practice of "emergency" certification illustrates. But its mere existence and its public stature—that is, its ability to be called to account—offer more leverage for enforcing quality than currently exists for alternative providers. Similarly, although public education is hardly saintly in adhering to agreements about appropriate child-adult ratios, its performance is better than most child-care operations and, again, has the capacity to be rigorously monitored and called to account. And no other existing arrangement can surpass the public schools' ability to deliver in-service training, which could keep the staff abreast of current child development theory and practices.

There are those who will argue that it is tantamount to madness to call for public school sponsorship of early childhood education during a time of intense criticism of public education. The education reform movement of the 1980s has produced a stack of reports documenting the shortcomings of the public schools. My own voice as president of the AFT has been loud and clear about the necessity of fundamental reform. But, as in the past, the response to the criticisms of the last few years, although not always adequate or thoughtful, illustrates that public education is a strikingly accountable institution. We do not hear much about what goes on in other institutions of government. We know even less about the private and other organizations sponsoring early childhood education that are subject only to loose controls or no democratic controls at all. Yet we always know the condition of public education, and we have an array of democratic policy mechanisms to improve its condition.

Still, the fears about the structural and educational rigidities that would beset early childhood programs under public school sponsorship are worth exhuming. According to the charges leveled during the 1970s, particularly around the time the federally proposed Child and Family Services Act of 1975 was being considered, public schools were bureaucratic, authoritarian institutions that revolved more around the interests of educators than the needs of children and their parents. Elementary education, critics contended, was narrowly conceived in terms of basic cognitive skills imparted through fixed lessons by teachers who essentially lectured to orderly rows and columns of too numerous children in self-contained classrooms. The schedule and time clock ruled expectations about the progress of children, as well as the day. Children who did not keep pace uniformly, usually according to the criteria of standardized tests, were labeled failures. The ideals of individualized instruction were espoused, but the legacy of the factory model of schooling prevailed.

Of course, this sterotypical image of the public schools ignored some important realities. For one, only the worst schools fit the sterotype.

Second, many public schools were already running exemplary preschool programs, none of which was "contaminated" by the rigidities of the upper elementary grades. And third, there were many factorylike preschool programs outside the public schools and others of such poor quality that introducing some of the worst features ascribed to the public schools would have represented an improvement. More than a decade later and with many more successful experiences with public schools sponsoring preschools, those realities are still with us.

Yes some of the groups that raised these criticisms about the rigidities of the public schools had a point. If the factory model of schooling is not pervasive, it nonetheless represents the dominant organizing principle of public education. It should under no circumstances be extended downward to the preschool level, and it should by all means be repudiated in the entire system. Given the recent report and efforts of the Carnegie Task Force on the Teaching Profession (1986) and considering the new tenor of the second stage of education reform in the 1980s, there is reason to believe that the structural and educational rigidities of the public school system will be addressed. Indeed, new models of school organization and learning are already being tried, and some of them owe much to the lessons learned from the flexible, developmental, child-centered approach that the best of the early childhood education community pioneered.

The renewed interest in early childhood education brings us another chance to reconcile the conflicts over early childhood. Our failure to do so will not stop mothers from working and needing quality child care. It will not materially harm the parties to the conflict. It will, however, hurt young children and perpetuate the problems of meeting their economic development, and custodial needs. There is no reason for the lack of coordination between day care and preschool education, save a set of policies that have irrationally fragmented the planning and administration of such programs and maintained the historic and unequally applied distinctions between a child's custodial and educational needs. There is every reason to expect more incidences of fatality, abuse, and just plain neglect if we continue to be indifferent to standards and implicitly delegate our responsibility for the welfare of the nation's children to organizations concerned only for their own welfare.

It is possible to have standards without standardization and flexibility without fragmentation in early childhood education policy. The solution lies in making a variety of quality early childhood education programs universally available to all parents who want these services. A large part of the means to that end involves the early childhood education community recognizing that the public education system is the best prime sponsor. Another part involves the continuing willingness of the public school system to recognize child development-based approaches to learning and to make the structural and educational changes indicated by the best of these approaches. By drawing on their strengths rather than hurling charges about their weaknesses, child advocates might this time actually cooperate on behalf of effective, caring policies toward children.

ALBERT SHANKER,
President, AFT

From: *Early Schooling: The National Debate*
Sharon L. Kagan and Edward F. Zigler, Eds.
Yale University Press, 1987

References

Berrueta-Clement, J. R. Schweinhart, I. J., Barnett, W. S. Epstein, A. S., and Weikart, D. P. (1986). Changed lives: The effects of the Perry Preschool Program on youths through age 19. In F. M. Hechinger (Ed.) *A better start: New choices for early learning* (pp. 11–40). New York: Walker.

Carnegie Task Force on the Teaching Profession. (1986). *Teachers for the 21st century (A Report of the Carnegie Forum on Education and the Economy).* New York: Carnegie Corporation of New York.

Grubb, W. N. (1986, August). "Young children face the states: Issues and options for early childhood programs." Draft paper for Rutgers University. The Center for Policy Research in Education.

Hechinger, F. M. (Ed.). (1986). *A better start: New choices for early learning.* New York: Walker.

National Governors' Association. (1986). *Time for results: The governors' 1991 report on education.* Washington, DC: Author.

Schweinhart, I. J., & Koshel, J. J. (1986). *Policy options for preschool programs.* Ypsilanti, Mi: High/Scope Early Childhood Policy Papers No. 5.

U.S. Bureau of Labor Statistics. (1986, August 20) "Half of mothers of children under three now in labor force." Washington, D.C.: U.S. Department of Labor 86-345.

U.S. Department of Labor. *Labor force statistics derived from the current population survey: A databook* (Vol.1. Table C-11). Washington, DC: U.S. Government Printing Office.

CHAPTER 2

Policy Options for Preschool Programs

Federal, state, and local policymakers find, these days, that they must take a position on early childhood development programs, especially those that are designed for children from low-income families. Based on evidence that these programs provide immediate, short-term, and long-term gains for young participants, legislators and school administrators in almost every state continue to deliberate about how to establish or expand programs for children under the age of 5. A recent Gallup poll indicated that 69 percent of the American public are willing to spend more taxes to pay for Head Start programs and 58 percent are willing to do the same to pay for day care for young children with working parents (Elam & Gallup, 1989, p. 52). Illustrative of the increase in activity—and financial commitment—in this area are these facts: In 1979, seven states funded public school prekindergarten programs and four contributed funds to Head Start. In 1989, 32 states provide funding in these ways or for statewide parent education programs, spending a quarter-billion dollars to serve over 135,000 children Mitchell, Seligson, & Marx, 1989). Head Start's 1990 budget is up $170 million, an increase of 12 percent over the previous year. Both houses of Congress passed major child care bills in 1989 and will probably agree to a final version in 1990.

The momentum for early childhood programs is still strong. State legislatures and other policymaking bodies throughout the nation seem more willing than they were a few years ago to consider investing in high-quality early childhood programs. A growing constituency that includes chief executive officers as well as welfare mothers considers public investments in such programs worthwhile. Consider these comments:

The Research and Policy Committee of the Committee for Economic Development (1985) noted, "It would be hard to imagine that society could find a higher yield for a dollar of investment than that found in preschool programs for at-risk children" (p. 44). Mayor Edward I. Koch, in announcing an initiative to provide early childhood education for all of New York City's 4-year-olds, said he was "struck by the near unanimity among experts that, of all the educational and social programs initiated in the last 20 years, there is one that holds more promise than any other, an intervention on which there is solid and compelling research indicating its measurable and long-term positive effects on children's success in school and in life." At the Education Summit in Virginia, President Bush agreed with all the nation's governors that "priority for any further [federal] spending increases be given to prepare young children to succeed in school" ("Text," 1989). A *Chicago Tribune* editorial ("The American Millstone," 1985) said of early childhood education: "A wealth of experimental projects proves that children from the most disadvantaged homes will thrive academically and socially if they are stimulated early enough in special preschool prgrams," and concluded that "in a few years, early learning programs will pay for themselves many times over in the reduced costs of school failures, delinquency, dependency, and violent behavior."

As state, local, and federal policymakers in greater numbers come to recognize the constituency that supports early childhood programs and the information that motivates it, public funding should give an increasing number of young children the opportunity to participate in high-quality early childhood development programs. But it is essential that those who are responsible for directing the debate and shaping the programs receive information from pertinent research and experience.

With the trend for increased early childhood programs continuing to gain momentum—and with public demand growing for more programs serving greater numbers of preschoolers—policymakers and educators must consider all the options available when conceptualizing and implementing programs. Among the questions central to the debate are: which children should be served, for what part of the day should programs operate, how much money should be invested in programs, and through what structures should the money be channelled.

Which Children Should Be Served?

Policymakers considering the question of which children should be served must determine the age range of children to be served, identify the category of children within that age range who will be served, and define the nature of the program's mandate.

Age Range

Policymakers may begin considering these questions by dividing early childhood into two age groups—birth to age 2 (infants and toddlers) and ages 3 and 4 (preschoolers). Approximately half of the mothers of children in each of these two age groups are employed outside the home, and about two-thirds of these employed mothers work full-time. Consequently, the need for child care in each of the age groups is roughly equivalent.

But although the supply of good child care programs for infants and toddlers is less than that for preschoolers (Ad Hoc Day Care Coalition, 1985), there is more evidence of lasting benefits for preschoolers enrolled in such programs than for infants and toddlers (Schweinhart & Weikart, 1980). Lawmakers and administrators would be wise, then, to commit funds first to programs for 4-year-olds from low-income families, with the next priority being expansion to 3-year-olds from low-income families.

Identifying Children to Be Served

Once an age range has been established, legislators and educators may choose to make the program universally available to all children within this age range. The principal disadvantage of this option is, of course, expense. New funds of this magnitude are difficult to find and, because the investment potential of early childhood programs has been documented only for children from low-income families, it is more difficult to make a persuasive case for public funding on the basis of documented benefits of programs for children from middle- and upper-income families.

Another option is for policymakers to provide early childhood programs that are open to all children, but fund only low-income children at particular risk of school failure. This option conserves public funds while maintaining the opportunity for universal enrollment.

If neither of these options is adopted, children must be selected for programs or for funding by certain criteria; they might be selected because they are living in poverty, they have been identified by a screening test as being at risk of school failure, or they meet both criteria. It may be helpful to recognize that the condition of poverty has proven to be a much better predictor of school failure than any existing screening test.

Policymakers involved in identifying selection procedures should take care to consider the political significance of their task: Serving children who are identified as being "at risk of school failure" may have wider acceptance than serving children who are labelled as "living in poverty." Perhaps the best option is to target children who are at risk of school failure and give considerable weight to environmental criteria in identifying children who fall into this category.

Nature of the Mandate

Legislators and school administrators must decide the nature of the program's mandate for school districts or community agencies, and for young children and their families. Among the questions to be addressed are whether the program is voluntary or compulsory, and whether it is permissive or required. Because government involvement in family and children's issues can be a sensitive topic, it is especially important to consider who is required to do what with respect to early childhood programs.

Illustrative of the range of options available to most policymakers today are public school kindergarten programs, which constitute the primary state efforts in early childhood education. State legislation calling for kindergarten programs falls into four categories: compulsory kindergarten attendance, demonstrated scholastic readiness as a condition for first grade entry, universal opportunity for kindergarten, and permissive provision of kindergarten.

For What Part of the Day Should Programs Operate?

Length of program day is the primary policy variable that determines whether early childhood programs meet families' child care needs. Policymakers have three options to consider—part-day (2 to 3 hours), full-schoolday (5 to 6 hours), and full-work-day (8 to 10 hours).

Part-Day Programs

Part-day programs, when they are offered at least four days a week for approximately eight months and meet other conditions of quality, achieve positive long-term effects. Chief among their immediate benefits are that they may spare children the fatigue that can come with full-day programs, and they may be less costly because there is less teacher-child contact time.

Part-day programs' disadvantages are that they do not fully meet families' child care needs, and in public schools, they may create special transportation demands. Particularly in rural areas, short program hours can mean children spend more time on the school bus than in class. These problems can, of course, be addressed; one solution is to organize satellite day care homes around a center-based part-day program so that children's transportation needs are met while also filling day care home providers' training and networking needs.

Full-School-Day Programs

A convenient option for public-school-based early childhood programs, full-school-day programs place preschoolers' public transportation demands on the same schedule as those of other schoolchildren. The full-school-day option also reduces families' child care needs, although if parents are employed full-time, the need for after-school child care remains.

One of the main disadvantages of full-school-day programs is that they can produce fatigue and behavior problems in young children, unless the program is a high-quality child development program that is responsive to children's needs.

As full-school-day programs grow in popularity, it is important to caution those who have interpreted early childhood research findings to show that full-school-day programs are superior to part-day programs in their effect on children's success in school. A recent study of Chicago kindergartens concluded that smaller class size was a better predictor of school achievement than length of school day (Department of Research and Evaluation, Chicago Public Schools, 1985). Ideal sizes are as low as 16, the study suggests. Those creating and monitoring programs should be concerned primarily with class size; only then can there be a payoff in expanding from part- to full-school-day programs.

Full-Work-Day Programs

Full-work-day programs are clearly the best option for meeting families' child care needs. They reduce transportation problems and help meet the child care needs of some of the 54 percent of mothers with children under age 6 who are in the workforce.

But full-work-day programs are costly. When they are of sufficient quality to meet child development needs, such programs can easily cost $5,000 per year per child (Clifford & Russell, 1989). In contrast, the typical family spends only $2,262 per year for a child in a day care centers (U.S. Bureau of the Census, 1987); and the typical state spends only $1,300 per year to support a child at home under its Aid to Families with Dependent Children payment schedule (Children's Defense Fund, 1986, p. 355).

Since funds are limited, policymakers are faced with a difficult choice. If they spend money to provide part-time early childhood development programs that are focused on the intellectual and social skills of economically disadvantaged children, they do little to meet the child care needs of parents who work full-time. If they allocate funds to full-work-day child care programs for low-income children, they run the risk of omitting essential developmental components and of failing to address the needs of children in families in which parents are not employed.

Policymakers and administrators might consider a compromise through which they could establish programs that provide high-quality, full-time care for children who live in poverty despite the fact that their mothers are in the labor force. In 1988, 1.1 million children under 5 lived in poverty even though their mothers participated in the labor force, yet remained impoverished because their earnings were insufficient to raise them above the poverty level (U.S. Bureau of Labor Statistics, 1988). This option meets the child care needs of some parents and the developmental needs of some disadvantaged children, while signalling a commitment on the part of the state or local government to addressing the increased incidence of poverty among children.

How Much Money Should Be Invested in Programs?

Perhaps the thorniest question public officials must consider when creating early childhood development programs is that of funding. Most states prefer to begin pilot projects at a few demonstration sites and then expand gradually to a statewide effort. The question of how to develop funding levels depends on a state's resources and its political will vis-a-vis the issue of early childhood. Policymakers implementing programs should take the time to consider the costs related to personnel and the costs of achieving program quality.

Personnel Costs

The cost of a fully implemented statewide early childhood program is the product of the number of children served multiplied by the average cost per child of the program (which is primarily the per-child cost of the teaching staff). Because the staff-child ratio depends in part on the number of children per classroom group, group size is a key determinant of both the cost and the quality of early childhood programs. Classroom group sizes of 20 or fewer and staff-child ratios of 1 to 10 and lower have been found to be associated with desirable classroom behavior and improved cognitive performance, according to the National Day Care Study (Ruopp, Travers, Glantz, & Coelen, 1979).

The National Day Care Study also found that the amount of job-related early childhood training a teacher has received—not the years of schooling completed, nor the amount of experience alone—was the only teacher characteristic that predicts program quality and effectiveness. Because such training is crucial to good programs, the undervaluing of the early childhood teaching field must end.

If this is an issue for teachers in general, it is much more of an issue for early childhood teachers. In 1988, the average annual salary of Head Start teachers was $12,074, $15,403 for Head Start teachers with bachelors' degrees, whereas the average salary of public school teachers was $27,423 (National Center for Education Statistics, 1989). Policymakers can help by working toward making early childhood teaching a hierarchical profession that permits career development and by emphasizing the vast potential of properly implemented early childhood development programs to contribute to the prevention of subsequent educational and social problems.

The Costs of Achieving Program Quality

Most policymakers familiar with early childhood research know that it is poor public investment policy to finance early childhood programs at per child levels insufficient to provide the high quality that assures effectiveness. Unless program quality is carefully defined and maintained, an early childhood classroom is just another place for a child to be. With limited funds, it is probably better to provide high-quality programs to some children than to provide inferior programs to more preschoolers.

If an early childhood program is to promote child development intellectually, socially, and physically, it must meet high standards of quality and be administred by competent child development professionals who establish an environment that supports children's active learning. This premise is supported by a 15-year study by the High/Scope Educational Research Foundation which found that preschool programs in which children initiate their own activities appear to be most effective in preventing later juvenile delinquency. Children who participated in child-directed programs, the study found, appeared to be better adjusted; those who took part in highly academic, teacher-controlled programs reported more social and educational problems as teens (Schweinhart, Weikart, & Larner, 1986).

Public officials working to develop early childhood programs should consider adopting staff-child ratios of 1 to 10 and classroom enrollment limits of 20 children; hiring teaching staff who are early childhood specialists—with academic degrees in early childhood development, competency-based Child Development Associate (CDA) credentials, or their equivalents; and using curriculum models, derived from child development principles, that have been evaluated and found to have positive intellectual and social outcomes.

They should also try to ensure that programs feature support systems to maintain the curriculum model, including inservice training and evaluation; collaboration between teaching staff and parents; and sensitivity and responsiveness to the children's health and nutrition needs and the families' needs for child care or other services.

Through What Structures Should Program Money Be Channeled?

One of the political issues facing government officials who are designing early childhood programs is deciding which agencies will receive funds to carry out the programs. As policymakers consider how to make public investments in such programs, they should keep in mind the diverse needs for child care and early childhood education of young children and their families. Any public investments in this area should be made with sensitivity to this diversity. In addition, public officials should remember that it is not necessary for one program to meet all the needs of all children.

Regardless of whether providers receive funds directly or parents receive funds and select programs through a voucher system, the question remains: Who should be authorized to receive funds to provide programs? The three types of agencies that policymakers should consider are public schools, federally funded programs such as Head Start, and other community agencies such as day care centers or associations of day care homes. They should also consider providing funding through open sponsorship, which permits funds to go to any of these agencies.

Public Schools

Those developing early childhood development programs might look to state-funded public school kindergarten programs as an example of public school sponsorship. However, lawmakers and school administrators should be aware that public school programs for 4-year-olds should be quite different from some existing kindergarten programs. Whether programs are created by enhancing existing kindergarten programs or using new models for younger children, policymakers should be aware that early childhood programs in the public schools carry with them all the advantages and disadvantages of other public school programs.

Advantages of funding programs through the public schools include their universal availability; their governance by elected community representatives (school boards); their professional standing, certification standards, and salary schedules; and their vested interest in having better-prepared students at kindergarten entrance.

Disadvantages include a tradition of high child-staff ratios (at least 20 to 1 in public schools, when 10 to 1 ratios have been found most effective for preschoolers) and their historic tendency to sometimes exclude parents from the educational process, to fail to meet the needs of non-white ethnic groups, and to be unresponsive to the child care needs of working parents. In addition, those concerned with investment in public schools point to their potential to adopt a narrow focus on direct instruction in academic skills rather than a broad child development focus, and to overlook and even threaten existing child care services in the community.

In order for public schools to serve a legitimate child development function, there must be innovation in addressing these concerns. Smaller class sizes, greater parental involvement, and stronger emphasis on broad intellectual and social development must be part of state kindergarten and prekindergarten public school programs if these efforts are expected to yield results similar to those of exemplary child development programs.

Federally Funded Programs

Another option for funding early childhood development programs is to provide supplemental state money for existing federally funded programs such as Head Start and compensatory education (Chapter 1 of the Education Consolidation and Improvement Act of 1981). Most federal programs require some state or local matching funds, so states may already be providing these dollars to some extent.

Sources of federal grants for programs for young children may also include special-education funds, the Social Services Block Grant, the Child Care Food Program, and several employment-related grants programs. Another source, the federal dependent care tax credit, retained in new federal tax policy, also has analogues in the income tax policies of various states.

Providing additional funding to a state's Head Start programs has several advantages. Head Start is the country's premier publicly funded program for meeting the child development needs of low-income children, and it has a relatively stable institutional structure. Designed to respond to the variety of needs of these children and their families, it focuses on education, nutrition, health care, social services, and parent involvement.

Disadvantages of providing funding through Head Start stem from the fact that, because state government has not been a real part of the Head Start system, policymakers are often unfamiliar with the program's operations in their state. Head Start dollars travel from Washington, D.C. through regional offices to local grantees and delegate agencies that operate programs. In addition, only two-thirds of Head Start teachers now have either an undergraduate degree in early childhood education or a Child Development Associate credential (Head Start Bureau, 1989).

Policymakers could work toward overcoming some of these disadvantages by earmarking state funds for Head Start for special purposes, such as training or evaluation, and for simple program expansion to serve more eligible children. Head Start and public school prekindergarten programs together serve 500,000, or 31 percent, of the 1.6 million 3- and 4-year-olds in poverty (Schweinhart, 1989).

Community Agencies

A third option policymakers should consider for funding early childhood development programs is providing funds to community agencies not associated with Head Start. Any program licensed for child care by the state's department of social services—both centers and homes—could be eligible. Limited funds could be allocated by employing competitive programs or conducting site visits to identify the agencies that run the best programs.

An advantage of this option is that private-sector agencies with experience in running good programs can expand to serve more children. A disadvantage is that private agencies are less subject to public scrutiny and control. In addition, the lack of sufficient public funding in the past has deterred private agencies from serving low-income neighborhoods, so programs funded through such agencies are not as well located as public school programs to meet these priority needs.

Open Sponsorship

A fourth option available to those developing programs is providing funding through open sponsorship to public schools, Head Start, and other community agencies. This approach helps minimize the turf battles that inevitably occur when funds are exclusively assigned to one type of agency. It also recognizes the variety of existing program providers. Of course, a designated agency or department must still be selected to distribute the funds, both at the state and local levels, in a demonstrably impartial manner.

The Early Childhood Challenge

There is increasing awareness among public officials that the rapid growth of early childhood poverty, at a time of reduced federal commitment to this population, poses serious near-future threats to our society. Because a variety of social problems—adult poverty, teen pregnancy, drug and alcohol abuse, and crime—can be associated with school failure, attempts to reduce children's risk of school failure can help.

For this reason, and based on research that has shown that good early childhood development programs for poor children help prevent school failure, more and more states and local governments are planning and implementing early childhood development programs for children from low-income families. Such programs help improve children's intellectual performance as school begins and can lead to various improvements in school achievement, placement, and motivation. High-quality early childhood education has even been shown to help children become more successful adults than children without such assistance. Consequently, it can reduce the incidence of major social and economic problems within a community, such as unemployment and welfare dependency. Because early childhood education improves the functioning of high-risk children early in their lives, it is a much more efficient investment than other interventions that address problems such as teen pregnancy, delinquency, and school failure after they have occurred.

The fact that financing high-quality early childhood programs leads to substantial economic benefits for the community is perhaps the most compelling benefit for state and local legislators and policymakers concerned about funding. According to an assessment of the High/Scope Educational Research Foundation's Perry Preschool Program, an investment in a good one-year preschool program for disadvantaged children (after adjusting for inflation and discounting 3 percent to estimate present value) returns to taxpayers six dollars for every dollar invested (Berrueta-Clement, Schweinhart, Barnett, Epstein, & Weikart, 1984).

It is essential that local, state, and national policymakers and leaders consider the research, viewpoints, and experiences of those in the field of early childhood. If that dialogue is held now, the programs that are developed can embody all that is known about high-quality programs and will go a long way toward producing beneficial effects for children and for society.

References

Ad Hoc Day Care Coalition. (1985). *The crisis in infant and toddler care.* Washington, DC: Author.

"The American millstone." (1985, October 8). *The Chicago Tribune.*

Berrueta-Clement, J. R., Schweinhart, L. J., Barnett, W. S., Epstein, A. S., & Weikart, D. P. (1984). *Changed lives: The effects of the Perry Preschool program on youths through age 19.* (Monographs of the High/Scope Educational Research Foundation, 8), Ypsilanti, MI: High/Scope Press.

Children's Defense Fund. (1986). *Analysis of the FY 1987 federal budget for children.* Washington, DC: Author.

Clifford, R. M., & Russell, S. D. (1989). Financing programs for preschool aged children. *Theory into Practice, 28,* 19–27.

Department of Research and Evaluation, Chicago Public Schools. (1985). *Meeting the national mandate: Chicago's government-funded kindergarten programs, Fiscal 1984.* Chicago: Author.

Head Start Bureau. (1989). Unpublished data.

Mitchell, A., Seligson, M., & Marx, F. (1989). *Early childhood programs and the public schools: Between promise and practice.* Dover, MA: Auburn House.

National Center for Education Statistics. (1989). *The condition of education 1989.* Washington, DC: U.S. Government Printing Office.

Research and Policy Committee, Committee for Economic Development. (1985). *Investing in Our Children,* New York: Author.

Ruopp, R., Travers, J., Glantz, F., & Coelen, C. (1979). *Children at the center: Summary findings and their implications,* Final report of the National Day Care Study, Volume 1. Cambridge, MA: Abt Associates.

Schweinhart, L. J. (1989). *How much do good early childhood programs cost?* An issue paper for the School Finance Study Group, North Central Regional Educational Laboratory. Chicago: NCREL.

Schweinhart, L. J., & Weikart, D. P. (1980). *Young children grow up: The effects of the Perry Preschool program on youths through age 15.* (Monographs of the High/Scope Educational Research Foundation, 7), Ypsilanti, MI: High/Scope Press.

Schweinhart, L. J., Weikart, D. P., & Larner, M. B. (1986). Consequences of three preschool curriculum models on youths through age 15, *Early Childhood Research Quarterly 1,* 15–45.

Text of final Summit statement issued by President, Governors. (1989, October 4). *Education Week,* p. 12.

U.S. Bureau of the Census. (1987). *Who's minding the kids? Child care arrange-*

ments Winter 1984–85, Series P-70, No. 9. Washington, DC: U.S. Government Printing Office.
U.S. Bureau of Labor Statistics. (1988, November). Unpublished data.

Larence J. Schweinhart, Jeffrey J. Koshel, and Anne Bridgman wrote this paper. Schweinhart is chairman of the Research Division, High/Scope Educational Research Foundation, Ypsilanti, Michigan. Koshel is a state human resource consultant. Bridgman is a free-lance writer specializing in early childhood issues. Earlier versions of this paper appeared in the *Phi Delta Kappan,* March 1987, *68,* 524–529; and as a 1986 policy paper of the High/Scope Educational Research Foundation and the National Governors' Association.

CHAPTER 3

Early Care and Education: Beyond the Schoolhouse Doors

In order to reform and improve education significantly, schools must reach beyond the schoolhouse doors to families, to communities, and to other social institutions that serve children and their families, Ms. Kagan reminds us.

Though some of us have grown wary (and others weary) of efforts to reform education, there is little doubt that "restructuring" is this era's main contribution to improving America's schools. Our growing experience with efforts to restructure schools suggests that teachers, parents, and communities must be more involved in school decision making and that children must be allowed more choice in curricular decisions.[1] At the heart of the restructuring movement, as at the heart of early childhood education, is a commitment to engage children, adults, and communities more actively and meaningfully in the decisions that affect education.

My aim in this article is simple. I wish to suggest that, in order to reform and improve education signficantly, schools must reach beyond the schoolhouse doors to families, to communities, and to other social institutions that serve youngsters and their families. I will show that a similarly open and holistic approach to classroom pedagogy and program paractice has historically characterized the care and education of young children and suggest that early childhood education may have some lessons to share with those who are concerned about the general restructuring of our education system. Finally, I will extract the lessons learned from two promising early childhood efforts (family resource and support and cross-program collaborations) and shape them into 10 "commandments" that may be useful in our efforts to restructure general education practice and policy.

Schools and Social Reform

The current efforts to expand early care and education and to restructure schools, though they use different nomenclature and appeal to different audiences, share common roots, goals, and strategies. Each stems from a concern that children are entering an increasingly pressured and technologically advanced world that will require complex social and cognitive skills. To ready children for the demands imposed by such a world and to enable them to cope with the effects of pervasive drug use, increasingly pressured and technologically advanced world that will require complex social and cognitive skills. To ready children for the demands imposed by such a world and to enable them to cope with the effects of pervasive drug use, increasingly fragmented family structure, and widespread poverty, educators recognize that schools must do more than simply teach the basics. Motivated by changes in demographics, in values, and in perceptions of social responsibility, schools are addressing the problems of society and are becoming effective agents of social reform.

Such responsibility forces schools to realize that they cannot remain isolated from other social institutions. Unquestionably, moving beyond the basics to embrace social and cognitive competences broadens education's mission and expands its perspectives and strategies.

Broadened mission. Throughout the history of American education, debate has focused on the purposes of schooling. To be sure, those working in the field have changed their visions of the aims of education radically over the centuries. The role of schools in Colonial times was narrowly defined: teaching the basics of reading, writing and arithmetic. Totally separate from schools, the family and the church were responsible for the ethical and moral development of children. By the time of Horace Mann in the 19th century, these aims were deemed narrow and dysfunctional. Encouraged by women activists, schools broadened their mission in order to improve life for new immigrants and children of the poor. Gradually, many parents formed coalitions and pressed for the introduction of play gardens and kindergartens; formal parent/school organizations were established to improve education. By the 1930s the community school movement had emerged. Though not widely accepted at the time, it advocated more active learning for children, greater involvement for parents, lifelong learning for adults, and the redefinition of the school as a hub of community services.

Over the past 25 years, three separate forces have hastened the realignment of relationships among schools, parents, and communities. First, the force of mandate—enunciated through the *Brown v. Board of Education* decision, through Head Start policy, through Title I of the Elementary and Secondary Education Act of 1965, and through the Education for All Handicapped Children Act (P.L. 94-142)—moved the spirit and molded the structure of various programs. Opportunities arose for more equitable and community-sensitive strategies. A second force, research in education and child development—guided by Urie Bronfenbrenner and others—

provided an ecological perspective that underscored the interdependence of parent, child, and community.

Emerging more recently, the final force is perhaps the most potent. Steeped in a growing uneasiness about the quality of family life in the U.S., liberals and conservatives alike have become concerned about the state of the nation's children and about the high cost of delivering public services in uncoordinated and fragmented ways. Concerned policy makers recognize that today's complex problems often cut across the rigid lines drawn to separate the authority of education, health, mental health, and social service agencies, and they are calling for the strengthening not only of family ties but of ties among agencies as well.

For most early childhood educators, commitments to uniting children, parents, families, and communities are hardly novel. Early educators have for a long time loudly proclaimed that parents are the first and most important teachers of their children. The long-standing commitment to involving parents in early care and education programs is manifest in the very structure of those programs, be they parent cooperatives for the children of the affluent or Head Start programs that mandate parent participation in decision making. The presence of parent coordinators and family and community workers in high-quality early childhood programs—particularly those for low-income youngsters—underscores the field's commitment to a linked mission: serving families and children together.

Equally important, early childhood educators recognize that the domains of development are intertwined. Fostering cognitive development in young children necessarily involves a simultaneous commitment to social, emotional, and physical growth. Consequently, the language of early childhood education is the language of the "whole child" and of integrated learning.

Although part and parcel of early care and education, such beliefs can pose considerable challenges for many educators and policy makers.[2] Burdened by tight budgets or overloaded agendas, some parties are reluctant to make more than rhetorical commitments to the whole child and to educating the child in the context of family and community. Understandably, others are unclear about the strategic consequences of such commitments.

Expanded perspectives and strategies. What do such commitments to the whole child in an ecological context really require in terms of altered perspectives and strategies? Clearly, they entail a vision of education as a shared resonsibility: shared with parents, with businesses, and with other agencies and providers of services. When education is viewed as a cooperative venture, with mandatory and meaningful input from the community, closed schoolhouse doors, barred gates, a quest for the one best system, and other forces that keep families, schools, and communities apart are excluded. Within this perspective, shaping the culture of the programs so that it is sensitive to parents, teachers, and the community is not only a democratic ideal but also an imperative for effectiveness. At a minimum, such a perspective demands a dedication to forging links between the school and its community, a revamped training program for school staff members, the establishment of vehicles for shared decision making, and regular communication with other service providers in the community.

Just as commitments to the child within the context of family and community have strategic implications for pedagogy, young children don't separate their learning by topic; they don't distinguish science or math as disciplines, distinct from one another or distinct from play. Blocks and sand, venerable tools of integrated learning, know no disciplinary boundaries. Withstanding decades of curricular fads in upper levels of education, integrated experiential learning has been the constant cornerstone of early care and education. With Dewey, Froebel, Piaget, and Pestalozzi as its pedagogical pioneers, early childhood education espouses the development of social competence, embracing and integrating children's physical, social, emotional, creative, and cognitive development.

Paradoxically, the very principles that have been treasured by early childhood education and that have traditionally set it somewhat apart from elementary education—extensive commitment to family, to community, to student choice, and to integrated learning—are now considered hallmarks of reform. As such, they are being incorporated into a variety of reform reports, projects and laws, including Right from the Start, from the National Association of State Boards of Education; the Casey Foundation's New Futures Project; the Joining Forces initiative; school-business partnerships; Schools Reaching Out, from the Institute for Responsive Education; and P.L. 99-457. Indeed, a new ethos is developing, one that supports integrated learning, interagency collaboration, and partnerships between schools and families.

Two promising efforts that are closely related to early childhood education—the family resource and support movement and early care and education collaboratives—are examples of important new approaches emerging from this ethos. Though distinct in purpose and structure, family resource and support programs and early care and education colloboratives both see schools as key levers in shaping services designed to improve child development, in enhancing the functioning of families, and in improving the delivery of social services to children and families. Both movements acknowledge the schools' potential as direct deliverers of service to parents and children. Finally, both movements, whether their programs are rooted within or outside the school walls, see themselves as potential vehicles for positive change.

Just what are these movements? What can we learn from them? And how do they further school reform?

Family Resource and Support Programs

Family resource and support programs are inventive responses to changes in the lives of families. Propelled into existence by changes in our social fabric that have left families more stressed, more isolated, and often poorer than ever before, thousands of family resource and support programs throughout the country offer services for parents (parent education, job training, respite care, adult education, employment referral, and emotional support) and services for children (health and developmental screening, home-based programs, and child care).

Recognizing the importance of this movement in its own right, as well as its importance to the education system, schools across the nation have begun to take part in it. To date, nearly one-third of the states include some form of parent education—an important component of family resource and support services—within their early childhood programs.[3] Not all of these efforts offer the complete array of services listed above. Indeed, many do not even call themselves "family resource and support programs." However, it is clear that educators are increasingly recognizing parents' substantial influence on their youngsters and are seeking innovative and practical ways to involve parents as educational partners.

This thinking has emerged, in part, from research on the relationship between children's home environments and family characteristics and their subsequent school performance. From James Coleman's work that suggested the important relationship between family status and student achievement to more recent studies that explore the differential effects of parenting styles on school performance, the case for closer ties between the home and the school has continued to grow. While research may not be sufficiently sophisticated to explain why such relationships occur or to pinpoint precisely which behaviors affect which outcomes, the evidence supports the critical role of families in the educational process.[4] Evaluations of early intervention programs that work directly with parents indicate that, despite variations in intent and strategy, they can have a considerable positive impact on children's lives, both in school and out.

Beyond their roots in research, family resource and support programs owe a debt to the self-help and parent education/parent involvement movements.[5] From the self-help movement, family resource and support programs have learned the importance of empowering individuals to improve their own lives. From the parent education and parent involvement movement, family resource and support programs have developed a strong commitment to enhancing the competence and confidence of parents.

Yet, in important ways, family resource and support programs are quite distinct from their historical antecedents. Family resource and support programs are not like the old-fashioned kinds of parent involvement that asked parents to bake cookies or accompany children on field trips; nor are they like more recent and often confrontational kinds of parent involvement that asked parents to concentrate not on themselves or their own families but on school reform in general. While family resource and support programs may remind us of many earlier efforts to link families and schools, they construe past lessons in new ways and represent the next frontier in home/school relations.

Two characteristics that distinguish family resource and support programs from past efforts are particularly important for schools. First, family support is seen as a developmental service for all parents. Family resource and support programs recognize that, even though families of all economic levels share such common concerns as drug abuse or sibling rivalry, not all families need precisely the same support at the same time. Thus, to meet the changing needs of families, family resource and support programs must be individualized, adaptive, and flexible. In addition, they must respect parents' values and schedules. Gone are the days when two daytime parent meetings per year constituted parent involvement. In their place, family support substitutes ongoing flexible programs that encourage parental input in planning.

Second, family resource and support programs stress egalitarian relationships between parents and school staff members. Parents are respected for their rich knowledge of their children, their culture, and their community, while teachers contribute knowledge of educational processes and systems. Working together as equals, parents and teachers plan and execute programs. Such realignment of relationships and roles alters the balance of power in schooling and challenges conventional working arrangements. Indeed, new job descriptions and new training programs may become necessary.

However, the greatest challenge, practically and financially, is integrating family resource and support programs into the mainstream of school life. Such programs report that, while acceptance is growing, they are still seen as *in,* but not *of* the schools.[6]

Part of this separation stems from the lack of a well-defined place for the programs in the educational bureaucracy. They may be part of early childhood education, or of vocational or adult education, or even of the social-service division of a school system. These tenuous links are further weakened by the precarious funding that characterizes many of the programs. The stability of family resource and support programs is sometimes threatened annually, a situation that requires staff members to devote valuable program time to fund-raising activities—perhaps even in competition with the school district. In some cases, funds for family support have been diverted from other funded programs, a practice that generates considerable animosity within school systems.

In spite of these challenges, school-based family resource and support programs are gaining currency in cities and states throughout the nation because they make important contributions to school life and to school reform. In addition to generating much community support, school-based family resource and support programs have rendered important services to children and families. They have demonstrated that it is possible and beneficial for schools to collaborate with community service agencies, and they have opened the schoolhouse doors a little wider, promoting the meaningful involvement of parents and other community members.

Likened to tugboats by David Seeley, family resource and support programs are small but mighty. They have the power to move entities many times their size. Just as tugs steer mighty ocean liners out of congested harbors toward open seas, family resource and support programs are one vehicle for guiding schools toward educational practices that are more open and responsive to the needs of families and communities.

Collaboration in Early Care and Education

As schools embrace a more comprehensive vision of the nature of the child and of their own role in society, the schoolhouse doors swing open ever wider. To meet the comprehensive needs of children, contacts with agencies rendering health, welfare, and social services have become routine. Special education legislation has propelled interagency collaboration to a new level, and the need to meet the before- and after-school child-care needs of children has fostered many connections between schools and communities. Collaborations between university scholars and school personnel have also helped mend town-gown schisms. And the existence of 40,000 partnerships between businesses and schools clearly indicates that the conventional vision of schools as isolated entities is outdated.[7]

Interestingly, such collaborations often involve agencies that deliver services that augment, but are clearly distinct from, the primary services offered by schools. For example, in addition to "special project" dollars, the private sector often brings new fiscal and management strategies to schools. Health agencies and the schools collaborate to provide health education, screening for health problems, and services to meet youngsters' specific health needs. Although each agency's raison d'etre is distinct, through collaboration each enriches the services offered by the other.

A second type of collaboration that is beginning to emerge in early care and education could have a dramatic impact on schools and school reform. These new collaborations involve agencies that share the same goals and missions and provide direct services to young children. In communities throughout the country, early care and education collaboratives are being established to bring together child-care programs, Head Start programs, profit and nonprofit programs, and the public schools.

Though still fragile, these collaborations in early care and education take the form of community councils, advisory groups, and resource and referral centers. In some communities, ad hoc councils have been converted into permanent bodies. Some collaborations have full-time staff members and funding; others have neither. But whatever their structure, these collaborations typically aim to: 1) increase the quantity and quality of available services, 2) insure more equitable distribution of services, 3) minimize expenses, 4) address shortages of staff and space, 5) equalize regulations across early childhood programs, 6) improve training opportunities, and 7) insure continuity for children. Many early childhood collaborations sponsor joint training for staff members in Head Start programs, child-care programs, and schools; others encourage cross-site visitation by staff members; still others join forces to buy materials and supplies. Collaborations often engage in community-wide data collection, cooperate in short- and long-term planning, and participate in advocacy efforts.

Given that public schools have played a comparatively minor role in the provision of preschool services and given that preschool services have remained quite distinct from one another, we might wonder why such interest in collaborations has arisen now and what school might gain from getting involved. Interest in collaboration has peaked for several reasons. First, funding for early care and education has increased. Second, because no empirical evidence has indicated a single "best" system and because of our national commitment to diversity, schools, child-care centers (public and private), and Head Start programs are all potential recipients of the new benefits that have been earmarked for childhood education.

Inevitably, this situation fosters competition. The stakes, after all, are quite high. To the victor go not only more slots for children but also typically the authority to control program regulations and staff requirements. Meanwhile, the losers lose doubly: they do not get program dollars, and, because of shortages of professionals in the field, their existing programs often lose staff members to better-funded programs. In truth, though they are conceived as separate entities, early care and education programs function on common pedagogical and physical grounds, a fact that makes collaboration all the more necessary.[8]

And finally, more important though less apparent, early care and education collaborations are emerging because communities are rejecting the segregated approach to funding and regulation that has yielded and inequitable system. Even the most cursory review of early care and education in the U.S. today reveals vast inequities and discontinuities for children, parents, and programs.[9] The children of the rich and of the poor do not have equal access to services. And even those youngsters who do receive services are blatantly segregated by income, with low-income children in subsidized programs and middle- and upper-income children in fee-for-service programs. Inequities exist, too, for providers of early care and education; those who work in public schools typically receive better salaries and benefits for fewer workdays per year and fewer working hours per day. Consequently, new school-based programs often act as magnets, attracting children and staff members away from other programs. Paradoxically, such competition for children, for staff, and for space, which is now well documented,[10] has spurred the drive for collaboration.

Yet early care and education collaborations are even more complex than public school collaborations because they involve more parties, many of which have longstanding acrimonious relationships. In addition, these collaborations can be somewhat suspect because they often act as external agents of change, initiating reform outside the school. Though this may sound ominous because the schools appear to forfeit control, such collaborations have been remarkably successful in broadening the schools' understanding of their important role within the early childhood system. Collaborations legitimate the sharing of responsibility. They do not allow any of the parties to avoid accountability, but they free schools to act as equal partners in crafting an equitable system of service delivery. Collaborations give schools options: they can improve their own early childhood services, they can add services, or they can join forces with community agencies. Furthermore, these collaborations give schools the opportunity to work in extremely productive ways with communities and providers who have tended to see the schools as rivals in the scramble for funding.

Whatever the motives, communities, cities, and states are embarking on collaborative strategies to influence the delivery of education services. For example, Florida is notable for its cooperative agreement between the departments of education and health and rehabilitative services; for its work on P.L. 99-457; for its prekindergarten Early Intervention Program, which was passed by the state legislature; and for its Central Agency system, which establishes city, county, and state collaborations that offer training, engage in joint planning and siting of programs, and coordinate service delivery. New Jersey's Urban Prekindergarten Program links Head Start, childcare, and the schools. In New York City, the Mayor's Office of Early Childhood Education, the board of education, and the Agency for Child Development plan the implementation of services for 4-year-olds.

Moreover, efforts such as these are not unique. They are taking root throughout the country, as services for preschoolers expand. Meanwhile, such efforts will increase as many pieces of federal legislation and most state legislation related to children and families call for establishing local or state-level collaborations or committees to address these issues.

Guiding Education Reform

Clearly, we need more experience with the programs before we can draw definitive conclusions regarding the efficacy of school-based family resource and support programs and early care and education collaborations. Yet each provides a stunning glimpse of the "restructuring" of American education. While neither effort originally set out to reform schools directly, each views education as a collective responsibility, each seeks equity for children and adults, and each recognizes the value of families and communities. Both efforts challenge conventional strategies, both ask schools to open their doors a bit wider, and both have altered the nature and amount of contact with parties one step removed from the schools.

However, more important than common intentions or creative strategies, family resource and support programs and early childhood collaborations share with each other and with advocates for reform a set of beliefs about the future of education in general and about the future of early care and education in particular. Though the following 10 "commandments" are not delivered from on high or carved indelibly in stone, they capsulate lessons to be learned from these efforts.

1. We cannot separate care and education. Together with the schools' involvement with young children and their families must come the recognition that high-quality care and education are inseparable. Whether labeled care or education, high-quality programs for preschoolers provide both. In spite of the similarity of services, we have seen that, within a community, different qualifications and salaries for teachers and different regulations for programs exist, diminishing the quality of care and education for children. To mitigate such differences, we must strive to link care and education.

2. We cannot segregate children according to family income. In many communities young children have unequal access to care and education, and, once in programs, youngsters are segregated according to family economic status. Thus our reforms will need to include strategies to foster

access to programs and to integrate services more equitably. Such is the spirit and the law of the land.

3. We cannot expect too much from poorly funded services. As discussed above, the inconsistent—and consistently low—funding of family resource and support programs has been one factor limiting their success. To permit early childhood services to achieve their proven potential, we must insure the stability and high quality afforded by sufficient and stable funding.

4. We must improve the infrastructure of early care and education along with increasing the number of slots. Because the expansion of services can exacerbate shortages of staff and space and because new slots and new needs generate increased demands for a coordinated system, funds must be devoted to planning and collaboration.

5. We must honor parents. Parents have a great influence on their children's development. Whether through Head Start's mandate for parent involvement or through family resource and support programs, educators must incorporate the family and the home culture into programs for children.

6. We must honor staff members. In early care and education programs, staff members are perhaps the most crucial component of program effectiveness. They facilitate learning, nourish active thinking and doing, and create environments in which children are cherished. We must support staff members by providing opportunities for continued professional growth, by involving them in decision making at the levels of program and school, and by compensating them fairly.

7. We must serve the whole child, within the context of family and community. Meeting children's needs demands that we address social, cognitive, emotional, and physical domains in an integrated fashion. Thus health, nutrition, psychological, social, special education, and parent support services must be included in early childhood programs.

8. We must foster developmentally appropriate pedagogy. Classroom practices that respect individual differences, that give children choices, and that foster the development of lifelong learning should be implemented. In addition to advancing the acquisition of skills, we must craft programs that foster social and cognitive growth and the development of curiosity, motivation, and other dispositions toward learning.

9. We must strive for the involvement of business, industry, and other groups. Recognizing that education is a shared responsibility, we need to make use of strategies that actively involve community members and organizations in school life. Although we should not allow the financial support of business to substitute for public responsibility, we must allow business to take its place along with other community organizations in our efforts to improve school effectiveness.

10. We must work together, not coveting the resources or children of other programs. Because policy strategies and funding have been largely categorical, early childhood education, like education in general, has matured in isolation. However, tighter resources, coupled with growing needs, make cooperation a necessity today. We must acknowledge that, as our problems transcend institutions and domains, so must their solutions. Reaching out is the key to reaching reform.

Sharon L. Kagan is associate director of the Bush Center in Child Development and Social Policy at Yale University, New Haven, Conn.; a member of the governing board of the National Association for the Education of Young Children; co-editor of Early Schooling; The National Debate (Yale University Press, 1987); and editor of the forthcoming yearbook on early care and education of the National Society for the Study of Education.

Endnotes

1. Elmore, Richard F. *Early Experience in Restructuring Schools: Voices from the Field*. Washington, D.C.: National Governors' Association, 1989.

2. For discussion of the challenges and strategies inherent in linking families and schools, see Donald Davies, ed., *Schools Where Parents Make a Difference*. Boston: Institute for Responsive Education, 1976. Hope Jensen Leichter, ed., *Families and Communities as Educators*. New York: Teachers College Press, 1979. Sara Lawrence Lightfoot. *Worlds Apart: Relationships Between Families and Schools*. New York: Basic Books, 1978. Milbrey Wallin McLaughlin and Patrick M. Shields. "Involving Low-Income Parents in the Schools: A Role for Policy?." *Phi Delta Kappan,* October 1987, 156–60. David Seeley. *Education Through Partnership: Mediating Structures and Education*. Cambridge, Mass.: Ballinger, 1981. Cynthia Wallet and Richard Goldman. *Home, School, Community Interaction*. Columbus, Ohio: Merrill, 1979.

3. Marx, Fern; and Seligson, Michelle. *The Public School Early Childhood Study: The State Survey*. New York: Bank Street College of Education, 1988.

4. Coleman, James, et al. *Equality of Educational Opportunity*. Washington, D.C.: U.S. Government Printing Office, 1966. Henderson, Ann. *Parent Participation and School Achievement: The Evidence Mounts*. Columbia, Md.: National Committee for Citizens in Education, 1981. Powell, Douglas, R. *Families and Early Childhood Programs*. Washington, D.C.: National Association for the Education of Young Children, 1989.

5. Weissbourd, Bernice. *"A Brief History of Family Support Programs."* In America's Family Support Programs: Perspectives and Prospects, edited by Sharon L. Kagan, Douglas R. Powell, Bernice Weissbourd, and Edward Zigler. New Haven, Conn.: Yale University Press, 1987.

6. Weiss, Heather, B. "Family Support and Education Programs and the Public Schools: Opportunities and Challenges," paper prepared for the Early Childhood Task Force of the National Association of State Boards of Education, 1988.

7. Otterbourg, Susan D.; and Timpane, Michael. "Partnerships and Schools."

In *Public-Private Partnerships: Improving Urban Life,* edited by Perry Davis. New York: Academy of Political Science, 1986.

8. Kagan, Sharon L. "Early Schooling: On Common Ground." In *Early Schooling: The National Debate,* edited by Sharon L. Kagan and Edward Zigler. New Haven, Conn.: Yale University Press, 1987.

9. Scarr, Sandra; and Weinberg, Richard. "The Early Childhood Enterprise: Care and Education of the Young." *American Psychologist,* October 1986, 1, 140–46.

10. Goodman, Irene F.; and Brady, Joanne P. *The Challenge of Coordination: Head Start's Relationship to State-Funded Preschool Initiatives.* Newton, Mass.: Education Development Center, May, 1988.

CHAPTER 4

How Best to Protect Children from Inappropriate School Expectations, Practices, and Policies

Since its inception in 1926, NAEYC's purpose has been to act on behalf of the needs and interests of young children. Toward that goal, most activity has been efforts to ensure the availability of high-quality, developmentally appropriate programs for all young children, and obversely to protect children from potentially harmful or inappropriate environments.

Two major trends in recent years have caused NAEYC to increase its activity in working toward its goals. First, the number of early childhood programs has increased rapidly, particularly with the advent of prekindergarten services in many public schools and the expanded need for child care for employed families. At the same time, there has been a negative trend toward escalated academic demand in kindergarten and preschool. In light of this trend toward more formal, teacher-directed drill and practice on isolated academic skills with younger and younger children, NAEYC members throughout the country petitioned the Association to provide guidance in defining developmentally appropriate practices for early childhood programs.

In 1986, NAEYC first published position statements defining developmentally appropriate and inappropriate practices in programs for young children, which were subsequently expanded to cover the entire age spectrum of early childhood, from birth through age 8 (Bredekamp, 1987). In the two years since initial publication, more than 85,000 copies of this important book have been distributed. For the first time, NAEYC described what is inappropriate as well as what is appropriate for children, in effect saying "Do this but also protect children from that."

Following the publication of NAEYC's positions on developmentally appropriate practice, the need was identified for a similar statement addressing the uses and misuses of standardized testing with young children (NAEYC, 1988). Many kindergarten and primary teachers expressed concern that, while they agree with the practices advocated by NAEYC, they are prevented from doing what is best for children by the need to ensure that their students produce specified scores on standardized tests. For example, many teachers reported experiencing "philosophy-reality conflicts" because of the discrepancy between their philosophical beliefs about what is appropriate for children and required instructional practices (Hatch & Freeman, 1988; Smith, 1986).

Unfortunately, high stakes testing is now the reality in primary schools. High stakes tests "are linked to decisions regarding promotion or retention, are used for evaluating or rewarding teachers and administrators, affect the allocation of resources to school districts, and result in changes in the curriculum (Meisels, in press)." Anyone who doubts that high stakes are involved in the testing of young children need only turn to commercial publishers who now produce curriculum kits on test-taking skills for pre-K, K, and 1st graders, or sponsor "CAT Academies" in Georgia to prepare kindergartners to take the required California Achievement Test, or publish books like *The Baby Boards: A Parents' Guide to Preschool and Primary School Entrance Tests* (Robinson, 1988).

The issues relating to inappropriate curriculum and assessment in the kindergarten and primary grades are complex and interrelated. In the March 1989 issue of Young Children (pp. 5–13), Rosalind Charlesworth addresses the pros and cons of various approaches to preventing school failure at an early age such as testing for readiness, transition classes, and raising the entrance age. The purpose of this article is to describe the research findings from which NAEYC derived its positions on these issues. A careful review of the research related to testing, retention, transition classes, and earlier entrance age cutoffs indicates that these increasingly common practices designed to protect "unready" children from inappropriately formal schooling are at best minimally helpful in the short run for some individual children, and hurt as many children as they help. In addition, these practices are harmful because they exacerbate the problem of inappropriate curriculum—that is, the downward shoving of what were next-grade expectations into the earlier grades (Shepard & Smith, 1988).

In brief, these strategies are all based on the same false assumption—that the kindergarten curriculum is a static, fixed entity and that if we can somehow better match children's readiness to the curriculum, their chances of success will increase. The truth is that the kindergarten curriculum is dynamic and has changed considerably in the last 20 years (Educational Research Service, 1986; Hiebert, 1988). For example, if children come to kindergarten apparently knowing more, then more of the first-grade curriculum is moved into kindergarten. When the school entrance age is raised by moving the cutoff date from January 1 to November 1, then academic expectations are adjusted upward in response to the new older group, and so forth. This article describes how well-intentioned efforts to protect children from inappropriate practices have had the opposite effect and proposes some alternative strategies to help us accomplish this important goal.

Policies that Promote Inappropriate Curriculum

Readiness Testing

Many school districts use standardized tests to obtain an "objective" measure of children's readiness for kindergarten or first grade. For example, the Gesell Institute reports that 18% of school districts use the Gesell School Readiness Test to assess readiness and place children. "Unready" children are usually given two options: to stay out a year before kindergarten or to enter a 2-year track, either developmental kindergarten or pre-first grade.

All tests have a degree of error. The reliability of a test is a measure of the degree to which the scores on the test can be attributed to real differences in individuals' abilities rather than to errors in measurement. The validity of the test refers to how accurately it measures what it says it measures. When a test is used for placement it must have predictive validity, that is, scores on that test must accurately predict how children will perform in the future. When a test is used to make an important decision about individual children such as school entrance, retention, or assignment to a special placement, that test must meet the highest standards of reliability and validity (Salvia & Ysseldyke, 1981). Unfortunately, the commonly used readiness tests are not sufficiently reliable or valid for such purposes (Shepard & Smith, 1988). The Metropolitan Readiness Test has the best predictive validity, reporting correlations of .70 to .78 with later first grade measures of achievement (Nurss & McGauvran, 1976). Although these correlatios are impressively high if the test is used for instructional planning or program evaluation as intended by its authors, they nonetheless indicate that as many as 1/3 of children would be misidentified as "unready" if the MRT were used for kindergarten placement. In the case of the Gesell test, predictive correlations from .28 to .64 have been reported (Kaufman & Kaufman, 1972; Popovics, 1982). Using even the most favorable data, the Gesell test misidentified 1/3 to 1/2 of children said to be unready. Practitioners should realize that correlations of this same size (about .50 to .60) would be obtained if parents were given an IQ test and the result correlated with each child's first grade achievement scores. Would it then be valid to place children on the basis of the parents' measured IQ? Of course not.

The psychometric properties of the Gesell test do not meet the standards of professional test development (AERA, APA, & NCME, 1985). For example, the test purports to measure an individual child's developmental age as compared to what is "normal," and yet the norms used by the test are inadequate, according to the *Ninth Mental Measurements Yearbook* (Bradley, 1985; Kaufman, 1985; Naglieri, 1985; Waters, 1985). The Gesell School Readiness Test was normed 20 years ago on a sample of only 50 boys and 50 girls per age level, most of whom were white and from Connecticut. A further psychometric aberration of the Gesell test is that it reports no scoring procedure nor standard deviation of scores. Usually, test developers report standard deviations to indicate the typical range within which individuals score compared to the average score. Lacking a standard deviation, it is not possible to tell whether a child's performance is normal. A 5-year-old child who performs like an average 4 ½-year-old is treated as if he were seriously deficient, yet for all the tester knows that child's score is at the 40th or 45th percentile of all 5-year-olds, and therefore quite normal.

This fact alone should make the test suspect to most early childhood educators, who readily accept the concept that there is tremendous developmental variation within an individual of a given age group as well as between different age groups.

Despite the lack of data supporting reliability and validity, the Gesell and other screening and readiness tests are being used for placement decisions. For instance, in 1988 the Norwood-Norfolk school district in New York assigned 61% of incoming kindergartners to the 2-year track called developmental kindergarten, on the basis of a single administration of the Gesell test. Parents brought suits against the district on the grounds that "developmental kindergarten" constitutes special placement and that federal and state special education statutes were violated when special placement was made on the basis of a single test administration, without individual educational evaluations, due process, or informed consent of parents (Center for Law & Education, 1988). The State Department of Education settled with the parents, returned the children to regular kindergarten, and has since revised placement procedures.

Our purpose here is not to bash specific tests, but to emphasize the importance of ensuring a test's validity for its intended use. As many early childhood educators know, the readiness tests discussed above are excellent tools for helping teachers assess children's individual abilities and needs and are very useful for planning individual instruction. The Gesell test, particularly, has helped early childhood teachers gain a better understanding of child development and improve observational skills. When a test is used to plan instruction within a classroom, it does not have to be as accurate as a test that is used for placement (Salvia & Ysseldyke, 1981). For example, suppose a readiness test determines that five children in the class do not know their colors. If the teacher initiates learning activities to teach colors and then discovers that the children already knows them she can easily adjust. Within the regular class placement, little has been lost by the error in measuring knowledge of colors. On the other hand, if those same five children are held out of kindergarten or assigned to a 2-year track because they failed to demonstrate required knowledge on a readiness test, then the situation is far more serious, much less easy to correct, and much less likely to be corrected.

Another major problem with the use of readiness tests for screening and placement is the inherent cultural and linguistic biases of such policies. Whether readiness tests measure pre-academic skills or "developmental" abilities, performance on such tests will be influenced strongly by past opportunities to learn. These tests cannot measure inherent or biological readiness. Therefore, children who do not have an English-language background and extensive experience with the forms of schooling, such as being questioned by a strange adult, will be at a disadvantage on the test. Legislators and school administrators must recognize that using standardized tests for entry or placement will undoubtedly further segregate children by economic class and ethnicity. Decision makers must be keenly aware of the implications of these policies for educational equity (Medina & Neill, 1988).

Using readiness tests for kindergarten entry or assignment to transition classes is harmful in two important ways. First, it harms individual children by labeling them as failures before they begin school. All children are ready to learn; learning begins at birth. Therefore, to label a child as "unready" can only mean that the child is not prepared for a particular curriculum or experience. Children are identified, often misidentified, as behind their peer group. The test puts the onus on the child, rather than requiring that the educational program be ready to serve the population for which it is intended.

The second major danger of readiness testing is that sorting children according to ability and assigning the most "ready" children to the regular kindergarten classroom feeds the escalation of the curriculum. It is sadly ironic that tests that are not accurate enough to make individual placements are reasonably accurate in describing groups on average. It is likely, then, that the average ability of the "ready" group will be higher than the average ability of the "unready" group. As has happened in the past, teachers will naturally teach to the new norm group and, therefore, the expectations in the regular kindergarten or regular first grade will shift again to become more like those of the next higher grade (Shepard & Smith, 1988).

Retention, Transition Classes, and Tracking

One of the most commonly used methods for "protecting" children from the increased academic demands of kindergarten and first grade is some form of extra-year program. Flunking kindergarten has become more commonplace. A supposedly more benign treatment than retention is the widespread institution of transition classes, either before kindergarten or pre-first grade. Each of these solutions is based on the assumptions that early retention does not have the same negative effects as later retention, that holding a child back early will help him or her to achieve more later, or that the same level of achievement will be achieved with less stress. Despite the fact that the research evidence contradicts these assumptions (Shepard & Smith, 1986; 1987; in press), they persist primarily because they are intuitively so powerful. Virtually every early childhood teacher can name specific children whom they recommended to be held back who subsequently did well in school. One of the major flaws in this reasoning is that the teacher or parent has no way of knowing how the child would have fared had he (and it is usually a male) been allowed to proceed normally. Many children selected for transition on the basis of immaturity are very able learners. They go on to become stars in their first grade classroom and the credit is given to the transition placement. What teachers cannot know is that an equal number of children, who were equally able learners and equally immature, but who went directly on to first grade, also became stars in their first grade class.

Controlled studies of kindergarten retention show that it does not improve achievement of the retained children. In a study conducted in Colorado (Shepard & Smith, 1987), control children were selected so that they started school with readiness scores just as low as the retained children. They were also mostly male and summer birthday children like the retained group. At the end of first grade, when the retained children were completing 3 years of school and the "unready" controls were completing only 2 years, the only significant difference was that the extra-year children were one month ahead on reading scores as measured by the Comprehensive Test of Basic Skills. There were no differences between the two groups on math scores or teacher ratings of academics, maturity, self-concept, and attention, despite the additional year of school for the retained children. An equal number of children in each of the two groups were at the top and bottom of their class. Many of the extra-year children were rated as immature by their first-grade teachers, causing the researchers to speculate that what is labeled as immaturity might actually be more enduring personality traits that are not changed by the extra year.

Advocates of kindergarten retention sometimes dismiss findings of no academic benefit, saying that achievement is not the issue. Rather the idea of an extra year is to remove children from the stress of a rigid curriculum so they will feel good about themselves. For example, in defense of retention, Ames argues that "even if it would be traumatic to keep them back, it's better to traumatize them once and get it over with than to face problems every day for the next 12 years (Kutner, 1988)." However, the lack of measurable deficiencies in unready children who refused extra-year placements in numerous studies (Gredler, 1984; Shepard & Smith, in press) raises questions about Ames's claim that these unready children who are not retained will struggle for the rest of their lives. Academics is always implicitly the issue since presumably the idea of relieving stress is based on the belief that academic tasks will be appreciably easier when the child is a year older.

The emotional effects of kindergarten retention or transition room assignment are of concern. In the Colorado study described above, parents reported that retained children had poorer attitudes toward school. In interview, parents of retained children reported positive perceptions of the experience such as being better prepared for school, not having to struggle so much, and preventing later retention, but even the majority of parents who supported the retention decision reported that they and their child suffered some trauma as a result (Shepard & Smith, 1985; in press). Contrary to popular belief, retained children do recognize that they are not making normal progress. One little girl thought that assignment to pre-first grade would mean that she would always be in the in-between class, pre-second, pre-third, and so on. Some of the most salient pieces of information about a child are her or his age and grade in school. Ask a child who has been retained what grade she is in and the probable answer will be, "I'm in the third grade, but I would have been in fourth if . . ."

Extra-year programs and kindergarten retention are examples of short-sighted policy. In our attempt to protect children from an inappropriate primary grade curriculum, we expose them to far greater hazard. We threaten their social and emotional development with a placement that is known to be traumatic in a vain hope that being a year older will reduce the damage to their self-esteem from excessive academic demands. We also extend the number of years required to remain in school to achieve a high school diploma. In an era when preventing high school dropouts is a major objective, we are instituting policies that will require keeping children in school until they are 19. Similarly, in an era of economic deficit, we are imposing the burden of financing an extra year of schooling for retained and transition children.

But the major point we want to make about retention and transition classes is that when less able or "immature" children are removed from the regular classroom by whatever means, license is given to further increase the academic demand of the curriculum. For example, the now older or more able group can sit still longer and complete more worksheets. By now, many readers are probably saying, "So? Isn't it a good thing to be able to challenge able learners to the utmost, and aren't these strategies actually ways of individualizing instruction?" Research says no. A vast number of studies have demonstrated that homogeneous ability grouping not only harms the less able children but does not help the brighter children (Heller, Holtzman & Messick, 1982; Oakes, 1986a, 1986b; Slavin, 1986). As far as very young children are concerned, increased academic demand hurts the children who can handle it as well as those who fail. Many of the brightest children, for whom school should be pleasurable, report stress-related symptoms, unwarranted fear of failure, and school-avoidance behaviors (Elkind, 1987). In some school contexts where standardized tests dictate the curriculum, children are often deprived of opportunities to develop reading comprehension or problem-solving abilities because of excessive drill on rote skills. Those who advocate kindergarten retention and extra-year classes as remedies for lack of "readiness" on the part of large numbers of children need to investigate why such drastic interventions are necessary and whether it is the children or the curriculum objectives that are to blame.

Raising the Entrance Age, or Older is Better
Because so many children struggle with the kindergarten and first grade curriculum, a common solution is to raise the entrance age or to recommend that children with "late bithdays wait a year before starting school. The concept of the "Gift of Time" (Uphoff & Gilmore, 1986) has been widely promoted. It has become popular wisdom that if your child is the oldest in the class, he or she will be much more successful in life than those who are the youngest.

This reasoning is based on the research on the "youngest" effect, which shows that children who are the youngest in the class are at a slight disadvantage academically. However, this disadvantage has been enormously exaggerated. The fact is that on average the youngest children are behind by 7 or 8 percentile points on achievement tests and this deficit disappears by the third grade (Shepard & Smith, 1986). This research should not surprise early childhood educators who recognize that during early childhood there is wide variance in what can be considered normal development, that young children are growing and changing rapidly, and that the rate of growth and the extreme variance in individual differences tends to slow down after third grade. Nevertheless, we cling to our exaggerated notion that older is better. "Because I held him back in preschool, he went from being at the bottom of his class to being at the top." "If I hadn't kept him back, he would have been a failure his whole life." Such impassioned statements greet any discussion of this emotion-laden issue. While being the youngest in the class may be a slight disadvantage in the most rigidly structured kindergartens, it does not follow that being the oldest ensures academic excellence or other forms of success, and yet the myth persists. It is ironic that a generation ago skipping grades was considered an intellectual status symbol (Baran, 1988) and now preschool "redshirting" is supposedly a sign of enlightened affluence. "Redshirting" is aptly named since some parents hold back children, especially boys, to ensure their chances as varsity athletes.

When parents voluntarily hold their children out of school to ensure that they are older, they contribute to the problem of escalating curriculum. These are usually middle-class parents (whose children would probably do fine in school), who then provide them an additional year of private preschool. The children enter kindergarten at age 6, sometimes reading fluently, and their parents demand that the kindergarten teach them something they don't already know. By holding a "bright, immature" boy out of school, parents might have raised his academic performance temporarily from the 80th percentile to the 87th percentile, although actually research shows that the youngness effect is less for very able learners than for below-average learners (Shepard & Smith, 1985). For this small personal advantage the school system has paid a heavy price. When middle-class children are the ones who come to school already 6 years old, they have a double advantage: the 7 percentile points due to age plus the much larger achievement advantage due to socioeconomic status. To the extent that this fashion is pursued by middle-class families, it greatly increases the heterogeneity of kindergarten and first grade classrooms. As more and more 6-year-olds come to kindergarten, teachers who are not trained to take advantage of multiage groups are stressed by too great a range of individual differences, which they seek to relieve by retaining normal but young 5-year-olds. It is a vicious cycle.

The institutional response to the youngness effect is to raise the entrance age. For example, in Missouri, children must now be 5 by July to enter kindergarten in September. Adjusting the entrance age is perhaps the easiest means of protecting children from inappropriate expectations, but is perhaps the most insidious in aggravating the problem. The adjustment simply creates a new youngest group. The very children in Missouri whom teachers will then complain about because they are "too young, too immature, and not ready" would be among the older children in Maryland (where the cutoff date is December 31), whom teachers would evaluate as normal.

Changing the entrance age is at best a very short-term solution. It is based on the false assumption that the kindergarten curriculum will remain fixed. In reality, teachers estimate that within two years the curriculum will adjust to the average ability of the older group, thus putting pressure on the new youngest group to keep up.

Policymakers should recognize that changing the entrance age creates inequity. A presumably minor adjustment such as raising the entrance age by 3 months actually denies schooling for one year to one-fourth of age-eligible children. The impact on middle-class families will be relatively minor, since their children are likely to spend that year in private pre-school. The burden falls on low-income children, for whom preschool services are much less widely available. For example, Head Start serves only one-fifth of eligible children. Therefore, raising the entrance age not only contributes to escalation of curriculum, but further divides the educational opportunity of the "haves" and "have-nots" in our society.

Alternative Strategies to Protect Children from Inappropriate Practices

Because of our positions and articles such as this one, NAEYC and the authors personally have been accused of recommending that "children be thrown to the wolves." In public forums, committed early childhood teachers describe kindergarten and/or first grade as a "hostile environment" against which they must protect young children. In these same meetings, teachers report frustration and impotence to influence curriculum and assessment revision. The discussion inevitably leads to blaming the source of external pressure, usually identified as parents, administrators, or legislators (Seefeldt & Barbour, 1988).

However, there are schools in which teachers and administrators resist these trends entirely. Smith and Shepard (in press) have identified two types of schools: schools with high retention rates that are characterized by an "accountability culture" where rigid proficiency standards and grade expectations prevail and testing and retention are prevalent; and schools with low retention rates where an atmosphere of collegiality among teachers and more fluid organization of grade expectations prevails. These schools cannot be distinguished by curriculum, instructional methods, or population served in terms of income, ethnic diversity, or student achievement. But the two types of school differ greatly. The high-retaining schools operate almost on a factory model where each grade-level teacher is expected to produce a predetermined product and teachers are held accountable for children's performance. On the other hand, in low-retaining schools the teachers tend to take the children where they are, move them along as far as they can, and then communicate clearly to the next grade teacher the child's strengths and needs.

We do not want to imply that accountability is not important. All children deserve the best education possible, and schools and teachers must be accountable for providing high-quality instruction and for recognizing and adapting instruction when children fail to learn. But the use of standardized test scores as the predominant indicator of accountability is ill-advised. The recent revelation that all 50 states report that their students' test scores are above the national average (Cannell, 1987) is one indication of the degree to which test scores are suspect. There is increasing evidence that when test scores take on too much political importance in schools, scores can go up without there being a real increase in student learning (Shepard, in press). We need alternative strategies that ensure excellence and equity, as well as accountability. Here are some suggestions to help guide educators in making decisions. We welcome other suggestions.

To Make Decisions About Entrance and Placement

1. Do not use standardized tests for entry to school or promotion in the primary grades.
2. Establish a uniform kindergarten entrance age whereby most children attending kindergarten are 5 years old and most first graders are 6.
3. Accept children for school on the basis of their chronological age and legal right to enter.
4. Use valid developmental screening tests as a first step in identifying children who may be in need of further diagnosis of a health, learning, or developmental handicap (Meisels, 1985).
5. Use valid standardized tests as one of many sources of information to conduct a complete diagnosis of a child's special needs and to suggest the cause of the problem and appropriate intervention and remediation strategies (Meisels, 1987).

To Evaluate Programs' Accomplishment of Goals

1. Do not conduct standardized achievement testing of all children until at least third grade.
2. Where standardized achievement tests scores are used in third grade as accountability measures and to compare individual schools and districts, do not test all children; use sampling to obtain the same results cost effectively without labeling individual children. If such testing is done, conduct it in the fall of the year to prevent "teaching to the test" and evaluating individual teachers with test scores.
3. Develop alternative assessment instruments and procedures to use instead of standardized tests, such as oral tapes of children's stories or reading progress and portfolios of students' writing and artwork. Recognize that currently available standardized tests provide very limited measures of school and student success and become invalid if children are drilled on questions just like the test items.

4. Increase the use of systematic observation of teacher and student performance and the systematic documentation of various sources of evidence of children's progress for use in curriculum planning, evaluation, and reporting to parents. Increase the use of measures that assess children's strengths as well as their deficits.

To Plan and Individualize Curriculum and Instruction

1. Use developmentally appropriate teaching methods to individualize instruction. For example, when children work in learning centers or in small groups on projects, the teacher is freed to work with individual children and to use techniques such as peer tutoring, coaching, and individual progress that use group heterogeneity as an instructional asset.
2. Clarify the terminology used to describe inappropriate practices. We realize that this article refers to "escalated" curriculum and that in some ways the curriculum expects too much, too fast for the age group, but in other ways it expects too little. Emphasis on drill and practice and worksheet-dictated curriculum is "shockingly un-stimulating to children and fails to extend their thinking (NASBE, 1988, p. 4)." Young children can actually engage in problem solving before they know their addition facts and sophisticated reasoning and questioning about stories before they can decode words if these opportunities are provided in ways meaningful to their level of understanding; (Palincsar & Brown, in press; Peterson, in press).

To Advocate for Appropriate Policies

1. Encourage concerned parents to join together and complain about inappropriate practices and policies. When children's rights are violated by testing abuses, vocal parents are the most effective agents of change.
2. Enhance collegiality within schools and across all sectors of the early childhood profession. Use the NAEYC Affiliate Group structure, which is organized by geography rather than special interest groups, to its fullest advantage by promoting membership and services to all teachers and administrators of programs serving children birth through age 8.
3. Use the many valuable tools currently available to advocate for appropriate practices in all early childhood programs. Following are some of the many position statements that strongly support sound practices for young children.

American Federation of Teachers. "Standardized Testing in Kindergarten. 1988 Convention Policy Resolution." In *AFT Convention Report* (p. 58–59), Washington, DC: Author, July, 1988.

Association for Supervision and Curriculum Development. *A Resource Guide to Public School Early Childhood Programs*. Alexandria, VA: Author, 1988.

California State Department of Education. *Here They Come: Ready or Not. Report of the School Readiness Task Force*. Sacramento: Author, 1988.

International Reading Association. "Literacy Development and Pre-First Grade: A Joint Statement of Concerns About Present Practices in Pre-First Grade Reading Instruction and Recommendations for Improvement." *Childhood Education*, 1986, 63: 110–111.

National Association of Early Childhood Specialists in State Departments of Education. *Unacceptable Trends in Kindergarten Entrance and Placement*. Lincoln, NE: Author, 1987.

National Association of State Boards of Education. *Right From the Start. The Report of the NASBE Task Force on Early Childhood Education*. Alexandria, VA: Author, 1988.

National Black Child Development Institute. *Safeguards: Guidelines for Establishing Programs for 4-Year-Olds in the Public Schools*. Washington, DC: Author, 1987.

Positions are currently being developed by the National Association of Elementary School Principals, the National Center for Clinical Infant Programs, and the American Academy of Pediatrics.

Conclusion

As mentioned earlier, NAEYC has devoted more than 60 years of activity to ensuring the best for children. We would never advocate subjecting children to inappropriate environments. At the same time, we cannot support policies such as readiness testing, transition classes, holding younger children out of school, or raising the entrance age, which we know at best are short-term solutions and at worst harm individual children and contribute to inappropriate expectations.

The early childhood profession must obtain better consensus about these issues and then act with one voice to influence policy. It is time that early childhood educators devote as much energy and commitment to fighting inappropriate practices, curriculum, and policies as they traditionally devote to protecting an individual child they feel is at risk.

As the next step in the process of articulating standards for appropriate practice, the early childhood profession has identified the need to develop guidelines for appropriate curriculum content and assessment in the early childhood unit, prekindergarten through third grade. NAEYC, in collaboration with the National Association of Early Childhood Specialists in State Departments of Education and other national organizations and experts, is currently beginning work on this project. Suggested resources should be sent in writing to Sue Bredekamp at NAEYC Headquarters.

This article is adapted from a seminar on Standardized Testing of Young Children presented by the authors at the 1988 NAEYC Annual Conference in Anaheim, California, and from "Escalating Academic Demand in Kindergarten: Counterproductive Policies" by Lorrie Shepard and Mary Lee Smith, which appeared in the November 1988 issue of Elementary School Journal.

Sue Bredekamp, PH.D., is Director of Professional Development at NAEYC. She directs NAEYC's accreditation system, and edited NAEYC's position statements on developmentally appropriate practice and testing.

Lorrie Shepard, Ph.D., is Chair of Research and Evaluation Methodology and Professor of Education at the University of Colorado, Boulder.

References

American Educational Research Association; American Psychological Association; and National Council on Measurement in Education. *Standards for Educational and Psychological Testing.* Washington, DC: Author, 1985.

Baran, K. "Schools Note Trend Toward Late Starters." *Washington Times,* May 16, 1988, E9.

Bradley, R. "Review of Gesell School Readiness Test." In *Ninth Mental Measurements Yearbook,* edited by J. V. Michael, Jr. Lincoln, NE: Buros Institute of Mental Measurements, 1985, 1: 609–610.

Bredekamp, S. (ed.) *Developmentally Appropriate Practice in Early Childhood Programs Serving Children from Birth Through Age 8* (expanded ed.). Washington, DC: NAEYC, 1987.

Cannell, J. J. *Nationally Normed Elementary Achievement Testing in America's Public Schools: How all Fifty Schools are Above the National Average.* Daniels, WV: Friends for Education, 1987.

Center for Law and Education, Inc. "Parents Win Challenge to Kindergarten Exam." *News Notes,* August, 1988, 2–3.

Educational Research Service. "Kindergarten Programs and Practices in Public Schools." *Principal,* 1986, 65: 22–23.

Elkind, D. *Miseducation: Preschoolers at Risk*. New York: Knopf, 1987.

Gredler, G. R. "Transition Classes: A Viable Alternative for the At-Risk Child?." *Psychology in the Schools*, 1984, 21: 463–470.

Hatch, J. A.; and Freeman, E. "Kindergarten Philosophies and Practices: Perspectives of Teachers, Principals, and Supervisors." Early Childhood Research Quarterly, 1988, 3: (2), 151–166.

Heller, K.; Holtzman, W.; and Messick, S. (Eds.). *Placing Children in Special Education: A Strategy for Equity*. Washington, DC: National Academy Press, 1982.

Hiebert, E. H. "Introduction." *Elementary School Journal,* 1988, 89: 115–117.

Kaufman, N. "Review of Gesell School Readiness Test." In *Ninth Mental Measurements Yearbook,* edited by J. V. Michael, Jr. Lincoln, NE: Buros Institute of Mental Measurements, 1985, 1: 607–608.

Kaufman, A. S.; and Kaufman, N. L. "Tests Built from Piaget's and Gesell's Task as Predictors of First-Grade Achievement." *Child Development,* 1972, 43: 521–535.

Kutner, L. "Repeating Kindergarten is Often Unnecessary." *The New York Times,* May 20, 1988.

Medina, Z.; and Neill, D. M. *Fallout from the Testing Explosion: How 100 Million Standardized Exams Undermine Equity and Excellence in America's Public Schools*. Cambridge, MA: National Center for Fair and Open Testing, 1988.

Meisels, S. J. *Developmental Screening in Early Childhood: A Guide*. Washington, DC: NAEYC, 1985.

Meisels, S. J. "Uses and abuses of Developmental Screening and School Readiness Testing." Young Children, 1987, 42: (2) 4–6, 68–73.

Meisels, S. J. (in press). "High Stakes Testing in Kindergarten." *Educational Leadership.*

Naglieri, J. J. "Review of Gesell School Readiness Test." In *Ninth Mental Measurements Yearbook,* edited by J. V. Michael, Jr. Lincoln, NE: Buros Institute of Mental Measurements, 1985, 1: 608–609.

National Association for the Education of Young Children." *Accreditation Criteria and Procedures of the National Academy of Early Childhood Programs*. Washington, DC: Author, 1984.

National Association of the Education of Young Children. "Position Statement on Standardized Testing of Young Children 3 through 8 Years of Age." *Young Children,* 1988, 43: (3) 42–47.

National Associaton of State Boards of Education." *Right From the Start. The Report of the NASBE Task Force on Early Childhood Education*. Alexandria, VA: Author, 1988.

Nurss, J.; and McGauvran, M. *Metropolitan Readiness Tests Teachers' Manual: Part 2. Interpretation and Test Results*. New York: Harcourt Brace Jovanovich, 1976.

Oakes, J. "Keeping Track, Part 1: The Policy and Practice of Curriculum Inequality." *Phi Delta Kappan,* September, 1986a, 12–17.

Oakes, J. "Keeping Track, Part 2: Curriculum Inequality and School Reform." *Phi Delta Kappan,* October, 1986b, 148–153.

Palincsar, A.; and Brown, A. (in press). "Classroom Dialogues to Promote Self-Regulated Comprehension." In *Teaching for Understanding and Self-Regulated Learning,* edited by J. Brophy. Greenwich, CT: JAI Press.

Peterson, P. (in press). "Alternatives to Student Retention: New Images of the Learner, the Teacher, and Classroom Learning." In *Flunking Grades: Research and Policies on Grade Retention,* edited by L. A. Shepard and M. L. Smith. Lewes, England: Falmer Press.

Popovics, A. J. "Total and Component Actuarial Scores of the Gesell Copy Form Test as Predictors of Achievement, Intelligence, and Creativity Measures." *The Journal of Psychology,* 1982, 110: 293–295.

Robinson, J. *The Baby Boards: A Parents' Guide to Preschool and Primary School Entrance Tests.* New York: Acro, 1988.

Salvia, J.; and Ysseldyke, J. *Assessment in Special and Remedial Education* (2nd ed.). Boston: Houghton Mifflin, 1981.

Seefeldt, C.; and Barbour, N. " 'They Said I had to . . .' Working with Mandates." *Young Children,* 1988, 43: (4) 4–8.

Shepard, L. (in press). "Redirecting Assessment: An Overview." *Educational Leadership.*

Shepard, L. A.; and Smith, M. L. *Boulder Valley Kindergarten Study: Retention Practices and Retention Effects.* Boulder, CO: Boulder Valley Public Schools, March, 1985.

Shepard, L. A.; and Smith, M. L. "Synthesis of Research on School Readiness and Kindergarten Retention." *Educational Leadership,* 1986, 44: (3) 78–86.

Shepard, L. A.; and Smith, M. L. "Effects of Kindergarten Retention at the End of First Grade." *Psychology in the Schools,* 1987, 24: 346–357.

Shepard, L. A.; and Smith, M. L. "Escalating Academic Demand in Kindergarten: Counterproductive Policies." *The Elementary School Journal,* 1988, 89: 135–145.

Shepard, L. A.; and Smith, M. L. (eds.). (in press). *Flunking Grades: Research and Policies on Retention.* Lewes, England: Falmer Press.

Slavin, R. K. *Ability Grouping and Student Achievement in Elementary Schools: A Best Evidence Synthesis.* Baltimore: Baltimore Center for Research on Elementary and Middle Schools, Johns Hopkins University, 1986.

Smith, D. *California Kindergarten Practices.* Fresno: California State University-Fresno, School of Education, Office of Research, 1986.

Smith, M. L.; and Shepard, L. A. (in press). "Kindergarten Readiness and Retention: A Qualitative Study of Teachers' Beliefs and Practices." *American Educational Research Journal.*

Uphoff, J.; and Gilmore, J. *Summer Children: Ready or Not for School.* Middletown, OH: J&J Publishing, 1986.

Waters, E. "Review of Gesell School Readiness Test." In *Ninth Mental Measurements Yearbook,* edited by J. V. Michael, Jr. Lincoln, NE: Buros Institute of Mental Measurements, 1985, 1: 610–611.

CHAPTER 5

The Impact of Policies for Handicapped Children on Future Early Education Policy

If Mr. Gallager's predictions are correct, early care and education programs for all young children will involve families to a greater extent, will be more multidisciplinary in character, and will make use of a variety of staffing patterns—three features of existing programs for young children with special needs.

Public influence on elementary and secondary education in America has traditionally been exercised at the local and state levels: through school board actions, budget reviews, certification standards, and the like. Only in the past three decades has the federal government exerted significant influence on the education community.

That influence has come largely through legislation directed at children with special needs: handicapped children or the children of low-income families. These children with special needs were chosen as the initial focus of federal legislation for two main reasons. First, the severity of their problems generated sympathy and made a positive response from legislators more likely. Second, by focusing on small subgroups of children, the legislators advocating these proposals could avoid huge expenditures that might frighten both the public and those members of Congress not totally committed to the purposes of the legislation. The congressional supporters hoped that obtaining limited legislative authority for special groups would eventually lead to a broader federal commitment to education.

The strategy worked. The magnitude of the problems that children with special needs and their families faced in the education system of the 1960s tended to overcome the traditional resistance to federal involvement in education policy. For example, much of the landmark Elementary and Secondardy Education Act (P.L. 89-10) of 1965 focused on economically disadvantaged students, while previous forays into federal legislation had been made on behalf of handicapped children.[3]

Need for Early Care and Education

The American education system and the American public have recently been showing increased interest in dropping the age for entering the public schools and in providing greater support for child-care programs. Two factors may explain this development. First, the number of women in the work force has risen dramatically. In the 1930s fewer than 15% of women worked outside the home; more than 50% of women now work outside the home, including almost half of all mothers with children under age 1.[4] The movement of mothers of young children into the work force has been one of the most dramatic social changes in American society, and it has raised the fundamental question, Who will care for the children?

The second factor stimulating public concern about early care and education is the growing realization that many young children from disadvantaged or culturally different families are not developmentally ready for school at the traditional age. They need specific skills and experiences in order to reduce the likelihood that many of them will fail in school and that the state will face greater costs later on.

Increases in the numbers of working mothers and of developmentally delayed children are compelling motivators for policy makers. As educational programs for all children under age[5] are developed, prior experience with legislation on behalf of children with special needs might be expected to play a major role in shaping and influencing these new programs.

Reform Legislation

One unexpected consequence of the increased public interest in education has been a more thorough public analysis of the manner in which education is conducted. In many cases this careful scrutiny has led to public dissatisfaction. Legislation for the education of the handicapped is a case in point. The earlier federal legislative initiatives for handicapped children were limited to expanding the resources available to special educators. Funding was increased for research, preparation of personnel, demonstration programs, dissemination, and the like.[6] When increased funds alone did not seem to achieve the desired goals, policy makers began to use legislation to create structural reform, and they required changes in educational settings and procedures as a condition for the allocation of future resources.

Legislators' growing involvement—perhaps even interference—in education policy making is not without irony, for the goals of legislators often coincide with the express wishes of many educational leaders. For example, educators have been saying for years that handicapped children should be better integrated into public school programs, that many professional disciplines (e.g., psychology, health, social work, education) should cooperate in delivering services to children, and that testing programs should consider the cultural backgrounds of the children being tested. These repeatedly proposed changes in educational practice have proved hard to institute, for a variety of reasons. Legislators finally took it upon themselves to mandate such changes, many of which will now affect preschool programs being initiated in the states.

At the state and federal levels, changes in services to handicapped children have traditionally served as a legislative wedge for the eventual provision of services to all children. For example, funds for educational research at the federal level were originally allocated to investigations pertaining specifically to the education of mentally retarded children. This research was then broadened to include all handicapped children and, eventually, all children in public education.

Legislation for the Handicapped

Legislation for the handicapped has also introduced the public to education policies that it might at first have found difficult to accept as applying to all children. The most dramatic example is the landmark Education for All Handicapped Children Act (P.L. 94-142), which has influenced all of American education. It is likely that its companion piece, the Education of the Handicapped Act Amendments of 1986 (P.L. 99-457), will do the same for services to all young children.

P.L. 94-142, introduced six key principles, all of which have had an impact on American education.

1. Zero reject. All children with handicaps must be provided a free and appropriate public education. Local systems do not have the option of choosing whether or not to provide needed services.
2. Nondiscriminatory evaluation. Each student must receive a complete and individual evaluation before being placed in a special education program, and tests must be appropriate to the child's cultural background.
3. Least restrictive environment. As much as possible, handicapped children must be educated with children who are not handicapped.
4. Due process. Legal due process procedures insure the fairness of educational decisions and the accountability of both professionals and parents in making those decisions.
5. Individualized education. An individualized education program (IEP) must be written for every handicapped child who is receiving special education. The IEP should describe the child's current performance, the educational goals for the child, and the manner in which services will be delivered to enable the child to reach those goals.
6. Parental participation. Parents are included in the development of the IEP and are guaranteed access to their children's educational records.[8]

The law governing handicapped preschool children (ages 3 to 5) provides an interesting example of the way legislative precedents can work. That law now requires that an IEP be provided for each child, extending the idea beyond the population originally targeted by P.L. 94-142.

A recent congressional initiative that has gone relatively unnoticed except by special educators is the Education of the Handicapped Act Amendments of 1986 (P.L. 99-457). This legislation is the most recent in a series of laws focusing on different aspects of educating handicapped children.[9] One of the provisions of P.L. 99-457 (Part H) deals with a group that had been previously overlooked: handicapped children from birth to age 3.

P.L. 99-457 (Part H) completes a long cycle of legislative efforts to provide a free and appropriate education for all handicapped children. This new legislation for infants and toddlers is also the latest step in an effort—spanning more than two decades—to focus attention on early childhood, a commitment that began with the Handicapped Children's Early Education Assistance Act (P.L. 90-538) in 1968. That law provided small sums of money to support demonstration models of early childhood programming for handicapped children.

This legislative cornucopia for children with handicapping conditions should be of interest to everyone concerned about children. Much of this legislation is groundbreaking: it establishes precedents for relationships among federal, state, and local education agencies. In addition, the most recent pieces of legislation extend beyond the provision of additional professional resources and attempt—specifically and deliberately—to effect reforms that will have an impact on all educators and all professionals who work with children and families.[10]

The stated purposes of P.L. 99-457 are:

- to enhance the development of handicapped infants and toddlers and to minimize the risk of developmental delays;
- to reduce educational costs by minimizing the need for special education and related services after handicaped infants and toddlers reach school age;
- to minimize the likelihood of institutionalizing the handicapped and to maximize their potential for independent living; and
- to enhance the capacity of families to meet the special needs of their handicapped infants and toddlers.

In many respects P.L. 99-457 is more specifically directed at reform than any previous legislation. The new law requires each state to develop and implement a statewide "comprehensive, coordinated, multidisciplinary, interagency program of early intervention services."[11] Public acceptance of this legislation was sought by appeals to broad themes: helping the child and the family, saving money through early intervention that reduces future costs, and developing the full potential of each child. Similar themes can easily be imagined as rationales for programs for all young children.

Handicapped Infants and Toddlers

The new legislation establishes precedents for providing comprehensive services to handicpaped infants and toddlers and to their families. The major reforms included in P.L. 99-457, (Part H) are:

1. Multidisciplinary approach. P.L. 99-457 requires that professionals organize multidisciplinary and multi-agency programs for young handicapped children and their families. Special educators have long seen the advantages of using teams of professionals— pediatricians, nurses, occupational therapists, physical therapists, speech/language pathologists, psychologists, and social workers—to work with handicapped children and their families, but such teams have rarely existed in practice. The law now mandates such multidisciplinary cooperation. The Individual Family Service Plan (also mandated for each child) will be required to contain evidence of this multidisciplinary approach.

Clearly, a young child who has cerebral palsy, a mild hearing loss, a delay in language development, and an inability to respond well to adults will need help from many sources. Working alone, the special educator, the psychologist, the pediatrician, or the physical therapist cannot provide the necessary program of coordinated treatment for such a child.

It should be equally clear that a mix of disciplines is needed to serve young children who are not handicapped. Social and health services have often been seen as desirable programs in the public schools, but not as partners in the educational program. At the preschool level, particularly for children from culturally different and economically disadvantaged families, some type of interdisciplinary teamwork among professionals would seem warranted. Jeanette Valentine and Edward Zigler note that the Head Start program is mandated to provide "education, health screening and referral, mental health services, social services, nutrition, and parent involvement."[12] To meet that mandate, public schools would need to include multidisciplinary teams that serve the special needs of the preschool population.

2. Family empowerment. Programs for handicapped children have long targeted parents and families for services: teaching parents

more effective parenting techniques, engaging them in the instruction of their own children, helping them become more effective public advocates.[13] P.L. 99-457 makes a major effort to included the family in planning for handicapped infants or toddlers. The notion of protecting the rights of parents is relatively new to general educators, many of whom have viewed the public schools as their exclusive domain, with parents limited to a visit on "parents' day." However, the emphasis on family empowerment in programs for handicapped children and in programs such as Head Start has already filtered into general education, and the influence will surely continue to grow.[14]

3. Personnel preparation. There is a chronic shortage of adequately trained personnel to provide multidisciplinary services for handicapped preschoolers.[15] This shortage can be circumvented by designing new ways of delivering services, whereby highly trained professionals supervise the work of other personnel rather than deliver the services themselves.

There are many variations on these personnel patterns, but they all seem to point the way to alternative models of service delivery for nonhandicapped preschoolers as well. It may not be possible to find sufficient numbers of certified preschool teachers to provide service to young children. However, alternative staffing models and personnel preparation models can help stretch the limited numbers of fully qualified preschool teachers.

Preschool Education for the Handicapped

Title II of P.L. 99-457 mandates full service to all handicapped children between the ages of 3 and 5 by the 1990–91 school year. In fiscal year 1989 the federal government provided $200 million to aid the states in meeting this requirement. A state that does not meet the deadline will lose its share of the $200 million and other discretionary funds that have been provided through the U.S. Department of Education's Office of Special Education Programs.[16]

It appears inevitable that financial support from the government produces rules and regulations that increasingly shape and control the expenditure of that money. Federal support for early care and education is likely to follow that pattern; for good or ill, federal guidelines and regulations will accompany these programs.

As the number of mothers of young children entering the work force increases and as the number of children with developmental deficiencies from economically disadvantaged families also increases, some type of public policy on early care and education seems inevitable. The provisions for such a policy will probably be shaped in part by existing programs for preschoolers with special needs. This would mean that programs for all young children will involve families to a greater extent, will be more multidisciplinary in character, and will make use of variety of staffing patterns—all features of existing programs for young children with special needs.

James J. Gallagher is Kenan Professor of Education at the University of North Carolina, Chapel Hill, and director of the Carolina Institute for Child and Family Policy. From 1967 to 1970 he served as the first director of the Bureau of Education for the Handicapped in the U.S. Office of Education.

Endnotes

1. Martin, Edward. "Lessons from Implementing P.L. 94-142." In *Policy Implementation and P.L. 99-457: Planning for Young Children with Special Needs,* edited by James Gallagher, Pascal Trohanis, and Richard Clifford. Baltimore: Paul H. Brooks, 1989.

2. Steiner, Gilbert. *The Futility of Family Policy.* Washington, D.C.: Brookings Institution, 1981.

3. Kirk, Samuel, A.; and Gallager, James. *Educating Exceptional Children.* Boston: Houghton Mifflin, 1989.

4. Weissbourd, Bernice. "A Brief History of Family Support Programs." In *America's Family Support Programs: Perspectives and Prospects,* edited by Sharon L. Kagan, Douglas R. Powell, Bernice Weissbourd, and Edward Zigler. New Haven, Conn.: Yale University Press, 1987.

5. National Commission on Excellence in Education. *A Nation at Risk: The Imperative for Educational Reform.* Washington, D.C.: U.S. Government Printing Office, 1983.

6. Martin, Edwin. "A National Commitment to the Rights of the Individual." *Exceptional Children,* 1976, 43: 132–35.

7. Kirk and Gallager, op. cit.

8. Abeson, Alan; and Zettel, Jane. "The End of the Quiet Revolution: The Education for All Handicapped Children Act of 1975." *Exceptional Children,* 1975, 44: 114–30.

9. Trohanis, Pascal. "Preparing for Change: The Implementation of Public Law 99-457." In *Early Childhood Special Education: Birth to Three,* edited by June Jordan et al. Reston, Va.: Council for Exceptional Children, 1988.

10. Gallagher, James. "The Implementation of Social Policy: A Policy Analysis Challenge." In Gallager, Trohanis, and Clifford.

11. Trohanis, op. cit.

12. Valentine, Jeanette; and Edward Zigler, Edward. "Head Start: A Case Study in the Development of Social Policy for Children and Families." In *Children, Families, and Government: Perspectives on American Social Policy,* edited by Edward Zigler, Sharon Lynn Kagan, and Edgar Klugman. New York: Cambridge University Press, 1983.

13. Gallagher, James; and Vietze, Peter. *Families of Handicapped Persons.* Baltimore: Paul H. Brookes, 1986.

14. Moroney, Robert. *Shared Responsibility: Families and Social Policy.* New York: Aldine, 1986.

15. Thorp, Eva; and McCollum, Jeanette. "Defining the Infancy Specialization in Early Childhood Special Education." In Jordan et al.

16. Gallager, Trohanis, and Clifford.

CHAPTER 6

Managing Child Care Programs: A Historical Perspective

What does an appropriate set of competencies for directors and managers of programs for young children consist of? What do early childhood administrators need to know in order to function effectively? How can supervisors and administrators in early childhood education fulfill their responsibilities to children, parents, families, teachers, the community, and themselves, without suffering burnout in the first month? These are some of the hard questions which the current set of training programs, curricula, written and audio visual materials attempt to answer. When one contemplates the growing wealth of resources for the administrator of an early education program, it is difficult to conceive of the fact that prior to 1971, few such materials existed. The development of training programs for, and published materials to aid the early childhood program manager in the United States, appears to have paralleled the growth of early childhood education programs in general.

Historically, prospective directors of programs for young children, typically women, learned how to teach young children by apprenticing themselves to schools such as those founded by Montessori, the Macmillan sisters, and Froebel. Upon completion of their training, they returned to their home community and opened a school based upon what they had learned during the internship period. At this point they became, at once, a teacher of young children, a manager of a program for young children, and often, a teacher-trainer. In the United States, this model of management training persisted into the 1920's, 1930's, and beyond.

It makes sense that such a model could persist, given the fact that a very small percentage of young children in the United States (U.S.) were in productive group environments prior to the 1960's. With the exception of the Federally funded WPA Nurseries of the 1930's and the Lanham Act Child Care Centers of World War II, both of which were closed immediately at the end of the crisis periods, there do not appear to be readily accessible written records describing the training of administrators in programs for young children in the U.S. The teacher training materials and methods used in those first two national child care programs have been documented by James L. Humes, Jr. (Braun & Edwards, 1972, p. 174;

70

Henig in Hymes, 1979, p. 4–27; Stolz in Hymes, 1978, p. 26–56). Publications detailing facility design and the procurement of appropriate materials existed. However, there were no published directors manuals, few privately written manuals, and little or no time to produce them. For example, as Humes and Stolz (1978, p. 40–1) recount, bathtubs and infirmaries were added by the new Director (Stolz) and Manager-on-the-spot (Hymes) to the plans for the Kaiser (demonstration) Centers (among the first documented employer sponsored child care centers) immediately prior to their opening in 1943. In fact, most directors made their rules as they went along, retained those policies and procedures that worked, and discarded the ones that did not work.

Programs for young children prior to 1965 consisted mainly of private nursery schools across the country, a few private or affluent public school kindergartens, and a handful of philanthropic day-care programs (Decker and Decker, 1988, p. 2–3). It was only with the advent of Head Start and its related Parent–Child center and Follow Through programs, and Title XX Day Care, that we began to see a systematic effort to guide and train the administrators of early childhood education programs. The terminology in the field is not standardized, so a director might be called a manager, coordinator, principal, administrator, supervisor, or by some other title (Hewes & Hartman, 1988, p. 1).

Host and Heller, in their 1971 publication, describe the ideal early childhood administrator:

> Creative administration requires both creative thinking and sound craftsmanship. The ability to think creatively is part of everyone's natural endowment. We, therefore, assume that those who read this book have already been challenged to apply their natural endowment to organizing and operating successful day care services.
> Craftsmanship, however, is learned. . . . It grows through study, dedication and experience but is never completely mastered. New materials, new techniques, new ways of seeing the world and of expressing what is seen constantly prod a craftsman to new efforts, new approaches to his craft. This is, and must always be, the attitude of those who would creatively administer such dynamic enterprises as day care services. (p. 3)

The earliest recent volumes in the field (published during the 1970's) were designed as "a guide for those interested or involved in organizing a private nursery school, or directing a day care center, cooperative nursery school, or kindergarten" (Butler, 1974, p. v.). These individuals came from diverse backgrounds in nursing, psychology, education, home economics, child development, early childhood education, and, more recently, business. Some books were written for "students in early childhood education who have had contact with a center through employment, student teaching, or volunteering" to "help them understand what is involved in managing a center . . . (and to) provide a knowledge base for future career development" (Sciarra & Dorsey, 1979, p. ix).

> The administrator in early childhood programs may have had little professional training for the job. Even the few with advanced degrees in early childhood education may have had no specific graduate training in administration. Most, particularly administrators of programs for children under five years of age, have mastered their administrative tasks through trial and error and much hard work. They often began as teachers, social workers, or perhaps nurses, and as programs grew and their professional commitment, interest, and competence increased, they assumed expanded responsibilities. However, early childhood administrators in the public schools, such as elementary school principals, have had substantial training in the theory and practice of school administration. Many, though, often lack direct experience and training in working with young children, children ages two to eight years. (Stevens & King, 1976, p. vii)

The role of the director of a child care program has changed drastically over the last several decades. In an interview with *Child Care Information Exchange (Exchange)* (June, 1984), Malcolm Host recounted that in the fifties administrators were hired primarily because of their program knowledge. Financial, regulatory, and administrative knowledge were minor requirements. (p. 21) In contrast, the director of the eighties needed to be well-versed in legislation, codes, and licensing requirements; finance; facility maintenance; and team building, with little time devoted to program issues. Host stated that the primary skills directors will need in the future are flexibility, program and staff assessment skills, and global thinking. (p. 23) Other professionals in the field considered assessment and improvement of organizational climate to be among the director's major roles. Such aspects as collegiality, professional growth, conflict resolution, and shared decisionmaking were deemed important factors in creating an affective organizational climate. (Jorde-Bloom, September, 1987, Neugebauer, February, 1989)

Humor is the powerful weapon often used in *Exchange* articles to soften the harsh realities of life in the director's chair. The July, 1986 issue of *Exchange* carried the tong-in-cheek, "Piaget's Theory of Director Development," in which the author proposed four stages through which directors pass at varying rates. The Pseudo-Managerial Stage, which begins on the first day and lasts until the first crisis, finds the director impressed with the trappings of power. In the Pre-Managerial Stage a director confronts reality by reaching "problem permanence" (the realization that problems do not go away). The "technician" of the Concrete Managerial Stage begins to "organize . . . random schema for responding to problems into concrete managerial skills. She is able to break tasks into subparts, arrange them in logical order, and address them sequentially." (p. 11) Upon reaching the Formal Managerial Stage, the director becomes a "philosopher" by taking a broader view of her role and of the issues. (p. 12) Clare Cherry's (January, 1984) classic view of one day in the life of a director confronts the stark reality of what life at the top of the organizational chart is really like.

During the last two decades publications have assisted directors with many aspects of their jobs. Materials dealing with personnel management, for example, have become increasingly more detailed, practical, and specific. Authors have advanced a number of different philosophical approaches to personnel policies and supervision practices, but all agree on the basic parameters for sound personnel management. Personnel policies should be presented in a written policy manual, with separate staff and parent manuals detailing the aspects pertinent to those persons. The hiring process should be carefully thought through and sequentially developed. An orientation and probationary period are helpful to the new staff members and to the administration and supervisor as the beginning of the staff development process. Staff members should be involved in an ongoing process of self development through staff meetings, training activities, and conference/workshop attendance. The process of supervision, observation, and evaluation should be spelled out in detail. Every staff member should be aware of the termination policies and procedures. Personnel records should be kept in a businesslike fashion, in computerized and/or "hard copy" formats. A usable discussion of these matters first appeared in the *Day Care Staff Training* manual (Parker & Dittmann) of 1971. Recent books on early childhood administration include at least a chapter or two devoted to personnel aspects. Of particular note in this regard are the *Preschool Director's Staff Development Handbook* (Watkins & Durant, 1987), which details the competency-based training program for the Child Development Associate, and the accreditation materials developed by the National Academy of Early Childhood Programs (1984, 1985), which include staff assessment criteria.

As a rule, the authors of training volumes developed them "in the course of many years of experience in teaching both undergraduate and graduate students, and working with teachers and directors of day care centers, 'Head start,' private schools and cooperative schools in a supervisory capacity" (Butler, 1974, p. v). Several authors reported that their writings are based on thirty or more years of experience in early childhood education.

Host and Heller's (1971) book was produced as part of a series of volumes authored by non-governmental child development experts, practitioners, and parents, and funded by the Child Development/ Day Care Resources Project, a cooperative venture of the Office of Child Development (under Dr. Edward Zigler), and the Office of Economic Opportunity. The volume includes the organization, components and business management of day care services. It contains one of the first references in early childhood education literature to an Operations Manual.

> An operations manual states the procedures by which a day care organization actualizes the policies and procedures discussed in the preceding chapters. It provides an organized body of procedural information in place of a flood of memoranda and directives emanating from all components of an organization at different times and, often, operating at cross-purposes. (Host & Heller, 1971, p. 163)

Hewes and Hartman (1988) developed a unique workbook approach to the subject matter in 1972. Their materials apply business management theory and principles to the administration of early education programs (p. 1). They, as well as Cherry, et al. (1987), moved from a hardbound format in the 1970's to a looseleaf format in the late 1980's. Such a format allows the practicing professional to insert current articles, workshop handouts and notes, research materials, bibliographies, and Center-developed materials into the book, thus making it an ongoing, working manual. Sciarra and Dorsey's (1979) "Working Papers" provided the Center manager with application forms, legal documents, budgets, and other items designed to make the director's life easier.

Streets (1982) edited a volume designed to bring the philosophy of the comprehensive, developmentally based, ANISA Model to bear on the areas of: design and administration of curriculum; organization of the environment; ethical, health and safety, and diversity issues; fiscal and other management functions; community support functions; and the selection and evaluation of personnel. Hildebrand (1984) added the ecological system framework to the director's repertoire. This model consists of the interrelationships among the natural, human constructed, and human behavioral environments in the child development center. The 1990 edition of Click and Click includes discussions of recent developments in managing infant-toddler classes, school-age child care, corporate, and employer-sponsored centers. The authors also present administrative guidelines for the inclusion of student teachers and volunteers in schools for young children. Grossman and Keyes (1985) promote the advocacy role of the director with a board, a sponsoring agency, business and industry, and various governmental levels and agencies. The director is also reminded of the necessity to be an advocate for humanism by engaging in professional activism. This role is increasingly supported by NAEYC publications, workshops, and Public Policy Alerts. (See LaCrosse in Hewes, 1979, and Brown). Recent publications by Seaver and Cartwright (1986) and Taylor (1989) emphasize program and personnel management. The Taylor volume, which is the result of years of field testing, discusses the humanistic needs of children and families for out-of-home care in the context of the services provided by child-care centers (p. v). Of particular interest are Taylor's provision of "stimulators," which "help the reader focus on particular principles," and "participators," which help the reader "to apply the principles" (p. vi). The intensive discussion of computer-assisted record keeping in the books by Taylor (1989) and Click and Click (1990) bring early childhood administration (kicking and screaming), into the technological era.

During the 1980's numerous practical guides, "survival kits," and articles have enhanced the knowledge base. These materials draw on the expertise of those actually working in the field who have put their ideas on paper to share them with colleagues across the country and around the world. Although *Child Care Information Exchange* is the only periodical solely devoted to the concerns of early childhood administrators, all of the early childhood education publications in the United States have devoted journal pages to related articles during the past decade.

There are currently a variety of human, print, and media sources available which detail appropriate competencies for directors, and assist supervisors and administrators in early childhood education programs in fulfilling their responsibilities to children, parents, families, teachers, the community, and themselves. Each individual can find the answers to the questions posed at the beginning of this chapter by utilizing these resources in his or her own way. Knowledge of past and present theory and practice helps us to avoid "re-inventing the wheel," and aids us in avoiding some of the pitfalls, as we strive to be the best early education administrator we possibly can be.

Dr. Blythe F. Hinitz, Assistant Professor, Early Childhood and Elementary Education, Trenton State College, Trenton, New Jersey 08650-4700

Selected Bibliography

Braun, S. J.; and Edwards, E. P. *History and Theory of Early Childhood Education*. Worthington, Ohio: Charles A. Jones, a division of Wadsworth Publishing Company, 1972.

Brown, J. F. (Ed.). *Administering Programs for Young Children*. Washington, D.C.: National Association for the Education of Young Children, 1984.

Butler, A. L. *Early Childhood Education: Planning and Administering Programs*. New York: Van Nostrand Company, 1974.

Cherry, C. "Just What Does a Director Really Do?" *Child Care Information Exchange*, January, 1984, 1–3.

Cherry, C.; Harkness; and Kuzma, K. *Nursery School and Day Care Center Management Guide*. Belmont, California: Fearon Teacher Aids, a division of David S. Lake Publishers, 1978.

Child Care Information Exchange. P. O. Box 2890, Redmond, Washington 98073. "Tenth Anniversary Issue." March, 1988, 60.

Click, P.; and Click, D. *Administration of Schools for Young Children*. 3rd ed. Albany, New York: Delmar Publishers, 1990.

Decker; and Decker. *Planning and Administering Early Childhood Programs*. Columbus, Ohio: Charles Merrill, 1988.

Grossman; and Keyes. *Early Childhood Administration*. Boston: Allyn and Bacon, 1985.

Henig, C. "The Emergency Nursery Schools and the Wartime Child Care Centers 1933–1946." In *Living History Interviews: Book 3: Reaching Large Numbers of Children*, edited by James L. Hymes, Jr. Carmel, California: Hacienda Press, 1979.

Hewes, D. (Ed.). *Administration: Making Programs Work for Children and Families*. Washington, DC: National Association for the Education of Young Children, 1979.

Hewes, D.; and Hartman. *Early Childhood Education A Workbook for Administrators*. San Francisco, California: R & E Research Associates, 1988.

Hildebrand, V. *Management of Child Development Centers*. New York: Macmillan Publishing Company, 1984, 1990.

Host; and Heller. *Day Care #7: Administration*. Washington, D.C.: United States Department of Health, Education and Welfare—Office of Child Development, 1971.

Jorde-Bloom, P. "Keeping a Finger on the Pulse Beat: the Director's Role in Assessing Organizational Climate." *Child Care Information Exchange*, September, 1987, 57: 31–35.

La Crosse, E. R. "New Thoughts for New Administrators." *Young Children*, 1977, 32: 4–13.

National Academy of Early Childhood Programs. *Accreditation Criteria and Procedures of the National Academy of Early Childhood Programs*. Washington, D.C.: Author, 1984.

National Academy of Early Childhood Programs. *Guide to Accreditation by the National Academy of Early Childhood Programs*. Washington, D.C.: Author, 1985.

Neugebauer, R. "When Friction Flares—Dealing with Staff Conflict." *Child Care Information Exchange*, February, 1989, 65: 3–6.

Neugebauer, R. "Step by Step Guide to Team Building." *Child Care Information Exchange*, June, 1984, 9–13.

Pagano, A. "The Role of the Manager of Early Childhood Programs." In *Early Childhood Education*, edited by Barry Persky and Leonard Golubchick. Wayne, New Jersey: Avery Publishing Group, 1977 [in cooperation with American Federation of Teachers and the Doctorate Association of New York Educators].

Parker; and Dittmann. *Day Care #5: Staff Training.* Washington, D.C.: United States Department of Health, Education and Welfare—Office of Child Development, 1971.

Piaget, Fred. "Piaget's Theory of Director Development." *Child Care Information Exchange,* July, 1986, 50: 10–13.

Sciarra, D. J.; and Dorsey, A. G. *Developing and Administering A Child Care Center.* Boston: Houghton Mifflin, 1979. [Albany, New York: Delmar, 1990.]

Seaver, J. W. and Cartwright, C. A. *Child Care administration.* Belmont, CA: Wadsworth Publishing Company, 1986.

Stevens and King. *Administering Early Childhood Education Programs.* Boston: Little Brown & Company, 1976.

Stolz, L. M. "The Kaiser Child Service Centers." In *Living History Interviews: Book 2: Care of the Children of Working Mothers,* edited by James L. Hymes, Jr. Carmel, California: Hacienda Press, 1979.

Streets, D. T. *Administering Day Care and Preschool Programs.* Boston: Allyn & Bacon, 1982.

Taylor, B. J. (1989). *Early Childhood Program Management: People and Procedures.* Columbus, Ohio: Merrill Publishing Company.

Watkins, K. & Durant, L. *Preschool Director's Staff Development Handbook.* West Nyack, New York: Center for Applied Research in Education, 1987.

CHAPTER 7

Origins of Early Childhood Education

Recognition of the importance of the early years in the life of a child is not new. The principles and practices of modern early childhood education are the direct descendants of the work of Comenius, Rousseau, Pestalozzi, and Froebel.

John Amos Comenius (1592–1670) set down in the *Great Didactic,* "General Postulates of Teaching and Learning" which appear to be the first step toward a branch of education specifically designed for young children. Comenius discusses the path to knowledge, and compares the brain to pliable wax. In a translation of the *Great Didactic* by Keating (1921), Comenius stated:

> This comparison throws remarkable light on the true nature of knowledge. Whatever makes an impression on my organ of sight, hearing, smell, taste, or touch, stands to me in the relation of a seal by which the image of an object is impressed upon my brain (p. 44–45).

Thus, Comenius advocated learning through the senses which we interpret as learning through experience. Comenius further states that these sense impressions will be internalized for future interpretation through reason. Curtis and Boutlwood (1961) state that Comenius believed "the acquisition of knowledge is essentially based on activity followed by reasoning. . . (p. 197)."

Modern principles of early childhood education stress the involvement of the child in an activity based on curriculum through the use of the senses. Rudolph and Cohen (1964), in a discussion of kindergarten state that

> . . . Only by building understanding of what his senses contact, will the child be ready for the symbolic learning that will come in time (p. 9–10).

In the above statement we see Comenius's ideas interpreted for application 300 years later. We find threads of his doctrine in the work of Dewey, Montessori, and Piaget.

In his book, Comenius further advocates different materials for children of different ages. He felt that nature establishes the order of development in the child step by step. Keating (1921) translates "all subjects that are to be learned should be arranged so as to suit the age of the students, that nothing which is beyond their comprehension be given to them to learn. This process begins with the universal and ends with the particular (p. 115–116)." Here we have the ancestor of Piaget's ideas about stages in cognitive development and sound principles of curriculum development for the early years of schooling. Comenius believed in giving the young child experiences and knowledge of the world through field trips, pictures, models, and real things. This background aids the child in future abstract learning.

Comenius suggested a system of education for all children, rich and poor, girls and boys. Pounds (1968) calls this the "ladder system" because all children would "take the same route and would merely stop at different levels (p. 154)." Comenius comments on the individuality and differences among children. Keating (1921) translates "There is a great difference between the minds of men as exist between various kinds of plants, of trees, of animals; one must be treated in one way, and another in another, the same method cannot be applied to all alike . . . Each one will develop in the direction of his natural inclinations (p. 181–182)."

In brief, Comenius' system of education consisted of four levels: 1) Infancy to age 6—School of the Mother's Knee. This is similar to nursery and kindergarten games, music, sensory experiences, body movement, and manual work; 2) Age 6–12—Vernacular School. The child is instructed in his native language. This was open to all children; 3) Age 12–18—Latin School. This was similar to high school. Students learn the classic languages, logic, mathematics, and art; 4) Age 18–on—University and Travel. Comenius believed in equal education for girls because, according to Braun (1972), "girls are equipped with the same industriousness and capacity for wisdom . . . There can be no reason why females should be excluded from studying (p. 32)."

Comenius was a man ahead of his time and the first to develop a special system of education for very young children. All those who followed him built their ideas around his work.

Jean Jacques Rousseau (1712–1778) rebelled against the formalism and artificiality of French society. He believed in naturalism in the education of children. His belief was, as stated in the Foxley (1911) translation, "Everything is good as it comes from the hands of the Creator of Nature; everything deteriorates in the hands of man (p. 1)." To Rousseau, naturalism was the belief in the goodness of the child as he developed free from the evil effects of organized society. According to Bayles (1966), Rousseau's naturalism meant protecting the child from "his man-made surroundings—science and civilization—that his innate tendencies would have the opportunity to grow and unfold in accordance with his own nature (p. 82)." The job of protector was assigned to education, but Rousseau believed that in order to be suited for this task, education had to be radically different from that of his generation.

In 1762 Rousseau's *Emile, Ou Traite de l'Education* was published. It was written as a novel and consisted of five books or parts. Each book deals with one of the developmental stages of the fictitious child, Emile. Rousseau felt that since the child, in the natural state was good, all his impulses and actions were good, therefore, the child must be free to develop and learn naturally. Pounds (1968) states, "Rousseau emphasized the necessity for the child to be free to develop according to his own natural impulses (p. 176)." Thus, to educate the child according to nature, Rousseau states, according to Duggan (1936), "we must study his nature and find out whether there are laws governing physical phenomena (p. 207)." Here Rousseau is suggesting that child study, a radically new concept at the time, should be the basis of education.

Rousseau reports the several states of Emile's development as separate and distinct, in each state the child is different. These states correspond to the stages in the history of human progress from savage to civilized society. According to Bayles (1966), Pounds (1968), Curtis and Boutlwood (1961), these stages are: 1) Infancy—birth to age 5. The child is a little animal not yet human. This is the period of body growth; 2) Childhood—age 6–11. The child is a human savage. This is the stage of social growth; 3) Adolescence—age 12–15. This is the Age of Reason when the child is civilized, but concerned only with himself. This is the period when the mind develops; 4) Youth—young adulthood. This is the period when the person becomes aware of and begins thinking of others. The youth is a social being. This is the period when the sex impulse arises, but reason takes over and morality governs life. This is the period of the development of the spirit (Bayles, p. 83; Pounds, p. 177–178; Curtis and Boutlwood, p. 277).

Rousseau's theory is based upon the idea of unfoldment development from within the child. Bayles (1966) states that this theory is based upon the belief that "the child's innate destiny (is) enfolded within him at birth and destined to unfold in the stage–order predestined at birth (p. 82)." This unfoldment concept is an important part of Rousseau's new education and from it Rousseau leads us toward a more important and lasting idea, that childhood is a special time. Rousseau stated a revolutionary idea for his time; children are different from adults. In the Foxley (1911) translation of *Emile* we find a plea for the rights of children to be children, not miniature adults. "Nature would have them children before they are men. If we try to invert this order we shall produce a forced fruit immature and flavorless, fruit which will be rotten before it is ripe; we shall have young doctors and old children (p. 54)."

From Rousseau's plea for the respect of childhood grew the concept of readiness to learn. Comenius hinted at this idea in his early work, but Rousseau states it clearly. Rousseau suggested an atmosphere that was permissive in which the child would experience the education of things and social situations at his own pace. The teacher must not force new things and new social situations on the child. Rather, the teacher must wait as Thut (1957) states, "for the signs of the internal strivings which signal the learners readiness to progress to new things and new social experiences before he is exposed to them (p. 133)."

In the Foxley (1911) translation, Rousseau states that the "most useful rule of education . . . is do not save time, but lose it . . . The mind must be left undisturbed till its facilities are developed . . . Therefore the education of the earliest years should be merely negative. It consists not in teaching virtue or truth, but in preserving the heart from vice and from the spirit of error (p. 57)." The heart of Rousseau's theory of education is let nature take its course, protect the child from well meaning adults and the vices of society.

Rousseau's *Emile* was a violent reaction against education that produced men of cold reason and made learning machines of children. Rousseau went to the other extreme making education a matter of nurture only. His system was an education of the emotions, an education of the person. Duggan (1936) states, "the work of the *Emile* was by necessity primarily destructive, and it performed a great service in clearing the ground of much educational rubbish preparatory to laying a new foundation . . . It is so full of suggestiveness concerning the aims, content, and process of education as to be the starting point of a new education (p. 214)."

Rousseau awakened Europe to the fact that a special type of education was needed for young children. Braun (1972) comments on Rousseau's impact on education, "The spirit of Rousseau may have been interpreted variously over the years, but certainly *Emile* has had an incalculable impact on education. In the move of teachers and students toward greater freedom and individuality, Rousseau's doctrine has taken root—though it has taken a multitude of different embodiments. No thinker after Rousseau could escape dealing with the ideas he set awing with a flurry of feeling . . . In harmony with Rousseau's belief in nature and the right of the child to grow untrammeled by society . . . Johann Heinrich Pestalozzi, was to express the counterpart of Rousseau's freshness of spirit in his own life a generation later . . . Rousseau's freshness of spirit in his own life a generation later . . . Rousseau's work prepared the mind of Europe to accept and to respect a man like Pestalozzi and Pestalozzi, in his turn, gave substance to what had been before him only hypothetical notions (p. 43)."

Johann Heinrich Pestalozzi (1746–1827), unlike Rousseau, was a teacher who put his theories into practice. Pestalozzi was one of the reformers upon whose work the movement to psychologize education was based. He initiated a movement which resulted in great changes in what Duggan (1936) calls "the aims, spirit, and methods of elementary education (p. 222)." It is with Pestalozzi that a change in teaching methods and a formalization of teacher training begins.

Pestalozzi's life and work fall into three periods. According to Duggan (1936) these were: 1) 1774–1780, Experiment in industrial education for orphans; 2) 1780–1798, Writing for social and educational reform; 3) 1798–1827, Reform in teaching elementary school subjects.

Period one was a time of experimentation at a small farm called Neuhof where Pestalozzi attempted to prove that one's character is shaped by the environment. He believed that the more natural the environment, the better the child's character will develop. Pestalozzi found that Rousseau's ideas needed great modification and concluded that, according to Duggan (1936), "the most natural environment for a child was a home dominated by a spirit of strict, but loving discipline (p. 226)." The orphanage experiment succeeded in helping the children, but failed financially in 1780.

In period two, Pestalozzi devoted himself to writing on educational and social reform. His works included pamphlets on the principles of the French Revolution which emphasized educational reform. In 1781 Pestalozzi wrote *Leonard and Gertrude* in novel form. It was accepted by the intellectuals of Europe and won honors from the French National Assembly.

In period three, Pestalozzi worked at several schools for war orphans. Pestalozzi believed in working from hand to head. Bayles (1966) states the children learned that "by the work of their hands they would get sense impressions out of which ideas (head) would form. Ideas, the assumed precursor of actions, hence habits, would then coalesce into habit patterns—Pestalozzi seeing of course, that they were the right ones—thereby begatting character (heart) . . . (p. 99)." Pestalozzi wanted to establish a school for poor children. Bayles (1966) states that in this school "love and kindness would reign and the intellectual powers of children would be fostered; beggers would grow into men and brutishness would give way to humanness . . . (p. 101)." Pestalozzi's chance came in 1798 at Stanz, a town ravaged by the French army. Pestalozzi set up an orphanage where he combined sense impressionism with kindness thereby modernizing teaching. At the Stanz school (1798–1799), later at the Burgdorf school (1799–1804), and at the Yverdon school (1805–1825) Pestalozzi further perfected his method.

Pestalozzi believed that educational reform would occur only when each child was allowed to develop his natural abilities to the fullest. This could not be accomplished without new methods and new materials of instruction. Duggan (1936) states "it was in this connection that Pestalozzi made his greatest contribution to educational reform . . . (p. 231)." Pestalozzi refused to believe that the only way to teach was to have children memorize material and then recite it. deGuimps (1890) states that Pestalozzi was convinced "that when the memory is applied to a series of psychologically graduated ideas, it brings all faculties into play (p. 150)." Pestalozzi believed, as Comenius did, that sense perception was the basis for all knowledge and that observation was the basis for all instruction. He developed object lessons which emphasized oral teaching in order to put Rousseau's ideas into practice. Pestalozzi suggested according to Duggan (1936), that "teaching through the observation of objective material within the child's experience gave him clear ideas and trained him in oral expression; not to gain knowledge of the object studied . . . but to train the powers of the mind, of expression as well as impression (p. 231)." Pestalozzi used music, art, spelling, geography, arithmetic, and a great many oral language activities in his teaching.

Pestalozzi went furthur using Rousseau's idea of readiness and Comenius' idea of graduated organization of knowledge to state, according to deGuimps (1890), that "in every branch teaching should begin with the simplest elements and proceed gradually according to the development of the child in psychologically connected order (p. 155)." Here we have what Dewey and Piaget would later call cognitive development.

Braun (1972) states that Pestalozzi's "life was devoted to human relationships, a life of the mind, but more a life of feeling and of service. More than what he said, or wrote, what Pestalozzi did was his doctrine. His educational doctrine is not easy to follow for it must be followed with devotion, self-forgetfulness, deep loving concern for children and for the essence of childhood (p. 60)."

Pestalozzi helped to humanize education. His schools were visited by scholars and statesmen from all over Europe and America. His ideas were put into practice in various ways throughout the world. Braun (1972) states, "there is a strand that links the modern kindergarten to Pestalozzi . . . it is in the affection and concern for children and in the attempt to protect them as well as instruct them (p. 61)."

Friedrich Wilhelm August Froebel (1782–1852) was the most influential of Pestalozzi's students. He studied Pestalozzi's method at Yverdon for two years. Froebel read the words of Comenius and Rousseau and he was greatly impressed by Comenius' description of the School of the Mother's Knee. Froebel decided to open a school for young children.

The *Education of Man*, (1826) contains an explanation of Froebel's educational theory, which according to Weber (1969), reflects several streams of thought: the absolute idealism of his time, some of the naturalism of Rousseau, aspects of the sense realism of Pestalozzi, his own tendency toward mysticism, and his understanding of the child's nature viewed in the context of the other influences (p. 1). Froebel developed the kindergarten as a garden rather than a school room in which young children could be free to learn about themselves and the world. He emphasized love and sympathy as the only relationship which should exist between teacher and pupil. Influenced by the desire for national unity in Germany, Froebel made the quest for unity part of his educational philosophy. Pounds (1968) states that Froebel developed his theory of unity from the idea that "the world is in a conscious cosmic evolution. God is the original, active source of all things and everyone and everything comes from this source . . . The essence of all things is found in God as his will is carried out on Earth. Froebel developed a theory . . . in which everything is a unity in and of itself, but is also part of a greater unity. This is a kind of part–whole theory. The unity of God's universe is best when all of its parts function together, but none of its parts would lose its identity within the larger whole (p. 179–180)."

Froebel felt that if we study the changes in the evolution of nature we would see similar changes in the development of man since man and nature are one. He found hidden meanings in natural objects which he felt were valuable in revealing the world to a child. Froebel felt that humanity as a whole is revealed in each child in a unique way. Froebel (1899) states ". . . As the germ bears within itself the plant and the whole man and the whole life of humanity? (p. 622)." Froebel interpreted the unity of God and man to mean that the child is innately good and felt, as Rousseau did, that the child is a behaving animal and the chief characteristic of the child was self-activity generated by the child's own interests and desires. Froebel (1899) states "all the child is ever to become lies—however slightly indicated—in the child, and can be attained only through the development from within outward (p. 68)." This is the aim of education according to Froebel about which Duggan (1936) states that "development of the inborn capacities of the child . . . hence education must provide for the development of the free personality of each child, it must guide but not restrict, it must not interfere with the divinity in each child (p. 258)."

Froebel believed that the child should learn by doing and education should build upon the child's interests. Froebel saw motor-expression as the method of education for the young. Froebel made motor-expression a vital part of the school program. Duggan (1936) states, "with Froebel motor-expression was not one step but all steps in the educative process . . . Motor-expression developed the powers of acquisition and accomplishment together, hence there was no break between thought and action (p. 259)." Froebel is stating that the child's development comes from inner strivings and their connection with outward expressions of these strivings.

The child's senses are involved. The child takes in stimuli through his sense and integrates the perceptions with activities he engages in. He internalizes events and the consequences of his actions in particular situations to form ideas and to help govern his actions. If a child is painting and accidentally puts the brush with red paint on it into the white paint, he finds a new color. He sees this and is moved to ask "Did I do this? What did I do to get the new color?" He may ask his teacher what happened. He may return to the paint corner and try other ways of getting the new color. When he discovers that red and white makes pink he is able to reproduce the color anytime he paints. The child has learned that he can mix colors to get a new one.

Froebel felt that social cooperation was the means of kindergarten education. He believed in Aristotle's theory that man was a social animal who can realize his humanity only in cooperation with his fellow beings. Thus, Froebel felt that the child has instincts that made him engage in cooperative actions based upon his observation of children at play. Froebel felt that the spirit of cooperation should be cultivated from early infancy and the school should be a society in miniature.

Froebel believed that creativeness or rendering the inner outer was a vital part of the child's learning. Thus, the child fosters the unfolding process through his impulses for creative activity. By expressing the beginning ideas within him the child is led, according to Froebel (1899) to "produce outside of himself that which he conceives within himself (p. 61)." Thus, the child's painting of a tree becomes important as a way of objectifying the vague idea of a tree. Froebel stated that the objects a child manipulates and handles awaken the inner world. Things help the child to imagine himself objectively and to be self-creative. Froebel suggested that children spend much of their time manipulating and constructing objects. Froebel was bold to suggest that children should play in school because play was a key factor in the development of the child. Through play the child achieves equilibrium between individuality and an organized curriculum designed to bring the child step by step through the subject matter of his education. Froebel (1899) states "play is the purest, most spiritual activity of man at this stage . . . it gives joy, freedom, contentment, inner and outer rest, and peace with the world . . . The plays of childhood are the germinal leaves of all later life; for the whole man is developed and shown in these, in his tenderest dispositions, in his innermost tendencies (p. 55)."

Froebel used several means of expression in his child centered curriculum; music and songs, gestures, and construction with language development a vital part of all of these. He believed in the integration of all of these forms through the use of paper, clay, blocks and his famous Gifts, and Occupations. The Gifts were designed to be handled by the child to lead him to an orderly sense of reality. The Gifts were materials that did not change form: cube, cylinder, sticks, and tablets. The Occupations were used to train the hand, the eye and the mind. The Occupations consisted of materials that changed form through use: clay, sand, and paper. *The Mother Play and Nursery Songs* was Froebel's book of songs with pictures and notes explaining use. The songs described the work of people and simple games, rather like modern kindergarten activities. Modern materials such as crayons, paste, the doll corner and other activities greatly enrich the kindergarten program, but grew directly from Froebel's original materials.

Froebel's work remains a vital part of education today. His unique contributions have withstood the test of time. Modern open classroom techniques, day care centers, and nursery schools can be traced directly to Froebel's original kindergarten. Braun (1972) states, "with Froebel, preschool education as a planned, organized portion of the school system begins. With Froebel, modern teaching of young children becomes an entity in its own right . . . The result of his work was the kindergarten, the true beginning of modern preschool education, created out of love and concern for children . . . (p. 61)."

From the work of Comenius, Rousseau, Pestalozzi, and Froebel modern early childhood education has evolved. Each of these scholars drew upon the work of those who came before him, shaping the ideas and practices in light of his own beliefs and in the context of his own times. Their work has been modified and amplified by John Dewey, Maria Montessori, and the American Kindergarten Movement, but remains the foundation upon which early childhood education has been built.

Dr. Barbara Ruth Peltzman, Assistant Professor of Education, Notre Dame College, St. John's University, Staten Island, New York

References

Bayles, Ernest E.; and Hood, Bruce L. *Growth of American Educational Thought and Practice*. New York: Harper & Row, 1966.

Braun, Samuel J.; and Edwards, Esther P. *History and Theory of Early Childhood Education*. Worthington, Ohio: Charles A. Jones Pub. Co., 1972.

Curtis, S. J.; and Boutlwood, E. A. *A Short History of Educational Ideas*. London, England: University Tutorial Press Ltd., 1961.

deGuimps, Baron Roger. *Pestalozzi: His Life and Work*. Translated by J. Russell. New York: D. Appleton & Co., 1890.

Duggan, Stephen. *A Student's Textbook in the History of Education*. New York: Appleton-Century Co., 1936.

Foxley, Barbare. *Emile by Jean Jacques Rousseau*. New York: E. P. Dutton & Co., 1911.

Froebel, Friedrich. *The Education of Man.* Translated by William N. Hailmann. New York: D. Appleton & Co., 1889.

Froebel, Friedrich. *Autobiography of Friedrich Froebel.* Translated by Emilie Michaelis and H. Keatly Moore. Syracuse: C. W. Bardeen, 1889.

Froebel, Friedrich. *Education by Development.* Translated by Josephine Jarvis. New York: D. Appleton & Co., 1899.

Keating, M. W. *The Great Didactic of John Amos Comenium.* London, England: A & C Black, 1921.

Pounds, Ralph L. *The Development of Education in Western Culture.* New York: Appleton-Century-Crofts, 1968.

Rudolph, Margurita; and Cohen, Dorothy H. *Kindergarten: A Year of Learning.* New York: Appleton-Century-Crofts, 1964.

Thut, I. N. *The Story of Education: Philosophical and Historical Foundations.* New York: McGraw-Hill, 1957.

Weber, Evelyn. *The Kindergarten: Its Encounter with Educational Thought in America.* New York: Teachers College Press, 1969.

Suggested Readings

Aries, Philippe. *Centuries of Childhood.* New York: Vintage Books, 1962.

Frost, Joe L. *Early Childhood Education Rediscovered.* New York: Holt, Rinehart & Winston, 1968.

Forest, Ilse. *The School for the Child from Two to Eight.* Boston: Ginn & Co., 1935.

Lambert, Hazel. *Early Childhood Education.* Boston: Allyn & Bacon, 1960.

N.S.S.E. *Forty-sixth Yearbook—Early Childhood Education.* Chicago: University of Chicago Press, 1947.

SECTION 2

Philosophical and Theoretical Issues

Introduction

The chapters in this section represent topics which have generated research in Early Childhood Education. An investigation of philosophical and theoretical issues in any field allows the researcher to go beyond the everyday necessity for practical application to ask "why?" and "what if?" Theoretical writings present the reader with material for speculation and stimulate thought.

Philosophy according to Dewey (1916) is ". . . Thinking what the known demands of us—what responsive attitude it extracts." It is an idea of what is possible, not a record of accomplished fact. Therefore, this section deals with what is possible or how might problems in Early Childhood Education be solved. These chapters present problems in an intellectual form asking the reader to think about what is presented and to look at problems from a new vantage point. Theory presents possibilities, suggestions, and new perspectives.

The chapters in this section will leave the reader with more questions than answers. However, that is their purpose. The reader may be provoked, angered or inspired by these chapters to reevaluate practice based on their ideas.

Dewey (1903) stated that analysis of human experiences leads to an understanding of how they are connected and how the practical develops into the scientific or the scientific develops into the practical. These chapters explore experiences, raise questions and challenge the reader to make the vital connections which lead beyond the practical to the scientific.

Barbara Ruth Peltzman, Ed. D. Assistant Professor of Education, Notre Dame College, St. John's University, Staten Island, New York.

References

Dewey, John. "Thought and Its Subject Matter." In *Studies in Logical Theory,* by John Dewey. Chicago: University of Chicago Press, 1903.
Dewey, John. *Democracy and Education.* New York: Macmillan, 1916.

CHAPTER 8

Developmentally Appropriate Practice: Philosophical and Practical Implications

True education reform will come about only when we replace the reigning psychometric educational psychology with a developmentally appropriate one, Mr. Elkind asserts. Unfortunately, the prospects for such a shift are not good.

The idea of developmentally appropriate educational practice—that the curriculum should be matched to the child's level of mental ability—has been favorably received in education circles.[1] However, this positive reception is quite extraordinary, for developmentally appropriate practice derives from a philosophy of education that is in total opposition to the "psychometric" educational philosophy that now dictates educational practice in the majority of our public schools. Perhaps for this reason developmental appropriateness has been honored more in word than in deed.

In what follows I highlight some of the differences between these two educational philosophies and contrast a few of their practical implications. My purpose in doing so is to argue that true education reform will come about only when we replace the reigning psychometric educational psychology with a developmentally appropriate one.

Two Philosophies

Any philosophy of education must include some conception of the learner, of the learning process, of the information to be acquired, and of the goals or aims of education. The developmental philosophy differs from the psychometric philosophy on all four counts. I should mention that the development philosophy that I present here derives from the research and theory of Jean Piaget.[2]

Conception of the learner. Within a developmental philosophy of education, the learner is viewed as having developing mental abilities. All individuals (with the exception of the retarded) are assumed to be able to attain these abilities, though not necessarily at the same age. For example, we expect that all children will attain the concrete operations that Piaget described as emerging at about age 6 or 7. These operations, which function much like the group of arithmetic operations, enable children who have attained them to learn and to apply rules. However, not all children will attain these operations at the same age. Accordingly, a developmental philosophy sees individual differences in ability as differences in rates of intellectual growth.

This concept of mental ability contrasts sharply with that of a psychometric philosophy of education. According to the psychometric position, the learner is seen as having measurable abilities. This philosophy assumes that any ability that exists must exist in some amount and must, therefore, be quantifiable. For example, intelligence tests—the flagships of the psychometric philosophy—are designed to assess individual differences in the ability to learn and to adapt to new situations. A psychometric perspective regards individual differences in performance as reflecting differences in amount of a given ability.

Both of these opposing conceptions of human ability contain some truth. However, they have far different pedagogical implications.

From a developmental perspective, the important task for educators is matching curricula to the level of children's emerging mental abilities: hence the principle of developmental appropriateness. Curriculum materials should be introduced only after a child has attained the level of mental ability needed to master them. This in turn means that curricula must be studied and analyzed to determine the level of mental ability that is required to comprehend them.

From a psychometric point of view, the most important task for educators is matching children with others of equal ability. Bright children are assumed to be able to learn more in a given time than less bright children. In practice, this philosophy leads to so-called "ability grouping," which in effect allows bright children to go through the material more quickly than slower children. This psychometric orientation also underlies the provision of special classes for the gifted and for the retarded.

Conception of the learning process. Within the developmental philosophy of education, learning is always seen as a creative activity. Whenever we learn anything, we engage the world in a way that creates something new, something that reflects both our own mental activity and the material we have dealt with. We never simply copy content; we always stamp it with our unique way of viewing the world. The child from Connecticut who heard the Lord's Prayer as "Our Father, Who art in New Haven, Harold be thy name" is not the exception but the rule. Everything we learn has both a subjective and an objective component.

The conception of learning as a creative or constructive process has a very important practical implication. It means that we cannot talk of learning independently of the content to be learned. The material to be learned will always interact with the learning process in some special way. Long after Piaget discovered the successive stages and organizations of mental operations, he continued to study the ways in which children attained different concepts, such as space, geometry, time, and movement and speed.[3] In so doing he emphasized the fact that merely knowing the stages of mental development does not provide special insight into how children use the operations at any given stage to attain any particular concept. The only way to discover how children go about learning a particular subject is to study children learning.

By contrast, the psychometric philosophy views learning as governed by a set of principles (e.g., intermittent reinforcement) and consisting of the acquisition of a set of skills (e.g., decoding) that are independent of the content to be learned. Early workers in this tradition enunciated such principles as "mass versus distributed" or "whole versus part" learning, which were presumed to operate independently of the content to be learned. Indeed, early studies of memory employed nonsense syllables in order to eliminate the effect of content on the study of memory.

The limitations of this approach were dramatically demonstrated by Jerome Bruner, Jacqueline Goodenough, and George Austin in their seminal work on problem solving.[4] Before the publication of their work, problem solving was spoken of in terms of "trial and error" or "sudden insight" because most of the work had been done with animals. What Bruner and his colleagues demonstrated was that human subjects, when presented with complex problems, employ complex problem-solving activities—in other words, "strategies." Put differently, the content influences the problem-solving activities that humans employ.

Nonetheless, this insight seems to have been lost. The current interest in teaching young children such things as thinking skills,[5] learning strategies,[6] or computer programming[7] reflects a regression to the idea that thought and content can be treated separately. It is assumed that—once children learn thinking skills or learning strategies or computer programming—these skills will automatically be transferred to different kinds of content. To be sure, transfer of training does occur, but it is far from automatic. Transfer happens when students are active, not passive, learners.[8] But what can we possibly mean by activity if not that students are consciously aware of the content they are thinking about or applying strategies to? Mental processes are always content-oriented.

The developmental approach implies that there is little or no automatic transfer from one subject to another, whereas the psychometric approach assumes that the skills and strategies of thinking often transfer spontaneously to new areas.

Conception of knowledge. From a developmental perspective, knowledge is always a construction, inevitably reflecting the joint contributions of the subject and the object. This is far from a new idea, and it harks back to the Kantian resolution of idealist (all knowledge is a mental construction) and empiricist (all knowledge is a copy of an externally existing world) interpretations of how we come to know the world.[9] Kant argued that the mind provides the "categories" of knowing, while the real world provides the content. Knowledge is thus always a construction of the mind's interaction with the world and cannot be reduced to one or the other.

What Piaget added to the Kantian solution—and what makes Piaget a neo-Kantian—was the demonstration that the categories of knowing (the mental operations of intelligence) are not constant, as Kant had supposed. Rather, the categories change with age. This idea adds a developmental dimension to the Kantian version of the construction of knowledge. As their mental operations develop, children are required to reconstruct the realities they constructed at the previous developmental level. In effect, a child creates and re-creates out of his or her experiences with the environment.

The reality of the young child—his or her knowledge of the world—is thus different from the reality of the older child and adult. For example, young children believe that a quantity changes in amount when it changes in appearance—that, say, the amount of liquid in a low, flat container is greater when it is poured into a tall, narrow one. Older children, whose reality is different, can appreciate the fact that a quantity remains the same in amount despite changes in its appearance. In other words, older children recognize that quantity is conserved. From a developmental perspective, the young child's conception of quantity is not "wrong." It is, in fact, as developmentally appropriate as the older child's grasp of conservation.

From the psychometric point of view, knowledge is something that a child acquires and that can be measured independently from the processes of acquisition. This separation is reflected in the distinction between intelligence tests and achievement tests. One consequence of the separation between learning and content is that knowledge is measured against an external standard that is independent of the learner. When compared to such an external standard, a child's responses can be assessed as being either "right" or "wrong."

Certainly, there is a right and a wrong with respect to some types of knowledge. The Bastille was stormed in 1789, not in 1650; two plus two equals four, not five. We have to distinguish here between what I have elsewhere termed fundamental knowledge, which we construct on our own, and derived knowledge, which is constructed by others and which we must acquire at second hand.[10] The terms right and wrong are useful only in connection with derived knowledge.

The developmental approach introduces the idea that there can be differences in knowledge without any reference to "right" or "wrong." The idea of difference, rather than of correctness, is important not only with respect to fundamental knowledge, but also with respect to creative thinking. For example, many bright children come up with ideas that are different from those of their peers and teachers. Unfortunately, these ideas are often regarded as wrong rather than as different and original. One bright child, when asked to write something about the color blue, wrote about Picasso's Blue Period and was teased and jeered. A greater appreciation for such differences would make the life of bright children in our schools a lot easier.

Conception of the aims of education. The aims of developmental education are straightforward. If the learner is seen as a growing individual with developing abilities, if learning is regarded as a creative activity, and if knowledge is seen as a construction, then the aim of education must surely be to facilitate this development, this creative activity, and this construction of knowledge. Piaget put the aims of education from a developmental perspective this way:

> The principal goal of education is to create men who are capable of doing new things, not simply repeating what other generations have done—men who are creative, inventive, and discoverers. The second goal of education is to form minds which can be critical, can verify, and not accept everything that is offered. The greater danger today is of slogans, collective opinions, ready made trends of thought. We have to be able to resist them individually, to criticize, to distinguish between what is proven and what is not. So we need pupils who are active, who learn early to find out by themselves, partly by their own spontaneous activity and partly through material we set up for them; who learn early to tell what is verifiable and what is simply the first idea to come to them (p. 5).[11]

The aim of developmental education, then, is to produce thinkers who are creative and critical. This aim will not be achieved, however, by teaching thinking skills to children and adolescents. Rather, the way to pursue this aim by creating developmentally appropriate learning environments that challenge the child's emerging mental abilities. Creative thinking and critical thinking are not skills to be taught and learned. They reflect basic orientations toward the self and the world that can be acquired only when children are actively engaged in constructing and reconstructing their physical, social, and moral worlds.

The aim of psychometric education is to produce children who score high on tests of achievement. In other words, the aim of education is to maximize the acquisition of quantifiable knowledge and skills. Perhaps former Secretary of Education William Bennett stated this view of the aims of education as well as anyone:

> We should want every student to know how mountains are made, and that for most reactions there is an equal and opposite reaction. They should know who said "I am the state" and who said "I have a dream." They should know about subjects and predicates, about isosceles triangles and ellipses. They should know where the Amazon flows and what the First Amendment means. They should know about the Donner party and about slavery, and Shylock, Hercules, and Abigail Adams, where Ethiopia is, and why there is a Berlin Wall (p. 3).[12]

In this statement Bennett echoes a theme that was also sounded in *A Nation at Risk,* which was published three years earlier and decried the poor performance of American students on achievement tests, especially when compared to the performance of children from other nations. Moreover, Bennett's remarks foreshadowed the best-selling critiques of U.S. education by Allan Bloom and E. D. Hirsh, Jr., which charged that American education was failing to provide children with the basic knowledge of western civilization.[13]

Young people should certainly be exposed to Shakespeare, they should know the basics of geography, and they should be familiar with current events. A developmental approach to education does not deny the importance of such knowledge. The difference between the two approaches is a matter of which acquisition comes first. Those who hold a developmental philosophy believe that children who are curious, active learners will acquire much of the knowledge that Bennett, Bloom, and Hirsch call for—and many other things as well. But, from a developmental perspective, the creation of curious, active learners must precede the acquisition of particular information. To put the difference more succinctly, the developmental approach seeks to create students who want to know, whereas the psychometric approach seeks to produce students who know what we want.

Implications of a Developmental Philosophy

Now that we have looked at these two contrasting educational philosophies, we can review a few of the implications for the practice of education of adopting a developmental perspective. Once again, my interpretation is largely based on the Piagetian idea of the development of intelligence.

Teacher training. Students of most disciplines must learn the basic material of their discipline. A physics student has to learn about the rules that govern the physical world; a chemistry student must learn how the basic chemical elements interact; a biology student must learn about plants and animals. Education is perhaps the only discipline wherein students do not learn the basic material of the discipline at the outset. Students take courses in curriculum, in methods, in educational philosophy, in assessment, and in classroom management. They take only one (or at most two) courses in educational or developmental psychology.

But the basic material of education is not curriculum. Nor is it assessment or methods. The basic material of education is children and youth. A teacher training program that is truly developmentally appropriate would have its students major in child development. Trained in this way, a teacher would be, first and foremost, a child development specialist. Students with a strong foundation in child development can integrate what they learn about curriculum, assessment, and management with what they know about how children of various ages think and learn.

From a developmental point of view, the recommendation of the Holmes Group that we do away with the undergraduate major in education and substitute a year or two of graduate training and internship will not produce better teachers. There is a need for teacher training at the undergraduate level—not in traditional education courses, but in child development.

Curriculum. From a developmental point of view, there are several principles that should guide the construction of the curriculum. First, a curriculum must be constructed empirically, not *a priori*. There is no way to figure out how children learn a subject without studying how they actually go about learning it. Thus it is truly a scandal that curriculum publishers not only fail to do research on the materials they produce, but also fail even to field-test them! In no other profession would we allow a product to be placed on the market without extensive field-testing.

In a truly developmental system of education, teachers would have the opportunity to construct and test their own materials. They could see what works and what doesn't, and they could try out different sequences and methods. The way curriculum materials work will always depend on the specific group of children in the classroom in any given year. So a curriculum should never be final; it should always be open, flexible, and innovative. Such a curriculum is exciting for the teacher and for the pupils and makes both learning and curriculum innovation cooperative ventures.

Second, I believe that a curriculum should be localized, particularly for elementary schools. I know that this is contrary to trends in other countries, which have uniform curricula for all children. Japan and France are but two of the countries with such uniform national curricula. England, too, will be initiating a uniform national curriculum in 1990. But such national curricula eliminate the possibility of localizing materials to include particulars from the environment in which children actually live and learn.

Such localized curricula hold a great deal of intrinsic interest for children. For example, in learning math, children living in Hawaii might be asked to match coconuts and palm trees, whereas children living in the Northeast might be asked to match acorns and oaks. Likewise, it would add to children's enjoyment if the stories they read took place in their own community or one similar to it. In social studies, too, children are delighted to find a picture of a building that they have actually been in, rather than one that they have never seen. To be sure, children like stories about places and events that are new to them. Nonetheless, they also enjoy reading stories that relate directly to the world they live in. Children, no less than adults, appreciate both fantasy and the realism of local reference.

Finally, we need to study curricula to determine their level of developmental difficulty. Developmental difficulty is quite different from psychometric difficulty. The psychometric difficulty of a curriculum or a test item is determined by the number of children of a particular age who successfully learn the material or who get the item correct. A curriculum or test item is generally assigned to the grade or age level at which 75% of the children can succeed.

Developmental difficulty, by contrast, must be determined by examining the actual "errors" children make in attempting to master a problem or task. For example, when young children who have been taught the short a sound are asked to learn the long "a" as well, they have great difficulty. The problem is that they are being asked to grasp the fact that the same letter can have two different sounds. Understanding that the same symbol can stand for two different sounds, however, requires the attainment of the mental abilities that Piaget calls concrete operations. A teacher who holds a developmental philosophy would thus avoid teaching phonics until he or she was quite sure that most of the children could handle concrete operations. Because the developmental difficulty of any particular problem or task can be determined only by active investigation, part of the experimental work of teaching would be to explore the developmental difficulty of the available curriculum materials and to try out news materials that might work differently or better.

Instruction. Developmentally speaking, it is as impossible to separate the learning process from the material to be learned as it is to separate learning from instruction. This is authentic teaching. From this perspective, the teacher is also a learner, and the students are also teachers. The teacher who experiments with the curriculum is learning about the curriculum and about the children he or she teaches. And children who work cooperatively and who experiment with curriculum materials are teaching as well as learning.

One way to highlight the difference between authentic teaching and psychometrically oriented teaching is to look at how each type of instruction handles the asking of questions. In psychometrically oriented teaching, the teacher often asks students questions to which the teacher already knows the answers. The purpose is to determine whether the students have the same information as the teacher. But asking questions to which one already has the answers is not authentic behavior. A much more meaningful approach is to ask children questions to which one doesn't have the answers. Finding the answers can then be a learning experience for teacher and students alike. The authentic teacher asks questions to get information and to gain understanding, not to test what students know or understand. Such questioning reflects the fact that the authentic teacher is first and foremost an enthusiastic learner.

Assessment. Developmental assessment involves documenting the work that a child has done over a given period of time. Usually this is done by having a child keep a portfolio that includes all of his or her writing, drawing, math explorations, and so on. In looking through such a portfolio, we can get a good idea of the quality of work that the child is capable of doing and of his or her progress over the given period.

Psychometric assessment involves measuring a child's achievement by means of commercial or teacher-made tests. A child's progress is evaluated according to his or her performance on such tests. Unlike a portfolio of work, the psychometric approach yields a grade that symbolizes both the quantity and the quality of the work that the child has done over a given period of time. Although some testing can be useful, it is currently so overused that many children and parents are more concerned about grades and test scores than about what a child has learned. The documentation of a child's work tends to avoid that danger.

I have tried to demonstrate that, while the idea of developmentally appropriate practice has been well received among educators, it really has little chance of being implemented. Without a change in underlying philosophy, changes in educational practice will be superficial at best. No classroom or school can truly be developmentally appropriate if its underlying philosophy is psychometric.

How can we change that underlying educational philosophy? It might seem that what is required is a paradigm shift of the sort described by Thomas Kuhn as characterizing major scientific revolutions.[14] Yet neither the developmental thinking of Freud nor that of Piaget has been sufficient to effect such a shift. This may reflect the fact that educational practice is dictated more by social, political, and economic considerations than it is by science. Unfortunately, a major shift in educational philosophy is more likely to come about as a result of economic necessity than as a result of scientific innovation.

David Elkind is a professor of child study at Tufts University, Medford, Mass. He is a past president of the National Association for the Education of Young Children and the author of *The Hurried Child* (Addison-Wesley, 1981), *All Grown Up and No Place to Go* (Addison-Wesley, 1984), and *Miseducation: Preschoolers at Risk* (Knopf, 1987).

References-Endnotes

1. Bredekamp, Sue. *Developmentally Appropriate Practice*. Washington, D.C.: National Association for the Education of Young Children, 1987.

2. Piaget, Jean. *The Psychology of Intelligence*. London: Routledge & Kegan Paul, 1950.

3. Piaget, Jean; and Inhelder, Barbel. *The Child's Conception of Space*. London: Routledge & Kegan Paul, 1956.

Piaget, Jean; Inhelder, Barbel; and Szeminska, Alina. *The Child's Conception of Geometry*. New York: Basic Books, 1960.

Piaget, Jean. *The Child's Conception of Time*. London: Routledge & Kegan Paul, 1967.

Idem. *The Child's Conception of Movement and Speed*. London: Routledge & Kegan Paul, 1970.

4. Bruner, Jerome S.; Goodenough, Jacqueline J.; and Austin, George A. *A Study of Thinking*. New York: Wiley, 1956.

5. Baron, Joan Boykoff; and Sternberg, Robert J. *Teaching Thinking Skills: Theory and Practice*. New York: Freeman, 1987.

6. Weinstein, Edwin; and Mayer, Richard Edwin. "The Teaching of Learning Strategies." In *Handbook of Research on Teaching*, edited by Merlin C. Wittrock (3rd edition). New York: Macmillan, 1986.

7. Papert, Seymour. *Mindstorms*. New York: Basic Books, 1980.

8. Perkins, David N.; and Salomon, Gavriel. "Teaching for Transfer." Educational Leadership, 1988, 46: 22–32.

9. Kant, Immanuel. *Critique of Pure Reason*. New York: Wiley, 1943.

10. Elkind, David. *Miseducation: Preschoolers at Risk*. New York: Knopf, 1987.

11. Quoted in Richard E. Ripple and Verne E. Rockcastle, eds. *Piaget Rediscovered: A Report of the Conference on Cognitive Studies and Curriculum Development*. Ithaca, New York: School of Education, Cornell University, 1964.

12. Bennett, William J. *First Lessons: A Report on Elementary Education in America*. Washington, D.C.: U.S. Department of Education, 1986.

13. Bloom, Allan. *The Closing of the American Mind*. New York: Simon & Schuster, 1987.

Hirsh, Jr., E. D. *Cultural Literacy: What Every American Needs to Know*. Boston: Houghton Mifflin, 1987.

14. Kuhn, Thomas S. *The Structure of Scientific Revolutions*, 2nd ed. Chicago: University of Chicago Press, 1970.

CHAPTER 9

Day Care and the Public Schools—Natural Allies, Natural Enemies

A blending of early childhood and elementary programs—as in Little Rock's Kramer Model—seems a logical way to benefit children, parents, and society.

My personal interest in day care began about 20 years ago at a time when any program of infant stimulation ran against the grain of theoretical ideas about proper upbringing for young children. To some extent this was true even if the mother was the "stimulator." It was especially true, however, if anyone other than the mother were the agent of stimulation and enrichment.

Our concern (Caldwell and Richmond, 1964) was primarily directed to young children of poverty who were known to be growing up in somewhat chaotic family circumstances. As many of the mothers were minimally available to their children, either physically or psychologically (Caldwell et al., 1963), our interest was in developing an enrichment program that would in some way supplement the experiences available to children in their homes. Our idea was to have teachers and other specially trained caregivers work with the children for a few hours each day and introduce them to various developmental events intended to excite and stimulate them.

The idea of bringing infants together in groups was totally unacceptable at that time. The common fear was that even short-term separation of infants from their mothers would be tantamount to creating "institutional" rearing conditions. The deleterious consequences of growing up in institutional care were constantly cited in the professional literature (see Bowlby, 1952) and publicized in the popular press. Our proposal to develop such a program in Syracuse, New York, was turned down, but we were offered a loophole. The Children's Bureau was willing to consider our request provided we used as subjects only those children who were already receiving some sort of substitute care and that we would not reduce in any way the daily time they spent in contact with their own mothers. In short, we could conduct our own project with children who were already in day care (see Caldwell, 1971).

103

Our center served children from six months through five years of age. It was affiliated first with the Department of Pediatrics of the Upstate Medical Center of the State University of New York and later with the College of Home Economics of Syracuse University. Although the resources of two great universities were behind it, it operated essentially in isolation from the mainstream of either university. It also operated in isolation from the public school system into which most of the children graduated.

While my professional concern centered on preschool children, I was personally involved with the public schools, having a set of twins who entered kindergarten at precisely the time that our project was "discovered" nationally. Occasionally I would be late picking them up from school, and Syracuse winters can be very cold. There I would find two forlorn twins with icy hands and frozen cheeks. I can remember reacting with horror to their not being allowed to wait inside to be picked up: when school was out, children were expected to go home immediately. To me it seemed the most logical thing in the world to think that their elementary school could have provided some sort of extended day care. It struck me as rather ironic that while I was working hard in one part of the city to provide both care and education for other people's children, no one was concerned about providing the care needed to supplement the education mine were receiving.

Shortly thereafter I moved to Arkansas and took with me something of an obsession about the need to develop child care programs in the public school. This obsession was no longer based only on my perception of the need for such care as a service to families but also on my awareness of the need to change the public conception of what day care was or should be. Considered by many people as a service that provided only "care and protection" for low-income children, child care was actually a comprehensive service that could and did provide education, access to medical care, and social services to large numbers of children from all levels of society. It was my conviction that an alliance with public education would help to "legitimize" child care and help it gain respectability with parents, professionals, and policymakers. Likewise, it was my hope that the provision of day care in a public school setting would make the elementary educational program more relevant to modern social realities.

Natural Allies—The Kramer Model

What developed from this obsession—with a great deal of help from Little Rock School District officials, personnel from the University of Arkansas, an interested granting agency (the Children's Bureau, shortly thereafter subsumed into the newly created Office of Child Development), and a favorable zeitgeist—was the Kramer Model. From 1969 to 1978 the project operated essentially as described here. Some of the major components are still in operation, although with slight programmatic changes and major administrative changes.

Early Childhood–Elementary Continuity

Continuity between early childhood and elementary educational programs should be as normal and routine as continuity between 2nd and 3rd grades. In most educational settings, however, this is definitely not the case. In fact, there is often a change in auspice (from private to public, or from one type of public funding, such as Head Start, to another); in location and size (from private home, church, or small-group center to large school); in educational philosophy and curriculum (from much free choice to a high degree of structure and adult control); and in training background of the personnel. Not infrequently there is distrust on the part of early childhood personnel of elementary personnel, and vice versa. Early childhood teachers often accuse elementary teachers of being concerned with subjects rather than children and of neglecting the "whole child"; elementary teachers sometimes assume and imply that their kindergarten colleagues "just play" with the children and do not "really teach" them anything.

If the transition is from anything other than a public school kindergarten, there is seldom any exchange of records. School personnel do not appear to be particularly interested in knowing much about previous educational experiences, and rarely do they send reports to teachers who previously worked with the children. Thus the new teachers receive no benefits from the insights gained by their predecessors, and the former teachers have no opportunity to confirm or disconfirm their predictions about future educational progress of individual children.

By having both an early childhood and an elementary program in the same building—with teachers from both segments serving on all committees, attending all meetings, and sharing the same lounge—we hoped to kindle a spirit of united effort directed toward common goals. Although it took some time for this spirit to develop, it unquestionably became an important feature of the Kramer Model.

Educational Day Care

The most important component of the Kramer Model was the conversion of the entire school to an "extended day school." That is, the school officially began at 6:45 A.M. and closed at 6:00 P.M. year round. The bells rang at the same time as in all the other elementary schools within the Little Rock School District, but the program operated for the full day. The extra hours and days were funded out of the program grant. Teachers at Kramer taught for the same number of hours and total days as all other teachers in the system (although they did have the option of applying for summer and holiday work for extra pay).

Extra hours were covered by part-time and split-time staff, or, for the early childhood segment, by staggering beginning and ending hours so that at least one certified teacher was on duty at all hours. In a situation like this it is easy to let "natural" preferences work themselves out instead of conforming to systemwide work hours. That is, there were always one or two early risers who preferred to begin work at 7:00, and there was always at least one person who preferred to begin work at 9:30 and stay later in the afternoon.

When day care in the public schools is discussed, concern usually is limited to children roughly in the age range of five or six to ten years. (Where kindergartens last only a half day, most working parents keep their children in a child care program until they reach 1st grade.) While this in itself is beneficial, it does not provide the range of coverage that many parents need. That is, a working mother may have children aged seven, four, and two, all of whom need day care. In many communities that can mean three child care arrangements (one school-age setting, one pre-school, and one infancy program) rather than one. The elegance of the Kramer extended care arrangements was that it accommodated children from 6 months to 12 years of age in the same physical location. The convenience of this arrangement for working mothers is truly remarkable—and quite rare.

Traditional starting and ending times for public school schedules, and dates for opening in the fall and closing in the spring, are entirely anachronistic in today's world. The times and dates we now have were not arbitrarily set; they were chosen to allow the schools to dovetail with the social realities of the children and families they served. The hours allowed children to complete chores before and after school, and the dates corresponded to times when the children would be needed to help in the fields. It is unfortunate that we are so bound to custom that we have lost sight of the fact that the custom originally corresponded to demographic realities. Once we fully understand today's demographic realities, the question of whether schools should provide day care will become totally obsolete.

Public School–University Collaboration

Other major features of the Kramer Model include having a university professor run the school and serve as its principal; establishing an advisory board to oversee school operation consisting of university and community personnel, in addition to representatives of the Little rock

School District; and establishing special work arrangements for Kramer teachers involving both extra requirements (take a certain inservice course of work and the late-day shift) and special privileges (having an aide in the classroom) not available to other teachers in the system. Although many of the special arrangements required for Kramer went far beyond the day care situation, the same flexibility may well be necessary if a public school day care program is to be anything more than an appendage to the existing operation without any curricular or developmental relevance.

One clear but often overlooked benefit of this university–public school alliance was the constant presence in the school of student teachers and a few doctoral candidates. Not only did their presence confer status on the Kramer teachers, but their excitement about the Kramer philosophy was contagious. For example, it was not uncommon for a 5th grade teacher to complain to an early childhood teacher that a mess "your" children made at the water fountain caused "our" children to slip down. To the students, all the children were far more likely to be perceived as "our" children, and they contributed to eliminating some of these exclusionary references.

Everything possible was done to help the students "think developmentally." For example, teachers had to spend some time with a class in each quadrant of the program—infancy, early childhood, primary (grades 1–3), and intermediate (grades 4–6). Obviously, they spent the greatest amount of time in the quadrant in which they expected or hoped to teach. Exchange times for teachers were also arranged so that intermediate teachers occasionally taught for a morning in an infancy or early childhood classroom, and vice versa. After such exchanges elementary teachers were rarely heard to complain that the early childhood teachers 'had it easy" or early childhood teachers to criticize elementary teachers for not understanding and loving the children enough.

Natural Enemies

When people ask me what we learned at Kramer, I usually tell them we learned that it isn't easy. Such an arrangement makes so much sense both socially and educationally that one could logically wonder why schools are organized any other way. And yet the two domains of child care and education are also natural enemies.

Conceptual and Philosophical Differences

The first basis for the adversarial relationship between day care and education relates to the concepts out of which each service pattern has grown and, if you will, to the way in which proponents of each service want the field to be identified. Having developed largely from a social service orientation, day care has been known as a service that provides "care and protection" for children. Schools, on the other hand, provide "education." Such sharp dichotomies represent a misunderstanding of both services, for it is literally impossible to care for and protect young children without educating them, and vice versa. The domain of education already includes many services that might seem to fit more comfortably under the rubric of care and protection: school nurses, health programs, nutrition programs, hot lunches, vision and hearing screening, requirements for immunization, and so on. Likewise, during a large part of the day, every high-quality day care program will provide educational experiences that are similar if not identical to school "teaching programs" for children of comparable age. Thus it is foolish to try to distinguish between the services in terms of shibboleths such as care versus education. In order for either service to be relevant to the needs of children and families, both components must be present.

Another conceptual distinction already mentioned is that day care is believed to be largely for "poor children from problem families," whereas public education is for "all children." There are now more families with young children whose mothers work outside the home than there are families in which the mother is available fulltime as a caregiver. And because all families supplement parental care with some extra-family child care, we recognize that the nature of the family situation no longer defines day care—if, indeed, it ever did. There are more commonalities between the fields than there are differences.

Both Institutions Held in Low Esteem

A second reason for the animosity that we sometimes find between representatives of public education and day care is that, unfortunately, both institutions are often held in low esteem. The current clamor for "educational reform" clearly implies that somehow public education has "failed." Likewise, day care has been denounced by conservatives as "weakening the family" and by liberals as being a "wasteland" of poor quality in which children's lives could be ruined. Leaders of the day care movement have often bristled at suggestions that an alliance between the field and education would be beneficial. A typically hostile objection might be, "The schools have already ruined the older kids; let's not help them do the same thing with the little ones." Natural resistance to such a union was increased by media reports of a national surplus of elementary and secondary teachers and by the suggestion that such teachers could be diverted into the burgeoning day care field if it were part of public education and thereby comparably lucrative for teachers. Early childhood and day care personnel were legitimately offended at the implication that no special training was necessary to work with young children. However, such an attitude on the part of professional educators was no different from that often expressed by the general public and given as a reason for failing to provide higher salaries for early childhood personnel.

The important point here is that the two fields, each of which had reason to doubt that it was held in esteem by the general public, took a stance against one another rather than forming what should have been a natural alliance. It was as though each sought to bolster its own self-esteem by asserting its independence from and superiority to the other.

Mutual Need—The Bonding Agent

The demographic realities of modern life have made this separatism and exclusivity on the part of both day care and public education entirely obsolete. Both fields have undergone travail, and both are dealing with increasingly sophisticated consumers who legitimately advocate education that fits modern urban rather than outdated rural patterns of family living, and day care that accepts its responsibility to provide developmentally appropriate education to young children.

Representatives of both domains must learn to find strengths and assets in one another. The biggest problems many people in the child care field face are low salaries and poor working conditions. Teachers certified in early childhood who work in public schools make, on the average, $5,000 more per year (often for fewer hours and days) than certified teachers who work in child care. Likewise, the public schools are having to try to withstand the major inroads in their clientele by private schools. It is fascinating to note that the new private academies springing up all over the country are not overlooking the profit potential associated with the provision of child care. Almost without exception, such schools are providing extended day care and summer programs. Unless public schools offer comparable services, they cannot hope to hold a major share of the market. And, though we might not want to admit it, marketing is as important for public education as it is for other products and services.

The inroads into support for public education made by this increasing network of private schools have weakened the infrastructure of our educational system. Likewise, allegations of sexual abuse and concerns about maintenance of healthful conditions in child care centers have generated increased concern about the quality and benefit of such programs. One might be tempted to suggest that attempts to unite the two domains are too late; the general public now sees both services as inadequate and flawed.

But, of course, it is never too late to develop a service program that is in harmony with patterns of human need. Because a blending of day care and education can meet the needs of children for developmental guidance and the needs of parents for effective supervision of their children more conveniently than any other pattern of service, I predict that the two domains will move ever closer to one another. The resultant merger will be symbiotic for the two fields and beneficial to children, to their parents, and to society.

Bettye M. Caldwell is Donaghey Distinguished Professor of Education, University of Arkansas at Little Rock, Little Rock, AR 72204

References

Bowlby, J. "Maternal Care and Mental Health." Geneva, Switzerland, World Health Organization, 1952.
Caldwell, B. M. "Impact of Interest in Early Cognitive Stimulation." In *Perspectives in Psychopathology,* edited by H. Rie. Chicago: Aldine-Atherton, 1971.
Caldwell, B. M., L. Hersher, E. Lipton, J. B. Richmond, G. Stern, E Eddy, R Drachman, & A. Rothman. "Mother-Infant Interaction in Monomatric and Polymatric Families." *American Journal of Orthopsychiatry,* 1963, 33: 653–664.
Caldwell, B. M., & J. B. Richmond. "Programmed Day Care for the Very Young Child: A Preliminary Report." *Journal of Marriage and the Family,* 1964, 26: 481–488.

CHAPTER 10

Uses and Abuses of Developmental Screening and School Readiness Testing

Public school involvement in early childhood education is growing rapidly, bringing with it new responsibilities for schools to identify children who may be at risk for learning problems and to place these children in appropriate educational environments. This process of identification and placement has been complicated by several basic confusions about screening and readiness tests that have resulted in young children being denied a free and appropriate public education. This exclusion is based not, as in the past, on being handicapped, coming from impoverished backgrounds, or being members of minority groups, but as a result of such labels as young, developmentally immature, or not ready. Moreover, these labels have been assigned on the basis of tests with unknown validity by testers who have had little training and usually no supervision.

One test that has been in widespread use nationally for identification and placement is the Gesell School Readiness Screening Test (Ilg & Ames, 1972). The purpose of this article is to analyze the uses and abuses that can be traced to the Gesell and other similar tests. I will first discuss developmental screening tests and readiness tests in general. Then I will focus on the Gesell tests, specifically addressing their validity, and questioning their current use, given the type of information the tests were designed to produce. This article will conclude with a discussion of the implications of using readiness tests for assigning children to particular school programs.

Uses and Abuses of Screening and Readiness Tests

Elsewhere I have defined and analyzed the differences between developmental screening tests and readiness tests and have listed examples of each (Meisels, 1984, 1985). The two types of tests are different and were designed to accomplish different objectives. Developmental screening tests provide a brief assessment of a child's developmental abilities—abilities that are highly associated with future school success. Readiness tests are concerned with those curriculum-related skills a child has al-

Table 1: Contrasts between developmental screening tests and readiness tests

	Developmental Screening Tests	Readiness Tests
Purpose	to identify children who may need early intervention or special education services	to facilitate curriculum planning
	to identify children who might profit from a modified or individualized classroom program	to identify a child's relative preparedness to benefit from a specific program
Content	items that display a child's ability or potential to acquire skills	items that focus on current skill achievement, performance, and general knowledge
Type of Test	norm-referenced	most are criterion-referenced; some are norm references
Psychometric Properties	reliability predictive validity	reliability construct validity

ready acquired—skills that are typically prerequisite for specific instructional programs. Table 1 compares the differences between the two types of tests in terms of purpose, content, type of test, and psychometric properties.

Screening Tests

During the years, professionals have misused and abused both screening and readiness tests. The most frequent abuse of developmental screening results from using tests that have no established reliability and validity. Reliability is an indicator of a test's consistency. It measures how often identical results can be obtained with the same test. Validity is a measure of a test's accuracy. Technically, validity concerns the overall degree of justification for test interpretation and use. It tells us whether a test does what it claims to do. Because young children grow and change so rapidly from day to day and week to week, it is critical that tests used to assess these children be stable and accurate.

Tests without reliability and validity are inherently untrustworthy and should not be used to identify and place children. We do not know if such tests provide different results when administered by different testers, whether children from certain socioeconomic or ethnic backgrounds are disadvantaged by them, or whether they are strongly related to some stable, external criterion or outcome measure—such as the results of a diagnostic assessment, a systematic teacher report form, or report card grades—that permits the test results to be interpreted and the findings to be generalized.

Yet, professionals persist in using invalid and unreliable tests. In a survey of 177 school districts in New York State, Joiner (1977) found that 151 different tests or procedures were used for screening. At best, only 16 of these tests could be considered even marginally appropriate. In a recent survey in Michigan, 111 tests were being used for preschool, kindergarten, and pre-first grade programs (Michigan Department of Education, 1984). Fewer than 10 of these tests were appropriate in terms of the age group and purpose to which they were being put. What is taking place in these two states, as well as elsewhere nationwide, is a proliferation of screening tests, many developed locally, that have never been assessed in terms of reliability, validity, or other general criteria that have been established for developmental screening tests (see Meisels, 1985). In the absence of satisfying these criteria—particularly the criterion of validity—children who need special services are being overlooked; some children who are not at risk are being identified as being at risk; parents are becoming alarmed, teachers and administrators upset, and resources squandered. More than 25 states currently mandate developmental screening for 3- to 6-year-olds (Meisels, 1986). A test with known, high-level validity and reliability should always be used when this type of testing is performed. Nothing less than strict psychometric standards are acceptable for other kinds of tests, such as diagnostic assessments or school achievement tests. Using screening tests that lack validity data is an abuse of testing procedures and of the trust the community places in professional educators (see American Educational Research Association, American Psychological Association, & National Council on Measurement in Education, 1985.)

Readiness Tests

Another major abuse is the substitution of readiness tests for screening tests. This substitution frequently occurs inadvertently, through confusion about the differences between screening and readiness testing. As a brief sorting device, readiness tests can be loosely considered screening tests. But, because of the type of information they yield and their lack of predictive validity, they cannot correctly be considered developmental screening tests. Readiness tests should be used to facilitate curriculum planning, not to identify children who may need special services or intervention.

One of the differences between developmental screening and readiness tests lies in the predictive relationships of these tests to such outcome measures as comprehensive developmental assessments and school performance. In general, individual readiness tests, as contrasted to multivari-

Figure 1: Relationship of screening and readiness tests to assessment and school performance

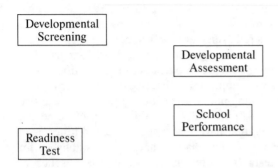

ate reading readiness batteries that incorporate several different kinds of assessments (see Barnes, 1982; Satz & Friel, 1978), do not have a strong predictive relationship to outcome measures. Most correlations between reading success and reading readiness tests are moderate at best (Knight, 1979). Figure 1 portrays the general relationship between developmental screening, individual readiness tests, developmental assessments, and school performance. The figure portrays the conclusions from several different studies, rather than a strict quantitative representation of specific empirical findings (see Lichtenstein, 1981; Rubin, Balow, Dorie, & Rosen, 1978; Wiske, Meisels, & Tivnan, 1982). The wide, dark lines represent strong relationships, the narrower dark lines suggest moderate relations, and the broken lines indicate weak relationships.

Figure 1 suggests that readiness tests have a much weaker relationship to developmental screening tests. At first glance, such a statement may seem counterintuitive because readiness tests are intended to assess readiness for a specific school program. Nonetheless, readiness tests best describe *child entry characteristics;* they are not intended to *predict child outcomes.* Thus, children who perform poorly on readiness tests may profit proportionately more from school programs than children with higher initial skills because they have more to gain. Conversely, those with well-developed entry level skills may profit less from kindergarten than children who do poorly on readiness tests. Hence, neither the potential of those who score well nor the potential of those who score poorly is accurately assessed by single-measure readiness tests. These tests are best used by teachers for making *initial curriculum decisions about individual children.* While this function is critically important, the data from readiness tests should not be used to attempt to identify developmental problems that may affect a child's chances for school success. Mistaking readiness tests for predictive developmental screening instruments misrepresents the purpose and scope of both tests.

Uses and Abuses of Gesell Testing

One of the most widely adopted tests used for both readiness and developmental screening is the Gesell School Readiness Screening Test (Ilg & Ames, 1972. Also known as the Gesell Preschool Test (Haines, Ames, & Gillespie, 1980), this test, or set of tests, is a shortened version of the Gesell Developmental Schedules—full-scale evaluations used to assess personal–social, fine motor/adaptive behavior; language and reasoning; and gross motor development of children younger than age 6. This article will focus on the Preschool Readiness Tests, not the Developmental Schedules.

In recent years the Preschool Tests have become increasingly popular. According to the Gesell Institute, thousands of public, private, and parochial schools nationwide have adopted them. In addition to the tests, the Gesell Institute conducts week-long workshops on developmental placement. These workshops prepare kindergarten teachers and other professionals to use the Gesell test results to place children in readiness or developmental kindergartens, to recommend that the child delay entering kindergarten for a year, or to suggest conventional kindergarten placement. In other words, the Gesell readiness tests are explicitly presented as performing the functions of developmental screening tests. According to Ames, Gillespie, Haines, and Ilg (1979), "perhaps 50% of school failures could be prevented or cured by proper placement based on a child's behavior age (p. 128)." Claims like these are responsible for the tremendous interest that educators have shown in Gesell testing in recent years.

Nevertheless, despite their widespread popularity and the amount of time and energy expended on them, the Gesell Preschool Tests are based on an outmoded theory of child development, lack reliability and validity, and use a concept of developmental age that has never been empirically verified. The remainder of this article will be devoted to substantiating these assertions and drawing conclusions from them.

Gesell's Theory

The Gesell tests reflect a maturationist theory of development. They view behavior as a function of structure, changing in a patterned, predictable way. The stages through which most behaviors develop are considered to be highly similar from child to child.

According to this theory, behavior is almost entirely the result of maturation, and neither chronological age nor environmental intervention is considered to be highly correlated with so-called developmental age (Gesell, 1954). In other words, maturational theory links behavior with pre-formed, genetically determined biological structures. In the absence of unusual environmental conditions, this theory focuses on time as the crucial variable in behavior change, not environmental stimulation or intervention, but time to grow, mature, and endogenously develop. According to Gesell, developmental diagnosis implies prognosis (Shonkoff, 1983).

Although the importance of maturational change in development cannot be ignored, this strict Gesellian approach is at odds with research ranging from Piaget to Perry Preschool Project. Numerous researchers have identified the ameliorative effects of environmental intervention on childhood development (see, for example, Berrueta-Clement, Schweinhart, Barnett, Epstein, & Weikart, 1984; Clarke-Stewart & Fein, 1983; Lazar & Darlington, 1982; Meisels & Anastasiow, 1982; and Zigler & Valentine, 1982). Modern-day researchers view maturation as only one aspect of development. Other factors include socioeconomic variables, familial factors, encounters with the physical and social environment, sex differences, and the internal regulations of new information with preexisting schemes of action. To assume, as do the Gesell theorists, that behavior is equivalent to age-related maturational growth is to confuse a description of experience with its cause. In other words, although it may be possible to describe development in terms of patterned sequential behaviors, doing so does not imply that development occurs because of these behaviors. Nor does it imply that teachers and other professionals are powerless to work with children until children spontaneously achieve these behaviors (i.e., school readiness). Few teachers today would willingly accept such a passive approach to education as that which is implied by a maturationist theory. Yet, unknowingly, that is what they are doing when they subscribe to the Gesellian approach to developmental placement and readiness.

Certainly, all children are not equally ready for school when they become 4 or 5 years of age. However, identifying these differences in readiness only suggests the need for differences in curriculum planning. Other information is required before a valid judgment can be made about whether a child should attend a particular program, or should be labeled at risk. This is particularly true for children from linguistic or cultural groups who may be at a disadvantage because of the limitations of the tests being used.

Validity of the Gesell Tests

Although the Gesell schedules were first published in 1940 (Gesell et al.) and have been used in numerous research studies and clinical investigations, no systematic study of the validity of these tests has ever been conducted. In 1966 a subset of items covering the first 2 years of life were selected as a developmental screening test for infants—the Developmental Screening Inventory (DSI) (Knobloch, Pasamanick, & Shepard, 1966). The data that accompanied this test were insufficient to support its validity as a screening test (see McCall, 1982, for a discussion of the DSI). No other validation studies have been published. Jacqueline Haines, director of training at the Gesell Institute, confirms that the Gesell tests have not been validated. In 1984 she noted that the Gesell "documents normative responses by age. The validity of the work has been through years of experience in application. A validity study has not been completed at the preset time" (personal communication, March 28, 1984).

This situation raises several problems for users of the Gesell tests. In the absence of predictive validity data, it is impossible to evaluate the claims set forth by Gesell theorist. For example, Ames and her colleagues state that "behavior develops in a patterned and highly predictable way and can be evaluated by means of simple, basic test situations (Ames et al., 1979, p. ix)." This may be true, but there is no evidence to support the position that the behavior evaluated by the Gesell Preschool Tests accurately predicts subsequent development.

A test that only "documents normative responses by age" cannot be used appropriately for prediction unless the predictive relationship has been tested and demonstrated. That is, children whose behavior is non-normative—either delayed or advanced—could, theoretically, be identified by means of the Gesell, but claims about their future performance would be purely speculative in the absence of studies that demonstrate the predictive accuracy of these normative assessments.

Another issue concerns the norms used by the Gesell tests. The original norms were developed by Gesell in 1928 and published in 1940. These norms were based on data obtained from a small, uncontrolled sample of primarily upper middle-class children and were rated by observers who were neither independent of each other nor free from potential bias. New norms have now been established for the Preschool Tests (Ames et al., 1979), but they still leave many questions unanswered. The norms are based on 640 children stratified by sex, age (eight 6-month intervals, from 2½ to 6 years), and parental occupational level. Unfortunately, nearly all of the children were Caucasian, and all·lived in Connecticut. Further, no effort was made to test for the effects of differences in birth order, parental education, number of parents in the home, or prior preschool or child care experience. Also, no data are provided concerning the reliability of the standardization procedure: We do not know how many examiners participated, what the level of interobserver agreement was, whether there was intertester stability, or what the standard error of measurement was. Thus, inadequate sampling procedures, absence of validity data, inattention to issues of reliability, and sources of variance in recording performances render the entire normative foundation of the Gesell tests questionable.

Developmental Age and School Placement

One of the foremost uses of the Gesell tests is developmental placement. Ames et al. (1979) note that "of all the possible uses of the Gesell Behavior battery, its use in relation to determining the most favorable time for starting school or for subsequent promotion of students may turn out to be one of its most substantial contributions (p. 184)." According to Gesell theorists, the purpose of Gesell testing is to make examiners aware of age-related behaviors. Children's responses then show the level, or developmental age, at which they are functioning. "Regardless of either birthday age or Intelligence Quotient, in most instances a child does best in school if started and subsequently promoted on the basis of developmental age (Ames et al., 1979, p. 6)."

Clearly, the validity of the concept of developmental age hinges on the mechanism for establishing this age. Because that mechanism is the Gesell Preschool tests—nonstandardized tests excerpted from the full-scale Gesell Developmental Schedules—the notion of developmental age is highly suspect.

Only one published study examines the predictive validity of developmental age by comparing results of kindergarten-age children on the Gesell School Readiness Screening Test with school success (Wood, Powell, & Knight, 1984). The study claims that developmental age provides a useful predictive measure of later school performance. Unfortunately, the study had major problems: the study population was small and not highly generalizable (N = 84, all Caucasian and middle class); the outcome measure of school success (special needs status versus nonspecial needs) was undefined and unvalidated; and the study was not predictive as claimed, but at best postdictive or possibly concurrent. That is, the children were first referred for special services, then 3 months later the Gesell was administered. Because the Gesell test was given after the special needs designation was assigned, the study authors linearly adjusted scores back by 3 months. This circular procedure assumes the validity of the developmental age concept, which is precisely what the study was intended to prove.

In short, the use of the Gesell School Readiness Screening Test—based as it is on a set of tests with unknown validity and reliability, a theory that is outmoded and unsubstantiated, and unverified notion of developmental age, and a racially and ethnically narrow normative base—for developmental screening and class placement is empirically unjustified and professionally suspect. The Gesell tests can be used effectively as school readiness tests for initial curriculum planning for individual children, but there currently is no evidence to support more extensive application.

Implications for Early Childhood and Kindergarten Educators

Testing in early childhood and kindergarten should only be used to make better and more appropriate services available to the largest number of children. There are several kinds of tests that, if used as designed and intended, can assist professionals in making appropriate decisions for young children. Children who need special services can be identified by developmental screening and assessment. Children in need of modified classroom programming or individualized attention in preschool or kindergarten can be identified by readiness tests and to a certain extent, by developmental screening inventories. Tests that exclude children from public education services or that delay their access to the educational mainstream, however, are antithetical to legal and constitutional rights to free education and equal protection. In addition, such tests and practices are incompatible with the belief systems, theoretical perspectives, and best practices of most early childhood educators.

The use of exclusionary tests suggests that children should conform to school programs, rather than schools adjusting to the needs of children. Nowhere is this reversal of the child-centered tradition more evident than in the Gesellian practice that recommends a year's delayed school entrance for children who are not ready for kindergarten. Ames and her colleagues claim that "if a 5-year-old child is still behaving like a 4- or 4½-year-old child, he will in all likelihood not be ready for the work of kindergarten, regardless of what the law allows (Ames et al., 1979, p. 6)." This approach is unjustified because it is based on the assumption that the Gesell tests are valid predictors of school performance—an assumption that has not been proven. Also unproven is the assumption that all not ready or developmentally immature children develop similarly and cannot benefit from kindergarten, even if their peers who are ready can. The reality of individual differences is that even in classrooms where all the children have been certified as ready some will be more ready than others.

Proponents of the developmental readiness concept frequently recommend that children who are immature or not ready be enrolled in developmental kindergartens instead of having to enter school late. These programs, also known as readiness kindergartens, usually precede a regular year of kindergarten.

Readiness kindergartens are a fast-growing phenomenon. In Michigan alone 161 school districts offered such programs during the 1983–84 school year, with 67 more districts slated to add them in the 1984–85 school year. These programs—most of which (65%) have existed for less than 5 years—served 5,700 students from 1983 to 1984 at a cost of $3,430,000 (Michigan Department of Education, 1984).

All developmental kindergartens do not subscribe to a Gesellian philosophy. Indeed, most of them are highly eclectic in approach, but they nevertheless share the same kinds of problems as Gesell-oriented programs. Specifically, these types of programs have not been systematically studied or evaluated. Among the questions that need further exploration are the following: On what basis are children placed in these programs? Are minority or poor children overrepresented in them? Are parents accorded due process in placement? What impact do these programs have on children's long-term development?

In practice, many developmental kindergartens contain a disproportionate number of younger children—those with birth dates late in the year. But the research evidence does not support this type of age grouping. Other factors in addition to simple immaturity play important roles in the explanation of school failure and learning problems (Diamond, 1983; Gredler, 1978; Maddux, Stacy, & Scott, 1981). Changing the standard of school readiness or the entry age cutoff only changes the composition of the group that is youngest or least ready—it does not eliminate it.

Many of these practices seem to result from pressures placed on kindergarten teachers to implement academically oriented programs in order to prepare children for the heavy academic emphasis seen in most first through third grades. The developmental readiness movement, as well as the widespread popularity of the Gesell tests, can be seen, in part, as well-meaning responses to these pressures, in which some children are excluded from kindergarten or enrolled in kindergarten for 2 years in order to reduce the likelihood of subsequent failure.

But this situation should cause grave professional concern. It signifies that schools are placing such institutional needs as obtaining higher achievement test scores and adopting more academically oriented early elementary curricula ahead of children's needs. To the extent that these priorities deny slowly developing or at-risk children access to public school programs, they are incompatible with child development research, contemporary social policy, and exemplary early childhood practice. Rather than label children, schools should devote their resources to helping teachers fashion individually responsive curricula that embrace a wide range of childhood activities and readiness levels.

The National Association for the Education of Young Children's Position Statement on Developmentally Appropriate Practice in Early Childhood Programs Serving Children Birth Through Age 8 (NAEYC, 1986) notes that high quality, developmentally appropriate programs typically include children with a range of developmental levels in a single classroom. The statement further notes that "It is the responsibility of the educational system to adjust to the developmental needs and levels of the children it serves; children should not be expected to adapt to an inappropriate system (p. 16)." Nor, it might be added, should children or their parents expect not to be served at all because children's skill levels do not conform to some external, preestablished norm or because they are being tested with an inappropriate instrument. In such situations, the schools and professionals who advocate these positions are demonstrating a failure of readiness, not the children.

Samuel J. Meisels, Ed.D., is Professor in the School of Education and Research Scientist in the Center for Human Growth and Development at the University of Michigan in Ann Arbor.

For comments on an earlier version of this paper the author would like to thank Nancy Klein, Kathy Modigliani, Robert Halpern, and Larry Schweinhart. This paper was completed while the author held a Mary E. Switzer Distinguished Fellowship from the National Institute of Handicapped Research, U.S. Department of Education. The opinions expressed are solely those of the author.

References

American Educational Research Association; American Psychological Association; and National Council on Measurement in Education. *Standards for Educational and Psychological Testing.* Washington, DC: American Psychological Association, 1985.

Ames, L. B.; Gillespie, C.; Haines, J.; and Ilg, F. *The Gesell Institute's Child from One to Six.* New York: Harper & Row, 1979.

Barnes, K. E. *Preschool Screening: The Measurement and Prediction of Children At-Risk.* Springfield, IL: Thomas, 1982.

Berrueta-Clement, J. R.; Schweinhart, L. J.; Barnett, W. S. Epstein, A. S.; and Weikart, D. P. *Changed Lives: The Effects of the Perry Preschool Program on Youths Through Age 19.* Ypsilanti, MI: High Scope, 1984.

Clarke, A. M.; and Clarke, A. D. B. *Early Experience: Myth and Evidence.* New York: Free-Press, 1976.

Clarke-Stewart, A. K.; and Fein, G. G. "Early Childhood Programs." In *Infancy and Developmental Psychobiology,* edited by M. M. Haith and J. J. Campos, (917–999). New York: Wiley, 1983.

Diamond, G. H. "The Birthdate Effect—A Maturational Effect?" *Journal of Learning Disabilities,* 1983, 16: 161–164.

Gesell, A. "The Ontogenesis of Infant Behavior." In *Manual of Child Psychology,* edited by L. Carmichael (335–373). New York: Wiley, 1954.

Gesell, A. et al. *The First Five Years of Life.* New York: Harper & Row, 1940.

Gredler, G. P. "A Look at Some Important Factors in Assessing Readiness for School." *Journal of Learning Disabilities,* 1978, 11: 284–290.

Haines, J.; Ames, L. B.; and Gillespie, C. *The Gesell Preschool Test Manual.* Lumberville, PA: Modern Learning Press, 1980.

Ilg, F. L.; and Ames, L. B. *School Readiness.* New York: Harper & Row, 1972.

Joiner, L. M. *A Technical Analysis of the Variation in Screening Instruments and Programs in New York State.* New York: City University of New York, New York Center for Advanced Study in Education (ERIC Document Reproduction Service No. ED 154 596), 1977.

Knight, L. N. "Readiness." In *Teaching Reading,* edited by J. E. Alexander. Boston: Little, Brown, 1979.

Knobloch, H.; Pasamanick, P. H.; and Sherard, E. S. "A Developmental Screening Inventory for Infants." *Pediatrics,* 1966, 38: 1095–1108.

Lazar, I.; and Darlington, R. (Eds.). "Lasting Effects of Early Education: A Report from the Consortium for Longitudinal Studies." *Monographs of the Society for Research in Child Development,* 1982, 47: 2–3, Serial No. 195.

Lichtenstein, R. "Comparative Validity of Two Preschool Screening Tests: Correlational and Classificational Approaches." *Journal of Learning Disabilities,* 1981, 14: 68–72.

Maddux, C. D.; Stacy, D.; and Scott, M. "School Entry Age in a Group of Gifted Children." *Gifted Child Quarterly,* 1981, 25: 180–184.

McCall, R. B. "A Hard Look at Stimulating and Predicting Development: The Cases of Bonding and Screening." *Pediatrics in Review,* 1982, 3: 205–212.

Meisels, S. J. "Prediction, Prevention and Developmental Screening in the EPSDT Program." In Child Development Research and Social Policy, edited by H. W. Stevenson & A. E. Siegel. Chicago: University of Chicago Press, 1984.

Meisels, S. J. *Developmental Screening in Early Childhood: A Guide* (rev. ed.). Washington, DC: NAEYC, 1985.

Meisels, S. J.; and Anastaslow, N. J. "The Risks of Prediction: Relationships Between Etiology, Handicapping Conditions and Developmental Outcomes." In *The Young Child: Reviews of Research,* Vol. 3, edited by S. Moore and C. Cooper. Washington, DC: NAEYC, 1982.

Michigan Department of Education. Superintendent's Study Group on Early Childhood Education. Lansing, MI: Author, 1984.

NAEYC. *Position Statement on Developmentally Appropriate Practice in Early Childhood Programs Serving Children from Birth Through Age 3.* Washington, DC: NAEYC, 1985.

Rubin, R. A.; Balow, B.; Dorie, J.; and Rosen, M. "Preschool Prediction of Low Achievement in Basic School Skills." *Journal of Learning Disabilities,* 1978, 11: 664–667.

Satz, P.; and Friel, J. "Predictive Validity of an Abbreviated Screening Battery." *Journal of Learning Disabilities,* 1978, 11: 347–351.

Shonkoff, J. "The Limitations of Normative Assessments of High-Risk Infants." *Topics in Early Childhood Special Education,* 1983, 3: 29–43.

Wiske, M. S.; Meisels, S. J.; and Tivnan, T. "The Early Screening Inventory: A Study of Early Childhood Development Screening." In *Identification of High Risk Children,* edited by N. J. Anastaslow, W. K. Frankenburg, and A. Fancei. Baltimore: University Park Press, 1982.

Wood, C.; Powell, S.; and Knight, R. C. "Predicting School Readiness: The Validity of Developmental Age." *Journal of Learning Disabilities,* 1984, 17: 8–11.

Zigler, E.; and Valentine, J. *Project Head Start: A Legacy of the War on Poverty.* New York: Free Press, 1979.

CHAPTER 11

Understanding School Readiness: The Bioplasmic Theory of Development

A new theory of human development based on energy forces in the human being seems to substantiate why early schooling is ineffective and may even reduce a child's learning potential. In brief, the theory of energy forces indicates that schools are wasting the energy needed for growth during a child's formative years by forcing premature intellectual learning of school subjects which could be more readily and easily mastered at a later age. It has an important bearing on the question, what are the effects of premature schooling?

Recent research goes one step beyond the growing protest against early schooling. In the last few years, many educators and psychologists have cited evidence that premature learning may actually create a permanent block to later learning (Moore, et al., 1979). It has been shown that later school entrants excel early school entrants by one or two years in academic achievement by the sixth and seventh year of school (Halliwell, 1966). Moore, et al., (1979) cited forty–fifty studies favoring late school entrances. Other studies have demonstrated that earlier school entrants who had been forced or persuaded to learn academic content prior to their readiness exhibited greater incidents of maladjustment than children who entered school at a later age (King, 1955). It is also well known that younger children have a much lower retention and attention span. As a result of premature academic learning by preschoolers or children with limited pre-educational experiences, such as socially deprived children, become academically "turned off," a "psychological dropout" (Jensen, 1969). Stanley's (1973) critique of the Hyman Blumberg Symposiums on preschool programs for disadvantaged children concluded there was little research evidence of elevated IQ's that persisted through the primary grades. Bissel (1973) also admitted that headstart findings were inconclusive and the effects of preschool programs problematic.

Forced learning can cause frustration, anxiety, alienation, and loss of interest in learning. The learning is not only inefficient or "pseudo-learning," but research indicates a resultant lowering of learning capacity. Forced learning may result in a permanent learning handicap—not only a distaste for a certain subject but permanent intellectual retardation (Moore and Moore, 1975). Why is this so?

Until very recently, educators have spoken about school readiness in generalities, e.g., as "the amount of learning that can transfer to new learning," or, "the child must be mature in terms of physical, mental, and emotional growth and social maturity." However, none of these points of view really explains readiness or the possible damaging effects of early schooling.

This lack of understanding of school readiness is reflected in the vagueness of educational objectives expounded by educators. Vague and general objective—"the harmonious development of the talents and capacities of the child," and so forth, cannot provide a realistic basis for educational methodology. It is not that these types of objectives are incorrect, but for providing a realistic foundation for education they are as viable as it would be to say of a machine that all its parts must be brought harmoniously into action. To operate a machine you cannot realistically approach it with truisms and phrases but with real and detailed knowledge of the operational functions of the machine. This lack of detailed knowledge of human development has led to a myriad of development and learning theories.

Let me explain. At this time educators do not have a total or realistic theory of human development. Mental and physical development are two separate phenomena. Psychological and physiological development are thought to be two ways of viewing human development. The physiologist is primarily concerned with the organic, somatic, and physical aspects of man, whereas the psychologist is concerned with mental, psychological, and motivational aspects of development. In regard to offering a unifying or total theory of human development, the two fields have remained separate and impotent. Attempts have been made to develop a mental/ physical conceptual model of human development using such theories as vitalism, mechanism, and the organismic and field theories (Bigge, 1964). These theories or models do not explain the relationship between physical and mental growth, mental maturation and readiness. One limitation of the theories was the attempt to apply concepts that explain the inorganic world to the organic world (Bigge, 1964). It is becoming increasingly evident that the forces operative in the inanimate world cannot explain the phenomenon of life.

Therefore, this paper offers a new theoretical model, based on the bioplasmic theory (Steiner, 1967).* Since bioplasmic forces are invisible,

---

*Rudolf Steiner (1862–1925) founded 500 Waldorf or Steiner Schools in 27 countries; 100 are in the United States. In addition, Steiner and his followers founded 250 residential and day schools for handicapped children and adults and 29 teacher training centers, located internationally. The fruits of his teaching and initiatives produced hospitals, clinics, medical research centers, biodynamic farms, pharmaceutical companies, scientific research center that study chromotography, crystallization and water purification, and a university with a doctoral program, law school and medical school.

though their effects are recordable, a theoretical model is necessary. A model is a perceptual aid to explain phenomenological relationships. In gaining greater insight, the model is refined and differentiated. It becomes the criterion by which we test and judge the accuracy of our reasoning and provide a sufficient comprehension of the subject to facilitate inquiry and possible validation of the model. Is this not a valid approach for a theory of human development based on invisible forces? After all, no one has ever seen magnetism, gravity, or electricity, only their results and effects. The same applies to the atomic theory; no one has seen an atom, electron, etc. Nevertheless, we borrow a model from the macrocosmic world—the planets and galaxy—to explicate our physical/chemical world through the use of the atomic theory, which is a microcosmic model of the universe. These models or scientific theories become laws when they consistently explain physical phenomena.

Bioplasmic Theory

The bioplasmic forces theory is based on the concept that all living matter is made up of an energy body and a physical body, as concluded by Steiner (1967), Russian scientists, and homeopathic and acupuncture physicians. Apart from the bioplasmic theory, biologists developed a term— "electrometabolic fields"—to explain the relationship between the electrical phenomenon and the metabolic processes in the body. The bioplasmic forces theory goes a step further; it is more comprehensive in its explanation of human growth and development. The Russians were not the first to develop the concept of the bioplasmic forces.

Rudolf Steiner (1967) over 50 years ago stated:

> The forces that hold sway in the etheric body (bioplasmic forces) are active at the beginning of man's life. . . , and most distinctly during the embryo period; they are the forces of growth and formative development (p. 15).

Recent Russian findings (Ostrander and Schroeder, 1971) gave visible proof to the premises of Steiner and the Chinese art of medicine—acupuncture—which works on the same principle that there are regenerative-energy currents flowing throughout the body. This energy is spent on the vital jobs of growing into maturity and keeping the body chemistry and organs functioning properly. It changes the minerals of the body from an inert to an active state, facilitating the reproduction and regeneration of organs and body cells. The energy used for maintaining bodily functions is measured as basal metabolism. The remainder is available for growth and activity. Basically, the source for this energy is nutrition and respiration. However, other factors can affect it, such as physical health, emotional well-being, and the environment. Mental health can affect physical health and growth, just as physical health can affect our emotions and behavior. The reaction is cyclical.

Energy output varies with age. As we grow older we are less energetic and physically active, whereas the child has an abundance of energy. He expends much energy through growth, play and other physical activity. We have observed this phenomenon in daily life and the organic world. Now Russian scientists have begun to explain it in new terms. They have actually photographed the bioplasmic forces. Ostrander and Schroeder (1971) visited research center in Russia and reported "a brand new concept in Soviet biology."

Russian research shows that the energy body we are talking about is not just a chaotic system of particles but a unified body which acts as a wholistic, structured, organized unit. Each organ of the body seems to have its own unified, specific etheric or bioplasmic forces. The forces are in continuous motion and metamorphosis. They are responsible for the maintenance of all the elements in the body to keep the organism going and to keep it healthy.

Acupuncture, a method of correcting bioplasmic energy imbalance, is based on energy levels or current flows, which sustain the development and replacement of cells in the body (Mann, 1972). Chinese physicians state that the skin, liver, kidneys, etc., are temporary deposits for a number of energy current flows which move at various rates throughout the body. Recent physiological studies have shown that the liver is changed in 10 days, the tongue in a longer period. The substance of the brain takes longer, while it is six months before new molecules are found in the bones. The hair and nails regenerate rapidly, whereas it takes seven years before all the skin cells have been replaced.

The basis of health, says the acupuncture physician, is the balance of energy currents in the body. "Good health is the free and unimpeded circulation of energy—the life forces—flowing from organ to organ along an invisible network of intercommunicating channels," which affects the flow of blood to the organs and tissues (Tiller, 1972). Illness is then the blockage and imbalance of the flow of these bioplasmic currents. The insertion of needles in one or more of the energy centers or acupoints on the skin revitalizes and facilitates the energy currents flow, putting the organism back in balance.

It is worth mentioning that these bioplasmic forces account for the phenomenon called 'the phantom limb." Persons who have a missing leg or arm as the result of a birth defect or an accident can sometimes sense the missing limb. A study by Weinstein, Sersen and Vetter (1964) showed that among 101 children born with missing limbs, 18 had clear perception of phantom limbs. Von Arnim (1967) theorized that the bioplasmic phantom limb is a phenomenon that accounts for the equal rate of body scheme acquisition by limbless, sightless, and normal children. In other words, the bioplasmic forces include a pattern or framework of the species for each part of the body. The forces facilitate the development of the physical limb when the physical material is present. The phantom or bioplasmic limb grows and develops just like the physical limb, except that it is nonmaterial, invisible. Steiner (1923) described the bioplasmic forces or body in a similar manner:

> All the organs of the physical body are maintained in their form and configuration by the currents and movements of the etheric body. Underlying the physical heart there is an 'etheric heart,' underlying the physical brain an 'etheric brain' and so on . . . And where in the physical body there are distinct and separate parts, in the etheric (bioplasmic) everything is in living flow and inter-penetrating movement (p. 11).

The Russian scientists who photographed the bioplasmic body confirmed that "the energy body didn't merely seem to be a radiation of the physical body. The physical appeared somehow to mirror what was happening in the energy" (Ostrander and Schroeder, 1971, p. 202).

Another characteristic of the bioplasmic forces in their regenerative function in lower animals, e.g., the flatworm, cut in half, completely regenerates itself; the same is true of an amphibian's legs and fins of a lungfish. However, man does not have this regenerative power. Instead, the bioplasmic forces are transmuted into the powers of cognition, the power or energy to control thinking (Mann, 1972).

The dual role of the bioplasmic forces in man is important to the understanding of its nature and function in human development. Part of the forces of the bioplasmic body is used for the development and maintenance of the physical body and the other part for cognition. Apparently the continuity between physical and mental development is evidently never broken. This relationship between thought and the physical body-forming process, has important educational significance. This bioplasmic or etheric force theory is the foundation of the learning theory and practices being used in the more than 750 Waldorf and handicapped schools that Rudolf Steiner and his followers founded.

What does all this mean for the child and readiness for schooling? As indicated, the energy or bioplasmic forces are used for human growth and maintenance of the body as well as for motor, emotional, and thinking activities. All of these require the expenditure of energy in one form or another. Each person has a certain amount of energy available. The crux of my argument regarding the damage school does to children is that, as a result of an inappropriate curriculum, activities, and assignments, children's energy forces are misused and atrophied prematurely, causing damage to their development. This is what Elkind (1981) calls a depletion of "clock energy," which we need for daily living. Pressure on young children to learn before they are ready causes "early symptoms of stress associated with clock energy," resulting in fatigue, loss of appetite and decreased efficiency.

Cognitive Development

Changes in thinking levels occur at about seven-year periods: preoperation (2–7), concrete operation (7–14), and formal operation (14 and older) (Piaget, 1969).* Certain major physical changes or plateaus also occur in seven-year periods. These are the change of teeth (second dentition) at age seven and puberty at approximately age fourteen. If we keep the theory of the transmutation of growth of bioplasmic forces in mind, it is no coincidence that at about age seven, second teething occurs at about the same time as the child's intellectual shift from the preoperational to the concrete operation level of thinking. Steiner (1928) described the relationship between second dentition and the releasing of the bioplasmic forces for cognition at age seven:

> Up to the change of teeth, this etheric body of formative forces is most intimately bound up with the physical body; it is the force which drives out the teeth. When the human being gets his second teeth, the part of the etheric body that drives the teeth out has no more to do for the physical body . . . the inner etheric forces which have pressed the teeth out are freed and with the etheric forces we carry on the free thought (concrete operational) that begins to assert itself in the child from the seventh year onwards (pp. 79–80).

Ilg and Ames (1973) reported the results of their study on second teething of 80 children in relation to school readiness. Those children who were ahead of schedule in teething (96%) were definitely ready for and could profit from academic school experiences. Of those children who were behind schedule in teething, 54% should have repeated (22% of their group did repeat), and 40% would have profited by repetition. Of those children who were in between—whether ahead or behind schedule in teething—64% would have benefited by repetition (14% of this group did repeat; 36% were hard workers, doing well). Their study indicates that subsequent to teething the children seemed to have reached a higher level of mental development, the concrete operational level of thinking.

---

*Piaget rejected the notion of vital or energy forces.

What does all this signify for the bioplasmic theory of maturation? It means that second teething is an indication of the culmination of physical growth of the head. The head has reached a plateau of physical maturation. The brain has reached 95% of its development, the head two-thirds of adult proportion. This signifies that the growth, energy, or bioplasmic forces have to a certain degree completed their task in the physical development of the head and brain. The physical forces are then released (gradually) from physical growth for the processes of thinking (subtle movement); this accounts for the transition from preoperational (noncontrollable) to concrete operational (controllable) thinking in the child. The child now has greater voluntary control over his thinking processes.

This same relationship applies to the onset of puberty and the child's change from the concrete operational to the formal operational level of thinking. Nisbet (1964) found that in England those adolescents who attained puberty scored higher on intellectual and academic achievement tests than those youngsters who were still at the prepuberty stage of development. During this time there is a growth spurt; the teenager is reaching adult proportions. The energy or growth forces are then released to be used for the higher level of formal operational thinking. There has not been much research on this level. However, there are indications that there is a delay in the attainment of the formal operational level of thinking even after the attainment of puberty. Physical maturation seems to have raced ahead of mental development at this later stage. No one really knows the reason; further research is needed. As indicated, the thinking process could be also conceived as the ability to control one's mind, a finer and more subtle form of cognitive mobility or movement.

Physical and speech development are controlled motor movement— one gross, the other fine. Thinking, which is a form of control over one's mind, is also a much finer and more subtle form of movement.

Piaget has shown that all children's minds evolve through a series of intellectual stages as they progress from early childhood through adolescence. He has classified these as follows:

1. Sensory-Motor Stage (0–2 years)
2. Preoperational Stage (2–7 years)
3. Concrete Operational Stage (7–12 years)
4. Formal Operational Stage (12–15 years and over)

Each of these stages has its own particular characteristics. Studies demonstrate that children's thinking shifts from the sense-bound to the emotional to rational forms of expression. The stages signify different centers of control. Piaget has devised tasks to determine the level of a child's thinking.

Before the shift from the preoperational to the concrete operational levels, the child "is involved in direct perceptual relationships with a minimum of reasoning or conceptual thinking." He is not able to distinguish between how things look and how they really are. If the form of an object is changed, he thinks the quantity is different. Using the earlier experiment—the changing of one of two spherical clay balls of equal size into a sausage shape, as indicated, the child does not understand that the sausage has the same quantity of clay as the ball from which it was rolled. The preoperational child will generally say the sausage shape is larger than the ball, even though he saw the experimenter roll the ball into a sausage. The child cannot conserve (retain a mental image of the two clay balls), nor reverse his thinking (compare the sausage with its prior ball shape, which should be retained as a mental picture if he was mature enough). The child who has attained the concrete operational level of thinking is able to perform this and similar tasks successfully. Following is an outline of the mental characteristics of the three major stages:

Preoperational (2–7 years)
1. Cannot conserve (hold or mentally manipulate mental images)
2. Thinking is perceptual or sense-bound
3. Thinking is nonreversible and centered*
4. Cannot deal with variables, changes
5. Has little control (voluntary) over thinking

Concrete Operational (7–12 or 14 years)
1. Can conserve (hold mental images)
2. Thinking is bound to emotional or affective life, but operational
3. Thinking is reversible and decentered
4. Has greater voluntary control over thinking
5. Thinking is more pictorial than analytic
6. Needs concrete props to support problem solving
7. Can deal with only one conceptual variable
8. Evolves logical thought process that can be applied to concrete problems
9. Cannot solve hypothetical problems that are entirely verbal.

Formal Operational (12–14 years and older)
1. Thinking is under voluntary control, i.e., it is operational
2. Thinking is relatively free of physical and emotional life, more objective

*Child is yet unable to explore (decenter) all aspect of what he sees (stimuli), only superficially. Cognitive activity is dominated by perceptual stimuli.

3. Can manipulate two or more conceptual variables
4. Thinking is more flexible and symbolic
5. Predictive problem solving is possible without concrete props
6. Can manipulate symbols and concepts without outer perceptual props
7. Can solve hypothetical and verbal problems.

As one examines these three stages in terms of their developmental sequence, it appears that the theme of increased voluntary control over thinking processes (movement) is just as applicable as it was to physical locomotion and speech development. However, in the Piaget stages, movement in cognition is more refined, sophisticated, and subtle. These transitional periods, from preoperational to concrete, and from concrete to formal, are marked by definite physiological and biological changes.

The terms used by Piaget are appropriate; they accurately describe the thinking characteristics and abilities at each level. Preoperational means the child cannot *operate (move)* his thinking, joining mental image to mental image, concept to concept, idea to idea. The child has not matured enough to be able to control his own thinking; his reasoning ability is limited. His thinking is nonoperational, uncontrollable, to a certain extent. At the concrete level, the older child can retain mental images and reverse his thinking; in short, his thinking is operational; he has greater cognitive mobility. He has control over his mind but needs concrete objects to solve problems. The same pattern of voluntarily controlled "movements" applies to the shift from the concrete to the formal operational level of thinking. Here the youngster can solve problems and predict solutions by making an educated guess—hypothesizing. He no longer needs concrete props to solve problems. He can solve such symbolic problems with several variables, e.g., when A is greater than B and B is greater than C, what is the relationship between A and C? His thinking is not only symbolic, but mobile.

The post-adolescent has developed full cognitive structures. He has control over the processes, essential to learning—assimilation, accommodation, conservation, equilibrium and the development of new and broader cognitive structures (conceptualized knowledge).

Effects of Premature or Forced Learning

As indicated, the child is not fully mature and ready for learning until age seven or eight. His brain is not fully developed, nor are his senses of hearing and sight. Therefore, if the child has not reached the indicated levels of maturity and is forced or persuaded to do intellectual (school) learning, there occurs a premature use of the bioplasmic or energy forces for thinking. The physical body is robbed of the growth forces needed to develop the brain to its fullest potential for physical growth. The learning is also of a pseudo or partial nature, incomplete; furthermore, physical development as well as emotional development has been sacrificed as a result. Portman (1966) reported that "whenever acceleration has occurred, there has been a noticeably increased susceptibility to certain diseases, especially those of psychological origin: (p. 786).

Shortened processes of maturation also cause later immaturity. This would account for the increased maladjustment of early school entrants found by King (1955) and Rowher (1971). Learning is hardly ever a purely cognitive process, particularly with children, but includes emotional involvement—interest, motivation, and preference. Children who are forced to learn subjects beyond their capacity and maturation develop anxiety and frustration; in short, they are "turned off." Emotional fatigue can cause physical fatigue, a dissipation of energy, mental and physical. Elkind (1981) agrees that when immature or young children are forced to keep up school work, they use up their reserve of "calendar energy" (energy needed for physical growth and maintenance of the body, etc.), the result of psychosomatic related illnesses—headaches, stomachaches, accompanied by anxiety, unhappiness and depression.

When Russian scientists photographed the energy or bioplasmic forces, they found that illness, emotions, fatigue, and particular thoughts and states of mind have a distinct effect on the flow of bioplasmic forces throughout the body. When a person was fatigued, tired, or emotionally overstrained, more energy appeared to pour out of the body than when he was in a healthy mental state of mind. So it is with the child who is forced prematurely into learning. It follows that as a result of the state of unreadiness for learning, the resulting frustration and anxiety cause the bioplasmic forces to dissipate. The bioplasmic forces available for physical growth and activity are accordingly reduced. Retardation may be the final result, for there are two factors working against the child: the depletion and ineffective use of the growth forces resulting from premature attempts at thinking (preoperational level), and the degradation of the growth forces resulting from frustration and anxiety.

The plasticity of intelligence decreases with age (Ausubel, 1965). Forced learning accelerates this loss of plasticity because of premature dissipation of the bioplasmic forces. Steiner (1928) agreed in that "if we force intellectual powers in the child we arrest growth . . . certain organic processes that tend inwardly to harden the body are brought into play" (pp. 136–37).

This means that the bioplasmic forces are too soon diverted from their primary task of the development of the physical body. Therefore, the physical body (also the brain) remains less plastic and mobile; physical maturation sets in prematurely.*

The child's intelligence and his learning capacity become differentiated and fixed early; this, in turn, limits the quantity and quality of experience he can have. His intellectual and learning potentials reach a plateau prematurely. If premature educational pressures have these kinds of effects on normally-reared or middle-class children, what must be the effect on children from socially and culturally deprived environments? The result is disastrous. Compensatory and Head Start programs have generally been a failure, despite enormous effort and the expenditure of considerable sums. As a result of poor environment, the deprived child begins school with a handicap. In short, he is environmentally retarded, which affects his mental and academic capacities. Here, too, the environment has depleted his bioplasmic growth forces. He therefore begins schooling with weakened and insufficient growth forces. Sieweke, a physician, stated:

> Any disturbance or change in the etheric (bioplasmic) forces during the formative years of childhood will have an impact on the emotional and intellectual constitution of the child. The metamorphosis of the etheric (bioplasmic) forces from physical development to emotional-cognitive development can be accelerated or retarded. There is a delicate balance between the two functions (physical and mental development) of the etheric forces (pp. 142–43).

When the child matures enough to shift from a lower stage of mental development to a higher level (e.g., preoperational to concrete) he does not possess enough bioplasmic energy to be changed into forces for thinking to make the transition complete. He is neither out of the preoperational stage nor in the concrete operational stage. He hovers somewhere in between. His rate of development is slowed down. When these developmental problems are compounded by forced premature learning, the result can only be further retardation. On the other hand, Elkind (1969) stated that there is no support for:

> The claims of the lastingness of pre-school instruction, (but there is) evidence in the opposite direction . . . The longer we delay formal instruction, up to certain limits, the greater the period of plasticity and higher the ultimate level of achievement (p. 336).

---

*Perhaps this is one reason that young people mature physically sooner than did their ancestors. In 1850 girls, internationally, reached menarche at age 17, today it is 13.5 years, a decrease of approximately 4 years in a century.

We need to conduct more basic research in child development on the basis of how he normally develops rather than on what we want him to become. We must work with the child's nature, not against it and cease attempts at acceleration in development. We must then reexamine our basic educational policies and curriculum schemes to truly meet the basic needs of the child.

Therefore the popular educational approaches of today, with their intellectual heavy-handedness, will never allow children to develop and blossom naturally. They can only do damage, making children into premature, unhappy adults. Such approaches will never be able to serve children from different and less desirable economic environments. Educators must begin looking at the dynamic needs of the growing child.

Commenting on Moore and Moore's *Better Late Than Early* (1975), Metcalf stated: "of what value is the educational process, if the very process, when prematurely introduced within the unfolding epigenetic field, distorts the developing psychic structure so as to interfere with future education, and learning to live and learning to love, let alone learning to learn" (jacket).

Our conventional approaches—pouring knowledge into the child, "fitting him into a curriculum" that is foreign to his nature—must cease. We must examine the needs of the child, *how* and *why* he develops as he does. Then what we need is to develop a curriculum and methods compatible with his unfolding and developing stages of growth. The bioplasmic or growth forces theory supports such an approach. It explains human growth, the development of thinking in children, and the rationale for readiness. If the theory is correct, it implies that the educational process should help the child to sustain and develop his bioplasmic body, his forces of growth. Curricular, extracurricular activities, etc., that are compatible with and supportive of these growth forces have been developed by the Waldorf School movement. The bioplasmic theory could be the key to human development and the basis for a universal method of education. The bioplasmic theory merits further research.

Earl J. Ogletree, Professor of Education, Chicago State University.

References

Ausubel, D., The Effects of Cultural Deprivation on Learning Patterns, *Audiovisual Instruction,* 1965, *10:* 10–12.

Bigge, M. L. and M. Hunt, *Psychological Foundations of Education.* New York: Harper & Row, 1964.

Bissell, J. S., Planned Variation in Headstart and Follow Through. In *Comprehensive Education for Children Ages 2 to 8,* Ed. J. C. Stanley, pp. 63–107. Baltimore, Md.: The Johns Hopkins University Press, 1973.

Elkind, D., "Piagetian and Psychometric Conceptions of Intelligence," *Harvard Educational Review,* 1969, *39:* 319–37.

Elkind, D., *The Hurried Child,* Addison-Wesley, Reading, Pa., 1981: p. 219.

Halliwell, J., "Reviewing the Reviews on Entrance Age and School Success," *Journal of Educational Research,* 1966, *59:* 395–401.

Ilg, F. and L. Ames, *School Readiness.* New York: Harper & Row, 1973.

Jensen, A., *Understanding Readiness: An Occasional Paper.* Urbana: University of Illinois Press, 1969.

King, I. B., "Effects of School Entrance into Grade 1 Upon Achievement in Elementary School," *Elementary School Journal,* February 1944, pp. 331–36.

Mann, F., *Acupuncture: The Ancient Chinese Art of Healing and How it Works Scientifically.* New York: Random House, 1972.

Moore, R., Moon, R. and D. Moore, "The California Report: Early Schooling for All?" *Phi Delta Kappan,* 1972, *53:* 617–19.

Moore, R., and Moore, D., *Better Late Than Early,* New York: Readers Digest Press, 1975.

Nisbet, J. D., "Puberty and Test Performance," *British Journal of Education Psychology,* June, 1964: 202–203.

Ostrander, S. and L. Schroeder, *Psychic Discoveries Behind the Iron Curtain* (Englewood Cliffs, N.J.: Prentice-Hall, 1971).

Piaget, J. and B. Inhelder, *The Psychology of the Child.* New York: Basic Books, 1969.

Poppelbaum, H., *The Etheric Body in Idea and Action.* London: Anthroposophical Publishing Co., 1955.

Portman, A., "Umzuchtung des Menschen? Aspekte heutiger Biotechnic," *Universitas,* 1966, *21:* 785–803.

Rowher, W., "Prime Time for Education: Early Childhood or Adolescence?" *Harvard Educational Review,* August 1971, pp. 316–341.

Sieweke, H., *Anthroposophic Medizin.* Dornach, Switzerland: Philoso-Anthroposophisches Verlag, 1959.

Stanley, J. C. Compensatory Education for Children, Ages Two to Eight: Recent Studies of Educational Intervention. Proceedings of the Second Annual Hyman Blumberg Symposium on Research in Early Childhood. Baltimore, The Johns Hopkins University Press, 1973.

Steiner, R., *Die Geheimwissenschaft, im Umris.*Dornach, Schweiz: Philosophisch–Anthroposophischer Verlag, 1923.

Steiner, R. and I. Wegman, *Fundamentals of Therapy.* London: Rudolf Steiner Press, 1967.

Steiner, R., *The New Art of Education.* London: Anthroposophical Press, 1928.

Tiller, E., *Energy and the Human Body,* Parts I & II; A.R.E. Medical Symposium on "Mind/Body Relationship in the Disease Process," monograph, Phoenix, Arizona: January 1972.

Von Arnim, G., *"Imitation and the Body Scheme,"* The Cresset, October, 1967, pp. 21–32.

Weinstein, F., R. Sersen, and A. Vetter, "Phantom and Somatic Sensations in the Cases of Congenital Aphasia," *Cortex,* 1964, *1:* 216–90.

CHAPTER 12

Lessons from Abroad: A Cross-National Survey of Policies Supporting Childbearing and Rearing

Because children are the future of a society, its developing work force and citizenry, the bearing and rearing of children benefits not only parents, but society as a whole. With this understanding, many nations have enacted policies both to encourage childbirth and to make public provision for the care and education of the young. In this respect, the United States differs, in principle and practice, from most nations of the world.

Historically, American social policy has been oriented toward individuals rather than families. As Anderson and Hula (1989) recently have written: "In contrast to most Western democracies, the United States Constitution makes no public commitment to the protection of family life, but rather defines rights and privileges solely in individualistic terms" (p. 573). One consequence is that parents are expected to bear and rear their children without public supports. Rosewater (1989) points out that "the United States is the only major industrialized nation other than South Africa that does not aid new parents upon the birth or illness of a child" (p. 11). U.S. domestic policy typically has targeted families with young children only when parents are failing to provide economic or social supports to their offspring (Grubb & Lazerson, 1982); in many nations, however, policies have been instituted to support *all* families with children.

In this chapter, we trace the growing concern among international organizations and nations to provide protection to women during the reproductive cycle. We proceed to present an overview of maternity leave policies in 121 countries derived from an International Labour Office Survey and review policies of selected European countries. We then describe policies and trends for these countries which extend public provisions to the early years of child rearing. In conclusion, we discuss the implications of these data for policymaking in the United States.

The Growing Concern

During the twentieth century, the International Labour Office and the United Nations have attempted to articulate policies to protect women before and after parturition. In Europe, pre- and post-natal care is provided through national health insurance systems (Kadushin, 1980), and, since the number of women in the paid workforce, always high in developing nations, has risen steadily in all developed nations of the world, there has been an increasing awareness of the need to establish policies which safeguard employment and guarantee a period of paid leave.

In 1919, the Maternity Protection Convention (No. 3) was adopted at the first session of the International Labour Conference. In 1950, maternity protection became one component of a broader effort to promote equality of opportunity and treatment for women workers (Paoli, 1982, p. 13). In 1981, an ILO Convention and Recommendation specifically urged that persons with family responsibilities not suffer job discrimination and be granted guarantees during a period of parental leave (ILO, 1981).

The first international conference on women was convened in Mexico City in 1975, leading to the U.N. Decade for Women (1976–1985). In 1979, the U.N. General Assembly adopted the Convention on the Elimination of All Forms of Discrimination Against Women. By 1980, over 60 nations had signed the Convention. With the ratification of the twentieth member nation late in 1981, the Convention became an international treaty. Specifically, the Convention recognizes that women have a unique role in reproduction. Written in the form of 16 articles, it requires paid maternity leave and job and seniority guarantees for working women who have children. Article 16 requires active efforts to eliminate all forms of discrimination against women and makes reference to women's right to choose a spouse and to own and dispose of property (Maternity Leave Policies, 1988, p. 174).

Nearly 60 percent of all countries in the world (90) had ratified the Convention by 1987. Another 20 had signed it.[1] Signing indicates that a country will not work against the principles set forth, while ratification binds a country to implement them. The treaty, the international equivalent of the Equal Rights Amendment, was signed, but never ratified, by the United States (Maternity Leave Policies, 1988, p. 173, note 7). As will be elaborated below, this is only one example of how the United States is strikingly out of step with efforts promulgated by a majority of nations.

Childbearing

Pregnancy and birth are among the most significant and vulnerable periods in the human life course. To determine how nations are responding to the needs of working women pre- and post-parturition, the International Labour Office (ILO) conducted a cross-national survey of legislative provisions on maternity benefits, including leave, cash benefits, job guar-

Figure 1: Total Amount of paid leave in weeks guaranteed in 121 countries

From data provided in the
ILO Global Survey, 1964–84;
Qualifying conditions and benefits vary

5< 7 Weeks

7< 9 Weeks

9<11 Weeks

11<13 Weeks

15<40 Weeks

13<15 Weeks

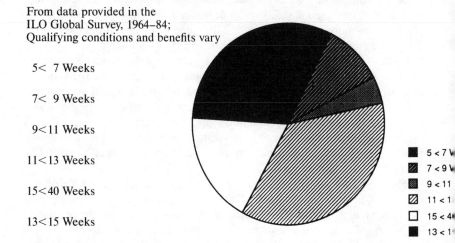

■ 5 < 7 Weeks
▨ 7 < 9 Weeks
▦ 9 < 11
▨ 11 < 1
□ 15 < 40
■ 13 < 1

antees, and nursing breaks (ILO, 1984). The survey provides an overview of legislation in 127 countries for which information could be acquired.

According to the Survey, fully 121 countries have established a period of paid leave, typically maternity leave, although a growing number of countries support leaves for fathers as well. As Figure 1 illustrates, the amount of time allotted varies, with the greatest number of countries (73) guaranteeing 11–14 weeks (roughly three months) leave in total.

Twenty-six countries have legislation which supports leaves of less than 11 weeks, and 22 guarantee more than 14 weeks (15 to 40). Additional paid or low-paid leave is available in some countries, with special provisions for women who are ill or who have given birth to a sick or disabled child. In Europe, 5 months following childbirth is the typical leave (Kamerman, in press).

Many countries allow women to decide when the leave period will begin, while others require that women take off for some specified number of weeks before or after birth. Typically the length of leave is stated as a specified time (e.g., 14 weeks (6 + 8)). However, countries which allow some degree of choice and flexibility may mandate a certain number of weeks post-parturition but will allow the mother to decide whether the additional weeks will be taken before or after giving birth.

Although it is useful to generalize from these data, it is nonetheless important to stress that laws and regulations vary widely in terms of qualifying conditions, cash benefits, sources of benefits, and employment guarantees. For example, countries typically specify how long a woman would need to be employed or contributing to the social security system before becoming eligible for coverage, a period typically ranging from 3 months to 1 year. A number of countries, notably the USSR and most communist bloc countries, however, do not have such requirements.

Similarly, cash benefits in some countries (e.g., Austria, Argentina) are provided through social security or insurance, while, in others (e.g., Jamaica, Kenya, and Jordan), they are provided by employers. In both developed and developing nations, many women are employed in the "informal economy," working part-time, multiple jobs, selling goods at market or doing farm labor, and they generally do not benefit from existing provisions.

The amount of benefit also varies from country to country, typically from 50–100 percent of wages during the leave period, although it might decrease over time. A few countries also provide differential benefit based on occupation. Finally, many nations have issued prohibitions of dismissal during and beyond the period of paid leave, with the actual time variable from country to country and frequently lengthened because of extenuating circumstances. The same or a comparable post is generally assured.

In addition to these policies, fully 67 countries, including all the nations of Europe, provide family or child allowances for each child to supplement the incomes of those raising children (Kamerman, 1980; Kamerman & Kahn 1989). In Europe, these allowances (for one child) typically amount to 5–10 percent of the median wage and are provided until the child finishes compulsory schooling (Kamerman & Kahn, 1989, p. 583).

The above discussion suggests some of the ways in which maternity policies vary cross-nationally. Table 1 illustrates the childbearing policies of 9 European countries and details this variability. Included are both centrally planned economies (Hungary, Poland, USSR) and market economies. As the table indicates, qualifying criteria for job protection and paid leave differ from one nation to another. All of these nations provide pre- and post-natal care through their national health insurance plans and care is not conditional on employment. All also guarantee some period of leave for working women, including 80–100 percent of wages and assurance of the same or a comparable position upon return to work.

The trend in Europe is toward extending the leave period through a supplementary period of unpaid or low paid leave and including fathers in the leave legislation. Thus, in Poland a woman can extend the leave to 2 years at a rate of 35 percent of the average female wage or to 4 years without pay. In Sweden, leave can be taken by either parent or alternated between them. In an effort to foster gender equality on a broad scale, moreover, the European Economic Community has proposed that all workers in all member countries be guaranteed a *minimum* 3-month leave

Table 1

Country	National Health Insurance Benefit	Qualifying Criteria	Job Protection/Leave Period	Cash Benefit During Leave	Supplementary Low Paid/Unpaid Leave
Italy	Yes	Must be employed and insured at start of pregnancy	5 months (2 before; 3 after); prohibition of dismissal for 1 year	80% of wages (social security)	6 months additional at 30% of wages
Netherlands	Yes	Social insurance coverage	12 weeks	100% of earnings	6 additional weeks unpaid
Norway[a,c]	Yes	6 months national insurance coverage during previous 10 months	18 weeks; 2 weeks paternity leave	100% of earnings and paternity leave paid by national insurance	Yes
Poland	Yes	None	16 weeks—first child; 18 for second; 26—multiple births	100% of earnings	To 2 years (35% of average female wage); to 4 years unpaid; 10 years if child ill or handicapped
Sweden[b,c]	Yes	Working 6 months prior to confinement; 12 months during past 2 years	9 months (both parents equally)	90% of wages of parent on leave (9 months); 3 additional months at flat rate 100% of earnings	To 18 months: right to part-time work until child is 8; sick leave—60 days/year
USSR	Yes	None	16 weeks[d]	100% of earnings	1 year—partly paid to 18 months unpaid
United Kingdom[a,c]	Yes	National social insurance coverage +2 years uninterrupted employment	6 weeks	6 weeks—90% weekly wage minus lump sum; at least 18 weeks—lump sum state allowance	To 40 weeks[d]
West Germany[b]	Yes	None	First 14 weeks limited to mothers; fathers thereafter	100% of earnings reduced monthly allowance during additional leave	To 1 year; 10 or more days sick leave for child

[a] ILO. "Protection of Working Mothers: An ILO Global Survey, 1964–84. *Women at Work* no. 2 (Geneva: ILO, 1984).
[b] Sheila Kamerman, "Parental Leave and Child Care: An Overview" (Paper presented at the Wingspread Conference on Parental Leave and Child Care, Racine, Wisc., September 1988) and Sheila Kamerman, "Maternity and Parenting Benefits: An International Overview," in *The Parental Leave Crisis: Toward a National Policy*, ed. Edward Zigler and Meryl Frank (New Haven, Conn.: Yale University Press, 1988.
[c] Sheila Kamerman, Parental Leave and Infant Care: U.S. and International Trends and Issues 1978–1988," in *Parental Leave and Childcare*, ed. Janet Hyde (Philadelphia: Temple University Press, in press).
[d] Extensions authorized for extenuating circumstances or if with same employer two years; see "At the Workplace," *Women at Work* no. 1 (Geneva: ILO, 1985).
[e] Also confinement allowance for each child; additional leave paid as a sickness or child allowance.

140

after the birth of a child. In a two-earner family, the leave would be granted consecutively and would not be transferable (Kamerman, 1988).

Child Rearing

The countries whose policies were discussed above have also made public provision for the care and education of preschool-age children. Programs differ cross-nationally according to the ages of children served, the length of time programs are in operation, the size of the group, teacher-child ratio, amount of teacher training, degree of subsidization, and administrative affiliation (Tietze & Ufermann, 1989) (see Table 2). In addition, new initiatives are currently underway to expand toddler care in Europe. By 1991 Sweden plans to guarantee places in centers and preschools to all children 18 months and over in need of care (Kamerman, 1989, pp. 135, 137). France serves most (97%) children aged 3 to 6 and approximately 45 percent of 2-year-olds. Germany accommodates about 75 percent of its 3–6-year-olds in half-day programs, and Eastern European countries provide for 75–90 percent of this age group in full-day programs (Kamerman & Kahn, 1989, p. 587).

Children typically enter at age 3, although in several countries children can begin at age 2 or 2½. Most programs operate 10 to 13 hours each day. Ratios vary from 1:5 in Sweden to 1:30 in the USSR. Postsecondary training is generally required of preschool teachers in each of these societies, and, in general, programs are run free of charge, with parents paying only for a child's food.

Generally programs are open to all children, regardless of need and regardless of the employment status of their parents. Continental Europeans view these programs as vital socialization experiences, as good for children in their own right (Kamerman, 1989, p. 136).

Lessons from Abroad

A cross-national appraisal of the policies and programs of other nations reveals that it is possible to reconstruct social needs in ways that suggest alternative solutions. Because of the American ideological commitment to private responsibility, public action, according to the English tenet of *parens patriae,* has seemed warranted only when parents have failed (Grubb & Lazerson, 1982).[2] U.S. policies for families and children—to the extent that they exist—largely reflect a concern "with social control and remediation: with inadequate families, severely disorganized and deprived families, handicapped, abused, neglected children in families where parents cannot fulfill their normal roles, and with some poor families, in particular those headed by women" (Kamerman & Kahn, 1989, p. 590).

Table 2

Country	Name of Program	Age Range	Hours Open (in hours/day)	Group Size	Age-Related Grouping	Teacher-Child Ratio	Teacher Training	Fees	Administrative Affiliation
Italy	*Scuola materna* (nursery school)	3–6	Full time, part time	Varies 15–30	Homogeneous	1:12	Vocational school 3–4 years	Food only	Ministry of Education
Netherlands	*Basisschool* (integrated preschool and primary school)	4–12	Mostly full time	25	Heterogeneous	1:28	College level 2 years	Food only	Ministry of Education
Norway	*Barnehage* (nursery school, day nursery)	3–7	Full time part time	Varies 4–18	Heterogeneous	1:8	College level	21% of operating costs	Ministry of Social Affairs
Poland	*Przedszkola* (nursery school)	3–7	Full time, part time	30 (often more)	Homogeneous	1:30	vocational school 4–5 years	Food only	Ministry of Education

142

Country	Program	Age	Time	Group size[a]		Ratio	Training	Parent cost	Ministry
Sweden	*Daghem* (day nursery)	2½–7	Full time 10–12 hours	12–18	Heterogeneous	1:5	College level 2½ years	10% of operating costs	Ministry of Social Affairs
	Deltidgrupp (nursery school)	4–7	Part time	20		1:10			
USSR	*Detskij sad* (nursery school)	4–7	Full time 9–12 hours	25	Homogeneous	1:25	Vocational school	Food only	Ministry of Education
United Kingdom	Nursery school	2–5	Full time	Varies	Heterogeneous	Varies 1:10	University 3 years	Food only	Ministry of Education
	Nursery classes	3–5	Part time						
West Germany	*Kindergarten* (nursery school)	3–6	Full time 10 hours Part time 4–7 hours	15–20 25	Heterogeneous	1:12.8	Vocational school 3 years	Varies between states	Ministry of Social Affairs

[a]denotes average group size.
Source: Reprinted, by permission, from W. Tietze and K. Ufemann, "An International Perspective on Schooling for 4-Year-Olds," *Theory into Practice* 28 (Winter 1989): 69–77.

143

European nations do address the special needs of troubled families. However, they also provide broad-based supports to *all* families. Rather than a narrow focus on the reform or re-education of stressed individuals, these nations have made sweeping efforts to transform the conditions of family life, in order to ensure that parents have the means and the flexibility to care for their children in the best way they see fit.

Income transfers, available to all families or on an income-tested basis, are a critical component. Income can be re-distributed horizontally (from those with no children to those with children) or vertically (from those with more to those with less). Importantly, Kamerman and Kahn (1989) note that: "low child poverty rates or the absence of child poverty as a policy issue is attributed largely to these and other child-related income transfers in the countries where they exist" (p. 584).

Policies supportive of childbearing and rearing constitute what Kamerman and Kahn (1981, 1989) have labeled a "family benefit package" and include pre- and post-natal care, paid job-protected leave, supplementary unpaid or low paid leave, and extra-familial child care in the form of publicly supported preschools. The breadth and scope of these supports effectively ensure that most parents can decrease the disjuncture between their work and family lives and provide adequately for their children.

Although issues related to work and child care have received widespread attention in the United States, policymakers continue to address these issues in a limited and piecemeal fashion. There is much to be learned from nations that mobilize both public and private resources to provide for the citizens of tomorrow.

Sally Lubeck, Ed.D., Senior Investigator, Frank Porter Graham Child Development Center, Clinical Assistant Professor, School of Education, University of North Carolina at Chapel Hill

Notes

1. Some countries have taken exception to certain articles of the Convention, especially Article 16. These countries are then not bound to implement these sections (Maternity Leave Policies, 1988, p. 174).

2. The authors claim that this is so, despite the obvious increase in public responsibility for the education of children 6–18, assistance to those in extreme poverty, and provision for the mentally retarded, delinquent, and aged (Grubb & Lazerson, 1982, p. 271).

Bibliography

Anderson, E. & Hula, R. (1989). Family policy. *Policy Studies Review, 8*(3), 573–580.

Grubb, N. & Lazerson, M. (1982). *Broken promises: How Americans fail their children*. New York: Basic Books.

International Labour Office (1981). *Convention (no. 156) and recommendation (no. 165) concerning equal opportunities and equal treatment for men and women workers: Workers with family responsibilities, no. 2*. Geneva: ILO.

International Labour Office (1984). Protection of working mothers: An ILO global survey, 1964–84. *Women at work*, no. 2. Geneva: ILO.

International Labour Office (1985). At the workplace, *Women at work*, no. 1. Geneva: ILO.

Kadushin, A. (1980). *Child welfare services*. New York: Macmillan Press.

Kamerman, S. (1980). Child care and family benefits: Policies in 6 industrialized countries, *Monthly Labour Review, 103*(11), 23–28.

Kamerman, S. (1988). Maternity and parenting benefits: An international overview. In E. Zigler & M. Frank (Eds.) *The parental leave crisis: Toward a national policy* (pp.   ). New Haven: Yale University Press.

Kamerman, S. (1988, September). *Parental leave and child care: An overview*. Paper presented at the Wingspread Conference on Parental Leave and Child Care, Racine, WI.

Kamerman, S. (in press). Parental leave and infant care: U.S. and international trends and issues 1978–1988. In J. Hyde (Ed.) *Parental leave and child care: Setting a research and policy agenda*. Philadelphia: Temple University Press.

Kamerman, S. (1989). An international overview of preschool programs. *Phi Delta Kappan, 71*, 135–137.

Kamerman, S. & Kahn, A. (1981). *Child care, family benefits, and working parents: A study in comparative policy*. New York: Columbia University Press.

Kamerman, S. & Kahn, A. (1989). Family policy: Has the United States learned from Europe? *Policy Studies Review, 8*(3), 581–598.

Maternity leave policies: An international survey. (1988). *Harvard Women's Law Journal, 11,*

Paoli, C. (1982). Women workers and maternity. *International Labour Review, 121,*

Rosewater, A. (1989). Child and family trends: Beyond the numbers. In F. Macchiarola & A. Gartner (Eds.) *Caring for America's Children* (pp. 4–19). New York: Academy of Political Science.

Tietze, W. & Ufermann, K. (1989). An international perspective on schooling for 4-year-olds, *Theory into Practice, 28*(1), 69–77.

CHAPTER 13

Teaching that Incorporates the Whole-Brain Teaches the Whole Child

"The classroom tends to seriously reduce the amount of input that students get, and thus the amount of raw material from which patterns may be extracted. The variety of activities permitted may be severely restricted . . . (whole-brain) instruction calls for a greatly increased amount of imput . . . imput should be random . . . first because what is logical to one person often makes little sense to another, and second because they need to come at a pattern . . . many ways, from many directions, in many contexts to flesh it out." (Hart 83, p.77)

Multiple studies have been done on how the human mind registers material from the outside and stores it as learning. Studies show that approximately 97% of the learning children do as they are entering the first grade is perceived first through the right hemisphere of their brain. By the time they are ready to begin third grade, two years later, the same percentage of learning children do has now become left hemisphere approach to learning. With the left hemisphere being the portion of the brain that also stores the "patterns of learning" the right brain is, in figurative language at least, phased out.

Much of learning research points out the fact that a child learns more in his first five years than in all the remainder of his or her lifetime. This being true and coupled with the use of the right hemisphere of the brain for nearly all learning until the age of five, emphasizes a need to teach more effectively. We must approach learning activities more through the right hemisphere of the brain.

Buzan (1979) summarizes the brain functions. First he says that "the two sides of you brain, or your two brains, which are linked together by a fantastically complex network of nerve fibres called the Corpus Collosum, deal with different types of mental activity." (14) In the major portion of people the left side of the brain deals with logic, language, reasoning, number, linearity, analysis etc. The left brain is also considered the storage of the brain. This is where the "patterns of learning" are held for future comparison and use.

In contrast to the type of activity in the left brain we find the right brain dealing with rhythm, music, images and imagination, color, daydreaming, fantasizing, face recognition, pattern recognition and parallel processing.

Further research has shown that (Buzan 79) "when people were encouraged to develop a mental area they had previously considered weak, this development, rather than detracting from other areas, seemed to produce a synergistic effect in which all areas of mental performance improved." (14)

It would appear that when we describe ourselves as talented, or as a visual learner, or as capable of certain feats we are actually stating the areas in which our potential has successfully been developed. Other areas we simply allow potential to lie dormant when with the right design in the strategies of learning they could become a very active part of the total learning and recall "package".

Studying the basic imput presented in our schools we note that beginning with day one of kindergarten there is a noticeable, strong increase in strategies that are left brain oriented. The child is trained to sit and listen, follow only the directions given by the teacher, not to ask any questions that are not directly answerable from the material being presented and to read and follow the directions. As the child progresses through the school system there is less comparative and interrelational learning allowed because time must not be wasted. Each of these separate textbooks must be covered this year. When in reality more could be covered over the total learning time if the learning were approached as a total and not just as so many different fragments.

This is not to say that these ways mentioned are not good methods in themselves. But rather, they are not to be the only way at the sacrifice of all other learning strategies. Studies show the brain is not as receptive to carefully organized, sequenced material as it is to random appropriation of the bits and pieces the mind picks up as the segment, at this point considered a whole, is actualized in the mind.

As an example of this I will give an illustration that is not from early childhood levels of learning. When I teach the process of rounding off a number, I write a twenty or thirty digit number on the board. We round to the nearest ten, then to the nearest hundred, then to the nearest thousand, etc. The class participates and does most of the rounding after only one or two illustrations of simple tens rounding. I then write a second twenty digit number and simply point to one of the digits. The name of the location is not important at this point. The students surprisingly enough can visualize the process and almost immediately are successful in rounding to any digit. To help the students visualize the concept of the digit to the right of the "rounding point" being above or below five I simply write the numbers from one to ten vertically on the board. This simplifies the concept of *above and below* five which is so critical to the concept of rounding.

In contrast to this approach for rounding off numbers, the approach recommended in the textbooks is to spend some days on rounding of tens, some days on rounding to hundreds, etc. These days are scattered throughout the text and many times throughout several academic years. The child may never see the relationships necessary and therefore not be able to store the information being presented. A teacher's first reaction is too often a reconsideration of his intelligence level.

> "The brain does not usually learn in the sense of accepting or recording information from teachers. The brain is not a passive consumer of information. Instead, it actively constructs its own interpretations of information and draws inferences from it. The brain ignores some information and selectively attends to other information" (Hart, 1983, p.78)

The key idea here is seeing the inferences or relationships. Thus being able to attach the unknown learning to known learning of the past. (More to be said about this later.) If the segments necessary for the total understanding of a basic concept are isolated, then the inferences for learning and the possibility of seeing the relationships are kept to a minimum rather than enhanced. An illustration of this point of inference might well be the fact that a large percentage of discoveries in the fields of mathematics, science, etc., come about by accidental blunders that produced unplanned experiments. These blunders could have been just as unfruitful as the original experiment had the researcher not seen the relationships and just ignored the blunder as being no part of the isolated experiment. (Hart, 83) To try to demand that this brain meekly put aside its mighty resources and go step-by-step down one path is to cripple and inhibit it." (52)

True teaching is the guidance of information available. Thus helping the child's brain achieve a selectivity approach enhancing the selection of more and better information. Therefore, due to more learning patterns for comparison, the child will be able to learn more effectively.

I would hasten to say that teaching with a stronger right brain approach does not necessarily argue for creative learning approaches as we know them. They should not be haphazard or uncontrolled. Putting a child at a learning center will not necessarily help the learning process. The end result desired must be clearly known by the teacher. The basic steps that are needed to arrive at the conclusion in learning and various relationships that enhance this segment of learning must be considered. The consensus of whole brain research estimates that the teacher must prepare ten times as much strategy presentation material, or even more, to effectively present a concept. The teacher will be directly involving far more of their time in guidance, answering questions, and introducing more avenues for imput.

Planning must have broad, clearly defined objectives with specific learning goals listed, rather than units to be covered. Planning should be for long periods of time not just a few hours or days. The end result being brought into focus in skeletal form, as the unit begins. The segmented parts of the whole should also be demonstrated as new material is added thus allowing the child the opportunity to see the end result. This is not to say that the child will indeed store this information but segments of it will be recognized in future portions of the study. Hart (83) says that "the ideal of neat, orderly, closely planned, sequentially logical teaching will in practice, with young students, guarantee severe learning failure for most." (56)

Hart (1983) states that, a teacher aggressively instructing a class of 25 is actually not addressing a group at all, but rather 25 individual brains each of which will attend to what it chooses, then process the input in an individual way, relating it (if at all) only to previous individual input, or experience. (78) Simply put, we in essence, have 25 lesson plans to teach. However, we really have only one concept to teach. We must teach it so the concept is not an isolated concept but rather enough interrelationships are illustrated so that the child can attach it to something that is known or already stored in the left brain. Without known relationships the brain will simply abort the material and it is lost as though nothing was ever attempted. (Hart 83) The learning process, by which patterns are sorted out so that increasingly more sense is made of a complex world, goes on incessantly, and each individual, in a purely individual way, gathers features and clues that gradually mount up. Progressively, the pattern is grasped more sharply and greater discrimination becomes possible." (77)

Before we can effectively work with our students we must understand where we are in our learning capabilities. Look back at your years in the formal education period of your life. Were you taught:

- How your memory functions?
- How to memorize?
- About your eye functions when learning and how to use this knowledge?
- About the ranges of study techniques and how to apply them?
- The nature of concentration and how to use it when necessary?
- About motivation, how it effects your abilities, and how you can use it to your advantage?
- Anything about thinking?
- Anything about creativity? (adapted from Buzan, 79)

By now the answer to learning needs is probably clearing somewhat. The reason why our performances of learning and its use do not match even a small part of our potential is because we are not taught but a minimal part of how we function during the learning process, or how to utilize our capacities to learn.

The problem is not with hard-working teachers who are dedicated to the classroom and teaching, but rather with the system that taught them to be assigners and warlords of the classroom which almost guarantees failure for so many. Becoming envolved in learning as an instructor is probably priority number one in being a successful teacher when the goal is teaching the child to his or her potential.

The problem is not in the fact that the child can not assimilate more learning. Research studies show that Einstein only used 20% of his potential brain available to him. The average person only uses approximately ten percent. This leads us to consider what the potential of our students might be.

Several factors can effect a child. Low self-concept due to continuous inability to relate learning segments and thus aborting them can have an overwhelming effect on the childs future learning. It is the relationship of the segment or patterns being learned rather than the segment itself that aborts the patterns or segment under consideration at the time. The need to relate the unknown segment to the known, already stored patterns, is the key to greater learning success. It must be remembered that several relationships must be fostered by the instructor so the child can attach the new patterns (segments of learning) to whichever patterns he has stored. This accumulation of patterns will vary with every child whether they have all learned under the same teacher or have previously never learned with each other in a formal setting.

Potential of the student may be disguised by this low self-esteem. We then interpret the child's potential, by I. Q. or otherwise, as being low and we too often treat him accordingly. We should rather believe that the known patterns available in the child's brain may simply not find appropriate relational patterns on which to tie this unknown imput.

It must be mentioned here that praise is not necessarily good. Success does not necessarily breed success. The student must be praised accurately. "Jeremiah, I see you have gotten three right on you spelling test. The last few weeks you have gotten only one right, if that many. You are making progress. I am glad to see it." Praise that is general and often not true, such as, "that is fantastic" when if the truth were known it was said from habit not in a sincere helping way, becomes bitter medicine to many low-concept students. I have had several students with whom I had to constantly guard myself when I praised them. One nine-year-old girl had spent more than two years in a school for severely retarded. Praise when given alone shut down all responses for two days or longer. Responses to her work were very important, but praise had to be very accurate and followed immediately by directions (almost in the form of demands) for further improvements. She did eventually become a low-average student. The change may have been greater had it begun sooner.

In some cases, students are led to believe they are doing well when in actuality their progress was very poor. Some students get the "smarts" from this type of praise treatment. Others withdraw or close down as the girl mentioned above was prepared to do.

(Hart 83) Feedback is essential to the learner to verify that learning has occurred. Realistic feedback will usually be clearer and more acceptable than second-person feedback" (77) or feedback that is the next day in being presented. Feedback, whether negative or positive in nature, is more profitable to the student the sooner he receives it. It has been said many times that it takes only three repetitions to make a bad habit, but ten repetitions of an act to correct that habit or form a good habit.

To put a child to work, say in a work center, only to find that he has not accomplished anything correctly has done two things. First, he has reinforced a bad habit. Secondly, he has lost valuable learning time. Even though there are times in which a child must learn independently, he needs frequent feedback to guide in the correct learning of concepts. This need would then eliminate using a classroom program set-up that "babysits" some of the students while others are being tended for long periods of time.

With effective design of the instruction strategies all the children can be more effectively involved and less inappropriate learning will take place. I will be saying more about this as the teaching example is presented.

As we look at a program for kindergarten level children we must evaluate the segments of learning which we are going to use as teaching strategies from the viewpoint of the student involved in the teaching situation. We will need to keep three things in mind:

- Evaluate the situation or need (identify the patterns.)
- Select the most appropriate program from those stored.
- Implement the program. (Hart 83, revised)

Now let's look at a teaching project for kindergarten children. This presentation will be to instruct the students in naming and recognizing geometric shapes. This could easily be broken down into different lessons or areas of learning. A child could recognize the shapes as the teacher names them, or simple place all the matching shapes together in the earlier stages of this instruction period.

To begin the study we must evaluate the need. What shapes are to be taught and learned? Will the students be able to recognize the shapes in the synthetic presentation such as a work sheet? Will the individual child recognize the shapes by name? Will the children be able to recognize the shapes in their environment? Will the children be able to name the shapes when discovered in their environment? How effectively will the child recognize these shapes and/or name them? What percentage of the time will the children recognize and/or name the shapes correctly? Will our expectations be limited by what we think the individual child might do or will our expectations be to challenge all of them? Will we give enough imput to the class so there will be a flexible number of choices to pick from and connect these unknown shapes to known (previously learned) patterns?

The four geometric shapes which we will work with are the circle, the triangle, the square, and the rectangle. The rectangle and square are very much alike and could be a challenge to many of the children. The need to be able to differentiate could be difficult if it is not carefully covered as the imput is given by the teacher.

The circle and triangle might be said to be much easier. I would agree that the circle is a great deal different from the triangle. But the triangle, from a childs point of view, does in some ways look like a square. I have found some children able to recognize the difference between a triangle and a square much more easily than differences between the square and rectangle. Other children more easily recognize the differences between a rectangle and a square. There is also the child who cannot recognize the circle and can recognize the other three. We are all different and as the instructor constantly tune your observation skills to *see*. Although the children may be attempting to learn the same basic patterns for mental storage they have their difficulties in different aspects of the concept presented.

I would like to have started this paragraph with, "Begin by doing thus and so." That, however, would have defeated the whole purpose of whole brain learning. I will present several strategies for presenting the concepts involved in recognizing the four geometric shapes. Most of these strategies should be incorporated in the beginning presentation.

Your first response may be, "Just one minute here. Can't you overload the child to the point of distraction?" The answer is no! We as teachers have been trained to segment, disect, slice into slivers, and guard the amount of learning imput available. However, let's go back to the fact that all human brains will pick and choose the bits and pieces that connect to previously acquired patterns they have already stored. The unknown patterns, concepts being presented, will abort if not relative to the known patterns in the mental storage. If the imput available is not varied and fairly broad the pattern assimiliation on the part of the children will be hampered.

- Using both hands and starting at the top make big shapes. Have the children watch at first. Then as they can see the shape they follow the teacher. Be sure they are doing the correct shape.
- Using only one hand make the shapes as large as is comfortably possible. First one shape, then as that shape is mastered do another. Do not always make the shapes in the same order. Order alone could accidently become a concept and thus be erroneous. When one hand is effectively completed, change to the opposite hand and repeat. It is not necessary to give the name, but simply tell the students to follow in making this given shape.
- Using both hands make the shapes going first in the same direction. Then make hands go in opposite directions while tracing the same shape in the air. This last approach may seem difficult. The teacher will have a harder time than the student.
- Have the students follow the teacher as they walk the different shapes. As the concept becomes more understood have a student leader do the leading. For very young children the corners may need to be taped.
- Have the students walk the shapes backwards. This will show the teacher a great deal about the level of motor skill function each student has acquired.
- Pass out cookies in these four shapes. You might put in one cookie which is a fifth shape. Use a shape that has come up in the learning process such as a diamond. This one may just be the one they remember the easiest. Candies, sliced fruit or vegetables, soda crackers or other foods can be substituted.
- Trace geometric shapes on board or vertical easel. Here is where the center idea can be employed for very short periods of time. Constant observation by the instructor is necessary to keep mistakes to an absolute minimum.
- Crawl through a series of patterns each representing one of the geometric shapes. Again the corners of the shapes may need to be marked.
- Trace large geometric shapes at desk on individual sheets of paper. The size can be reduced and more than one shape can be on each page.
- Cut geometric shapes from printed patterns. If one or two other geometric shapes seem extremely interesting do not be afraid to add them anywhere along the line of presented imput.
- Have the student sort pre-cut geometric shapes. Have from twenty to thirty pre-cut pieces to a group. This could first be done as a total group then in two or three smaller groups of students. Remember

that when working with tangible two or three dimensional geometric shapes make sure to change the size, the color and the number of a given shape. Shape is what you are teaching. Size, color, and the number of that given shape must be kept random or difficulty may arise as they are grasping the idea. Also all the geometric shapes in a given set could be of a given color to add a bit of change.

- Facing the child and touching finger tips with him/her draw the different geometric shapes in the air. This is extremely helpful when the child has missed some of the presented material or when it first appears to be too difficult.

- Have the children find the geometric shapes in the environment. This is best started at the end of the presentation. Finding them in the environment can then be extended to individual students during play time or during activity time. A note home for the students to find the geometric shapes and name them as a homework assignment is also effective. It may be best to request a note saying how the child did on the homework assignment. Very soon the students will want you to see these shapes on the playground and anywhere else you may both meet.

- Put hard cardboard geometric shapes into "feeler box". This is a box where the child can insert his arms into sleeves and can not see what is in the box. The back side of the box may be made so that it can be opened for teacher observation. This approach takes away the visual portion and in turn increases the senses.

- Find the geometric shapes in magazines and newspapers. The children could even add these to a journal type activity book. This can also be a homework assignment. Be sure to write a explanation of what the parent should look for in the child's responses.

- Draw them with first a sample, then a dotted sample, and then space enough to draw two or three on their own. This can extend to drawing simple pictures using these geometric shapes. An example might be a house drawn with a square and a triangle. The children might need a few samples, but they will soon be on their own and wanting the teacher to see this or that geometric shape in a drawing outside of the regular presentation time.

So it takes more than 15 minutes to present the imput package, don't worry. The ideas presented for imput include art, fine motor skills, shape recognition which is part of reading, concept of same and different, and physical education. If more time is needed the catagories of imput certainly merit the time increase.

Using imput methods from the above list for only fifteen minutes, the children completed an assignment with near perfect accuracy in another eight minutes. These kindergarten students had not previously been taught the geometric shapes within a formal setting. A teacher across the hall using the standard small segment presentation approach stated that her class took eight work sessions over a three day period to complete the same material. Her biggest frustration was that her class did not achieve near the level of function with all that extra time given to teaching.

Making sure all of one geometric shape is not the same color can cause frustration. This list is not attempting to give all the ways that can be used to present this topic. Nor am I saying any given number of input strategies should be used. The child will pick and choose those bits and pieces that will "attach" to his store of known patterns. It is safe to say that the more approaches at a given time the better will be the learning for the whole group, not just the fast or top groups. The presented material should not necessarily be in this order. Use your own imagination. Just be careful not to give inappropriate clues that could ditch a child's thinking such as mentioned in the first line of this paragraph.

Be thrilled with teaching and your enthusiasm for learning will help win many of the learning battles. Get into the learning arena with the children and learning will take on a whole new dimension for you as well as the students.

Teaching with the whole-brain approach will take far more preparation. Research indicates at least ten times as much preparation and teaching aids are necessary. This same research also indicates that the learning will increase more that the tenfold teacher preparation that is necessary.

Try always to look at the strategies and ideas to be used for imput from the eyes and ears of the children. Observe the children. Do not teach down to them. Expect great changes in their capabilities and you won't be disappointed.

Bibliography and Suggested Readings

Buzzan, Tony, 1983, *Use Both Sides of Your Brain,* E. P. Dutton. New York, New York.

Buzan, Tony, 1977, *Make the Most of Your Mind,* Simon and Schuster, Inc. New York, New York.

Edwards, Betty, 1979, *Drawing on the Right Side of the Brain,* J. P. Tarcher, Inc. Los Angeles, California.

Hart, Leslie A., 1983, *Human Brain and Human Learning,* Longman, Inc. New York.

Pflaum, Susanna, 1978, *The Development of Language and Reading in Young Children-Second Edition,* Charles E. Merrill Publishing Company. Columbus, Ohio.

Williams, Linda Verlee, 1983, *Teaching for the Two-sided Mind,* Prentice Hall
    Inc., Englewood Cliffs, New Jersey.

Dr. James E. Bale, PhD in Education
Learning Disabilities Consultant
Yakima Valley Schools

CHAPTER 14

Kindergarten Education in the Public Schools: Developmental vs. Academic

Why are many kindergartens adopting an academic approach to teaching, when current research indicates typical kindergarten-age students function best with a non-academic environment (Bredekamp, 1986)? The situation can begin to be explained by defining academic kindergarten and developmental kindergarten.

> FORMALIZED, ACADEMIC KINDERGARTENS. Formalized, academic kindergartens adopt a philosophy of systematic organization, direct-instruction and mastery learning. The curriculum is teacher-centered with a focus on paper/pencil activities, phonics instruction, detail in handwriting, repetition and reinforcement in math concepts. The teacher's role is one of preparing and directing lessons with involvement in expository teaching while the children gain knowledge through the process of reception learning (Patterson, 1977; Gagne, 1974, Craig, 1989).

> DEVELOPMENTAL KINDERGARTENS. Developmental kindergartens adopt a philosophy of inquiry-learning. The curriculum is child-centered with most of the instruction accomplished through the use of learning centers and developmentally appropriate, manipulative materials. The teacher's role is one of facilitating learning by encouraging students to pursue interests and explore the classroom environment (Maxim, 1977). The teacher prepares the classroom environment, realizing that children learn intrinsically, through self-initiated actions (Patterson, 1977; Piaget, 1973; Craig, 1989).

The research of James J. Hymes (1974), in his excellent book, *Teaching the Child Under Six*, indicates that typical five-year-old children function better with a developmental approach to learning. Many kindergarten teachers in America realize a developmental approach to kindergarten is best for children, yet they are pressured to teach with an academic approach. Why? Kindergarten teachers view themselves as being placed in the role of preparing children for the pressures of first grade. They indirectly feel as though they must produce children who can recite letter sounds, read words and perform beginning addition and subtraction by the time they leave kindergarten. Many kindergarten teachers feel they, alone, cannot change a system which expects phonics instruction, writing mastery and number concepts at the conclusion of kindergarten.

Teaching at the kindergarten level should be a position of facilitating growth in children and creating environments which will inspire children to learn as much as they can. Kindergarten teachers should not be placed in the role of arriving at and maintaining competency standards for five-year-olds.

All schools today feel pressure to teach information more quickly and cover more material in a shorter time-span (Elkind, 1981). These pressures fall heavily on kindergarten and primary teachers. Teachers alone, cannot change the pressures of academic instruction in the kindergartens of America. The burden of responsibility for change in the public schools lies with four groups: (1) teachers; (2) administrators (superintendents and principals); (3) parents; and (4) state departments of education.

TEACHERS. If we are going to see changes in education, teachers must focus on the characteristics of typical five-year-old children and educate themselves to current research in the area of child development. They must choose materials and activities appropriate for five-year-old development. Teachers need to grow professionally in knowledge and skills related directly to early childhood education. Kindergarten and primary teachers must initiate a child-centered approach to teaching which meets the needs of individual children. Kindergarten teachers must work closely with parents to educate parents regarding the nature and stages of child development and proper school experiences which facilitate growth at the various stages of child development.

SUPERINTENDENTS AND ADMINISTRATORS. Administrators must facilitate change by becoming knowledgeable regarding current research in the area of child development and appropriate kindergarten practices. They need to encourage professional growth in the area of early childhood education for kindergarten teachers and provide opportunities for knowledge growth in the area of early childhood education. Administrators need to be committed to employing teachers (who will be involved with young children) with current background in or degrees in the field of early childhood education. Superintendents and principals must discourage the purchase of textbooks, workbooks or materials which do not correlate with a developmental approach to dealing with primary children. Administrators must listen to kindergarten teachers' requests for manipulative materials and encourage the purchase of developmentally appropriate materials. Finally, superintendents and administrators must eliminate standardized, paper and pencil placement tests at the conclusion of kindergarten.

Involvement

PARENTS. To facilitate change in the public kindergartens, parents must eliminate the pressure of paper and pencil activities in the classroom. Parents must learn to accept the developmental kindergarten philosophy and understand how it differs from instructional programs for older children. Parents must not pressure today's teachers to produce mastery learning in areas of math and reading; rather, they must understand early curiosity, discovery and proper activities produce enthusiasm for a lifetime of learning. Parents need to enroll in parenting or child development courses which will assist them in understanding the developmental stages of human growth.

STATE REQUIREMENTS. To promote change in public kindergartens, state teacher requirements must require early childhood degrees of all kindergarten and primary teachers or ensure all certified kindergarten and primary teachers have completed a vast amount of appropriate coursework in the area of early childhood education. Instruction in early childhood education prepares teachers in the area of child development; thus, educates them to appropriate teaching strategies for kindergarten and primary students.

The appropriate environment for five-year-old children will nurture growth in all areas of development, such as physical, emotional, social, and intellectual. This is accomplished with a nurturing, accepting, flexible and knowledgeable teacher. Concrete, manipulative materials arranged in learning centers will inspire child-initiated activities, while creating the optimal learning environment for young children. Children learn with intrinsic motivation rather than extrinsic motivation (Hohmann, Banet and Weikart, 1979); therefore, active exploration and manipulation of one's environment will enhance learning (Piaget, 1973). Children are naturally curious and eager to explore their environmen (Moore and Moore, 1979). The learning center approach to teaching creates a total learning environment which supports the development of each child as an individual.

Children need space to learn through their own actions such as building, sorting, experimenting, counting and pretending (Hohmann, Banet and Weikart, 1979). An environment of this nature lets children make choices and act on them. According to Jean Piaget, freedom to actively manipulate materials in one's environment helps to develop a specific base for learning (Bybee and Sund, 1982). Early experiences appear to be a key influence in determining children's abilities for further learning.

Value of Play

The importance of play for educational purposes has been overlooked in the public schools. Recently, however, considerable material has been documented on the value and purpose of play environments for children (Fein and Rivkin, 1986). It is difficult to determine how the action of play became a non-existent part of the public schools. However, it is clear to see that as students progress through the educational system children seem to equate activity related to learning as activity which is repetitious, tedious and time-consuming. Most students do not generate pleasure or play with learning in the school environment.

For most people, play is spontaneous. Play is not generally thought of as a teacher-directed activity (Gottfried, 1986). Frost and Sunderlin (1985) assert that the process of play significantly prepares children for the future by facilitating the development of well-rounded people. Play is not a common activity in schools today; thus, teacher advocates of play environments must be prepared to defend the theory and cite the research behind the value of play for holistic development when administrators, parents and other teachers ask, "Is that all they do—play?" or "When will they start learning something?"

In the book, *The Whole Child,* by Joanne Hendrick (1988), she cites five positive aspects of play as:

1. *Fosters Physical Development.* On a very simple level play promotes the development of motor skills. Piaget (1973), asserts that physical competence is the foundation of which later intelligence is built; thus, when children master their environment through physical development they build self-esteem and develop cognitive abilities.

2. *Fosters Intellectual Development.* Piaget (1962) contends that the imagination is one of the purest forms of symbolism. Imaginative play allows children to assimilate reality in terms of interests and knowledge of the world. Imaginative, symbolic play contributes to cognitive growth. Opportunities for free play have been linked to the ability to solve problems (Sutton-Smith and Roberts, 1981). Play

also offers opportunities for children to acquire information that is formed into later learning (Elkind, 1976).

3. *Play Enhances Social Development.* Play and involvement with other children prepare children for social experiences which will arise in the process of maturation (Moffitt, 1972). Social play helps children develop successful group interaction which is important for children and crucial for adults. The environment has a powerful influence on the development of children.

4. *Contains Rich Emotional Values.* The emotional value of play is utilized as children express feelings. Play can serve as a relief from the pressures of growing up quickly in a world of busy environments. Play offers children opportunities to achieve mastery of their environments and develop healthy concepts of self. Children's play leads to the memory development of repeated events and an understanding of further complex thinking (Elkind, 1981).

5. *Develops the Creative Aspects of Personality.* Play allows the expression of personal and individual responses to situations. This in turn leads to growth in emotional aspects. Studies have shown that play experiences and the ability for creative, divergent thinking are related (Pepler, 1986). Play appears to be the lifeblood of childhood.

In conclusion, if we are truly going to see changes in kindergartens of the 90s we must educate America to the concept of developmental kindergartens. We must see more play and more environments directed at teaching strategies which allow children to be involved in self-initiated learning and less teacher-directed learning. Children must be allowed to develop at their own pace and in their own way. Teachers, administrators, parents and state boards of education must adopt philosophies of meeting educational needs by creating optimal environments for children which first meet developmental needs.

Deva Ward is an instructor of early childhood education at the College of Southern Idaho in Twin Falls, Idaho. She has been involved as a primary teacher with the public schools in Idaho for fourteen years. Deva holds a bachelor's degree of elementary education and a master's degree of early childhood education. She is a doctoral candidate and anticipates a Ph.D. of education in 1991.

References

Bybee, Rodger and Robert Sund. *Piaget for Educators,* Second Edition. Columbus, Ohio: Charles E. Merrill Publishing Co., 1982.

Bredekamp, S. *Developmentally Appropriate Practice*. Washington, D.C: National Association for the Education of Young Children, 1986.

Craig, Grace J. *Human Development*. New Jersey: Prentice-Hall, Inc., 1989.

Elkind, David. *The Hurried Child*. Reading, Massachusetts: Addison-Wesley Publishing Co., 1981.

Elkind, David. *Child Development and Education: A Piagetian Perspective*. New York: Oxford University Press, 1976.

Fein G., and M. Rivkin. *The Young Child at Play: Reviews of Research,* edited by G. Fein and M. Rivkin. Washington, D.C: The National Association for the Education of Young Children, 1986.

Frost, J. L. and S. Sunderlin, *When Children Play: Proceedings of the International Conference on Play and Play Environments*. Wheaton, Md.: Association for Childhood Education International, 1985.

Gagne, Robert M. *Essentials of Learning for Instruction*. New York: Holt, Reinhart and Winston, 1974.

Gottfried, A. E. "Intrinsic Motivational Aspects of Play Experiences and Materials." In *Play Materials and Parental Involvement to Children's Development,* edited by A. W. Gottfried and C. C. Brown. Lexington, Mass.: D. C. Heath and Co., 1986.

Hendrick, Joanne. *The Whole Child*. Columbus, Ohio: Merrill Publishing Co., 1988.

Hohmann, Mary; Banet, Bernard and Weikart, David P. *Young Children in Action*. Ypsilanti, Michigan: High/Scope Press, 1979.

Hymes, James L. Jr. *Teaching the Child Under Six*. Columbus, Ohio: Charles E. Merrill Publishing Co., 1974.

Maxim, George. *Learning Centers for Young Children*. New York: Hart Publishing Company, Inc., 1977.

Moffitt, Mary W. "Play as a Medium for Learning." *Journal of Health, Physical Education, Recreation,* June 1972, 45–47.

Moore, Raymond S. and Dorothy N. Moore. *School Can Wait*. Provo, Utah: Brigham Young University Press, 1979.

Patterson, C. H. *Foundations for a Theory of Instructional and Educational Psychology*. San Francisco: Harper and Row, 1977.

Pepler, D. "Play and Creativity." In *The Young Child at Play: Reviews of Research,* edited by G. Fein and M. Rivkin. Washington D.C: The National Association for the Education of Young Children, 1986.

Piaget, Jean. *To Understand is to Invent*. New York: Grossman Publishers, 1973.

Piaget, Jean. *Play, Dreams and Imitation in Childhood*. New York: W. W. Norton and Co., 1962.

Sutton-Smith, B. and J. M. Roberts. "Play, Toys, Games and Sports." In *Handbook of Developmental Cross-Cultural Psychology,* edited by H. C. Triandis and A. Heron. Boston: Allyn and Bacon, 1981.

CHAPTER 15

Developmental and Experimental Programs—Key to Quality Education and Care of Young Children

Given the well-established fact that young children learn differently, the conclusion that educators must draw is a straightforward one: the education of young children must be in keeping with their unique modes of learning (Elkind, May, 1986).

At the heart of the educational process lies the child. No advances in policy, no acquisitions of new equipment have their desired effect unless they are in harmony with the nature of the child, unless they are fundamentally acceptable to him.

Knowledge of the manner in which children develop, therefore, is of prime importance, both in avoiding educationally harmful practices and in introducing effective ones (Plowden Report, 1966).

These statements, written twenty years apart, by Elkind and Plowden, summarize succinctly the rationale for early childhood programs that are developmental in nature. What happens when this rationale is translated into reality? What are the characteristics of developmentally appropriate early childhood programs? Are such programs effective?

There is significant body of research based on scientifically valid explanations of how children develop, and how learning occurs, that supports a change of paradigms. This model embraces what is widely referred to as developmentally appropriate practice and utilizes what the National Association for the Education of Young Children (1988) terms:

> ". . . active, experiential learning in a meaningful context" where emphasis on "all domains of development—the physical, social emotional and cognitive—are integrated."

The developmentally appropriate model of early childhood education is being advocated by a variety of prominent educators (e.g., Elkind, Katz, Day, Kamii and Duckworth) and officially sanctioned by a number of professional organizations (e.g., the Association for Supervision and Curriculum Development [1988], the National Association of State Boards of Education [1988], as well as the NAEYC [1988]).

The reality of a Developmental Early Childhood Classroom for five-, six-, seven- and eight-year-olds may look like the following: Outside the classroom is a busy patio with children engaged in a variety of activities. Two childen are building a log cabin with a kit of large linking boards. Next to them two more children are creating their own rolling toy with a giant set of plastic nuts, bolts, wheels and tools. At the sand and water tables, children are pouring, mixing and molding. An "interstate highway" winds its way around and through the tables and tools as two "highway engineers" construct a roadway with bridges, cars and trucks. Bubbles float through the air, drifting over from children at a small picnic table equipped with soap solution and wands. One meditative child rides a rocking seesaw alone, while on another seesaw a girl and a boy rock higher and higher. On the waterway "canals," boats float in the sun waiting for the next ship's "captain" to come along. A small basket holding balls and jump ropes attracts the attention of a small boy.

Inside, the classroom hums with energy, yet the noise level remains low. Small cubbies filled with games, books, and materials divide the large room into child-sized nooks and spaces. Colorful bulletin boards display children's drawings, stories and projects. Children move purposefully from place to place as they finish one activity and start another. In one corner children are balancing blocks, feathers, sponges, and crayons on a scale. Beside them four children are engaged in a cooperative sorting activity. First, they determine the criteria for their groupings. Will the arrangement be based on size, shape, color or kind? The tub full of attribute blocks lends itself to a variety of arrangements. The children reach an agreement; the groups will be sorted first by shape and then re-arranged by color.

In the writing corner, the teacher assistant reads a poem, "Mommies," by Nikki Giovanni, to a six-year-old girl. The child then starts her own "Mommy" poem: "Mommies make you eat spinach and carrots. But I like them anyway!" She adds a picture of her own Mommy to her page. Next to her a five-year-old boy is cutting and pasting a silhouette of Abraham Lincoln. The assistant moves over to him and writes as he dictates, "Abraham Lincoln was a famous president." On the floor three other five-year-olds make up their own fairy tale by arranging the picture cards from a "Shufflebook" set.

Two small cars whiz past as experiments with inclined planes take place in the science center. In the block corner another log cabin is taking shape as its two builders discuss whether or not Abe Lincoln needed a chimney to go along with his fireplace.

At an easel, a rainbow of red, green and pink valentines appear beneath the brush of a little boy. At the nearby table, a variety of heart designs are taking shape from the hands of several young artists.

Puzzles and board games occupy some children, while inside a wooden "Wendy house" one child reads a book of riddles to a large stuffed rabbit.

The classroom teacher chats with two children serving plastic cupcakes, scrambled eggs, and ice cream to the doll collection in the dramatic play corner. "Is this brunch?" she asks, adding a brief definition of the term. The children giggle with delight and invite another friend in for "brunch." The teacher moves around the room, collecting a small number of children for math skills work. She settles down with them on the floor in an area of the room reserved for group work. The children create equivalent and non-equivalent sets using a colorful collection of small toys. Then they try drawing their own equivalent sets. Another group of children now gathers in the work/study area with the teacher and begin a language/reading skills group. These first graders do an oral game with consonant blends and complete reading assignments from a variety of books. Each child then adds a picture and story page to his/her booklet on famous Black Americans. Today's emphasis is on Black inventors and scientists. Astronauts begin to appear along with illustrations on huge ice cream sundaes in honor of Alfred Cralle the inventor of the ice cream scoop.

Another small group is organized, ready to begin a whole language activity with a "big book." Today's selection, *Clifford the Big Red Dog,* is greeted with excitement as a stuffed version of "Clifford" participates in the reading of the story.

In another corner are cubbies filled with reference books. One child uses the playground page in the *Sesame Street Word Book* to identify a variety of simple machines such as the slide, the seesaw, and the swing. Another child researches Sojourner Truth and writes a brief summary of her accomplishments. Yet another child has the *Afro-Bets Book of Black Heroes* open to the page on Mary McLeod Bethune, known for establishing her own school. This child is meticulously designing *her* own school room on drawing paper.

The lights blink in the classroom and the children respond to this signal for cleaning up. Materials are returned to shelves, papers put in folders, crayons and pencils sorted and put away. A few children keep working, clearly intent on adding the final touch to their projects. Children retrieve folders from small boxes placed in each center. They get out their "contracts" and "check-off" completed tasks. Rainbows of color-coded clothespins appear and are attached to similarly colored charts hanging in each learning center. Center "helpers" double check the clean-up job completed by their peers. Within five minutes the entire class has gathered in the homebase circle area and is enjoying a brief appearance by "Mr. Elephant," a thoroughly grouchy and hungry puppet. "Mr. Elephant" reminds everyone that it is indeed lunchtime. Lunch is followed by storytime, singing and "show and tell." While the children listen to *Mufaro's Beautiful Daughters,* a parent volunteer is setting up a special presentation. Using an egg beater and cookie cutters, both designed by black inventors, she will engage the children in cooking and eating no-bake peanut butter fudge. They will also have the opportunity to enjoy the benefits of the ice cream scoop as a gallon of lime sherbet is scheduled to be equally divided. Recipes are given to each child so that they may try making this treat at home.

The children then return to either learning centers or small skill groups until the Spanish teacher arrives for a twenty minute session with everyone. After a final "adios" from Carlos, the children are ready for a brief rest time, and then outdoor play. Today the parachute is out and excited cries greet the ups and downs of the chute as children try to avoid being draped in its folds.

The Characteristics

Basic characteristics that distinguish a developmentally designed early childhood program evolve from its philosophy, planning, and implementation.

Philosophy

Just as a weaver takes threads of different colors, textures, and lengths and weaves them into a tapestry by using creative patterns and knots, educators planning quality early childhood programs must incorporate many elements into a coherent whole. They must weave parents' needs, society's expectations, research, and most importantly the concepts of child development into a creative, intelligent, working program. The best place to start such a program is with the child. Early childhood educators must have a clear, strong sense of children as growing, dynamic individuals with needs and capabilities appropriate to various stages of development. Developmental programs allow for a flexible and varied curriculum to permit the planning and evaluation of activities designed to meet a broad range of developmental, socioeconomic, and cultural needs (Leeper, S. H., Witherspoon, R., & Dy, B., 1984).

Planning

There are four major areas to be considered when planning quality developmental programs.

The first area involves the child's opportunities to practice developmental tasks. The concept of developmental tasks as developed by Tryon and Lilienthal (1950) contend that there are major common tasks that face all individuals in a given society. The first task involves gaining appropriate dependence-independence patterns. This concerns the child's adjustment to less private attention and the initiation of more independent actions such as putting away his/her own toys or sharing the teacher's attention. A quality program addresses this task by providing facilities scaled to the children's size so as to encourage independence, time for children to perform these tasks, and an atmosphere of acceptance where a child feels secure enough to act independently. Another developmental task involves establishing healthy patterns for giving and receiving affection. This can be done by providing opportunities for greetings, sharing, and friendship among children. Relating to social groups is another important task. The program can help children develop this skill by allowing opportunities for group planning and sharing, and by valuing cooperative effort through praise. Another task involves the development of conscience. Opportunities for choices within limits and explanations by teachers and staff. Physical growth is an important area where children's developmental needs must also be met. Quality programs should provide ample space for running, climbing, painting, etc. Finally, communication opportunities will address the child's development of an ability to use and understand symbols.

The second major area in planning for a quality program concerns teachers and staff. The teacher's knowledge is a critical factor in determining the success of a developmental program. Teachers need to be informed about the physical, social, and cognitive development of children. Teachers' interactions with students are also important elements in providing quality programs. A study by Perkins (1981) reveals that where teachers participated more with the children and were less directive, the children exhibited higher levels of cognitive play, task involvement, and verbal interaction. Teachers should also take care to have their nonverbal behavior consistent with their verbal messages to students. The philosophy of discipline and guidance should be based on respect for the inherent dignity and worth of each child. Teachers need to recognize that options are available. Behavioral approaches to discipline are options focused on correcting inappropriate behavior by conditioning patterns of appropriate behavior. Finally, the teacher should combine his/her knowledge of research, child development, and the home environment of the children to plan opportunities which use the child's own experiences as a spring board for learning.

Academics have an important place in the quality program. However, the curriculum for four-year-old children should not be first grade or kindergarten moved down, often referred to as the "trickle down" syndrome. Children from two to seven are in the concrete stage of cognitive development. They learn from concrete experiences. Applying this to the school setting means that learning should be experiential. Since children do not have the cognitive ability of reversibility, and since they are bound by the perceptions, academic learning should use concrete experiences as a starting place. The focus of academics in preschool should be to make children aware of reading, writing, and mathematics. Stories, dictation to the teacher, and counting can be creatively used by teachers to expose children to experiences of reading, writing, and math. First and second graders also need continued concrete learning experiences as they begin to make the transition to the more sophisticated symbolisms required in formal reading and math instruction. The suggestion that preschool curriculum should "trickle up" into the primary grades is developmentally quite appropriate.

The fourth major area considered in planning a quality program is the physical setting. Since one developmental goal is to encourage children to be independent, the facilities of the school should be designed for this purpose. Child-size toilet facilities and closets for putting away clothes are examples of scaled facilities. The physical environment should provide opportunities for children to have hands-on learning experiences. Centers for math, sciences, reading, writing, art, cooking, listening, etc., can be set up so that children can engage in experiences which allow them to use their hands, eyes, ears, and minds to learn about themselves and the world around them.

Implementation

In implementing a good early childhood program consideration must be given to curriculum organization and classroom management. Curriculum organization is made up of three components: learning centers, skills groups, and units of study. Classroom management components include the use of color coding, contracts, and internal and external methods of discipline (Day and Drake, 1983).

Curriculum Components

1. Learning centers are created when classroom space is physically divided into a number of small areas (i.e., art, blocks, math, reading, listening and viewing, science, social studies, outdoor centers, dramatic play, writing, etc.), each of which is equipped with materials specific to the development of a skill or concept. Materials in each center may range from the concrete to the abstract. Centers typically provide children with many opportunities for interaction with one another and for experiential learning.
2. Skills groups provide for flexible groupings for basic instruction and the opportunity for direct teaching in areas such as language experience, reading and math.
3. Units of study are organized to teach specific topics in areas such as science and social studies (i.e., animal habits, self-concept, dinosaurs, the circus, etc.). In the developmental classroom, activities

are designed for large and small group instruction and for learning centers. The unit approach serves as a mechanism for integrating the curriculum throughout the entire classroom. It allows children the opportunity to draw, read, write, and create within a content area.

Management Components
1. Color coding is the systematic use of color to organize games, books, activities, etc. Its use helps young children manage a multi-task environment.
2. The contracts, a pictorial (later written) plan for the child's day, helps ensure that each child stays on task. The contract includes a variety of activities each day in order to provide a balanced program for the child.
3. Discipline is divided into two aspects, external and internal. The external aspect of discipline refers to how the child's classroom environment influences his or her behavior. Providing a developmentally appropriate learning environment facilitates appropriate behavior. The internal aspect of discipline refers to the child's own ability to behave in appropriate ways. Clear expectations, consistent use of rules, and frequent feedback are techniques early childhood educators can use to help the young child develop internal discipline. These four basic rules ensure a workable classroom: Children must (1) have a job, (2) use soft voices, (3) walk as they move about the classroom, and (4) respect the feelings and property of others.

Effectiveness

A brief review of the literature suggests that developmental classrooms do work. Early childhood programs have been examined in terms of their physical arrangement, and their management techniques and teaching strategies as follows:

Physical Arrangement of the Classroom
Much of the research on classrooms that operate learning centers have been done in preschool settings rather than in elementary school classrooms. These studies include measurement of the effects of classroom spatial features and the arrangment of equipment on children's behavior, as well as inquiries into how various types of materials affect on-task behavior.

Kritchevsky and Prescott (1977) identified several principles concerning the relationship between spatial arrangement and behavior in young children. The teacher-arranged spaces in classrooms encourage children to move in one direction or another, enter or leave an area, to pause or to pass by without attending. Space invites children to talk with others, hurry or move calmly, touch others or leave them alone, combine materials or keep them separated. When behavior encouraged by the environment is expected and desired, teachers are more likely to respond in positive ways that support activities and learning. When the resulting behavior is unexpected or unwanted, teachers tend to recite rules, redirect, scold, or restrain children. In either situation, spatial organization is a strong influence on both teacher and child behavior.

Jones (1973) found that providing learning areas with materials of a high level of complexity usually promoted involvement and a fairly long attention span for pupils, combined with independence from teacher-led segments of the school day; however, there was a substantial relationship between high variety and pupil involvement when children were working independently. Children in first and second grades were much more involved in high variety segments than children in low variety segments.

Rosenthal (1974) found that length of stay in an activity setting (i.e., learning center) was attributable to the activity's holding power rather than to the child's attention span. Weinstein (1977) found that changes in the physical setting of a classroom can produce changes in student behavior in predictable, desirable directions. Changes in the classroom environment modified children's spatial patterns (children moved into centers they had previously avoided), broadened the range of behaviors previously exhibited (children exhibited less "large physical activity," for example). However, she too found that environmental factors only influenced the children's behavior if the activities/materials available were of interest to the children. She concluded that environmental changes intended to increase a desirable behavior will have maximum impact when the inclination to engage in the activity is already present. Weinstein (1979) in a review of the research on the physical environment of the school, also suggests that the learning centers of "subsettings" of early childhood classrooms do indeed exert "coercive power" over the inhabitants, constraining certain behaviors and encouraging others. She states that different types of environmental activities have varying environmental requirements, that different individuals may require different types of environment in order to function effectively, and the "susceptibility" to different environmental factors may vary with developmental stage.

Altman and Wohlwill (1978) point out that young children may be particularly sensitive to modification of the environment. Morrow and Weinstein (1982) suggest that if this is true, then the opportunity for achieving a positive impact on development may be correspondingly greater in the case of the young child. They contend that a well-designed classroom facilitates behaviors that enhance cognitive development. They agree with Phyfe-Perkins (1979) who suggests that the "skill of arranging the early childhood environment to support the maximum involvement of children with materials and with each other is a skill that can and should be taught."

Classroom Management Techniques and Teaching Strategies

Research indicates that there is close relationship between classroom activity formats and student involvement. While the variety of activity formats that could be used in the classroom might appear to be endless, only a few formats are actually used in practice. Jackson noted that:

> Despite the diversity of subject matter content, the identifiable forms of classroom activity are not great in number. The labels: "seatwork," "group discussion," "teacher demonstration;" and "question-and-answer period" (which could include work at the board) are sufficient to categorize most of the things that happen when class is in session. "Audio-visual display," "testing session," and "games" might be added to the list, but in most elementary classrooms they occur rarely.

Other researchers have confirmed Jackson's claim, documenting that in American schools, three instructional formats dominate the classroom: recitations, seatwork, and small group instruction (which may only be a variation of the recitation) (Gump, 1967).

Investigations have shown that pupil involvement can be related to whether or not the activity format calls for active input of stimuli or passive availability of materials and events. In a study of third graders the average pupil involvement scores in all active input segments was 85 percent. It was 75 percent during passive availability segments (Gump, 1967). Another study involving grades one through five showed pupil involvement in recitation segments (active input) to be 85 percent, yet only 65 percent in seatwork (passive availability) segments. Misconduct beyond simple non-involved behavior was almost four times as frequent in the seatwork segments (Kounin et al., 1966).

Another aspect of classroom activity formats concerns the extent to which teachers operate overlapping segments or activities. When simultaneous segments operate, the teacher has created a relatively complex structure which must be coordinated and supervised. Gump (1967) notes that overlapping segments are common in elementary classrooms (for example, a small group of children may be reading with the teacher, while the rest of the children are engaged in seatwork). Doyle (1977) has noted that beginning teachers try to adapt to the complexity of the classroom by localizing attention to one region of the classroom and being engrossed in one activity at a time. He found that this strategy was not generally successful. Kounin (1970) found that where teachers were able to deal with simultaneous segments without becoming immersed in one situation to the exclusion of the others, pupils were more involved in the teacher-led segments and less deviant in the pupil-initiative segments. It was especially important that the pupil-initiative segments have activities that the students could manage.

Numerous studies have addressed the effect of various grouping structures on student behavior. These studies have reported conflicting findings. Many investigations have concluded that there are no demonstrated differences between student engagement rates during different classroom groupings (Cooley and Leinhardt, 1980; Probst, 1980; and Cornbleth and Korth, 1980). However, other studies have reported that large group structures are superior in producing higher engagement rates (Ruff, 1978; Filby, 1978; and Easton et al., 1979).

Still others have found that engagement rates of students are higher during small group work than during independent seatwork or conventional large group instruction (Petersen et al., 1978; Slavin, 1980; Sharan, 1980; Hess and Takanishi, 1974). For example, Webb (1982) found that the degree of giving and receiving help in small groups is positively related to student achievement. Petersen (1979) found that only small effects on achievement were attributable to large group, teacher-led, direct instruction, with the difference between this instruction and an individual or open approach only one-tenth of a standard deviation. Further, Petersen found that non-direct rather than direct instruction was more associated with creativity and problem solving.

Linn (1980) found that a combination of direct instruction, such as lectures and demonstrations with the teacher functioning as group leader followed by free-choice experiences such as those found in learning centers, increased the children's learning in science more than either direct instruction or free-choice experiences alone.

Wasik and Day (Day and Drake, 1983) studied a multi-aged kindergarten and first grade classroom that created a multi-task, active input type of learning environment through the use of learning centers and contracts. These students spent over half their time working independently (Kindergarten 54.97 percent; first grade 54.50 percent) without direct adult supervision. Wasik and Day reported that the overall rate of appropriate, on-task behavior exhibited by the children while working independently was over 88 percent. The overall rate of on-task behavior exhibited by the children while working under the supervision of an adult was over 94 percent. The children had the least amount of aggressive/resistive behavior when they were in learning centers. Some centers showed no instances of aggressive behavior over a two year period. The work-study areas (used for completing independent seatwork) were the least productive places in the classroom for the first graders in this study.

However, even the intrinsic interest and strong signal systems of small group tasks and learning center activities may not keep students attentive unless the activities are well managed. For this reason, classes having a wide range of concurrent activities sometimes show lower achievement gains than classes with only one or two activities occurring simultaneously (McDonald and Elias, 1976; Stallings, 1980). This is because some teachers in multi-task settings are unable to supervise the work behavior of all students (Rosenshire, 1979; Berliner, 1979). These findings have led some researchers to recommend less small group work and more whole class instruction (Medley, 1979; Brophy, 1979).

Wilson (1983) suggests that in highly differentiated classrooms complex strategies of management and coordination are necessary. The classroom characterized by high task complexity differs markedly from the more routine classroom since more activities take place and since children change activities more often. He states that engagement in a class with complex task arrangements depends on the fit of the management system with the task arrangement. He also hypothesized that student engagement would be higher in well managed complex classrooms because teachers would, of necessity, foster interdependency among the children by encouraging them to take over some of the management functions usually performed by the teacher. These children would be sharing information with one another and working together to solve problems. He designed a study which investigated the engagement rates of students who were taught science through the use of learning centers (a "high complexity" task arrangement) and students in math classes where everyone was working on the same assignment at a given time (a "low complexity" task arrangement). The area of greatest difference in management between high and low complexity task arrangements was in the delegation of authority. Significantly more working together and peer task talk occurred in high as compared to low complexity task arrangements was in the delegation of authority. Significantly more working together and peer task talk occurred in high as compared to low complexity task arrangements. Students set up materials, allocated necessary resources and answered each other's questions regarding what to do next and how to do it. Engagement was also higher in the high complexity condition.

Just as certain academic skills don't happen on their own, the desired socio-emotional outcomes cannot be expected to emerge entirely unaided. The classroom environment and curriculum must be explicitly constructed to actively support the optimum development of the whole child.

What then are the characteristics of an environment that fosters a child's balanced development? Many of the research findings of the last decade support Katz's advocacy for educating the whole child.

Weikart (1978) and his colleagues suggested that "important social consequences of preschool curriculum choices were showing up in the elementary school years." Children from teacher-directed programs consistently were rated lower (on sociability, cooperation, and academic orientation) than children from more child-centered programs.

There were also pronounced differences on the socio-emotional side between the different groups studied as part of a widely publicized and discussed report on preschool curriculum (Schweinhart, Weikart and Larner, 1986) *High/Scope Foundation*. This study followed the children enrolled in three well-implemented preschool curriculum models through the age of fifteen.

The researchers found marked differences in behavioral and social outcomes among the three groups. The group in which teacher-directed experiences were predominant (when compared to the groups that were encouraged to initiate their own activities) reported significantly higher rates of juvenile delinquency and other associated problems. These problems included 1) lower participation rates in sports, 2) a lower likelihood of being appointed to an office or special job at school, and 3) a higher incidence of poor relations between students and their families.

Marshall (1989) found that: "Children in classrooms that supported autonomy had higher perceptions of their own cognitive competence, self worth and mastery motivation than those in classrooms where teachers retained control." This research challenges the commonly-held belief that teacher-directed instruction raises academic achievement, and thereby, most effectively promotes a child's positive self concept. The implication here may be that socio-emotional development should be addressed directly, rather that through academic achievement.

In summary, active involvement by pupils creates higher engagement and multi-task classrooms that encourage active involvement need more complex management techniques than classrooms with only one or two on-going activity segments.

A recent study in developmental programs for five- and six-year-old children found that children in classrooms that featured eight or more learning centers, that opened the learning centers for the entire day, that were multi-aged (with five- and six-year-old children grouped together) and that used contracts had on-task behavior rates of 92 percent. As a result of these high rates of on-task behavior, children in the developmental classrooms actually received 120 more hours of schooling over the entire school year than did children whose organization did not include learning centers or contracts. This translated into 20 more school days per year for the children in the development programs.

This study (conducted by Day and Drake, 1983) investigated the relationship between various types of early childhood classroom environments and the on-task behavior rate generated by the children in each program.

Classroom environments can be defined in terms of the number of simultaneous segments (i.e., activities) operating at any one time (Wilson, 1983). Classrooms that rely primarily on teacher-led group instruction are the least complex, with only one activity segment in operation. The next level of complexity involves two activity segments operating simultaneously in the classroom. In early childhood programs this typically consists of teacher-led small group instruction (i.e., reading or math skill groups) and an independent seatwork segment planned for children who are not working with the teacher in the skills group.

Classrooms with more than two segments operating simultaneously are the most complex and also the most difficult to manage. Early childhood classrooms that are organized so that children have the opportunity to work in both teacher-led and independent small groups, have hands-on learning activities, and have the opportunity to move at their own pace, often using learning centers as the mechanism for implementing this approach. Classrooms with learning centers are multi-task settings, with the number of segments in operation at any one time varying from three to fifteen or more.

In this study, eighteen kindergarten and first grade classrooms were observed and then categorized into five different organizational patterns as follows:

Type 1. Six-year-old children in classrooms that operated for most of the school day with only one or two simultaneous activity segments.

Type 2. Five-year-old children in classrooms that operated multiple activity segments (including eight or more learning centers) for the first hour of the school day, and then operated only one or two simultaneous activity segments for the rest of the school day.

Type 3. Six-year-old children in classrooms that operated multiple activity segments (including eight or more learning centers) for the morning half of the school day (using a twenty minute rotation period for each activity segment). The afternoon pattern included only one or two simultaneous activity segments.

Table 1: Percentage of On-Task Behavior by Classroom Type

Type	Activities	Time	Contract	On-Task Behavior
1	1–2	——	no	79%
2	multiple	1 hr/day	no	79%
3	multiple	1/2 day	no	78%
4	multiple	all day	no	81%
5A	multiple	all day	yes	85%
5B	multiple	all day	yes	87%
5C	multiple	all day	yes	92%

Type 4. Five-year-old children in classrooms that operated multiple activity segments (including eight or more centers) all day and used written contracts as a management technique.

Type 5. Five- and six-year-old children in classrooms that operated multiple activity segments (including eight or more learning centers) all day and used written contracts as a management technique.

Children in Type 5 classrooms were grouped in five-year-old kindergarten programs (Type 5a), six-year-old first grade programs (Type 5b), and in multi-aged five- and six-year-old programs (Type 5c).

Empirical accounts of the on-task behavior of the children in the various classroom environments was collected by using the Wasik-Day: Open and Traditional Learning Environments and Children's Classroom Behavior Instrument. This instrument categorized children's behavior as appropriate or inappropriate and also gave detailed information on the child's place in the classroom, the number of children in the group at any given moment, the academic behavior being observed, etc.

Ten students per class were selected at random and observed over a two day period. Each child was observed for four ten minute sessions (twice on day one, twice on day two). The 7200 observations generated by the study created a detailed portrait of life in early childhood classrooms.

Table 1 shows the on-track behavior rates generated by each type of classroom.

Type 2 and Type 3 classrooms featuring limited use of multiple activity segments (including eight or more learning centers) had similar on-task rates to Type 1 classrooms that conveyed instruction by using only one or two activity segments (such as group work or seatwork) throughout the school day (78.9 percent and 78.38 percent versus 79.01 percent). Small positive changes in on-task behavior rates were produced by Type 4 classrooms that operated multiple activity segments (including eight or more learning centers) for the entire day (81.25 percent). However, pronounced changes in on-task behavior rates were observed in the Type 5 classrooms that combined the all day use of multiple activity segments (including eight or more learning centers) with the use of written contracts. This interaction of written contracts and multi-task classroom environment generated on-task behavior rates of as high as 92 percent for five- and six-year-old children.

One possible implication of these data is that the presence or absence of learning centers may not influence on-task behavior rated in early childhood classrooms as much as does how the learning centers are used. Teachers in Type 4 classrooms by using learning centers for the entire day made the centers an integral part of their program. As a result, these classrooms may have created a more diligent attitude on the part of the children toward the centers and their materials, may have provided activities with greater holding power, and may have reduced the overall amount of time that was spent in seatwork, and in small and large groups.

While the Type 4 classroom results hint at possible positive changes in on-task behavior rates due to the use of learning centers, the Type 5 classrooms also operated learning centers for the entire school day. However, they added a specific management technique, a written contract, to their programs. Type 5 classrooms achieved total on-task rates from 84.96 percent to 92.00 percent, the highest in the study. These results suggest that written contracts function effectively as a mechanism for helping children stay on-task in a multi-activity setting. The results also suggest that a complex early childhood environment featuring learning centers in conjunction with an appropriate management system can achieve rates of on-task behavior higher than those achieved in less complex classrooms that rely extensively on large or small group instruction and seatwork assignments.

As seen in Tables 2 and 3, five- and six-year-old children in this study had higher on-task rates when working in learning centers than when engaged in seatwork activities. On-task rates were highest for centers that required "hands-on" involvement by the child, such as art, blocks, water and music. Centers such as writing and research that require specific correct written responses from the children has on-task rates that were similar to the rates produced by classroom seatwork segment. These results suggest that young children need classrooms that feature a variety of learning experiences, including kinesthetic, auditory, and visual activities and materials, as well as traditional pencil and paper activities.

A particularly interesting example of the interaction between the developmental readiness of children for an activity and the on-task behavior rates generated by that activity was seen in the reading centers studied. Five-year-olds in this study had on-task rates of 29.03 percent when

Table 2

Percentage of On-Task Behavior
5-Year-Olds

Music	100	Water	100	Outside	98
Listening	93	Sensory/Motor	88	Math	84
Housekeeping	81	Science	80		
		Study Area	78		
Research	75	Writing	75	Cooking	72
		Reading	29		

Table 3

Percentage of On-Task Behavior
6-Year-Olds

Math	100	Sensory/Motor	100	Outside	100
Reading	93	Art	97	Sand	91
Science	89	Blocks	88	Listening	86
Writing	85			Cooking	82
		Study	78		
		Housekeeping	60		

observed in reading centers. Six-year-old children in this study had an on-task behavior rate of 93.03 percent in reading centers. Clearly, reading centers as they are typically designed in early childhood classrooms are not involving five-year-old children, most of whom are nonreaders. Implications of this data suggest the reorganization of reading centers for five-year-olds so that stimuli other than print are included. For example, books with tape recordings of their content might be more involving to five-year-olds than books alone.

Even though the study areas were among the least productive places in the classrooms observed in this study, children in these study areas actually had higher on-task rates than children in other research studies. For example, Rosenshine (1980) found that children were on-task during 68 percent of their seatwork time. Kounin et al. (1966) found on-task rates of 78.83 percent for five-year-olds and 77.87 percent for six-year-olds engaged in seatwork. In contrast, the first grade children in this study spent 46.50 percent of their day in seatwork activities. Conceivably, fewer seatwork assignments resulted in higher on-task behavior because repetitive, non-meaningful tasks were eliminated.

Table 4 presents interesting contrasts in how time is actually spent in kindergarten and first grade classrooms. First grade children spent a much higher proportion of their day in the study area (46.50 percent) than did the kindergarten children (8.61 percent). First graders were observed in fewer centers than were kindergarteners, with no observations at all recorded for six-year-olds in woodworking, water, or music centers. The first grade children spent less total time in centers than did the kindergarten children (13.63 percent versus 26.15 percent). The typical first grade day in this study is clearly structured quite differently than the typical kindergarten day.

Table 4

Percentage of Time by Place

Activity Centers	
Homebase Circle	
Homebase Other	
Study Area	
Other	

■ 6 year old
▒ 5 year old

0 5 10 15 20 25 30 35 40 45 50

Percentage of Time

Conclusion

Quality early childhood programs must allow for exploration, experimentation, and inquiry all within a structured, yet creative, learning environment. Such an environment is based on the following beliefs (Day, 1988):

1. Children grow and develop at unique, individual rates that are often unrelated to chronological age. (Many learning activities at a variety of challenge levels should be provided in an effort to meet the needs of all children. Even within the range of preoperational learning, there are many levels).
2. Children's natural curiosity and eagerness to learn are enhanced if children are free to follow many of their natural interests. (Piaget has said that children learn best through direct, immediate involvement with the environment. They learn through sensory input of observation, manipulation, and testing).
3. Learning is what children do; it is not something that is done to them. (The child must be directly involved in doing the learning. Telling the child may result in empty verbalizations).

4. Play is the child's way of working and learning. (Children acquire many skills through play. They try new roles, solve problems, learn how to make sense of the environment, and practice social skills).

5. Children learn many things from each other, including respect for themselves and others, ways of learning how to learn, and a sense of responsibility and achievement. (Bloom [1981] has described "such basic characteristics of 'learning to learn' as the ability to receive instruction from adults, deferring gratification of reward, and the more generalized motivation to learn. It also includes the basic attitudes toward school and teacher.")

6. A specially constructed, rich learning environment, filled with concrete and sensory learning materials, is essential in helping children to learn. (The environment is the vehicle for learning, and it must provide the materials the child needs for exploration and learning).

7. The integrated day, involving centers-oriented, simultaneously occurring activities within the learning environment, is one of the creative approaches to the development of basic skills fit into a broader realm of experience, thus providing a reason for learning. Children can see how learning "school skills" will help them in everyday life).

8. In a learning atmosphere based on trust and structured freedom, children are encouraged to use their own initiative and to be self-reliant. (Children need reassurance and security, but they also need intriguing challenge. They need and respond to praise for a job well done).

9. The uniqueness of the child, as reflected in his or her individuality and learning style, should be appreciated and valued.

Finally, our first and most important challenge is to focus on the individual needs of the young children we serve. We can provide the resources and opportunities to meet those needs. Specifically, schools can provide children with:

- a comfortable, safe, and stable environment every day, year round, for all of the hours that parents are at work.
- consistent and nurturing care and education.
- the opportunity to be physically active.
- opportunities to explore and meaningfully interact with the world around them.
- opportunities to interact with, learn from, and be appreciated by other children.
- stimulation and support to develop cognitively, socially, emotionally, and physically in their own time and in their own ways.

Barbara D.Day, Professor and Chair Curriculum and Instruction, School of Education, University of North Carolina at Chapel Hill.

Kay N. Drake, Teacher, Seawell Elementary School, Chapel Hill—Carrboro City Schools.

References

Altman, I.; and Wohlwill, J. F. *Children and the Environment. New York: Plenum, 1978.*

Berliner, D. C. *All the Children Learning.* New York: McGraw Hill, 1979.

Bloom, B. S. *All the Children Learning.* New York: McGraw Hill, 1981.

Bredekamp, S. (Ed.). *Developmentally Appropriate Practice in Early Childhood Programs Serving Children From Birth Through Age 8.* Washington, DC: National Association for the Education of Young Children, 1987.

Brophy, J. E. "Teacher Behavior and its Effects." *Journal of Educational Psychology,* 1979, 71: 733–750.

Carroll, J. B. "A Model of School Learning." *Teachers College Record,* 1963, 64: 723–733.

Cooley, W.; Leinhardt, G. "The Instructional Dimensions Study." *Educational Evaluation and Policy Analysis,* 1980, 2: 7–24.

Cornbleth, C.; and Korth, W. "Context Factors and Individual Differences in Pupil Involvement in Learning Activities." *Journal of Educational Research,* 1980, 73: 319–323.

Day, B. "What's Happening in Early Childhood Programs Across the United States." In *A Resource Guide to Public School Early Childhood Programs,* edited by C. Warger. 1988.

Day, B. D. *Early Childhood Education: Creative Learning Activities,* 2nd Edition. New York: MacMillan, 1988.

Day, B. D.; and Drake, K. N. *Early Childhood Educatoin: Curriculum Organization and Classroom Management.* Alexandria, VA: Association for Supervision and Curriculum Development, 1983.

Doyle, W. "Learning the Classroom Environment: An Ecological Analysis." *Journal of Teacher Education,* 1977, 28: 51–55.

Duckworth, E. *"The Having of Wonderful Ideas" and other essays on teaching and learning.* New York: Teachers College Press, 1987.

Easton, J. Q.; Muirhead, R. W.; Frederick, W. C.; and Vanderwicken, S. *Relationships Among Student Time on Task, Orientation of Teachers, and Instructional Grouping in Elementary Reading Classes.* Paper presented at the meeting of the American Educational Research Association, San Francisco, 1979. (ERIC Document Reproduction Service No. ED 169 503).

Elkind, D. "The Resistance to Developmentally Appropriate Educational Practice with Young Children: the Real Issue." In *A Resource Guide to Public School Early Childhood Programs,* edited by C. Warger. Alexandria, VA: Association for Supervision and Curriculum Development, 1988.

Filby, N. "How Teachers Produce 'Academic Learning Time': Instructional Variables Related to Student Engagement." In *Selected Findings from Phase III-B of the Beginning Teacher Evaluation Study,* edited by C. W. Fisher. San Francisco: Far West Laboratory for Educational Research, 1978. (ERIC Document Reproduction Service No. ED 160 639).

Gagne, R. M. *The Conditions of Learning* (3rd ed.). New York: Holt, Rinehart, and Winston, 1977.

Gump, P. V. *The Classroom Behavior Setting: Its Nature and Relation to Student Behavior.* (U.S. Office of Education Final Report, Project No. 2453.) Lawrence, KS: University of Kansas Press, 1967.

Hess, R. D.; and Takanishi, R. *The Relationship of Teacher Behavior and School Charactership to Students Engagement.* (Technical Report No. 42). Stanford, CA: Stanford Center for Research and Development in Teaching, 1974.

Jackson, P. W. *Life in Classrooms.* New York: Holt, Rinehart, & Winston, 1968.

Jones, E. *Dimensions of Teaching—Learning Environments: Handbook for Teachers.* Pasadena, CA: Pacific Oaks College Bookstore, 1973.

Kamii, C. "Leading Primary Education Toward Excellence: Beyond Worksheets and Drill." *Young Children,* 1985, 40: (6), 3–9.

Katz, L. G. "Engaging Children's Minds: the Implications of research for Early childhood Education." In *Resource Guide to Public School Early Childhood Programs,* edited by C. Warger. Alexandria, VA: Association for Supervision and Curriculum Development, 1988.

Kounin, J. W. *Discipline and Group Management in Classrooms.* New York: Holt, Rinehart and Winston, 1970.

Kounin, J. S.; Freisen, W.; and Norton, A. E. "Managing Emotionally Disturbed Children in Regular Classrooms." *Journal of Educational Psychology,* 1966, 57: 1–13.

Kounin, J. S.; and Sherman, L. W. "School Environments as Behavior Settings." *Theory Into Practice,* 1979, 18: 145–151.

Kritchevsky, S.; Prescott, E.; and Walling, L. *Planning Environments for Young Children: Physical Space* (2nd Ed.). Washington, DC: National Association for the Education of Young Children, 1977.

Leeper, S. H.; Witherspoon, R. L.; and Day, B. D. *Good School for Young Children* (5th Ed.). New York: MacMillan Publishing Company, 1984.

Linn, M. C. "Free-Choice Experiences: How do they Help Children Learn?" *Science Education,* 1980, 64: 237–48.

Marshall, H. "The Development of Self-Concept." *Young Children,* 1989, 44: 44–49.

McDonald, F. J.; and Elias, P. J. "The Effects of Teaching Performance on Pupil Learning." *Beginning Teacher Evaluation Study, Phase II, Vol. 1.* Princeton, NJ: ETS, 1976.

Medley, D. M. "The Effectiveness of Teachers." In Research on Teaching (11–27), edited by P. L. Petersen and H. J. Walberg. Berkeley, CA: McCutchan, 1979.

Morrow, L. M.; and Weinstein, C. S. "Increasing Children's Use of Literature Through Program and Physical Design Changes." *The Elementary School Journal,* 1982, 83: 131–137.

Petersen, P. L. "Direct Instruction Reconsidered." In *Research on Teaching* (57–69, edited by P. L. Petersen & H. J. Walberg. Berkeley, CA: McCutchan, 1979.

Petersen, P. L.; Marx, R.; and Clark, C. "Teacher Planning, Teacher Behavior, and Student Achievement." *American Educational Research Journal,* 1978, 15: 417–432.

Phyfe-Perkins, E. *Children's Behavior in Preschool Settings: A Review of Research Concerning the Influence of the Physical Environment.* (ERIC Document Reproduction Service No. ED 168 722), 1979.

Piaget, J. *The Origins of Intelligence in Children.* New York: International Universities Press, 1952.

Piaget, J. *Psychology of Intelligence*. (M. Piercy & D. E. Berlyne, Trans.). Totowa, NJ: Littlefield, Adams, 1966.

Plowden, Lady Bridget, and others. *Children and their Primary Schools: A Report of the Central Advisory Council for Education*. London: Her Majesty's Stationery Office, 1966.

Probst, D. *A Study of Time on Task in Three Teachers' Classrooms Using Different Instructional Modes*. (Technical Report No. 562). Madison, WI: University of Wisconsin, Research and Development Center for Individualized Schooling, 1980.

Rosenshine, B. V. "Content Time and Direct Instruction." In *Research on Teaching* (28–56), edited by P. L. Petersen & H. J. Walberg. Berkeley, CA: McCutchan, 1979.

Rosenthal, B. A. "An Ecological Study of Free Play in the Nursery School." (Doctoral Dissertation, Wayne State University, 1973). *Dissertation Abstracts International*, 1974, 34: 4004A–4005A.

Ruff, F. *Instructional Variables and Student Achievement in Reading and Mathematics: A Synthesis of Recent Process-Product Research*. Unpublished manuscript, Research for Better Schools, Philadelphia, 1978.

Schweinhart, L. J.; Weikart, D. P.; and Larner, M. B. "Consequences of Three Preschool Curriculum Models Through Age Fifteen." *Early Childhood Research Quarterly*, 1986, 1: (1), 15–45.

Sharan, S. "Cooperative Learning in Small Groups: Recent Methods and Effects on Achievement, Attitudes, and Ethnic Relations." *Review of Educational Research*, 1980: 50: 241–271.

Slavin, R. W. "Effects of Student Teams and Peer Tutoring on Academic Achievement and Time on Task." *Journal of Experimental Education*, 1980, 48: 253–257.

Smith, R. F. "Early Childhood Science Education, A Piagetian Perspective." *Young Children*, 1981, 36: 7–9.

Stallings, J. A. "Allocated Academic Learning Time Revisited or Beyond Time on Task." *Educational Researcher*, 1980, 19: (11), 11–16.

Tryon, C.; and Lilienthal, J. W. *Developmental Tasks: The Concept and its Importance, Fostering Mental Health in our Schools*. Alexandria, VA: ASCD, 1950.

Webb, N. M. "Student Interaction on Learning in Small Groups." *Review of Educational Research*, 1982, 50: 421–445.

Weinstein, C. S. "Modifying Student Behavior in an Open Classroom Through Changes in the Physical Design." *American Educational Research Journal*, 1977, 14: 259–260.

Wilson, B. K. *Effect of Task and Authority Structures on Student Task Engagement*. Paper presented at the meeting of the American Educational Research Association, Montreal, Quebec, Canada, April, 1983. (ERIC Document Reproduction Service No. ED 230 416).

SECTION 3

Critical Issues

Introduction

The Council of Supervisors & Administrators of the City of New York maintains that collaboration must take place in the communities and the districts where the action is. We emphasize the importance of networking between Day Care Directors and public school supervisors. We advocate the public school program which is a comprehensive model, similar to the ACD model, that stresses parent involvement, social services, health and nutrition services and developmentally appropriate experiential curriculum. The public school program deals with the children from birth to age eight—270,000 children in New York City public schools. Parents are getting younger, but there is a program through the Health and Hospitals Corporation that is designed to help them finish school. There is a teacher on site in many hospitals who contact these teenage mothers at the birth of their child. Emphasis is placed on the mother going back to school and the baby is cared for in a quality day care setting.

Life Program—The child is brought to school and cared for while the parent finishes her education. The parent has to be 18 years old or younger and former high school student. This program services about 300 babies and mothers. Legislative grants are needed to expand upon these programs. Note the various public school programs.

Pre-K Program—the most comprehensive program. It's in 27 out of 32 districts, but only 12,500 children. This is funded by the New York State Department of Education.

Project Giant Step—Geared to four-year-olds, funded by City tax levy funds.

Project Child—involves 153 schools and fosters linguistic English, problem solving skills. Class size is reduced to 22 children. A committee composed of principals, teachers, and UFT Chapter Chairmen plan and implement the program and purchase materials.

All Day Kindergarten—established in 1983. Hours are from 8:30 A.M.– 2:30 P.M. and 60,000 children are serviced. Parents need more services. For example, some children may come from a home where another language is spoken. One hundred and six languages are spoken by New York City school children.

Summary Primary—There are 1,194 classes servicing 24,000 children for six weeks in Kindergarten, 1st and 2nd grades, not a promotional program. Parents are a part of the program.

Project Sail—developed by UFT in public schools which emphasize school based management and shared decision making by people on site. It is an unstructured program for five, six, seven and eight year olds.

Satellite Schools—encourage businesses to develop school settings on site for Kindergarten–2nd grade. Satellite schools relieve some of the overcrowding and lead to economic and ethnic mixing in the school setting.

Curriculum Guides—For Pre-K, 1, 2, 3, 4 are available from the Board of Education.

Training is a different task—the Chancellor's office initiatives pinpoint multicultural, interdisciplinary education which includes children, parents, teachers, and principals and takes feelings and needs into account. Many children after 3rd grade go into special classes. Special needs must be identified early. We dream of a better day and more services for children and families.

*Donald Singer is President of the Council of Supervisors and Administrators

CHAPTER 16

An Acute Shortage of Qualified Early Childhood Teachers: A National Disaster

If Ravitch and Finn asked a sample group of 17 year olds what our nation's most valuable resource is going into the 21st century, and they gave the wrong answer, we wouldn't be at all surprised. However, when America's industrial, political and educational leaders cite vital energy and mineral resources, sufficient food supplies for a burgeoning population, and a healthy biological environment, we have reason for grave concern. Clearly, our nation's most vital resource is our children in whose hands we place our world future. Theirs is not an enviable task. They must grapple with inherited global problems and seek the means of rectifying generations of wanton mismanagement of our natural resources.

As professional educators, our primary task must be to shore-up the sagging infrastructure of our American public school system. Our involvement must transcend the much needed allocation of additional funds, it requires creative restructuring and risk-taking. If there is one thing that we learned from Lyndon Johnson's Great Society, it is that financial commitment to our schools alone will not significantly change our dinosaur-like educational system. The use of much needed funding requires careful preplanning prior to implementation. The one program still remaining as a proud beacon of what the Johnson administration attempted is head start. The classic Ypsilanti, Michigan, longitudinal study comparing adults with Head Start experience with a control group overwhelmingly demonstrated the imporance of quality preschooling. While most of the Head Start group were gainfully employed, their counterparts were either on the welfare rolls or incarcerated. The message appears to be clear to policymakers that the diversion of vast funds to guarantee quality early childhood services pays off in the long-run in terms of more productive students entering into the work force. The alternative scenario is the reinforcement of a nonproductive under-class of welfare recipients and criminal offenders, whose cost to society is far greater than early educational intervention programs would be.

Alternative life styles that characterized the 1980's have seriously threatened the traditional nuclear family. While the large majority of

American families are still headed by married couples, the number of families headed by single women or divorcees is growing rapidly (U.S. Census Bureau, 1989). Overall, 79% of all family households were headed by married couples in 1989; 17% were headed by women, and 4% by men. A further breakdown showed sharp racial differences existed in the proportion of families maintained by women. In 1988, 44% of Black families were headed by women as compared to 23% in Hispanic families and 13% in White families. Urie Brofenbrenner (1986) started that approximately 60% of the working mothers returning to the work force were women with children under six years old (p. 278). These statistics coupled with the double-digit inflation rate of the early 1980's forced most household adults into the workforce.

This perhaps laid the foundation for one of the most far-reaching societal changes in a decade marked by rapid change. The entrance of double or single household heads into the world of work created a dire need for competent early childhood services. Our societal needs cut across socio-economic boundaries and equally affected residents of Brownsville and Bronxville, the rich and poor alike. As a consequence, societal change in family needs fostered the rapid proliferation of child care centers, pre-kindergarten programs and the national adoption of the all-day kindergarten.

Traditionally, the main source of financial support for childcare programs has been the federal government, but that pattern was altered by the Reagan administration's emphasis on decentralization. Between 1980 and 1988, the federal government's annual contribution to the State of New York went from between $3 million and $4 million to about $450,000 according to Deb Adler of the State Department of Social Services. Part of those monies was allocated for enabling many minority-group women to go back to school and get the degrees necessary to become New York City day-care teachers. Eventually, many of these women joined the ranks of the public schools. The federal government's answer to this loss of huge chunks of funding was the offering of child-care initiatives, focusing on encouraging the private sector to fill the void left by their fiscal retrenchment.

It's estimated that some 2,000 employers currently provide some form of child-care. Among the corporations and hospitals with on-site centers, the consensus of opinion is that providing child-care services positively impacts recruitment, reduces turnover, absenteeism and tardiness, and improves employee morale. However, most employers are reluctant to establish on-site centers because of high start-up costs which can range between $100,000 to $1 million. The major provider of child care services remains religious institutions. As much as 50% of the child-care services in this country is housed on religious property (Smith, 1984, p.210).

Once considered the stepchild of child-care, day care in private homes has gained a new respectability. Many parents are attracted by the home-like environment, which can cater to school-aged children after school along with their younger siblings. This new found popularity has resulted in the growth of family day-care associations. This banding together provides mutual individual benefits such as child-care training, effective business management practices, and bulk ordering of supplies and equipment.

Private schools like Alphabetland, Children's World, Kinder-Care, La Petite Academies, and Montessori have franchised and are found in most of the affluent suburbs. Some of these newly spawned operations not only offer day-care services, but also offer around the clock baby-sitting and snack bonuses.

Although there is a large variety of service providers in this burgeoning new service area, the overriding grave concern by parents is their children's safety. The nightmarish epidemic of child abuse and sexual molestation has been graphically depicted by the media for the last decade. There are few parents who haven't been exposed to the blaring headlines of supermarket magazines or television feature reports. The case that received the most notoriety was that of the highly regarded Virginia McMartin Preschool in the affluent southern California community of Manhattan Beach. The owner Virginia McMartin, 76, and several family members were indicted on 115 counts of child molestation.

The nationwide shock and revulsion following the Manhattan Beach case triggered what appears to be a media exposé of child-molestation incidents of epidemic proportions. A few days following the McMartin indictments, incidents were reported in three major cities. In Chicago, a janitor at a day-care center was charged with taking indecent liberties with children at the center; in Minneapolis, the artistic director of the famed Children's Theater Company was arrested and charged with sexually abusing three male students, and Los Angeles authorities were investigating possible sexual abuse at two other preschools.

The experts appear to concur in their belief that sexual molestation of children has always been a much more serious problem than almost anyone realizes. Experts vary in their estimate of the extent of sexual abuse. Conservative estimates place the number at one in ten, and more extreme estimates are as many as one in five children being the victims of some kind of sexual abuse, from fondling to rape. In addition, many practitioners working directly with child abuse reports are noting a trend of more and more reported victims being 5 years old or younger. In the United States in 1985, reported cases of child abuse totaled 1.7 million (Dept. of Social Services, 1986). Their sordid findings indicate that the victimization of innocent children is skyrocketing, and increasingly, their molesters are teachers, youth leaders, and day-care professionals entrusted with their care. Parents are asking what must be done to protect our children?

Quality by most child-care services providers is being threatened as low teacher pay drives trained instructors away in droves. According to the National Child Care Staffing Study (1989), nearly half of all child-care teachers leave their jobs each year, many seeking better-paying jobs. The study found that child-care teachers earn an hourly wage of $5.35, the equivalent to an annual income of $9,363 for full-time employment. This is far more distressing when measured against the 1988 poverty threshold for a family of three, which was $9,431.

Yale psychologist Sharon Kagan (1989) reflects the sentiments of many teachers when she posed the question as to why teachers should remain in day-care when they can earn more at McDonalds. Robert Granger (1989) cites the high number of teaching positions that are filled by temporaries and the annual turnover rate estimated as high as 40%. It is difficult to recruit and retain qualified personnel outside the public schools at starting salaries ranging between $11,000 and $12,000.

There were approximately 664 vacancies in New York City's day-care and Head Start system at the beginning of the 1989 school year. Robert Granger (1989) estimates that only 150 newly-graduated teachers will apply for these openings—far short of the number required to fill these vacancies. In addition, it's estimated that 450 current teachers will leave for greener pastures. New York City made a major commitment last year toward retaining its day-care and Head Start teachers by negotiating a contract with the day-care union that raised starting salaries to $24,500 for fully certified teachers. The contract also established a pension plan for Head Start teachers for the first time in the program's 24 year-old history. According to the Bank Street survey (1989), this resulted in a reduced turnover rate of 32% and a reduced vacancy rate of 12%, as teacher morale and a sense of improved future prospects increased.

There is a bill currently being debated in Congress earmarking Federal Funds for Early Childhood Programs. While deployment of large scale funding is necessary to ensure quality day-care services, it must be disseminated to only those service providers who upgrade their salary levels to competitive rates with the public schools and screen their staff more effectively. It seems apparent at this time that the only child-care provider that's doing a reasonably good job in screening new teachers in terms of educational preparation and psychological profiles are the public schools. Whether it is because more rigorous college preparation itself weeds-out many misfits or close screening procedures within the hiring process identify undesirables, the fact remains that the public schools provide a reasonably safe environment. It is safe to predict that higher wages and better fringe benefits will attract the type of early child-care teachers that this country so desperately needs.

Dr. Barry Persky is President of the Doctorate Association. He is Chairman of the Education Department at Walden University and an Adjunct Assistant Professor at Brooklyn College.

References

Fallows, Deborah. "Mommy, Don't Leave Me Here!" *Redbook,* October 1985, 160–164.

Fischer, Mary A. "Crime: In Search of Justice." *Life Magazine,* May 1988, 164–166.

Friedman, Dana. "The Child-Care Challenge: How Are We Really Doing?" *Working Woman,* November 1984, 210–215.

Gerger, David. "Can the Abused Kids be Believed." *U.S. World News,* July 27, 1987, 10.

Granger, Robert C. "Twelve Reasons for the Low Wages in Child Care." *Young Children,* March 1988, 14–15.

Rosenthal, Herman M. "Baby." *The Newsday Magazine,* January 14, 1990, 15–23.

Rowen, Carl T.; and Mazie, David M. "Day Care in America." *Reader's Digest,* June 1985, 103–108.

Smith, Richard M. "Assault on the Peaceful." *Newsweek,* June 10, 1988, 44.

CHAPTER 17

Design of a New York City Validity Study for the NTE Specialty Area Test in Early Childhood Education*

Introduction

The following provides a research plan for a study which is required to assess the validity of the NTE Speciality Area Test in Early Childhood Education as it is used by the New York City public school system. This plan can be used as a prototype for other school systems because such validity studies are required wherever the NTE tests are used. The three components of this study are: 1) content review of the test as it is related to college and university teacher education programs, 2) content review of the test as it is related to the entry-level job requirements of New York City Teacher of Early Childhood Education, and 3) identification of potential criteria, standards or passmarks which reflect minimally acceptable performance of an entry-level New York City Teacher of Early Childhood Education.

The study described below is necessary because the NTE Specialty Area Test in Early Childhood Education is required by the New York City school system. The *Guidelines for Proper Use of NTE Tests* (Educational Testing Service, 1985b) specify that validity and standard setting studies must be conducted as prerequisites for the use of NTE tests. As indicated below, this requirement is consistent with newly promulgated New York State law. Consequently, the Educational Testing Service—publisher of the NTE examinations—has apprised the New York City Board of Education that such studies must be conducted.

The NTE Specialty Area Test in Early Childhood Education

The NTE Specialty Area Tests are two-hour tests designed to measure the knowledge and academic skills generally acquired by examinees in preparing for teaching careers in specific fields. These tests focus on areas covered by most teacher education and training programs. The examination in Early Childhood Education is designed for examinees who have

194

completed their undergraduate preparation in this field. As delineated in Educational Testing Service (1988), the purpose and uses of this test are: 1) to measure the examinees' academic competence in Early Childhood Education, 2) to aid educatonal institutions in their efforts to improve teacher preparation, and 3) to provide one type of quantitative information useful in the certification of teachers. A more detailed description of this 150 item test is presented in Table 1.

APPENDIX I

Table 1: Test Content Description—Early Childhhod Education

The examination in Early Childhood Education is intended primarily for candidates who have completed their undergraduate preparation in the field. In keeping with trends in the field, the examination focuses on the candidates' understanding and recognition of appropriate applications of early choldhood education knowledge and theory related to the development of the whole child. Major dimensions of the examination include the following areas:

Content Topics	*Approximate % of test*
I. *The nature of growth, development, and learning of young children*—including aspects of cognitive development (concepts, skills, language), physical development, and personal-social development	30%
II. *Factors that influence growth and development*—including biological, familial, nutritional-hygienic, and cultural factors	10%
III. *The contributions of developmental and curriculum theory to early childhood education practices*—including major streams of developmental theory (e.g., cognitive, behaviorist, social-learning) and major streams of curriculum theory (e.g., Bank Street, Bereiter-Englemann, Kamii, Montessori)	12%
IV. *The planning and implementation of curriculum*—including the planning, selection, and implementation of appropriate curriculum experiences; management of the physical learning environment; behavior management issues and practices; and utilization of family-community resources in the learning program	29%
V. *The evaluation and reporting of student progress*—including the selection and use of formal and informal assessment instruments or procedures, the maintenance of records of a child's progress, and effective communication with parents about a child's total developmental progress	13%
VI. *Professional and legal responsibilities of the early childhood teacher*——including effective teacher interaction with other adults in the learning setting and cognizance of legal regulations that impact on teaching in the early childhood setting	6%

Source: Educational Testing Service (1988)

The Use of NTE Specialty Area Tests in the New York City School System

A passing score obtained on the NTE Specialty Area Test in Early Childhood Education is an essential criterion in one of the routes by which an individual may become licensed to teach prekindergarten through grade two in some New York City public elementary schools (New York City Board of Education, 1986; 1989a). This is an alternative route for teacher licensure, in compliance with the New York City School Decentralization Law 2590-j (McKinney's Consolidated Laws of New York—Annotated, 1981). Currently, this NTE Specialty Area Test route for licensure applies only to those New York City public elementary schools which are ranked in the bottom 45 percent of the annually administered citywide reading test (see, for ranking of schools, New York City Board of Education, 1989b).

In general, the primary route for teacher licensure in New York City includes satisfactory performance on a test administered by the Board of Examiners (see, for Teacher of Early Childhood Education examination announcement, Board of Examiners, 1989). Currently proposed legislation, however, may provide the basis for NTE Specialty Area Tests to replace the written component of some Board of Examiners tests. Should this legislation be implemented, the NTE Specialty Area Tests may be used as the written component of procedures which establish pools of teacher candidates in several disciplines, including Early Childhood Education.

The New York State Education Department has demonstrated the validity of several of the NTE Specialty Area Tests (see, for studies: Educational Testing Service, 1985a; 1985c; 1987). These studies have not included the examination for Early Childhood Education. At this time, none of the NTE Specialty Area Tests has been adopted by the New York State Education Department for use in New York State. Consequently, New York State passmarks have not been mandated for any of these tests. It is noted, however, that the New York State Education Department has: demonstrated the validity of the three NTE Core Battery tests (Educational Testing Service, 1983), established passmarks and adopted the NTE Core Battery for use in New York State.

The manner in which NTE passmarks are established in New York State is defined by New York State law. Specifically, under Chapter 628 of the Laws of 1989, signed by Governor Cuomo on July 21, 1989, the New York State Commissioner of Education has the responsibility of setting NTE passmark scores. Where the Commissioner has not established such passmarks, the Chancellor of New York City public schools may set the passmarks based upon appropriate validity studies. In this instance, the Commissioner has not established a passmark for the NTE Specialty Area Test in Early Childhood Education. Consequently, New York City public schools must conduct a validity study in order to use this test.

Methodology and Objectives of This Study

No single process leading to the setting of standards for certification is generally acknowledged by professional educators and measurement specialists to be either the best or the only defensible method for conducting this type of study. The methods proposed for this particular study are based upon those implemented previously by the Educational Testing Service (1983; 1985a; 1985c; 1987) in validity studies commissioned by the New York State Education Department. In addition, these methods are in accordance with accepted measurement guidelines (e.g., American Educational Research Association, *et al.,* 1985) and federal "Uniform Guidelines" (Equal Employment Opportunity Commission, *et al.,* 1978; 1979). A survey of selected literature dealing with content validity studies, standard setting, and validity-study related issues can be found in Educational Testing Service (1985c, Chapter II). Discussion of related methodology and issues can be found, also, in Angoff (1971) and Livingston & Zieky (1982).

Specifically, the objectives of this study are:

1. To assess the appropriateness of the content of the NTE Specialty Area Test in Early Childhood Education, as it relates to New York City college and university teacher education programs in Early Childhood Education,
2. To assess the appropriateness of the content of the NTE Specialty Area Test in Early Childhood Education to relevant entry-level job requirements of Teacher of Early Childhood Classes in New York City public schools, and
3. To recommend a score (or provide options) on the NTE Specialty Area Test for Early Childhood Education which will serve as the foundation for informed decision-making. It is anticipated that policy-makers will use the recommendation to establish the minimum qualifying score or passmark for licensure. The passing score reflects the minimal level of knowledge required by teachers of Early Childhood Education in New York City and, in addition, other policy related issues such as "supply and demand" and affirmative action goals.

Study Design and Procedures

The suitability of using the NTE Specialty Area Test in Early Childhood Education will be assessed by a representative group of experienced New York City educators who will comprise the following panels: 1) the *Teacher Education Panel* which will review the content of this test in relation to the content of curricula used in the academic preparation of

APPENDIX II

Table 2: Overview of Project Tasks

Advertise panel positions for Board of Education teachers and supervisors

Contact colleges and universities for nomination of teacher educator panel members

Nominate teacher and supervisor candidates (Community School District Superintendents)

Select and confirm participation of panel members (Project staff)

Prepare packets of test materials (Educational Testing Service)

Develop data collection material including: instructions to panel members, teacher education panel questionnaire, job relevance questionnaire, knowledge estimation questionnaire, and related response sheets for each questionnaire

Proof-read and print panel instructions, questionnaires and answer sheets

Prepare background information sheets, rosters, payroll forms and site packets for panel members

Conduct Panel meetings

Perform quality control on forms

Scan forms

Analyze panel data

Prepare tables with panel data

Obtain from Educational Testing Service computer tapes with NTE Early Childhood Examination item and total test data

Statistically analyze test data

Relate panel judgments to actual test data

Prepare report

---

teachers in New York City; 2) the *Job Relevance Panel* which will judge the relevance of the content of the test questions to the job of beginning teacher in New York City; and 3) the *Knowledge Estimation Panel* which will estimate the test performance required of minimally qualified applicants for New York City licensure. An overview of the tasks which comprise this project is presented in Table 2.

To obtain expert judgments, approximately 47 New York City classroom teachers, school administrators and teacher educators will be organized into the three abovementioned panels to review one form of the NTE Specialty Area Test in Early Childhood Education. In all instances, panelists will make their judgments independently. There will not be any attempt to come to consensus of judgment.

At all times, appropriate procedures will be implemented to ensure test security. For example, the test itself will always be carefully monitored and stored in a securely locked closet. No opportunity will be provided for anyone to copy test questions. In addition, all panel members will be required to sign confidentiality forms.

Different Forms of the Test

Currently, there are three forms of the NTE Specialty Area Test in

Early Childhood Education and a fourth form is being developed. In past validity studies, panels reviewed items from several forms of a given subject area test. However, the Educational Testing Service currently supplies only one form of a test for validation studies. Questions from this particular form of the Early Childhood Education test may be grouped according to topic in order to make the task easier for the panel members and to enhance the reliability of the estimates. Should it be deemed advisable to review more than one form of the test, questions from the different forms will be treated as a single pool and will be grouped according to topic. This procedure will be followed to avoid the "order effects" that might occur if one form of a test is judged after the other edition and, also, to avoid the administrative problem of counterbalancing the orders of judgment to control for possible "order effects."

Determination of the Size of the Panels

Several factors will be taken into consideration when the size and nature of the membership of each of the three panels is finalized. These factors include: the availability of qualified teachers, administrators and teacher educators; the need to represent appropriately the diversity of New York City's public school personnel, Community School Districts, and higher education institutions; and the need to obtain sufficiently reliable judgments about each question in the test.[2] On the basis of these considerations, it is proposed that: the Teacher Relevance Panel consist of 15 teacher educators; the Job Relevance Panel consists of 32 public school teachers (i.e., representing 32 New York City Community School Districts); and the Knowledge Estimation Panel consist of 15 teacher educators and 32 public school teachers or administrators.

Nomination and Selection of Panel Members

The objectives which we will attempt to meet in the nomination of panel members are:

- (a) designation of individuals with the requisite expert qualifications. This includes individuals: who are currently serving in New York City public schools as teachers, supervisors or administrators of Early Childhood Education, have had a minimum of two years experience in Early Childhood Education, and have New York State certification or its equivalent; or who are currently serving as a college or university faculty member and teaching courses, for at least two years, in which students planning to teach (or who are currently teaching) are enrolled.
- (b) representation from each New York City Community School District;
- (c) reasonable representation of males and females;
- (d) reasonable representation of diverse racial and ethnic groups; and

(e) reasonable representation of faculties from New York City colleges and universities which offer Early Childhood Education teacher education programs.

Test Content Review and Teacher Education Programs

A *Teacher Education Panel* comprised of New York City college and university-based teacher educators will be established. This panel will review the appropriateness of the content of both individual questions and the test as a whole, as related to the curriculum of teacher education programs.

Teacher Education Panel members will be asked to make judgments on four dimensions: one for each test question and three for the test as a whole. For each question, panel members will be asked to respond *yes, no* or *don't know* if at least 90 percent of all students completing teacher education programs in Early Childhood Education would have had an opportunity to acquire the knowledge or academic skill being tested. For the test as a whole, panel members will be asked to: 1) compare the emphasis given to each major topic in the test with the emphasis given to that topic in the relevant college curriculum; 2) identify any major topics that were covered in the curriculum but were not included in the Test Content Description; and 3) provide an overall evaluation of the similarity between the test and the curriculum offered at their institutions.

For the review of individual test questions, it is anticipated that a question will be classified *content appropriate* if more than 50 percent of the panel members who gave an evaluative response indicated that approximately 90 percent of all students who completed their teacher education program had an opportunity to acquire the knowledge or academic skills tested by that question.

Item data will be analyzed for each of the panel members who provided judgments. Specifically, items evaluated by each panel member will be classified as either *content appropriate* or *not content appropriate*. Subsequently, the percentage of items judged content related will be calculated and reported for each panel member.

For the review of the test as a whole, panelists will be asked to review content areas of the test and to match the curriculum areas. Panel members will be asked to identify important curriculum areas prior to their review of the actual test content specifications. In this manner, areas not covered by the test will be noted. A valid test does not necessarily measure every relevant curriculum area, but every area measured must be relevant.

Specifically, Teacher Education Panel members may be asked to indicate for each test content area if their curriculum emphasized the area *more, less,* or *about the same* than in the test. Panel members' assessments of the degree to which the test content is similar to the relevant curriculum will be summarized.[3] Descriptive statistics (e.g., numbers, percentages, medians and modes) will be reported to summarize panel member judgments of the correspondence between the teacher education and training programs and this test. Panel members will be asked, also, to identify important curriculum areas that were not tested. Curriculum areas identified by more than two panelists may be considered significant.

A high degree of correspondence between the test and the teacher education and training programs is demonstrated when the: 1) *percentage of questions judged content appropriate,* 2) *overall similarity,* and 3) *overall emphasis* between the test and curriculum content are high; and 4) *numbers of major content areas not covered by the test* are low.

The Educational Testing Service (1985c, page V.8) has used broad guidelines to characterize and summarize the overall degree of correspondence between the test and the appropriate portions of the teacher education programs. These guidelines specify that, in order to be characterized as: *very closely related* to the curriculum, the test must satisfy all four indicators of correspondence; *closely related,* the test must satisfy three indicators including both content appropriateness *and* overall similarity plus one additional indicator; *reasonably related,* by satisfying the indicator of content appropriateness *or* of overall similarity, plus at least one additional indicator. The remaining lowest category reflecting the weakest correspondence is described as *questionable relationship.*

Test Content Review and Job Requirements

A *Job Relevance Panel* will be established to judge the extent to which knowledge or skills tested by individual questions are appropriate to the job requirements of an entry-level Teacher of Early Childhood Education in New York City. This panel will be comprised of practicing professionals, such as New York City public school Early Childhood Education classroom teachers and school administrators.

Job Relevance Panel members will be asked to judge whether each test item or question is relevant to competent performance required of the job of a beginning Teacher of Early Childhood Education. In addition, panel members will be asked to judge the importance of test content areas for the first year of teaching. For both item and content area judgments, panel members will be asked to select one of the following four judgment categories: *essential, important, questionable,* and *not relevant.*

Panel members may be asked, also, to indicate the frequency that first-year teachers would apply knowledge in each content area using a scale of: *daily, weekly, yearly* or *less than yearly.*[4] In addition, they may be asked to

list any job relevant skills or knowledges that are not tested. Areas identified by more than two panelists may be considered significant.

Each item will be designated as either *job relevant* or *not job relevant*.
An item will be designated not job relevant if a majority of the panel
judged the item either *questionable* or *not relevant*. The number and
percentages of items found relevant will be presented. The percentage of
job relevant items will be considered the primary evidence of job related-
ness of the whole test.

In accordance with Educational Testing Service (1985c, pages V. 16–
17), the relationship of the test to the job of a beginning Early Childhood
Education may be summarized and described as follows: *very relevant*
(percent of questions judged relevant greater than or equal to 90), *relevant*
(percent of questions judged relevant less than 90 but greater than or equal
to 80), of *questionable relevance* (percent of questions judged relevant less
than 80 but greater than or equal to 65), and *not relevant* (percent of
questions judged relevant less than 65).

Item level data may be obtained and analyzed for each of the panel
members who provided judgments.[5] In this analysis, responses of *essential* or *important* will be considered *job relevant* responses. Responses of
questionable or *not relevant* will be considered *not job relevant*. Each item
will then be considered as *job relevant* or *not job relevant* for each panel
member. Subsequently, the percentage of job relevant items will be calculated for each panel member.

Setting the Minimum Passmark

A *Knowledge Estimation Panel* will be established and will be comprised of both teacher-educators (e.g., college professors) and New York
City public school practicing professionals (e.g., classroom teachers, administrators). Each of these two groups will bring a different perspective
to the task of judging the minimum knowledge and skills necessary for
competent performance. It is expected that the Knowledge Estimation
Panel will include those individuals who had served previously on the
Teacher Education and Job Relevance Panels.

The Knowledge Estimation Panel will identify either a single score, or
more than one score from which policy-makers will select one score, to
serve as the passmark. This passmark will serve as the minimum qualifying score which estimates the minimal level of knowledge and skills
required by entry-level New York City Teachers of Early Childhood Education.

Specifically, panel members will estimate the proportion of minimally
knowledgeable first year teachers who would be expected to know the

answer to each test question. They will use an eight-category scale, as follows: 2%, 10%, 25%, 40%, 60%, 80%, 98%, and DNK (Do Not Know). For questions characterized as *content appropriate* (i.e., by the Teacher Education Panel) and, also, as *job relevant* (i.e., by the Job Relevance Panel), the study-derived passing raw score will be estimated by averaging the percentages (converted to proportions) selected by Knowledge Estimation Panel members across questions and then summing these values for the entire test. Summary statistics and the distribution of scores will be reported.

The relevance and implications of additional issues may be assessed. These may include, for example: 1) corrections or adjustments related to guessing, and 2) estimation of the potential effects of shortening the test by eliminating questions judged *not content appropriate* (to teacher education programs) and/or *not relevant* (to entry-level job of Teacher of Early Childhood Education). In addition, reliability of the panel judgments will be assessed.

Subsequently, the obtained mean raw score will be converted to a corresponding mean scaled score using an NTE score conversion table and equation provided by the Educational Testing Service. This mean scaled score will be rounded to the nearest "10" to match the manner in which the Educational Testing Service reports individual scores. Consequently, passmarks will be three digit scores that end in zero.

In addition to taking into account the Standard Error of Measurement for the Early Childhood Education test, other factors may be considered when establishing passmarks. These factors may include the: need for adequate numbers of qualified new teachers, supply of new teachers, need to maintain an adequate pool of teachers from all segments of the New York City population and risks of certifying unqualified applicants compared to risks of not certifying qualified applicants (see, for discussion, Educational Testing Service, 1985c, chapter IV).

In addition to judgmental data provided by the panels in this study, empirical data (i.e., actual test scores) will be requested of the Educational Testing Service. Specifically, the Educational Testing Service will be asked to provide computer tapes of item and total test performance on the Early Childhood Education test for examinees designating the New York City Board of Education as a score recipient. Both panel judgments and actual test scores will be helpful in establishing minimum passmarks.

In conclusion, federal "Uniform Guidelines" (Equal Employment Opportunity Commission, *et al.,* 1978, Section 5.H., page 38298) indicate that: "where cutoff scores [i.e., passmarks] are used, they should normally be set so as to be reasonable and consistent with normal expectations of acceptable proficiency within the work force." It is the purpose of this study to provide information which will be helpful for establishing such cutoff scores for entry-level New York City Teachers of Early Childhood Education.

Bibliography

American Educational Research Association, American Psychological Association, National Council on Measurement in Education (1985). *Standards for Educational and Psychological Testing.* Washington, D.C.: American Psychological Association.

Angoff, W. H. Scales, Norms, and Equivalent Scores. In R. L. Thorndike (ed.), *Educational Measurement.* Washington, D.C., American Council on Education, 1971, pp. 514–515.

Board of Examiners (1989). *Examination Announcement—Examination for License as Teacher of Early Childhood Classes in Day Elementary Schools (Grades Pre—KG—2) Men and Woman Examination Code No. 787B.* Brooklyn, New York: Board of Education of the City of New York.

Educational Testing Service (1983). *Report on a Study of the NTE Core Battery Tests By The State of New York.* Princeton, New Jersey.

Educational Testing Service (1985a). *Content Validity Analysis of the NTE Specialty Area Test in Special Education.* Princeton, New Jersey.

Educational Testing Service (1985b). *Guidelines for Proper Use of NTE Tests.* Princeton, New Jersey.

Educational Testing Service (1985c). *Report on a Study of Selected NTE and GRE Tests by the State of New York.* Princeton, New Jersey.

Educational Testing Service (1987). *A Study of the Content Validity of Three NTE Specialty Area Tests and Five Consortium Tests.* Princeton, New Jersey.

Educational Testing Service (1988). *NTE Programs: The Examination in Early Childhood Education.* Princeton, New Jersey.

Equal Employment Opportunity Commission, Civil Service Commission, Department of Labor, Department of Justice (1978, August). Adoption by Four agencies of uniform guidelines on employee selection procedures. *Federal Register, 43* (166).

Equal Employment Opportunity Commission, Office of Personnel Management, Department of Justice, Department of Labor, Department of the Treasury (1979, March). Adoption of questions and answers to clarify and provide a common interpretation of the uniform guidelines on employee selection procedures. *Federal Register, 44* (43).

Livingston, S. A., & Zieky, M. J. (1982). *Passing Scores: A Manual for Setting Standards of Performance on Educational and Occupational Tests.* Princeton, New Jersey: Educational Testing Service.

McKinney's Consolidated Laws of New York—Annotated (1981). St. Paul, Minn.: West Publishing.

New York City Board of Education (1986). Pedagogical personnel—local selection of teachers. *Regulation of the Chancellor,* No. C-221, issued 6/26/86. Brooklyn, New York.

New York City Board of Education (1989a). Appointments through alternative teacher selection method to Community School Districts for school year commencing September 1989. *Personnel Memorandum,* No. 37, 1987–88. Brooklyn, New York: Division of Personnel.

New York City Board of Education (1989b). *Ranking of Schools by Reading Achievement—Spring 1988*. Brooklyn, New York: Office of Educational Assessment.

Endnotes

1. Appreciation, for their assistance, is expressed to Ms. Catherine Havrilesky (Executive Director, Teacher Programs and Services) and Ms. Marlene Goodison (Director, NTE Programs) of the Educational Testing Service in Princeton, New Jersey.

2. In some past validity studies, panels were divided into comparable halves for purposes of analysis. The Educational Testing Service has recommended that the panels not be split in half and that the split-half comparisons are not required.

3. In some past validity studies, a Degree of Relative Emphasis (DRE) statistic was calculated for these data. However, difficulty in interpreting this statistic was reported in Educational Testing Service (1985a).

4. These procedures are optional in the sense that they are not required by the *Guidelines for Proper Use of NTE Tests* (Educational Testing Service, 1985b).

5. These procedures are optional in the sense that they are not required by the *Guidelines for Proper Use of NTE Tests* (Educational Testing Service, 1985b).

*Dr. Gary M. Kippel is a Certified Psychologist. He is Assistant Director of Educational Research at Headquarters of the New York City school system and Adjunct Associate Professor of Management at Pace University's Lubin Schools of Business.

CHAPTER 18

On Redshirting Kindergartners

No one would consider it a new experience to find that one person takes more time than another to perform with equal success the same kind of task. As a matter of fact, probably all of us have been exhorted to take our time in a given situation, the assumption being that taking more time would increase our chances of success. Nowhere is this more dramatically illustrated than in the area of intercollegiate athletics, where a practice called "redshirting" is standard procedure.

Success in athletics has become a high priority for most colleges. Consequently much effort is expended in helping each athlete develop maximum potential. Redshirting is based on the assumption that such development may take more time in some cases. An athlete may, therefore, spend an entire year concentrating on increased development of physical strength and skills rather than participating in competitive sports. The extra time is likely to lead to greater future success.

Curiously, though, this principle has been completely abandoned by those who plan and implement the education of young children. The child who takes longer than others to accomplish a given task becomes immediately suspect. Consistently taking more time eventually labels a child as a "slow learner" with accompanying limitations on future achievement. There does not appear to be a compelling reason why the redshirt principle cannot be applied with equal success to the educational development of young children.

In almost every case, schools admit children once per year to begin their formal education. In most kindergarten classes, upon entrance to school, there will be about a year's difference in maturity between the youngest and the oldest. At the end of the school year, however, all children are expected to have reached roughly the same standard. For many children the time allotted is insufficient for such achievement. It would appear that the redshirt principle would provide the ideal solution. Elson (1989) reports that in some cases redshirting is most effective if done before the child enters kindergarten on the assumption that poor performance in a first school experience could do permanent damage to that child's chances for success. Others suggest that redshirting may be more effective at the conclusion of the kindergarten year. (Frick, 1985).

At this point there is not enough evidence available to draw any meaningful conclusions regarding academic redshirting. It is not clear to what extent this practice can interact positively with the many forces active in a child's school life. Most of the forces operating in the case of athletic redshirting tend to support the high priority given to athletic success. Such is not the case in the educational arena.

No educational policy or strategy can operate outside the societal setting in which it exists. The assumptions which members of a society accept without often thinking about them and certainly without questioning them profoundly affect the success or failure of educational practices. The attitudes and values of society in general determine how much pressure is put on educational decision makers to address any one particular issue. For example, many educators and politicians have expressed great concern over the escalating problems of children referred to as "at risk." Yet little is heard from an aroused public about this issue (Olson, 1988). A public as aroused over "at risk" children as it is over abortion, for example, is still to be heard from.

Accepted life styles of society's members likewise provide a setting in which educational practices are more or less successful. McLanahan (1988) referred to such life styles. While her focus was on single parenthood, she nevertheless pointed out that the life styles of the entire community help determine the educational and economic future of its members.

These two examples help emphasize the influence of society's attitudes on educational practices. There are, however, some much more widespread attitudes which have the kind of effect that profoundly influences education nationwide and has critical implications for the practice of redshirting.

The first of these is the generally accepted attitude toward that which we call ability. This word represents a concept used universally; yet a satisfactory definition continues to elude us. When applied to children, especially in school, the concept ability means for most, if not all, people the fact that one person can accomplish something in less time than it takes another person to accomplish the same thing. For about a century psychologists have been claiming to measure ability. Children are given a task to achieve, and those who complete the task in less time or at an earlier age than others are considered to have more ability. Such a definition is completely arbitrary. It is based on the notion that by combining predetermined quantities of achievement and time one can infer the qualitative variable, ability. The fact that such inferences have been wrong countless times does not deter their continued use.

The practical result of all this is that many children have become victims of an educational system that claims to have determined their ability and then educates them accordingly. The education of children having been defined as "low ability" children or "slow learners is not pursued as aggressively as that of those identified as "high ability" or "fast" learners.

The concept of redshirting is based on the assumption that with respect to mastering the necessary skills, all children enter kindergarten with equal ability. Ability is defined as potential, with no reference at all to time. Thus a kindergartner who has sat out a year has the opportunity to reach a high degree of mastery of the requisite skills and become an eminently successful student without being burdened by artificial time restraints. Implementing such a common sense strategy is extremely difficult in a setting which reflects a societal insistence on accepting faulty definitions and an educational system which has made time its highest priority.

But the mischief doesn't stop here. The damage wrought by indefensible assumptions about ability is compounded by the educational practices pursued in schools. Teachers and administrators have taken a perfectly sound concept like individualized instruction and completely distorted it to fit a scheme designed to account for perceived differences in ability.

Individualized instruction as an idea has been around forever. Its use as a carefully planned and implemented educational procedure is more recent. The idea, of course, is that teachers should develop instructional methods that take into account variations in children's maturity, interests, and dispositions. What has happened is that individualized instruction has become individualized curriculum. Teaching procedures remain the same, but the curriculum is varied to accommodate differences in children.

Already in kindergarten children are sorted out according to their "ability." Those who need more time than others are quickly labeled and taught accordingly. This early labeling continues throughout the educational career of these children. They are categorized and grouped and tracked for the next twelve years. Instead of receiving variations in their instructional experiences so that they can master the same curriculum as other children, they receive the same instructional experiences, but the curriculum is watered down so that they can appear to be successful in school. This charade culminates in high school where each student is in one of three tracks—college preparatory, vocational, or general. Obviously the general curriculum is not the same as the college preparatory curriculum.

Redshirting implies that each child is given the most challenging curriculum and provided the necessary time and instruction, without penalty or stigma, to master the same curriculum as everyone else.

Another widespread societal attitude that has profound implications for anything that goes on in education, including redshirting, is the notion that schools must be organized into grades. The concept of the non-graded school has appeared occasionally in the past and even had fairly strong support at the time of the focus on the "open school" during the late 60s and early 70s. But the idea never really caught on, and today the huge majority of schools use the graded structure (Cuban, 1989).

While many children have achieved great success in the graded school, a significant number have serious problems with such a structure. The difficulty arises when a child has not mastered the curriculum for a given grade. Such a situation requires that the teacher consider whether the child in question might be more successful in the next grade or would be more successful given an opportunity to master the necessary information and skills by repeating the grade just completed.

Promoting a child to the next grade unready—often called social promotion—has always been looked upon with some skepticism. The whole idea seems to violate common sense. Consequently, retention in a grade has become a much more accepted procedure, especially during the 1980s. Unfortunately, retention has no more positive effect on achievement than social promotion. Years of research have demonstrated that retention in a grade does not accomplish its purpose (Doyle, 1989).

Children who have not satisfactorily completed the work in a given grade are, therefore, faced with two losing alternatives. They may be socially promoted or they may be retained in the previous grade. Neither of these options is likely to be successful. Society has decided to call such children "at risk." Cuban (1989) insists that maintaining the graded structure makes educational improvement for these children impossible. He states:

> No significant improvement will occur in the school careers of at-risk students without fundamental changes in the graded school, and current restructuring proposals will not achieve that end. (p. 799)

Cuban goes on to warn that simply abolishing the graded structure and changing nothing else will not achieve the desired effect. Changes in other facets of school operation are necessary if the elimination of grades is to lead to school improvement. Such changes, of course, will require first of all a change in attitudes among all members of society, educators and non-educators alike.

But what are the chances of changing societal attitudes toward this kind of issue? Doyle (1989) sheds some light on this question. He attempted to convince various people, including educators, that research evidence regarding retention in a grade contradicted conventional wisdom. Yet he was only slightly successful. Many of his subjects maintained the position that retention would be helpful, even in the face of evidence to the contrary.

Clearly, then, public attitudes and values constitute a social environment which must always be considered when contemplating the potential effectiveness of a change in educational strategies. It is no different with the redshirt concept. Certainly redshirting would be significantly more successful in a non-graded than a graded school. However, eliminating the grades without changing prevailing attitudes, especially among teachers, would prevent the redshirting operation from being as successful as it might. This suggests still another prevailing attitude which has serious implications for the entire endeavor, and that is expectations.

The public in general has certain expectations of schools and the children who attend them. Educational reform efforts are the result of a public perception that schools have not lived up to expectations. But far more influential on a given child's achievement are the expectations teachers have of that child. A great many things teachers do in the classroom, including little things, convey the message that tells children whether or not they're expected to do well (Good and Brophy, 1989). These expectations are strongly related to prevailing attitudes about ability and individualization of educational procedures.

As indicated earlier, when a group of children enters kindergarten, the teacher is likely to begin the school year by using various measurements to determine something about those children. Presumably the results of such measures give the teacher information about the maturity, past achievements, and readiness of each child. All too often, however, these activities result in a decision about the "ability" of each child, and the teacher quickly adjusts expectations to fit this presumed "ability." It doesn't take children long to figure out what the teacher thinks of their potential for success. Such expectations eventually are reinforced by parents and finally the children themselves adopt a position of limited expectation for themselves (Comer, 1988).

As also referred to earlier, at this point the teacher decides that individualized attention is in order. Such individualization is not likely to make it possible for all children to master the same skills. It is more likely to modify the curriculum for those who have been labeled as being "low ability," and from then on these children, knowing that not much is expected of them, perform accordingly. These procedures are then repeated in grade after grade until such children have completed their school careers, miseducated and underachieving.

The redshirting program is designed to maintain high expectations of children who require additional time to master the curriculum. It is clear, however, that current public attitudes, including those of educators, about ability, grades, and individualized curriculum may present an insurmountable obstacle for a program that might otherwise have great promise. Convincing all the teachers in a school, and they must all be convinced if redshirting is to succeed, that all children can master the most challenging curriculum seems remote. Nevertheless, with the fate of so many children at stake, the effort must be made to change such attitudes, and redshirting may very well be a vehicle to help accomplish this change.

The redshirting concept is probably most relevant early in the child's school career. There appears to be considerable agreement that school reform ought to begin at the earliest possible age on the theory that you don't need to remediate at age 12 what you prevented at age 5. The child's early developmental experiences are, of course, critical to continued positive development in school. Transition from home to school represents an important stage in the young child's life. The child's success or failure during the first year or two in school has serious implications for that child's future emotional health. All the more reason that children ought to feel successful in school, and if any children have not developed the maturity needed to master the kindergarten tasks, for example, there ought to be a way for them to take the additional time necessary without being stigmatized.

For many years educators have bandied about the term "readiness." But there seems to be less discussion aimed at answering the question, "Ready for what?" Readiness for reading has been rather taken for granted as a useful term. Readiness for school in general is likewise a popular concern. Gold (1987) reports on a meeting of the National Association of Early-Childhood Specialists where the concept of readiness received considerable attention. Instead of the question, "Is the child ready for school?", it was suggested that a more appropriate question would be "Is the school ready for the child?" Many schools have intensified their focus on academic skills in kindergarten, resulting in a curriculum that is really quite inappropriate, says the Association.

Everyone is aware of the continuing debate about what constitutes a desirable curriculum for children in kindergarten. The redshirt idea is a response to the combination of emphasis on academic skills in kindergarten and a rigid graded structure. Given prevailing societal attitudes, it is in fact difficult to provide an extra year of study for kindergartners, irrespective what it is called, without running the risk of a sense of failure and the accompanying stigma. The National Association of Early-Childhood Specialists has strong reservations about any kind of program requiring an additional year of study unless it qualifies as a "decent developmental program" (Gold, 1987).

A word needs to be said about social development and its relation to readiness for experiences the child is likely to meet in school. Many children, particularly from low income areas, miss the kinds of activities in their early years that would enhance their social development and prepare them more effectively for school life. Comer (1988) suggests that such children may indulge in behavior which is appropriate in their community but looked upon as bad behavior in school. Teachers' responses are likely to be to "punish the bad behavior rather than close the developmental gap."

The redshirt experience is designed to assist children in their social as well as emotional and intellectual development. But, again, its effectiveness depends entirely on the degree to which teachers can shed negative attitudes and become imbued with a positive spirit that breeds success.

Many teachers have taken the position that the school cannot be all things to all children. If that is so, the logical question then becomes, "What can the school be to all children?" The worrisome part of this issue is the uncomfortable feeling that there are teachers who do not believe the school can be *anything* to some children, even though it can be all things to other children. At this point it appears again that teachers fail to rise above the commonly accepted attitudes of society. People in general simply do not expect all children to be successful in school. The entire educational system is structured and operated in the interest of a particular segment of the population. A report by the William T. Grant Foundation Commission (1988) on the forgotten half of America's youth laments:

> Our society has become so preoccupied with those who go on to college that it has lost sight of the half of our young people who do not. More and more of the non-college bound now fall between the cracks when they are in school. Then they either drop out or graduate inadequately prepared to fill their adult roles as parents, workers, and citizens. (p. 283)

But in addition to examining their attitudes, it behooves teachers and administrators to examine teaching practices as well. The concept of effective schools, for example, has developed into a movement which has attracted many followers. Criteria for effectiveness are established and schools are measured against those criteria to reveal the degree of effectiveness attained. Glickman (1987) points out that effective schools are not necessarily good schools. He found that even educators have different standards for a good school from those they have for an effective school.

What promoters of effective schools are actually fostering is *efficient* schools, particularly academically efficient schools. No wonder, then, that time becomes such a high priority. Teachers are evaluated on how well they remain on task; students are evaluated on how well they score on tests. The whole operation becomes as mechanized as any factory. Teachers begin each day by entering the school assembly line and keeping it moving relentlessly the entire day. Children embark on their educational adventure as if enclosed in a vehicle with no windows, only a front view. There are no opportunities to enjoy the scenery along the way and no stops to engage in unplanned experiences, however pleasant and desirable they might be. When tests show that the school has met the demands of the normal curve and half of the children score at the national average, there are congratulatory handshakes all around. Such a school might very well be efficient, but by no stretch of the imagination can it be called good.

Early childhood advocates have long protested against such a focus on academic efficiency at an early age (Gold, 1987). Since early development has such a profound effect on later school success, the demand that kindergarten children meet standards of intellectual mastery many times leads to situations opposite of those sought by the school. In spite of misgivings by many teachers about the wisdom of including social and emotional development in the curriculum, Comer (1988) insists that this is in fact an important role of the school. The whole point of redshirting is to provide an opportunity for children with a developmental lag to reach the kind of maturational status which ensures success in school.

Educational reform during the 1980s has become part of the agenda of the nation as well as of individual states. State and local legislation, university projects, local district reforms, and public inquiries have characterized the educational scene through most of the decade. And yet, *ETS Developments* (1987) reports:

> . . . our high schools graduate 700,000 functionally illiterate young people every year—and another 700,000 drop out.

The educational reform movement of the 1980s has been broader and deeper than most previous movements. Nevertheless, membership in a miseducated underclass has, if anything, become larger. These questionable results of what appear to be genuine efforts can perhaps be explained by what Glass and Ellwein (1986) call a distinction between instrumental and symbolic reforms. Instrumental reforms reach the fundamental processes of teaching and learning, while symbolic reforms convey the message to the public that things have changed for the better when they in fact have not. Glass and Ellwein conclude:

> . . . the system can undergo a thorough revolution without any changes occurring in outsiders' perceptions of it; *more often (emphasis added) outside perceptions of the system change without any real changes in the system itself.*

The redshirting issue is no different. Unless the program is accompanied by necessary changes in attitude and procedure, a promising concept will produce no real changes in the lives of children who need alternative routes to an education. If the redshirt year is no more than another year of more of the same—another year of academic drudgery—it, too, will be no more than symbolic reform of those practices that lead to the miseducation of a significant proportion of American youth.

Bibliography

1. Comer, James. "Teaching Social Skills to At-Risk Children." *Education Week,* Nov. 30, 1988, 28.
2. Cuban, Larry. "The 'At-Risk' Label and the Problem of Urban School Reform." *Phi Delta Kappan,* June, 1989, 70:10, 780-4, 799–801.
3. Doyle, Roy P. "The Resistance of Conventional Wisdom to Research Evidence: The Case of Retention in Grade." *Phi Delta Kappan,* Nov. 1989, 71:3, 215–20.
4. Elson, John. "The Redshirt Solution." *Time,* Nov. 13, 1989, 134:20, 102.
5. Educational Testing Service. "National Effort Needed to Raise the Quality of Literacy in America." *ETS Developments,* Summer, 1987, 33:1, 2.
6. Frick, Ralph. "In Support of Academic Redshirting." *Education Week,* Jan. 16, 1985, 24.
7. Glass, Gene V.; and Ellwein, Mary Catherine. "Reform by Raising Test Standards." *Evaluation Comment,* December, 1986, 1–6.
8. Glickman, Carl D. "Good and/or Effective Schools: What Do We Want?" *Phi Delta Kappan,* April, 1987, 68:8, 622–4.
9. Gold, Deborah. " 'Readiness' Goal Seen Producing Harmful Policies." *Education Week,* Dec. 2, 1987, 1, 6.
10. Good, Thomas L.; and Brophy, Jere E. *Looking in Classrooms.* 3rd ed. New York: Harper and Row, 1984.
11. McLanahan, Sara. "The Consequences of Single Parenthood for Subsequent Generations." *Focus* Fall, 1988, 11:3, 16–21.
12. Olson, Lynn. "Despite Years of Rhetoric, Most Still See Little Understanding, Inadequate Efforts." *Education Week,* Sep. 21, 1988, 1, 16.
13. William T. Grant Foundation Commission on Work, Family and Citizenship. "The Forgotten Half: Pathways to Success for America's Youth and Young Families." *Phi Delta Kappan,* Dec. 1988, 70:4, 281–9.

CHAPTER 19

Flunking Kindergarten: Escalating Curriculum Leaves Many Behind

Next year Michael Lee will repeat kindergarten because he flunked the Georgia readiness test for first grade. Judging from his fidgety behavior and inability to cope with scissors and other fine-motor tasks, his teacher confirmed that Michael Lee could benefit from another year before going on to first. Across the country the practice of kindergarten retention for many children like Michael Lee is increasing dramatically. In some districts, 10%, 25%, 33%, or as many as 60% of kindergartners are judged to be unready for the academic rigors of first grade. Unready children are provided alternative programming: developmental kindergarten (followed by regular kindergarten), transition or pre-first grade, or repeating kindergarten.

An extra year before first grade is intended to protect unready children from entering too soon into a demanding academic environment where, it is thought, they will almost surely experience failure. Depending on the philosophical basis of kindergarten retention, which differs profoundly from one district to the next, the extra year is meant either to be a time for immature children to grow and develop learning readiness or a time to work on deficient prereading skills.

The advocates of kindergarten retention are undoubtedly well intentioned. They see retention as a way for the school to respond to the enormous differences in background experiences, developmental stages, and aptitudes of the young children who present themselves at the schoolhouse door. They view it as a policy that has the child's best interests at heart and as a means, as they would put it, to prevent failure before it occurs. The question is: Are they right? Is kindergarten retention a helpful remedy for the problems it is intended to address?

For the past four years we have conducted research on the issues surrounding kindergarten retention: What are current practices? What problems are encountered by children who are youngest in their grade? How accurate are the tests used for screening? What are the effects of extra-year programs? What are the differences in school cultures that account for low incidence of retention in one school and high incidence in the next?

In this article we summarize three of our major findings: 1) Kindergarten retention does nothing to boost subsequent academic achievement. 2) Regardless of what it is called, the extra year creates a social stigma. 3) and most ironically, the practice of kindergarten retention actually fosters the problem it was intended to solve—it feeds the escalation of inappropriate academic demand in first grade.

We have been able to locate 14 controlled studies that document the effects of kindergarten retention: 6 studies that were included in Gredler's 1984 major review of the research on transition rooms and 8 newly identified empirical studies.[1] The dominant finding is one of no difference. Gredler concluded that at-risk children, promoted to first grade, achieved as well as or better than children who spent an extra year in transition rooms. The additional studies we located confirmed Gredler's conclusion. Children who spend an extra year in transition rooms are no better off at the end of first grade than comparable children who were recommended to repeat but whose parents refused.

In the study we conducted in Colorado, extra-year children were matched with control children on sex (mostly boys), birth month (mostly near the entrance-age cutoff), and measured readiness at the start of kindergarten. Measured at the end of first grade, there was again no difference on standardized math scores or on teacher ratings of reading and math achievement, learner self-concept, social maturity, and attention span. The only significant result was on standardized reading scores, where the retained children were only one month ahead of promoted children. These no-difference findings are surprising considering that by this time the retained children were a year older and had had an additional year of schooling compared to the control children who began equally at risk. That is, each group of children was tested at the end of first grade. But by the time the retained children were tested, they had had two years of kindergarten and one year of first grade, as compared to one year of kindergarten and one year of first grade for the promoted children.

When parents are asked to agree to retention or transition placement they are often told that, give the extra year to grow, their children will move to the top of their class and become leaders. Research evidence from controlled studies does not support this claim.

How could there be such a discrepancy between research findings and the practical experience of many teachers who watch children blossom and grow during their transition year? For example, a study conducted by Dr. Judith Ford in Norman, Okla., is often cited by the Gesell Institute to support its advocacy of extra-year programs.[2] During their year in transition class, the 27 children in the Norman program gained an average of 55 percentile points on the Metropolitan Readiness Test. Thus children who were in the bottom half of their class at the end of one year of kindergarten were remarkably more ready after an extra year, now with readiness scores more like those of their more mature peers who had gone directly on to first grade.

Though many cite findings such as these as convincing, this study is fatally flawed. As is typical of studies cited by transition advocates, the Norman study had no control groups, which would have been critical in determining what those children would have been like if they had been promoted rather than retained or placed in transition. Nor were children in the Norman study followed up in first grade. Studies with control groups consistently show that gains such as these in readiness do not persist into the next grade. Eventually children end up at approximately the same percentile rank compared to their new grade peers as they would have been had they stayed with their age peers. Young or at-risk students who are promoted perform equally well in first grade.

Kindergarten teachers, however, are generally unaware of these end results. They know only that the retained children are doing better than they did in their first year of kindergarten. In the short run, teachers see progress: longer attention spans, better compliance with classroom rules, and success with paper-and-pencil tasks that were a struggle the year before. Furthermore, many of the transition children are above-average achievers in their first grade class (but, unseen by their teachers, so are an equal number of the matched control children). Some of the transition children are still acting out and doing poorly with worksheets (as are an equal number of control children). After retention has been tried and children are a year older than their classmates, disruptive behaviors that were once thought to be signs of immaturity are now seen as relatively enduring personality traits.

For these few transitory academic benefits, retained children pay with a year of their lives. And, they understand that they could not go on with their classmates because of something that was wrong with them. Many educators believe there is no stigma attached to kindergarten retention, especially if it is "handled properly" by parents. Many especially deny that transition placement—which has a different name and does not involve recycling of curriculum—could be harmful. But children know that they are not making normal progress in the same way they know the meaning of placement in the bluebird reading group. One little girl understood the meaning of her pre-first placement so well that she thought she would also need to go to pre-second before second grade, and pre-third, and so on.

Our conclusion that kindergarten retention is traumatic and disruptive for children is based on interviews at the end of first grade with parents who had previously agreed to developmental or transition placements for their children. The majority of parents said that on balance the extra year had been the correct decision. Even if their children were doing poorly in first grade, they believed they were ahead of where they would have been without the extra year (and we did not tell them that the control group made equal progress). A majority of parents also reported significant negative emotional effects associated with the retention. The apparent contradiction was created by the substantial group in the middle who reported both positive and negative experiences.

The following quotations typify the ambivalent feelings of parents who have a positive "vote" to the program but revealed an undercurrent of regret:

> I knew he was struggling and he knew that he wasn't doing what the other kids were doing so I thought this was right. He's OK now. He does refer back once in a while. He says, "If I would have made it through kindergarten, I would be in second grade instead of first."
>
> Well, the only [problem] was that he wasn't going to be going with the rest of his class into the next grade. But it was only because I told him that he was so special that his teacher wanted to keep him.
>
> I think the biggest drawback is the attitude of other children and adults. Not so much from the teachers, but parents of other children remarking on how he looks so much older, "he should be here," "he should be there," and other children picking up on the fact that he was going to remain in kindergarten, giving him a hard time about that.

> I think it was more of a social thing. It was really hard to explain to her that her friends would be going on and she wouldn't be. That was a real hard part of it. I think it helped her more than it hindered her.
>
> I personally think it's better that we've held her back and she has the possibility of being a little closer to the top than being a grade ahead and being at the very bottom. Some of the negative aspects of it are her own problems dealing with it and saying that she's been held back.

Kindergarten retention is similiar in many respects to tracking and special education placements for mild learning problems. The logic of providing instruction tailored to individual learning needs is admirable, but research has not confirmed the efficacy of separate placements. Instead, research has documented negative side effects such as social stigma, lowered expectations, and watered-down instruction. From findings in these other literatures it is possible to speculate about why kindergarten retention does not produce the expected boost in academic achievement. For example, in a review of research on ability grouping, Robert Slavin found that homogeneously tracked classrooms are ineffective but that within-class groupings do improve learning.[3] He reasoned that within-class grouping for each subject provides a closer fit between student learning and instruction than does a one-time assignment to separate classes on the basis of ability. Similarly, we might reason that kindergarten retention is a very gross and inaccurate way to individualize instruction because it requires a 12-month dislocation. Children who are judged to be unready by three months are treated the same as those who are 12 months behind; a child who seems immature in only one area of development is treated the same as a child who suffers developmental lags in all areas of development.

Kindergarten retention also resembles tracking and special education placement in that a disproportionate number of minority children are selected for extra-year placements.[4] Thus, children who most rely on public education for the opportunity to learn are segregated from their peers on the basis of prior learnings.

Tests used to determine readiness are not sufficiently accurate to make their use for extra-year placements defensible. For example, Kaufman and Kaufman have provided the only reliability data on the widely used Gesell School Readiness Test.[5] They found a standard error of measurement equivalent to six months, meaning that a child measured to be four and one-half years old developmentally and unready for school could very likely be five and fully ready. Although various readiness tests are correlated with later school performance, predictive validities for all available tests are low enough that 30 to 50 percent or more of children said to be unready will be falsely identified.[6]

Over the long term, kindergarten retention has a final negative consequence. Children who are over age for their grade have a much greater likelihood of dropping out of school. The Association of California Urban School Districts reported that children failed in their first two years of school have substantially reduced chances of completing high school.[7] When background factors and achievement are taken into account, children who have been retained or are otherwise over age for their grade are 20 to 30 percent more likely to drop out.[8] These findings hold true in both rich and poor school districts.

The current fad to flunk children in kindergarten is the product of inappropriate curriculum. Over the past 20 years there has been a persistent escalation of academic demand in kindergarten and first grade. What were formerly next-grade expectations are shoved downward into the lower grade. In a recent survey, 18 percent of principals reported that it is district policy to teach reading to all kindergartners; an additional 50 percent of schools teach reading to kindergartners who are "ready and able"; 85 percent of elementary principals say that academic achievement in kindergarten has medium or high priority in their schools.[9]

In a forthcoming article for the *Elementary School Journal,* we document the societal factors behind the escalation: universal availability of kindergartens, pervasiveness of preschool, and Sesame Street. If everyone has had kindergarten, then first grade teachers assume as prerequisites those letter sounds that previously were taught in first grade. If kindergartners already know their letters from Big Bird, then they must be taught something more, or so the argument goes. In addition, our interviews with teachers reveal more immediate sources of pressure: accountability gates in later grades and demands from middle-class parents that children move faster and faster along the track of preprimers and graded workbooks. Schools with high rates of retention in kindergarten are characterized by an "accountability culture." Promotional gates at third grade or sixth grade are translated downward into fixed requirements for the end of first grade. If a first grade teacher is visited by the principal and reprimanded for any child who is below national norms on standardized tests, this teacher in turn communicates to the kindergarten teacher an unwillingness to accept children for first grade who are not ready to read.

Kindergarten teachers also describe the demands imposed by parents. Many middle-class parents visit school and convey that their only criterion for judging a teacher's effectiveness is her success in advancing their child's reading accomplishments. They ignore other evidence of enriching experience and cognitive development. "My child was reading when he came to school. You haven't taught him a thing." What counts for many parents is the number of first grade primers completed in kindergarten because this is a clearly quantifiable measure of progress, like an SAT score for a five-year-old.

More academics borrowed from the next grade is not necessarily better learning. A dozen national organizations, such as the National Association for the Education of Young Children, the International Reading Association, and The National Association of Elementary School Principals, have issued position statements decrying the negative effects of narrow focus on literacy and numeracy in the earliest grades.[10] Long hours of drill-and-practice on isolated skills are detrimental to all children, even those who are able to meet the demands, because tiny, boring proficiencies learned by rote are substituted for conceptual understanding and enthusiasm for learning. Highly formalized activities that occur too early deprive children of time to learn from play, substitute inappropriate symbolic learning for manipulative learning, detach reading from normal language development, stifle natural exploration, and increase stress.[11] More seriously, fixed, higher standards injure at-risk pupils, causing many more children to fail who would have, in due course, done quite well. The clearest victims of inappropriate curriculum are the children who are judged inadequate by its standards, children who can't stay in the lines and sit still long enough.

Many kindergarten teachers acknowledge that extra-year programs would not be necessary if children were being sent on to a more flexible, child-centered first grade. But faced with what they expect will be a punishing experience for the child (and holding generally rosy opinions about the effects of retention), keeping the child in the safety of kindergarten is clearly preferred. Educators do not express awareness, however, that the practice of retention might acutally contribute to the escalation of curriculum. The more that unready children are screened out of school or put in pre-K, the more that kindergarten becomes a place for six-year-olds. Teachers naturally adjust what they teach to the level of the children in their class. If many of the children are older and reading, teachers do not continue to teach as if the room were filled with five-year-olds. Likewise, as more and more "unready" children are removed, first grade becomes a place for seven-year-olds, and instruction is paced accordingly. The subtle adjustment of curricular expectation to the capabilities of an older, faster-moving group can be demonstrated in the research literature on school entrance ages.[12] Each time a district or state raises the cutoff date for school entry, the hope is to eliminate the youngest children who seem unready for school. In a very short time, instruction is adjusted to the new age range and a new youngest group appears inadequate.

One alternative to escalation, retention, and more escalation can be found in the schools we observed that practiced virtually no kindergarten retention. Instead of highly stratified curricula, strict promotion standards, and an insistence that teachers adhere rigidly to the authorized curriculum rather than exercising their creativity, these schools had developed a culture where teachers and principal shared a commitment to adapting curriculum and instructional practices to a wide range of individual differences. They were able to manage heterogeneity without the need to sort, label, track, and retain. Although these non-retention schools were also very academic and teachers had goals for skill development in kindergarten, a child who was not yet proficient would not be failed. Instead there were cooperative understandings between teachers. The kindergarten teacher would begin at the child's level and move him along to the extent possible, and the first grade teacher would pick up where the kindergarten teacher left off. These schools also had more flexible between-grade arrangements. Children moved more freely across grade boundaries, as exemplified by cross-age tutoring or a child visiting the next-higher grade three hours a week for reading instruction.

Our observations indicated that the non-retention schools were neither richer nor poorer than those schools with rigid grade-level expectations; nor did they serve less diverse populations. It should also be noted that the more flexible and individualized arrangements in the non-retention schools did not come at the expense of higher standards. The average standardized achievement test scores for third graders in these schools were no different from those in the high-retaining schools that had become preoccupied with the accountability tests.

When these research findings are presented to groups of educators across the country, we are told that all of our conclusions are credible except the implication that current practices can be changed. A kindergarten teacher stands up in the audience and gives yet another account of what will happen to children who cannot keep pace in first grade. In a workshop for first grade teachers the story is told of the principal who visits each May, test scores in hand, seeking an explanation as to why several of the children are not above national norms. In a state conference of elementary principals, the principals point to their superintendents, who post standardized test scores by school. As long as each group feels powerless to intervene and persists in practices that contribute to the problem, the problem will get worse. More and more children like Michael Lee in Georgia will be told, in one of their earliest encounters with schooling, that they are inadequate.

The answer is still to be found in the schools with appropriate curriculum and collegial understandings among teachers and principal that make retention unnecessary. Once the larger context of curriculum escalation is understood, then perhaps groups of early-grade teachers and their principal will have greater incentive to resist the myriad pressures and reject the factory-model, accountability culture that is rendering more and more children "unready."

Lorrie Shepard is chair of Research and Evaluation Methodology in the School of Education at the University of Colorado, Boulder. Her research focuses on uses of tests in educational settings. Mary Lee Smith is professor in the College of Education, Arizona State University. She specializes in qualitative research methods and studies of diversions in pupils' careers.

References

1. Gredler, G. R. "Transition Classes: A Viable Alternative for At-Risk Child?" *Psychology in the Schools*, 1984, 21: 463–470.

Dolan, L. "A Follow-Up Evaluation of a Transition Class Program for Children with School and Learning Readiness Problems." *The Exceptional Child*, 1982, 29: 101–110.

Jones, R. "The Effect of a Transition Program on Low Achieving Kindergarten Students when Entering First Grade." Unpublished doctoral dissertation, Northern Arizona University, 1985.

Kilby, G. A. "An Ex Post Facto Evaluation of the Junior First Grade Program in Sioux Falls, South Dakota." Unpublished doctoral dissertation, University of South Dakota, 1982.

Shepard, L. A. "Evaluation of Transition Room." Prepared for Kirkwood School District, January, 1984.

May, D. C., and Welch, E. L. "The Effects of Developmental Placement and Early Retention on Children's Later Scores on Standardized Tests." *Psychology in the Schools,* 1984, 21: 381–385.

Mossburg, J. W. "The Effects of Transition Room Placement on Selected Achievement Variables and Readiness for Middle School." Unpublished doctoral dissertation, Ball State University, 1987.

Stapleford, D. C. "The Effects of a Second Year in Kindergarten on Later School Achievement and Self-Concept." Unpublished doctoral dissertation, Michigan State University, 1982.

Turtley, C. C. "A Study of Elementary School Children for Whom a Second Year of Kindergarten was Recommended." Unpublished doctoral dissertation, University of San Francisco, 1979.

2. Ford, J. "The Transitional Classes: A Report to the Elementary Principals." Norman, OK, Norman Public Schools, October 22, 1985 (mimeographed).

3. Slavin, R. E. "Ability Grouping and Student Achievement in Elementary Schools: A Best-Evidence Synthesis." *Review of Educational Research,* 1987, 57: 293–336.

4. California School Readiness Task Force. "Here They Come: Ready or Not." Sacramento, California State Department of Education, February, 1988.

5. Kaufman, A. S., and Kaufman, N. L. "Tests Built from Piaget's and Gessell's Tasks as Predictors of First-Grade Achievement." *Child Development,* 1972, 43: 521–535.

6. Shepard, L. A., and Smith, M. L. "Synthesis of Research on School Readiness and Kindergarten Retention." *Educational Leadership,* 1986, 44: (3), 78–86.

7. Shepard, L. A. "Dropouts from California's Urban School Districts: Who Are They? How Do We Count Them? How Can We Hold Them (Or at Least Educate Them)?" Association of California Urban School Districts, October, 1985.

8. Grissom, J. B. "Structural Equation Modeling of Retention and Overage Effects on Dropping Out" (in press).

9. Educational Research Service. "Kindergarten Programs and Practices in Public Schools." Principal, May 22–23, 1986.

10. National Association for the Education of Young Children. "NAEYC Position Statement on Developmentally Appropriate Practice in the Primary Grades, Serving 5- through 8-Year Olds." *Young Children,* 1988, 43: (2), 64–84. International Reading Association. "Literacy Development and Pre-First Grade." Childhood Education, 1986, 63: 110–111.

11. Elkind, D. *Miseducation: Preschoolers at Risk.* New York: Alfred A Knopf, 1987.

International Reading Association. "Literacy Development and Pre-First Grade: A Joint Statement of Concerns About Present Practices in Pre-First Grade Reading Instruction and Recommendations for Improvement." *Childhood Education,* 1986, 63: 110–111.

Kamii, C. "Leading Primary Education Toward Excellence: Beyond Worksheets and Drill." *Young Children,* 1984, 40: (6), 3–9.

National Association for the Education of Young Children. "NAEYC Position Statement on Developmentally Appropriate Practice in Early Childhood Programs Serving Children from Birth Through Age 8." *Young Children,* 1986, 41: (6), 4–29.

Winn, M. *Children Without Childhood.* New York: Random House, 1983.

12. Shepard, L. A., and Smith, M. L. "Escalating Academic Demand in Kindergarten: Counterproductive Policies." *Elementary School Journal,* Fall 1988 (in press).

CHAPTER 20

"Behind" Before They Start?

Deciding How to Deal With the Risk of Kindergarten "Failure"

Kindergarten was originally a year of relatively informal education designed to form a bridge from home to more formal schooling in the elementary grades (Hill, 1926/1987). Currently, there is concern because it appears that more and more children are at risk for kindergarten failure. Until recently, failure prevention for potential high-risk students focused primarily on children from the lower socioeconomic levels who might not have the necessary background experiences for school success and on children with special needs due to learning disabilities, hearing or vision impairments, or other handicapping conditions that might hinder their potential for learning. Programs such as Head Start (Morrison, 1988) and the Handicapped Children's Early Education Program (May, Meyer, & Trohanis, 1981) were designed in part to help high-risk children get ready for the academic demands of kindergarten or first grade. Through the 70s, for the majority of young children, kindergarten retained its focus on developing school readiness through socialization experiences and learning through play. Readiness for elementary education was defined in terms of attitude and motivation rather than specific academic achievements.

During the 80s, there has been a trend toward identifying high-risk children at all socioeconomic levels who may not be ready for kindergarten. Rather than serving a readiness function in the sense of socializing children for future schooling, kindergarten has become an experience for which children need to be ready when they arrive (Smith & Shepard, 1987). Some critics of the current trend in kindergarten instruction, including NAEYC, believe that expectations have become increasingly high and unrealistic as the curriculum from upper grades has been pushed down to lower levels, thus dooming large numbers of young children to inevitable failure. Others, usually professionals with backgrounds in areas other than child development ages zero to 8, believe that the instructional expectations are appropriate and that many children should enter school when they are older and more mature so that they have a better chance of meeting current academic expectations. While some early educators agree that today's young children are ready for a more academic program than in years past, they caution that the program must fit the children's developmental level (Marzollo, 1987). For whatever reason, many children today

225

are not meeting initial educational expectations, and early childhood educators are faced with using one of the available options for preventing kindergarten failure.

From the traditional early childhood developmental view, the solution appears obvious: Match the curriculum to the children (Bredekamp, 1987; Meisels, 1987). Unfortunately, it is currently more popular to fit the children to the curriculum. With large classes and increasing administrative paperwork responsibilities, teachers find it difficult to treat a broad range of children individually, especially when many are behind the levels expected by fixed state and local standards, Rather than developing more flexible standards, school systems have sought methods that will ensure that children enter kindergarten capable of reaching required objectives prerequisite to success in today's first grade.

Four currently popular, but not necessarily equally efficacious, methods designed to make kindergartners sure winners in the classroom are:

- providing more prekindergarten programs,
- adopting a later school entrance age,
- moving to a developmental placement system, and
- going to a continuous-progress plan, usually with multiage grouping.

Before adopting any of these approaches, educators must consider the implications for the young children whose lives will be touched. Each method offers a procedure for eliminating kindergarten failure; however, potential pitfalls are associated with each.

Programs for Prekindergartners

The results of the long-term studies of children who attended Head Start (Schweinhart & Weikart, 1986) and other experimental early childhood education programs (Lazar & Darlington, 1982; Schweinhart & Weikart, 1985; Schweinhart, Weikart, & Larner, 1986) show academic and personal success and cost effectiveness and support increasing the numbers of programs for prekindergartners. State-funded programs for prekindergartners have been in place in New York, California, Pennsylvania, and New Jersey for more than 10 years; many more states have implemented programs in the 80s (Kagan, 1988). A joint study by Bank Street College of Education and Wheelock College identified 2,800 school districts nationwide having prekindergarten programs (Strother, 1987). Most of these programs are for children from low socioeconomic households and for exceptional children, but many may enroll children from a higher economic level than those in Head Start. Of the programs identified,

> 33% serve special education students, 11% are Head Start programs, 16% are prekindergarten programs funded by the state, 8%

are locally funded prekindergarten programs, 9% are Chapter 1 prekindergarten programs, 6.5% are child-care programs, 2% are child-care programs operated by high school students, 3% are parent education programs, and 8% are magnet school or summer programs (Strother, 1987, pp. 306–307).

Simultaneously, private and parochial prekindergarten programs are rapidly increasing in number. The National Governors' Association Task Force on Readiness identified programs for high-risk 3 and 4 year olds as high priority for state-level action (Riley, 1986).

Many early childhood educators have major concerns about these programs, especially public school programs (Morado, 1986). Although some public school preschool programs are excellent or at least good, there is very serious concern regarding the educational appropriateness of some of these programs. Many are watered-down versions of developmentally inappropriate kindergarten curricula. Too much structure too soon can lead to "elementary school burnout (Elkind, 1987b; Sava, 1987)." Prekindergartens are commonly funded on year-to-year basis, so continuity is not ensured. In many cases, the programs available under various sponsorships are not coordinated and may either overlap or miss providing needed services (such as programs for 3s or parent education). Eligibility criteria frequently rely on family income and place of residence. Some programs also use tests to determine placement. Morado (1986), Meisels (1987), and Peck, McCaig, and Sapp (1988) point to a need for caution because test results are unreliable measures of young children's potential for school success or failure. Finally, Morado (1986) warns against expecting prekindergarten programs to solve problems created by overly academic kindergartens; early childhood educators, including the hundreds who participated in drafting NAEYC's position statements on developmentally appropriate practice (Bredekamp, 1987), insist that all programs for young children—preschool or kindergarten—be geared to the developmental level of the children in the program.

Later School Entrance

The most easily implemented and least expensive method intended to ensure success in the first year of school is having children enter at a later age. That the intention is good does not guarantee that the approach is flawless. Moore and Moore (1975), the foremost advocates of later school entrance, suggest that children enter school between ages 8 and 10. They feel that children are neither neurologically nor physiologically ready for formal schooling until at least age 8. Most educators find this suggestion extreme. What is the quality of care and learning for a nation of children, many with employed mothers, who stay home until they are 8? Money may be saved by school systems, but someone would have to pay for the care and education of the children before they would enter school at 8; it would not be inexpensive.

DiPasquale, Moule, and Flewelling (1980) studied children referred for psychological services. The greatest frequency of referrals was for children in the primary grades, most often children with late birthdates. Most were boys, and most were referred for academic problems. However, DiPasquale et al. believe that because of the possible self-esteem and emotional damage, these children should not be held back a grade but should be given remedial help until they catch up.

Few child developmentalists accept the concepts of behind and catch up. Children can be helped to develop further from wherever they are. Gredler (1980) suggests that the children identified in the DiPasquale et al. study may just have needed a more appropriate instructional approach than they were receiving rather than conventional remediation.

Comparing age of admission to first grade and trends in achievement for a sample of Black and White children, Langer, Kalk, and Searls (1984) found that the oldest school entrants stayed ahead until age 9, but in both ethnic groups the older and younger entrants were equal in academic achievement by age 17. Shepard and Smith (1986) also conclude from their review of research that the effects of age on achievement overall are small and disappear by third grade. Langer et al. (1984) believe that an age-of-entrance change would not solve the problem of some children being "behind grade level standards" because even in the groups where the mean age of the children was higher the younger males were still "behind." Langer et al. (1984) estimate that school systems using kindergarten entrance age cutoffs of 5 years of age by December, January, and February should expect 50% of males and 25% of females to be developmentally "not ready." Systems using September, October, and November cutoffs should expect 33% of the males to be not ready. After reviewing age-effect research, Simner (1983) concluded that raising entrance age is less productive than using a screening program and gearing special instruction to the needs of the children most likely to fail. Once again, child developmentalists generally believe that there is no such thing as "not being ready"; as NAEYC publications often observe, it's high time schools became ready for children (Bredekamp, 1987; Meisels, 1987; Peck, McCaig, & Sapp, 1988).

Developmental Placement

Developmental placement has been popularized by the Gessell Institute (Ames, 1978; Ames, Gillespie, & Streff, 1972; Carll & Richard, undated). This approach hinges on the concept of developmental age as measured by a developmental readiness test. The child is placed in a class appropriate to his or her developmental age. Different approaches may be used depending on whether the readiness test is given before or at the end of kindergarten. A school system that tests before kindergarten may place the children judged not ready in a prekindergarten class or in a so-called developmental kindergarten class, or may ask them to stay home for another year. Children tested at the end of kindergarten and judged not ready for first grade may be placed in a pre-first grade (or transition class).

Most public school systems do not have prekindergarten or developmental kindergarten classes. Therefore, many of the children who need optimal experiences most, often because their home environment is lacking in intellectual simulation, find themselves at home getting farther "behind." (In fact, the initial impetus behind Head Start, for example, was to get children at risk for lack of success in school into appropriate programs that would ultimately enhance their school performance). Both prekindergarten and pre-first grade classes provide children with an extra year to grow before entering first grade. The pre-first grade, however, by offering the extra year after the children have had a year of school experience (i.e., kindergarten), affords the advantage of additional information besides that obtained from the developmental readiness test. Observational and informal assessment test information collected during kindergarten also aids in making placement decisions (Brewer & Simmons, 1984; Peck, McCaig, & Sapp, 1988); teachers can identify and document classroom behaviors such as perceptual/motor deficiencies, daydreaming, short attention span, and other signs of immaturity. Further, children who come from backgrounds that lack prekindergarten enrichment experiences have the opportunity to grow during the kindergarten year and may in fact prove ready for first grade by the end of the year.

Developmental placement has a serious pitfall. The available tests have not been proven consistent and accurate (Meisels, 1987). A major problem with placement by developmental readiness is what is referred to as hit rate. That is, how reliable is the test (to what degree can scores be attributed to differences in test takers' performance rather than to errors in measurement) (National Association for the Education of Young Children, 1988)? Every test includes some error of measurement resulting in some false positives (children identified as ready who are not) and some false negatives (children identified as not ready who really are) (Wilson & Reichmuth, 1984). Further, giving children an extra year is much the same as retaining them, and retention has not proven advantageous for children (Byrnes & Yammamoto, 1986; Holmes, 1986; Shepard & Smith, 1986; Smith & Shepard, 1987). Retention has no academic advantage and may be emotionally damaging to children (Smith & Shepard, 1987).

Morado's (1987) survey of Michigan school districts that had instituted developmental placement documents some of the weaknesses of this approach. Her data reflect a number of factors for serious concern. Morado notes the weaknesses of relying on a single screening test to determine placement because it places a major decision about the children on a very limited behavior sample.

The Michigan teachers rated the importance of various types of activities that might be included in the kindergarten program. Teacher ratings indicated that the activities considered very important for kindergartners in the developmental classrooms were the concrete experiences conventionally viewed as essential for all kindergartens. Activities rated as very important for the regular kindergartens focused much more on formal academics.

Morado also asked teachers to rate each child's behavior. Teachers viewed the children in the developmental classrooms as less socially mature than those in the regular classrooms, but their ratings of both groups' academic behavior were similar. This finding raises the question of whether it is fair to hold children back on a social basis if they are academically ready.

Another problem Morado identified was that typically the children who completed the developmental program were not retested at the end of the year to determine if they were ready for first grade entrance. They were automatically sent on for a second year of kindergarten. Thus, as pointed out by Smith and Shepart (1987), they were locked into being a year behind their agemates for the rest of their school days.

Continuous Progress and Multiage Grouping

In the fourth approach, two or more grades are integrated and children progress at their own rates through an ungraded block. This model has its roots in Montessori (Morrison, 1988), the British Infant School (Devaney, 1974; Short & Burger, 1987), Dewey (1902/1964), and Piaget's developmental theory (Piaget, 1969/1970). Continuous progress and multiage grouping were basic components of open education as implemented in this country in the 70s. With the demise of open education under the onslaught of back to basics in the 80s (Morrison, 1988), continuous progress and multiage grouping lost popularity in elementary education but live on in Montessori and some other prekindergarten and kindergarten programs (Morrison, 1988).

Currently there seems to be a resurgence of interest in continuous progress and multiage grouping (Elkind, 1987a; Goodlad, 1986; Smith & Shepard, 1987). For example, a contemporary version is being implemented at the L. J. Campbell School in Atlanta (Frick, 1985). The Campbell program began by dividing the kindergarten program into four stages and will gradually add grades until K-3 is divided into 13 stages. The traditional grade divisions will disappear. Children will enter school as usual at the age mandated by state law and progress through the stages at their own pace. There will no longer be retention; each year each child will pick up where she or he left off the year before. For example, if a child completes three out of the four kindergarten stages the first year, rather than repeating what he has completed, he begins the second year where he left off, with the fourth kindergarten stage. On the other hand, a child who completes the four kindergarten stages before the end of the first year can move into work that might otherwise have been held off until the second year of elementary school. Children might move through the K-3 block in 2 to 5 years, depending on their capabilities.

Donna Reid Connell reports on her personal experience with a multiage group of kindergarten, first, and second-grade students (Connell, 1987). She taught in a two-room rural primary school that enrolled students from backgrounds ranging from fairly enriched to very impoverished relative to school readiness. She and the other teacher in the school divided the children into two groups with age spans of 3 years each, based on the Montessori and British primary school models. They developed a curriculum suited to the children's cultural and experiential backgrounds and capabilities that fares well when compared with NAEYC recommendations (Bredekamp, 1987). The children could complete the 4-year primary curriculum in 3, 4, or 5 years. There were no grade levels, no retention, and no acceleration as we usually define them. The end-of-year achievement test scores for these children went from the next to the lowest in the district to the highest.

Mounts and Roopnarine (1987) documented another advantage of multiage grouping, comparing the cognitive level of play behaviors of 3 year-olds and 4 year-olds in same-age and mixed-age classrooms. The 3-year olds in the mixed age classrooms engaged in more cognitively mature play than those in the same-age classrooms. In the mixed-age group, the children chose playmates at random; thus, the older and younger children did integrate. Further, the cognitive level of the play of the 4 year-olds was the same in both classrooms. Mounts and Roopnarine (1987) believe that while the younger children are learning higher level play behaviors, the older children are refining the skills they have already learned. They conclude that their study, along with other research in the area, supports the value of mixed-age grouping in classrooms for young children.

David Elkind (1987a), a strong supporter of multiage grouping, summarizes the advantages. First, multiage grouping accommodates to the child's biological clock rather than relying on age as the primary factor in instruction. It gives all children the opportunity to be the oldest and most mature at some point in their school career. Research shows peer cooperation and peer tutoring increase the achievement of both the more advanced and the less advanced children (Tudge & Caruso, 1988). Multiage grouping offers a greater opportunity for this type of interaction. It also supports increased flexibility and learning experiences adapted to individual needs. Finally, teachers and students benefit from being together for more than one year and from having only part of the class be new each year, which provides for more educational continuity and less time spent each fall teaching classroom routines.

Continuous progress and multiage grouping also present problems. Individualized instruction and regular monitoring of progress are essential to its success. Teachers in this type of program must be skilled diagnosticians and planners. In many such programs, though not all, they must also be able to operate in a team teaching situation. A great deal of training and experience is required for success. Many primary specialists, among them myself, believe that open education faded in this country not only because of the back-to-basics movement, but also because teachers were not in on the initial planning, were not thoroughly trained, and did not receive needed support once they got started. Also, this developmental approach has difficulty surmounting the resistance of the behaviorist approach that dominates elementary education today (Smith & Shepard, 1987). However, a continuous progress/multiage grouping approach affords children the opportunity to enter school with their peers and proceed at their own rate so they never have to be separated from important friendships and suffer the humiliation of repeating a grade.

Is There a Best Choice?

Each of these methods for dealing with the risk of kindergarten failures has its weaknesses:

1. To ensure excellence, prekindergarten programs require large amounts of funding, particularly to guarantee teachers well trained in a developmentally appropriate approach, and a good staff-child ratio.
2. There is increasing evidence that age is a somewhat arbitrary criterion for school entrance. Whatever the entrance age, there will always be younger and older children entering school each year and there will always be a wide range of maturity and prior life experience. Again, if the program offered is developmentally appropriate, entrance age is not a problem, as long as every child is allowed to enter by the eligibility date.
3. The use of developmental age as the criterion for kindergarten entrance is questionable in that we don't have reliable and valid assessment tasks to guide decision making. Also, it seems unfair to make such an important decision based on such a minimal behavior sample.
4. Continuous progress with multiage grouping demands exceptionally

skillful and creative teaching in order to work successfully. Also, continuous progress and multiage grouping alone don't ensure that curriculum and teaching methods will be developmentally appropriate.

Whichever method is selected for dealing with the risk of kindergarten failure, the program needs to fit the preoperational child's learning style. For example, reliance on paper-and-pencil activities with young children is never appropriate. The truly developmental classroom offers concrete materials and experiences, choices, and an emphasis on children being allowed to construct their own actions most of the time (Bredekamp, 1987; Charlesworth, 1985; Greenberg, 1987; Kamii, 1985).

Surveying the four available choices, we are left with the difficult task of weighing the pros and cons and deciding which direction to take. Where does this leave us?

Summary and Recommendations

In recent years, concern has grown regarding increased pressure and more and more inappropriate academic expectations being placed on young children. Childhood seems to be disappearing, and children are being pressured to grow up before their time (Doremus, 1986; Elkind, 1987a; Postman, 1981). Kindergarten teachers find it increasingly difficult to provide developmentally appropriate programs due to the pressures to reach specified objectives and "get through" designated workbooks (Castle, 1984; Subcommittee on Public Policy in Kindergarten, 1984; Webster, 1984). First grade teachers pressure kindergarten teachers to teach skills and use materials that have conventionally been introduced in the first grade so that entering first graders will be prepared to reach the goals prescribed for them. (Great pressure is put on first grade teachers, too!) The current practice of setting the same objectives for all children in the same grade and using workbooks and ditto sheets is in direct contradiction to the traditional early childhood view that children should be treated as individuals and guided to bloom in their own good time (Charlesworth, 1985; Doremus, 1986). Early childhood educators' concern about the risk of kindergarten failure and retention of more and more children has resulted in the search for a solution to this problem.

Because it will probably be some time before all states have prekindergarten programs statewide, because bypassing the problem of kindergarten failure by keeping children home until they are 10 or 8 or even 6 is unlikely to become our national policy, and because placement solely on the basis of developmental tests is both unfair and unsupported by research as a useful approach, we should focus our energies on improving our schools so that kindergartens and primary grades are developmentally appropriate for each individual. A definition of appropriateness for K-3 appears in the NAEYC Position Statement on Developmentally Appropriate Practice in the Primary Grades, serving 5-Through 8-Year-Olds (National Association for the Education of Young Children, 1987), and an explanation of how to assess children appropriately can be found in Meisels (1987). NAEYC's book Kindergarten Policies: What Is Best for Children? (Peck, McCaig, & Sapp, 1988) discusses entry age, curriculum appropriateness, testing, and length of day.

To achieve appropriate education, we should match the curriculum to the child. The prerequisites for making this match would include the following:

- A belief that the classroom environment can have a supportive effect on every child's growth and development
- Flexible promotion standards that do not lock children into meeting strict and often unrealistic requirements in order to progress to the next level
- An opportunity for children to benefit from a rich school experience before formal assessment is incorporated into the program. Standardized testing using conventional achievement tests should be held off until after the primary grades. (See NAEYC Position Statement on Standardized Testing of Young Children 3 Through 8 Years of Age, National Association for the Education of Young Children, 1988).
- Adoption of the NAEYC Developmentally Appropriate Practice guidelines for the kindergarten and primary levels
- Provisions for parent support, education, and involvement
- Provision of necessary support services such as speech and language therapists, psychologists, social workers, and curriculum coordinators
- Classrooms staffed with teachers who have strong educational backgrounds in early childhood education and child development
- Principals who understand and support appropriate educational practices for young children

Observing teachers in schools with low rates of retention, Smith and Shepard (1987) found that these teachers managed their heterogeneous groups of children "without the need to sort, label, track, and retain—all practices that may meet the needs of the system, but fail to address the needs of the students (Smith & Shepard, 1987, p.134)."

Combined with a child-centered, developmentally appropriate approach to education that matches learning to experiences to children, continuous progress and multiage grouping merit serious consideration as a means for offering the best opportunity for success in kindergarten eliminating the stigma of failure. To accomplish the changes many of us seek, parents and teachers must be involved in the planning and decision making from the beginning so that they really own the program and understand its purposes and practices.

Rosalind Charlesworth, Ph.D., is Professor of Curriculum and Instruction and Assistant Chairperson for Graduate Studies in the College of Education, Louisiana State University.

References

Ames, L. B. *Is Your Child in the Wrong Grade?* Lumberville, PA: Modern Learning Press, 1978.

Ames, L. B., Gillespie, C., & Streff, J. W. *Stop School Failure.* New York: Harper & Row, 1972.

Bredekamp, S. (Ed.). *Developmentally Appropriate Practice in Early Childhood Programs Serving Children From Birth Through Age 8.* Washington, DC: NAEYC, 1987.

Brewer, J. A., & Simmons, B. "Taming the First Grade Monster." Transitional programs. Presentaton at the annual conference of the National Association for the Education of Young Children, Los Angeles, November, 1984.

Byrnes, D., & Yammamoto, K. "Views on Grade Repetition." *Journal of Research and Development in Education,* 1986, 20: (1), 14–20.

Carll, B., & Richard, N. *One Piece of the Puzzle.* Lumberville, PA: Modern Learning Press.

Castle, K. "Readers Speak Out!" *Childhood Education, 1984, 61, 80.*

Charlesworth, R. "Readiness in Early Childhood Education: Should We Make them Ready or Let them Bloom?" Day Care and Early Education, 1985, 12: 25–27.

Connell, D. R. "The First 30 Years were the Fairest: Notes from the Kindergarten and Ungraded Primary (K-1-2)." *Young Children,* 1987, 42: (5), 30–39.

Devaney, K. "Developing Open Education in America." Washington, DC: NAEYC, 1974.

Dewey, J. "The Child and the Curriculum." In *John Dewey on Education: Selected Writing,* edited by R. D. Archambault. New York: The Modern Library, 1964.

DiPasquale, G. W., Moule, A. D., & Flewelling, R. W. "The Birthdate Effect." *Journal of Learning Disabilities,* 1980, 13: 4–8.

Doremus, V. P. "Forcing Works for Flowers, but not for Children." *Educational Leadership,* 1986, 44: (3), 14.

Elkind, D. "Multiage Grouping." *Educational Leadership,* 1987a, 43: (1),2.

Elkind, D. "Superbaby Syndrome can Lead to Elementary School Burnout." *Young Children,* 1987b, 42: (3), 14.

Frick, R. "In Support of Academic Redshirting." *Education Week,* January 16, 1985, 24.

Goodlad, J. *Ungraded Primary.* New York: Teachers College Press, Columbia University, 1986.

Gredler, G. R. "The Birthdate Effect: Fact or Artifact?" *Journal of Learning Disabilities,* 1980, 13: 9–12.

Greenberg, P. "Ideas that Work with Young Children. Child Choice-Another Way to Individualize-Another Form of Preventive Discipline." *Young Children,* 1987, 43: (1), 48–54.

Hill, P. S. "The Function of the Kindergarten." Reprinted from "Report of the Department of Superintendence Meeting," 1926. *Young Children,* 1987, 42: (5), 12–19.

Holmes, C. T. "A Synthesis of Recent Research on Nonpromotion: A Five Year Follow-Up." Paper presented at the meeting of the American Educational Research Association, San Francisco, April, 1986.

Kagan, S. L. "Public Policy Report. Current Reforms in Early Childhood Education: Are We Addressing the Issues?" *Young Children,* 1988, 43: (2), 27–32.

Kamii, C. "Leading Primary Education Toward Excellence: Beyond Worksheets and Drill." *Young Children,* 1985, 40: (6), 3–9.

Langer, P., Kalk, J. M. & Searls, D. T. "Age of Admission and Trends in Achievement: A Comparison of Blacks and Caucasians." *American Educational Research,* 1984, 21: 61–78.

Marzollo, J. *The New Kindergarten.* New York: Harper & Row, 1987.

May, M. J., Meyer, R. A., & Trohanis, P. L. "Demonstration Projects for Handicapped Children: A Review." *Young Children,* 1981, 36: (6), 27–32.

Meisels, S. J. "Uses and Abuses of Developmental Screening and School Readiness Testing." *Young Children,* 1987, 42: (2), 4–6, 68–73.

Moore, R. S., & Moore, D. N. "Better Late than Early." New York: Reader's Digest Press, 1975.

Morado, C. "Prekindergarten Programs for 4-Year-Olds: Some Key Issues." *Young Children,* 1986, 41: (5), 61–63.

Morado, C. "Kindergarten Alternatives for the Child who is 'Not Ready': Programs and Policy Issues." Paper presented at the biennial meeting of the Society for Research in Child Development, Baltimore, April, 1987.

Morrison, G. S. *Early Childhood Education Today.* Columbus, OH: Merrill, 1988.

Mounts, N. S., & Roopnarine, J. L. "Social-Cognitive Play Patterns in Same-Age and Mixed-Age Preschool Classrooms." *American Educational Research Journal,* 1987, 24: (3), 463–476.

National Association for the Education of Young Children. NAEYC position statement on developmentally appropriate practice in the primary grades, serving 5-through 8-year-olds. In S. Bredekamp Edition, *Developmentally Appropriate Practice in Early Childhood Programs Serving Children from Birth Through Age 8.* Washington, DC: NAEYC, 1987.

National Association for the Education of Young Children. "NAEYC Position Statement on Standardized Testing of Young Children 3 Through 8 Years of Age." *Young Children,* 1988, 43: (3), 42–47.

Piaget, J. *Science of Education and the Psychology of the Child.* Translated by D. Coultman. New York: Viking, 1970.

Peck, J., McCaig, G., & Sapp, M. E. *Kindergarten Policies: What is Best for Children?* Washington, DC: NAEYC, 1988.

Postman, N. "Disappearing Childhood." *Childhood Education,* 1981, 58: 66–68.

Riley, R. "Can We Reduce the Risk of Failure?" *Phi Delta Kappan,* 1986, 68: 214–219.

Sava, S. G. "Development, not Academics." *Young Children,* 1987, 42: (3), 15.

Schweinhart, L., & Weikart, D. P. "Evidence that Good Early Childhood Programs Work." *Phi Delta Kappan,* 1985, 66: 545–551.

Schweinhart, L., & Weikart, D. P. "What do we Know so Far? A Review of the Head Start Synthesis Project." *Young Children,* 1986, 41: (2), 49–55.

Schweinhart, L., Weikart, D. P., & Larner, M. B. "Consequences of Three Preschool Curriculum Models Through Age Fifteen." *Early Childhood Research Quarterly,* 1986, 1: (1), 15–46.

Shepard, L. A., & Smith, M. "Synthesis of Research on School Readiness and Kindergarten Retention." *Educational Leadership,* 1986, 44: 78–86.

Short, V. M., & Burger, M. "The British Infant/Primary School Revisited." *Childhood Education,* 1987, 64: 75–79.

Simner, M. L. "Will Raising the School Entrance Age Reduce the Risk of School Failure?" Paper presented at the annual meeting of the American Educational Research Association, Montreal, Canada, April, 1983.

Smith, M. L., & Shepard, L. A. "What Doesn't Work: Explaining Policies of Retention in the Early Grades." *Phi Delta Kappan,* 1987, 69: 129–134.

Strother, D. B. "Preschool Children in the Public Schools: Good Investment? Or Bad?" *Phi Delta Kappan,* 1987, 69: 304–308.

Subcommittee on Public Policy in Kindergarten. "Kindergarten: What Should Be?" (draft position paper). Chicago: Author, 1984.

Tudge, J., & Caruso, D. "Cooperative Problem Solving in the Classroom: Enhancing Young Children's Cognitive development." *Young Children,* 1988, 44: (1), 46–52.

Webster, M. K. "The 5s and 6s go to School revisited." *Childhood Education,* 1984, 60: 325–330.

Wilson, B. J., & Reichmuth, S. M. "Early Screening Programs: When is Predictive Accuracy Sufficient?" Paper presented at the annual meeting of the American Educational Research Association, New Orleans, April 1984.

CHAPTER 21

Educating Language-Minority Children: Challenges and Opportunities

Teachers facing the challenge of teaching children from different cultural communities find themselves hard pressed to decide what constitutes an appropriate curriculum. Ms. Bowman identifies a few developmental principles that can provide a conceptual framework.

Why can't all Americans just speak standard English? This plaintive question reflects the distress that many citizens feel about the linguistic diversity that has become a source of divisiveness in society and a source of failure in the schools. In many school districts, the number of languages and dialects spoken by children and their families is staggering, as the languages of Central and South America, Africa, and Asia mix with various American dialects to create classrooms in which communication is virtually impossible. Across America, language-minority children are not learning the essential lessons of school and are not fully taking part in the economic, social, and political life of the country.

And the problem will soon become even more serious. Over the next decade or two, language-minority children will become the majority in our public schools, seriously straining the capacity of those institutions to educate them.

In a nation that is increasingly composed of people who speak different languages and dialects, the old notion of melting them together through the use of a common language is once again attractive. Requiring all children to speak the same language at a high level of proficiency would make the task of educating them a good deal easier. Unfortunately, what seems quite simple in theory is often difficult to put into practice. One of the most powerful reasons in this instance is the interrelationship of culture, language, and the children's development.

Culture, Language, and Development

Christian men show respect for their religion by removing their hats but keeping their shoes on in church, while Muslim men show similar respect by keeping their hats on and removing their shoes in a mosque. But

238

differences in how groups think and act are more than a matter of using different words or performing different actions for the same purposes. Differences in culture are more substantial than whether members of community eat white bread, corn pone, or tortillas. The behavior of people varies, and the beliefs, values, and assumptions that underlie that behavior differ as well. Culture influences both behavior and the psychological processes on which it rests; it affects the ways in which people perceive the world—their physical environment, the events that surround them, and other people. Culture forms a prism through which members of a group see the world and create "shared meanings."

Child development follows a pattern similar to culture. The major structural changes in children—changes that arise form the interaction of biology and experience, such as language learning—are remarkably similar in kind and sequence across cultural groups. However, the specific knowledge and skills—the cultural learning—that children acquire at different ages depend on the children's family and community.

Learning a primary language is a developmental milestone for young children and is, therefore, a "developmentally appropriate" educational objective. Moreover, the informal, social method by which children learn their primary language is also "developmentally appropriate." However, the specific uses to which that language is put are determined by the culture.

As the ideas from a child's social world are brought to bear through the guidance of the older members of the community, children come to know, to expect, and to share meanings with their elders. Children acquire scripts (sequences of actions and words) for various interactions with people and things, and the adults in their families and communities structure these scripts for children to help them learn. Gradually, children internalize the adult rules for "making meaning."

Classroom discourse presents a challenge to children to learn new rules for communication. The use of formal language, teacher leadership and control of verbal exchanges, question-and-answer formats, and references to increasingly abstract ideas characterize the classroom environment, with which many children are unfamiliar. To the extent that these new rules overlap with those that children have already learned, classroom communication is made easier. But children whose past experience with language is not congruent with the new rules will have to learn ways of "making meaning" all over again before they can use language to learn in the classroom.

When teachers and students come from different cultures and use different languages and dialects, the teachers may be unaware of the variations between their own understanding of a context and that of their students, between their own expectations for behavior in particular contexts and the inclinations of the children they teach. When children and adults do not share common experiences and do not hold common beliefs about the meaning of experiences, the adults are less able to help children encode their thoughts in language.

Children are taught to act, believe, and feel in ways that are consistent with the mores of their communities. The goals and objectives presented, the relationships available, and the behavior and practices recommended by family and friends are gradually internalized and contribute to a child's definition of self. Language is an integral part of a group's common experience. Speaking the same language connects individuals through bonds of common meaning and also serves as a marker of group membership; it is the cement for group members' relationships with one another. The shared past and the current allegiances of the group are the bedrock for the "common meanings" taught to children through language.

Teaching Culturally Different Children

The idea of a developmentally appropriate curriculum is inherently attractive. It evokes a vision of classrooms in which experiences are synchronized with each child's levels of maturity and experience, so that what is taught is consistent with the child's capacity to learn.

But teachers facing the challenge of teaching children from different cultural communities find themselves hard pressed to decide what constitutes an appropriate curriculum. If the children speak different languages and dialects, how should teachers communicate with them? If children from some groups are hesitant to speak up in school, how can teachers organize expressive language experiences? If children from some groups are dependent on nonverbal cues for meaning, how can teachers stress word meaning? If different groups have different ways of expressing themselves, how can teachers know what children understand of what teachers and other children say? How can teachers test for mastery of the curriculum if children do not speak a standard language or use the same styles of communication? Cultural diversity makes it hard for teachers to assess each child's developmental status, to find common educational experiences to promote further growth, and to measure the achievement of educational objectives.

Given the complexity of the interaction between culture and development, is it possible to design a developmentally appropriate curriculum at all? If that question implies that the same curriculum can be used for all children, the answer must be no. Children who have been socialized in different worlds will not understand material in the same ways. On the other hand, recognizing a few developmental principles can provide a conceptual framework for the culturally sensitive teacher. The following list of principles is not meant to be exhaustive; it merely provides a beginning for teachers who are trying to bridge the gap between children's cultural backgrounds and the school's objectives.

First, teachers need to learn to recognize developmentally equivalent patterns of behavior. Before they come to school, all children have learned many of the same things—a primary language, categorizing systems, interpersonal communication styles. Although these developmental accomplishments may look quite different, they can be said to be developmentally equivalent. There are a number of "equally good" ways to shape development. When a child does not respond to the social and cognitive expectations of the school, the teacher should look first for a developmentally equivalent task to which the child will respond. For instance, a child who does not talk in the classroom can be observed on the playground or at home. A child who does not separate buttons correctly can be asked to sort car logos or other personally relevant artifacts. A child who does not listen to stories about the seasons may be spellbound by a story about a basketball player.

Teachers who have doubts about the development of culturally different children should assume that the children are normal and look at them again, recognizing that their own vision may be clouded by cultural myopia. By assuming the developmental equivalence of a variety of tasks, adults can begin the search for the mismatch between their own and a given child's understanding of a situation or of a task to be performed.

Second, it is essential not to value some ways of achieving developmental milestones more highly than others, because young children are particularly sensitive to the ways in which adults view them. Asa Hilliard and Mona Vaughn-Scott point out that, because the behavior of African-American children is so different from that of their white peers, such children are often judged to be deficient in their development, rather than just different. The result is that normal, healthy children are sometimes diagnosed as sick or retarded.*

Speaking a common language is the cement that binds individuals to groups. Thus young children who speak languages other than English (or nonstandard dialects) are reluctant to give up this connection to the members of their own group. When such children find that the way they talk and act is not understood or appreciated in school, they are apt to become confused or disengaged. And their rejection by the school presages their rejection of school.

Third, teachers need to begin instruction with interactive styles and with content that is familiar to the children. Whether this entails speaking in the child's primary language, using culturally appropriate styles of address, or relying on patterns of management that are familiar to and comfortable for children, the purpose is to establish a basis for communication. While fluency in a child's primary language may not be an achievable goal for many teachers, they can nonetheless become more adept at understanding, planning, and implementing a culturally sensitive curriculum. Such a curriculum must encompass more than tasting parties and colorful ethnic costumes; it must be more than shopworn introductions to the odd and amusing practices of people from different nations or different racial groups. In order to teach such a curriculum, teachers must have come to grips with their own ethnocentricity and must be able to deal with themselves and others fairly; teachers must know the difference between style and substance.

Fourth, school learning is most likely to occur when family values reinforce school expectations. This does not mean that parents must teach the same things at home as teachers do in school. However, it does mean that parents and other community members must view achievement in school as a desirable and attainable goal if the children are to build it into their own sense of themselves. This means that interpreting the school's agenda for parents is one of the most important tasks for teachers.

Fifth, when differences exist between the cultural patterns of the home and community and those of the school, teachers must deal with these discrepancies directly. Teachers and children must create shared understandings and new contexts that give meaning to the knowledge and skills being taught. The challenge is to find personally interesting and culturally relevant ways of creating new contexts for children, contexts in which the mastery of school skills can be meaningful and rewarding. Learning mediated by teachers who are affectionate, interested, and responsive—teachers who are personally involved in the lives of young children—has greater "sticking power" than learning mediated by an adult who is perceived as impersonal and socially distant.

Sixth, the same contexts do not have the same meanings to children from different racial and ethnic groups. The meanings of words, of gestures, and of actions may be quite different. The assessment of learning outcomes presents a formidable problem when children misunderstand the meaning of the teacher's requests for information and for demonstrations of knowledge and skills. The same instructional materials and methods may take on meanings different from those that the teacher intended. Formal assessment should be delayed until teachers and children have jointly built a set of new meanings, so that the children understand the language and behavior called for in school.

A developmentally appropriate curriculum can never be standardized in a multicultural community. Thoughtful teachers, however, can use the principles of child development to make the new context of school meaningful, to attach new kinds of learning to what children have already achieved, and to safeguard the self-image and self-confidence of children as their knowledge and skills expand. It is not easy, but it is the only workable system.

Barbara T. Bowman is director of graduate studies at the Erikson Institute, which is affiliated with Loyola University, Chicago, where she teaches courses in public policy administration and early childhood curriculum. She is a past president of the National Association for the Education of Young Children and currently serves on a committee on day care for the National Research Council.

*Asa Hilliard & Mona Vaughn-Scott. "The Quest for the Minority Child." In *The Young Child: Reviews of Research,* Edited by Shirley G. Moore and Catherine R. Cooper. Washington DC: National Association for the Education of Young Children, 1982.

CHAPTER 22

Helping Children to Acquire
Standard English

Teachers often find that the English language spoken by children in their classrooms varies from the Standard American English of the schools. Should the schools promote the teaching of Standard English to children who speak a Nonstandard English dialect? Unquestionably, the answer is "yes." The schools should teach Standard English to children who speak Nonstandard English. The acquisition of Standard English by children should be an important educational goal in programs for young children in the United States. Standard English need not be viewed by the schools as the ideal language form, but as a language form important for educational and social advancement.

Children who are fluent only in a nonstandard form of English are likely to have problems in academic pursuits. Morrow (1988) states that children who speak only Nonstandard English often have difficulty reading and writing with proficiency in Standard English. Available data and expert judgement suggest that only those Nonstandard English speakers who develop some mastery of Standard English proceed successfully through the educational systems of the society (Smitherman, 1985). It has also been reported that many cultural and linguistic minority youth manifest educational deficiencies because they have been denied the opportunity to acquire the language skills necessary to achieve in school (Adler, 1988). Children who do not acquire skill in standard English usage frequently encounter problems in educational achievement and, as a result, have limited chances for participation in the mainstream literate culture.

Dialectal Differences

Dialect refers to a distinct variation in how a language is spoken. Speakers of a particular dialect usually form a speech community that reflects the members' family, ethnic, or national background (Zintz and Maggart, 1984). In a particular linguistic community, everyone understands everyone else. When subgroups within a language community speak with differences in pronunciation, vocabulary, and syntax yet the different subgroups understand one another, their language variations are considered to be dialects (West, 1975). Any dialect, as long as it serves its purpose of communication, is a functional language system.

Socially, dialects may reflect different levels of education, social position, cultural background or national origin. From a social point of view, there are generally two broad classes of dialect—standard and nonstandard (West, 1975). The standard dialect is that used by authors, newspaper and magazine writers, television commentators, the well educated, and by educational systems. It is usually the dominant dialect or the official speech for a broad language community. Other dialects are collectively labeled as nonstandard (Zintz and Maggart, 1984).

At one time nonstandard speakers were considered cognitively and linguistically deficient (Bereiter and Engelmann, 1966). However, more recent research has shown that standard speech is not more rule-governed or more logical than nonstandard speech (Labov 1962; Robinson, Strickland and Cullinan, 1977; Steffensen, 1978). Nonstandard English should not be treated as an inferior form of communication. The schools must be sensistive to the differences in language among children. They must respect language differences while helping children to acquire Standard English.

Young children usually speak the dialect of their family, neighbors, and friends. If children grow up in a language learning environment filled with standard speakers, they are likely to speak a standard dialect. If they are surrounded by speakers of a nonstandard dialect, they will develop nonstandard speech. Words and sentences are given meaning because they are embedded in the context of social and cultural interaction.

Yet, children who speak a nonstandard dialect need not be limited to speaking that one dialect for the remainder of their lives. They should be taught Standard English forms so that they can gradually become able to "style shift" from one dialectal form to the other depending on the situation. Baker (1988) points out that varying of language forms to fit different social contexts is called "register change" or "register switching." A register is a set of linguistic forms used in given social circumstances. Each register may be signaled by changes in phonology (sounds), syntax (structure), and lexicon (vocabulary). Generally, a person controls a range of registers extending from informal ones used within his or her own folk group to formal ones used in educational and other formal contexts (DeStefano, 1974).

The idea of register switching is very important to teachers of children because it suggests that variations in language use is natural. Viewing language variations as register switching is more enlightening than considering nonstandard dialectal patterns as deviations from standard speech. Most children who speak Nonstandard English have control of some Standard English patterns. The aim of teachers should be to help children control even more forms of Standard English and to become aware of situations appropriate for the use of standard forms. The school should try to modify and extend what has already been learned informally by children from family and friends. Therefore, information on the manner in which children acquire language can be helpful in teaching standard English patterns.

How Children Acquire Language

How do young children acquire their language? Although the complete answer to this question is not known there are theories that help explain language acquisition. These theories have implications for promoting language development. The major language acquisition theories include the behaviorist theory, the innatist theory, the cognitivist theory, and the learnability theory.

The behaviorists define language as the observed and produced speech that occurs in the interaction of speaker and listener. Thinking is the internal process of language. Both language and thought are initiated through interactions in the environment such as those between a mother and a child (Skinner, 1957). According to the behaviorist theory, adults provide a language model that children learn through imitation. The child's acquisition of language is enhanced and encouraged by the positive reinforcement of an adult. Positive reinforcement encourages practice which helps language development to continue. Conversely, negative responses from an adult interferes with or inhibits a child's exploration of language.

A second theory, the innatist theory, is sometimes referred to as the nativist theory. Chomsky (1965), Lennenberg (1967), and McNeil (1970) have described this theory and maintain that language develops innately because children are preprogrammed genetically to acquire language. They contend that the onset and accomplishment of minimal language development seems unaffected by linguistic and cultural variations. Children learn their language even without the practice reinforcement and modeling offered by adults. Innatists say that language acquisition is motivated inside children; language learning is a natural ability (Morrow, 1988).

Proponents of the cognitivist theory believe that language development is dependent on cognition. They believe that children develop knowledge of the world generally and then map this knowledge onto language relations and categories. Any teaching, therefore, aimed at intellectual development will simultaneously promote language development. In other words, children develop language through their activities. Their early language as well as their development overall is related to actions, objects, and events they have experienced in their environments (Piaget and Inhelder, 1969).

The final theory, the learnability theory, proposes that language acquisition occurs because of the special interaction between the child's cognitive abilities and the learnability of language. According to Vygotsky (1978), the leading proponent of this theory, adults gradually withdraw the amount of help they need to give. The learnability theory suggests that in order to promote language development, adults need to interact with children, and they need to encourage, motivate, and support children in language learning (Sulzby, 1986).

The cognitivist and learnability theories have come to be the more accepted ideas concerning language acquisition (Morrow, 1988). For many, the learnability theory is especially acceptable since it presents a unified theory of language acquisition which incorporates both innate predispositions and cognitive development. In all, theories of language development suggest that the process of acquiring language is continuous and interactive. This process takes place in the social context of interacting with others and it takes place as children play with language in their own monologues (Cazden 1972; Smith, 1973).

The acquisition of language varies from child to child depending on social, cultural, and linguistic factors (Jagger, 1985). Using theoretical information about language acquisition, educators can provide experiences to nurture young children's language development. As teachers become familiar with the theories, they will see that each can account for some language behavior in young children, and that language instruction strategies can be based on suggestions generated by the theories. It must be noted, however, that none of the theories gives a comprehensive explanation of the way a child acquires language. Moreover, group differences have not been explored to any significant extent in the research on language acquisition. Dialectal differences, ethnic differences in learning and thinking styles, and emotionally related factors are all areas for further study in language development. Using what is known and understood, however, educators have attempted to design specific strategies for helping children acquire Standard English.

Techniques for Teaching Standard English

The literature offers a few techniques for teaching Standard English to children who speak Nonstandard English. These techniques may help teachers in their work with children. Traditionally, two approaches have been followed. First, some educators use instruction which involves adapting techniques from teaching English as Second Language (ESL).

Pattern Books to Teach the Standard/Nonstandard English Contrasts (Figure 1)

SE/NSE Contrast	Sample Book	Book's Pattern	Step 2 and 3 Sample Activities	Other Books
Person-Number Agreement	The Judge	Each prisoner describes the horrible thing in more detail: It growls, it groans It chews up stones It spreads its 　　wings And *does* bad 　　things	Have children use collage materials to construct their own horrible things. Then record children's descriptions of their horrible things.	Over in the Meadow The Green Grass Grows All Around Seven Little Monsters
Past Tense	I Know an Old Lady Who Swallowed A Fly	This is a cumulative tale about an old lady who swallows a fly and a series of other animals to catch the fly.	Have the children make a set of finger puppets use in retelling the story	Elephant in a Well Too Much Noise Goodnight, Owl Where the Wild Things Are
Negative	A Flower Pot Is Not A Hat	This pattern is repeated on each page: A ——— is not a ———.	Have children compose new sentences and record them on a chart or in individual booklets. Have children draw pictures to illustrate sentences.	It Looked Like Split Milk Never Hit A Porcupine Have you Seen My Cat?

Adapted from: Gail E. Tompkins and Lea M. McGee. "Launching Nonstandard Speakers into Standard English." *Language Arts.* Vol 60 (April 1983), pp. 466–467.

This instruction points up differences between Standard English and Nonstandard English expressions. Then, teachers provide systematic practice in specific standard expressions through pattern practice or drills (Steward, 1970). In keeping with the behaviorist theory, adults must provide the speech models and they must provide positive reinforcement to motivate continued practice of the speech patterns.

A second type of instruction uses children's literature as a model for language. Activities such as dramatization, storytelling and discussion are used for expansion of language patterns encountered in literature (Cullinan, Jagger and Strickland, 1974; Jalongo and Bromley, 1984). With this approach, it is believed that children can more naturally develop an intuitive sense of standard patterns of expression. Consistent with the learnability theory and the cognitivist theory, this approach attempts to capitalize on the interactive, contextual nature of young children's language acquisition.

One innovative program for early childhood education combines features of both approaches above. This program comprises three basic steps: 1) introducing a pattern of expression from eight major contrasts between Standard English and Nonstandard English through children's literature, 2) providing practice with the new Standard English pattern through activities such as puppetry, story dramatization or storytelling, and 3) providing activities for internalizing the new Standard English form. Children may engage in activities such as composing new episodes or additional verses for a story which they have heard utilizing the target Standard English pattern (Thompkins and McGee, 1983). Figure 1 illustrates how the Standard English patterns are presented and reinforced. In addition to the literature selected by Tompkins and McGee, it would be advisable for teachers to incorporate culturally relevant literature into this approach whenever possible. Studies suggest that the use of culturally relevant literature with children can increase both motivation and learning (McEachern, 1987).

In addition to the techniques discussed above, Gillet and Gentry (1983) have proposed a variation that values the language and culture of children while providing exposure to Standard English. With this approach the teacher accepts a language experience story from a group of children exactly as it is dictated, but later writes another version of the story using Standard English. The teacher presents his or her story as another story, not as a better story. The students then revise their story to make the sentences longer, more elaborate, and more consistent with Standard English. Choral reading and echo reading are used with the revised version to aid in the development of fluency and the learning of new sight words. Here again, as the behaviorists point out, modeling by the teacher is important. The students gain ideas for the revised version from the

Standard English story of the teacher. From a cognitivist point of view, this approach recognizes that language is intimately related to expressing ideas based on one's background of experiences.

Teachers must synthesize the information available on language acquisition and on language development techniques for Nonstandard English speakers to establish their own approaches for working with children in the classroom. Although more study and research in the area of teaching Standard English to nonstandard speakers are needed, some ideas for classroom practice are offered in the literature. For those who work with nonstandard speakers, the following guidelines are suggested.

Provide children with Standard English speech models. Children need appropriate speech models if they are to develop the patterns of any language or dialect. Overwhelmingly, the language of the teacher, the language of children's literature, and the language of the school environment should be that which stress the pronunciation, vocabulary, and syntactic patterns of Standard English.

Allow children to be active learners. Language acquisition theory indicates that language learning is an interactive process. Children must be regarded as active participants in that process. Children need many opportunities to practice language learnings. Activities such as singing, word games, storytelling, dramatizations, and conversation periods insure active language involvement on the part of young learners. Teachers must provide a rich program of language activities for children.

Use child-centered speech to encourage and support children's language development. Teachers should talk with young children in a manner which facilitates the communication efforts of children and which encourages the language development of children. Teachers use child-centered speech when they use techniques such as maintaining the child's topic, but adding other important information to what was raised by the child; using open-ended questions to stimulate thinking and to allow the child to respond without fear of being wrong; and listening to the child's language in questions and comments, but modeling Standard English in responses to the child.

Create an accepting atmosphere in the classroom. Teachers should be open and responsive to the communication efforts of young children. They should be sensitive and attentive listeners who show interest in what each child has to say. Emphasis on a child's verbal message should outweigh the focus on the form of the child's language.

Selected Bibliography

Adler, Sol. "A New Job Description and a New Task for the School Clinician: Relating Effectively to the Nonstandard Dialect Speaker." *Language Speech and Hearing Services in Schools,* 1988, 19: 28–33.

Baker, Ronald. "Folk Speech: Doing What Comes Naturally." *Contemporary Education,* 1988, 59: 91–93.

Bereiter, Carl, and Siegfried Englemann. *Teaching Disadvantaged Children in the Preschool.* Englewood Cliffs, N.J.: Prentice Hall, 1968.

Cazden, Courtney. *Child Language and Education.* New York: Holt, Rinehart and Winston, 1972.

Chomsky, Carol. *Aspects of a Theory of Syntax.* Cambridge, Mass.: MIT Press, 1965.

Cullinan, Bernice, Angela Jagger, and Dorothy Strickland. "Oral Language Expansion in the Primary Grades." *In Black Dialects and Reading,* edited by Bernice Cullinan. Urbana, Ill.: National Council of Teachers of English, 1974.

Flatley, Joannic, and Adele Rutland. "Using Wordless Picture Books to Teach Linguistically/ Culturally Different Students." *The Reading Teacher,* 1986, 40: 277–88.

Gillet, Jean, and J. Richard Gentry. "Bridges Between Nonstandard and Standard English with Extensions of Dictated Stories,." *The Reading Teacher,* 1983, 36: 360–65.

Jagger, Angela. "Allowing for Language Differences." *In Discovering Language with Children,* edited by G. S. Pinnell. Urbana, Ill.: National Council of Teachers of English, 1985.

Jalongo, Mary, and Karen Bromley. "Developing Linguistic Competence Through Song Picture Books." *The Reading Teacher,* 1984, 37: 840–45.

Labov, William. *Language in the Inner City: Studies in Black English Vernacular.* Philadelphia: University of Pennsylvania Press. 1972.

Lennenberg, E. *Biological Foundations of Language.* New York: John Wiley, 1967.

McEachern, William. "Culturally Relevant Reading Materials: Addressing a Need." *Reading Improvement,* 1987, 24: 96–100.

McNeil, D. *The Acquisition of Language: The Study of Developmental Psycholinguistics.* New York: Harper and Row Publishers, 1970.

Morrow, Lesley. *Literacy Development in the Early Years.* Englewood Cliffs, N.J.: Prentice Hall, 1989.

Padak, Nancy. "The Language and Educational Needs of Children Who Speak Black English." *The Reading Teacher,* 1981, 35: 144–151.

Piaget, Jean, and B. Inhelder. *The Psychology of the Child.* New York: Basic Books, 1969.

Robinson, V., Dorothy Strickland, and Bernice Cullinan. "The Child: Ready or Not?" In *The Kindergarten Child and Reading,* edited by L. Allila. Newark, Del.: International Reading Association, 1977.

Skinner, B. F. *Verbal Behavior.* Boston: Appleton-Century-Crofts, 1957.

Smith, Frank. *Psycholinguistics and Reading.* New York: Holt, Rinehart and Winston, 1973.

Smitherman, Geneva. "What Go Round Come Round, Keep in Perspective." In *Tapping Potential: English and Language Arts for the Black Learner,* edited by C. K. Brooks. Urbana, Ill.: Black Caucus of the National Council of Teachers of English, 1985.

Steffensen, Margaret. *Bereiter and Englemann Reconsidered: The Evidence from Children Acquiring Black English Vernacular* (Technical Report No. 82). Champaign, Ill.: Center for the Study of Reading, University of Illinois, March 1978.

Stewart, William. "Foreign Language Teaching Methods in Quasi-Foreign Language Situations." In *Teaching Standard English in the Inner City,* edited by Ralph Fasold and Roger Shuy. Washington, D.C.: Center for Applied Linguistics, 1970.

Sulzby, Elizabeth. "Children's Elicitation and Use of Metalinguistic Knowledge About 'Word' During Literacy Interactions. In *Metalinguistic Awareness and Beginning Literacy,* edited by P. Yaden and S. Templeton. Exeter, N.H.: Heinemann Educational Books, 1986.

Tompkins, Gail, and Lea M. McGee. "Launching Nonstandard Speakers Into Standard English.: *Language Arts,* 1983, 60: 463–68.

Vygotsky, L. S. *Mind in Society: The Development of Psychological Processes.* Cambridge, Mass.: Harvard University Press, 1978.

West, Fred. *The Way of Language.* New York: Harcourt Brace Jovanovich, 1975.

Zintz, Miles, and Zelda R. Maggart. *The Reading Process: The Teacher and the Learner.* Dubuque, Iowa: Wm. C. Brown, 1984.

Children's Literature References

Ets, Marie Hall. *Elephant in a Well.* New York: Viking Press, 1972.

Hoffmann, Hilde. *The Green Grass Grows All Around.* New York: Macmillan, 1968.

Hutchins, Pat. *Good-night, Owl!* New York: Macmillan, 1972.

Langstaff, John. *Over in the Meadow.* New York: Harcourt, Brace and World, 1957.

McGovern, Ann. *Too Much Noise.* New York: Scholastic, 1967.

Sendak, Maurice. *Seven Little Monsters.* New York: Harper and Row, 1963.

Sendak, Maurice. *Where the Wild Things Are.* New York: Harper and Row, 1947.

Shaw, Charles. *It Looked Like Spilt Milk.* New York: Harper and Row, 1947.

Zemach, Margot. *The Judge.* New York: Farrar, Strauss and Giroux 1969.

Dr. Louise R. Giddings is an Associate Professor, Education Division, Medgar Evers College, The City University of New York.

CHAPTER 23

Bringing the 'Moral' Back In

Parents have always cared about giving their children moral standards. Now consensus on the purposes of schooling has eroded. What's the school's proper role in this delicate endeavor?

The thunder about moral education has been heard in the last decade mostly from voices on the right. Until quite recently, most liberals have tended to dismiss this rhetoric as a reiteration of nineteenth-century morality, complete with appeals for restoration of school prayer. But then, from the other side of the political spectrum, New York Governor Mario Cuomo began to give a more prominent place to the role of schools in shaping public morality, and Jesse Jackson's Presidential campaign further rehabilitated the topic. It should not now come as a shock to find so trenchant a voice on the democratic left as Christopher Jenks weighing in recently to defend moral rhetoric (granted, the moral rhetoric of Black leaders and teachers, not Ronald Reagan). In a penetrating analysis of William Julius Wilson's *The Truly Disadvantaged,* Jencks writes:

> In poor communities, as well as in rich ones, clergymen, teachers, mothers, and other moral leaders must continually struggle both to limit and redefine self-interest. Censoriousness and blame are their principal weapons in this struggle: blame for teenage boys who steal from their neighbors, blame for drunken men who beat up their wives, blame for young women who have babies they cannot offer a 'decent home,' blame for young men who say a four-dollar an hour job is not worth the bother, blame for everyone who acts as if society owes them more than they owe society.
>
> The unwritten moral contract between the poor and the rest of society is fragile at best. We usually treat the poor badly, they often treat us badly, and perhaps worst of all, they often treat one another badly. But the solution cannot be to tear up the moral contract, or the deny that the poor are responsible for their behavior. That approach must eventually lead to a Hobbesian war of all against all. The only viable solution is to ask more of both the poor and the larger society.

Jencks agrees with Wilson that more job training, children's allowances, subsidized child care, and other programs are needed to make good on American society's obligations to the poor, but he also argues that "moral ideas and norms have a life of their own." Thus institutional reforms of the type just enumerated must be complemented by "a self-conscious effort at cultural change, of the kind that Jesse Jackson and others have promoted." Although Jencks does not discuss the role of schools in such a transformation, his analysis signals a remarkable shift in discourse about the problems of moral education.

A consensus is developing from both the right and the left that the topic of moral education needs to be brought back into the dialogue. The difficult questions involve defining what we mean by moral education and defining how it should be brought back in: In what manner, at what level, and by whom?

Privatizing Virtue

In one sense, the topic of moral education never dropped out of the dialogue. Parents have never been unconcerned about morality, nor has any first grade teacher been able to avoid the topic. But shifts in emphasis, in the broader policy discourse, can be marked out.

A comparison of two points in history illustrates one such broad shift. The first is the Northwest Ordinance of 1787, which expressed the federal motive in this language: ". . . religion, morality, and knowledge being necessary to good government and the happiness of mankind, schools and the means of education shall forever be encouraged." The second came in 1958, when Congress, stung by the Soviet success in launching Sputnik, "hereby finds and declares that the security of the nation requires the fullest development of the mental resources and technical skills of its young men and women." By the time the National Defense Education Act was adopted, the close connection between morals and education that the founders assumed was seldom expressed in legislative intent.

The Revolutionary generation in America saw the need of linking virtue and intelligence. Thomas Jefferson and Benjamin Rush advocated expanded schooling devoted to citizenship and common culture. The developers of common schools in pre-Civil War America were not secularists. Horace Mann and others, Carl Kaestle reminds us, "assumed that moral education required the sanction of religion and that moral education was the most important task of the common school."

But as America became more diverse and stridently sectarian, the problem became to define moral education in such a way as to win the assent of those of many faiths (albeit mostly Protestant ones). The nineteenth-century discourse about moral education moved from Puritanism to Protestantism to general Christian beliefs based upon Bible reading.

The compromise did not please Roman Catholics. They objected both to the use of the King James version of the Bible and to the Protestant practice of reading the Bible without comment and without the benefit of illumination by Catholic teaching. Many Catholics (and some Lutherans and, later, Jews and others) went their own way, founding schools where specific religious doctrines could inform the entire educational enterprise.

By the 1880s some educators saw the faults of the pan-Protestant approach and attempted to develop a more universalistic creed. A report in the Wisconsin Journal of Education claimed:

> There is a secular morality which is not opposed to religious morality . . . but is the result of human experiences, is recognized by all civilized people, is taught by the philosophers of all nations, and is sanctioned by all enlightened creeds.

Schools eventually began using "morality codes" sponsored by the Character Education Institution, a private organization founded in 1911.

John Dewey sought to go beyond code-like solutions to moral education and to bury the religious divisions of the nineteenth-century in a new philosophy of pragmatism. He aimed to lay the philosophical foundaton for a common democratic faith based on logical premises of shared life in schools. Criticized by traditional moralists for being a relativist and by radicals for focusing too much on process and too little on ends, Dewey nevertheless provided new justifications for the moral basis of public schooling and helped to shape what researcher Robert Bellah has called the "civil religion."

Dewey's framework did not end the defection of some Catholics and other dissenters from the public schools. But it did become grist for the conventional morality, freely mixed with elements of the Boy Scout oath and local sentiments in a nation that managed to assimilate large waves of immigrants (although Blacks, who were increasingly migrating to urban areas of the North, were still a pariah caste) and to survive the economic shock of the Great Depression.

By the 1950s, America was a newly self-confident and prosperous world power. We were the "first new nation" and the first to put a nearly universal system of primary and secondary schools in place. We felt (at least until Sputnik) that our success was due in good measure to our success as educators.

This was also, as Daniel Bell's widely noted book proclaimed in 1960, supposed to be the "end of ideology." By this title Bell indicated that traditional divisions between the left and the right were attenuating, the moral fervor of McCarthyite anti-communism in the United States was on the wane, and technical issues had become more salient.

The language of the National Defense Education Act reflected this shift. International competition was to be waged in terms of brainpower and technical expertise. In the schools, this translated into an emphasis on cognitive development and intellectual achievement. The formal content of the curriculum was stripped of moral justifications, and the schools increasingly reflected the separation between the public and private realms that became common currency in American society. In this division the discussion of religion and morals was classified as personal and relegated to the private realm, although most schools routinely engaged in some form of school prayer through the 1950s and into the 1960s.

The End of Consensus

This was the status of moral education through the Eisenhower years: a bland consensus (occasionally marked by protests from Blacks, Jews and Catholics) in which wide variation was permitted in a system of local control that honored local traditions. Teachers were confident of their moral authority and of the community's support. Americans—even those Americans whose children went to separate schools established for Blacks and whites—overwhelmingly assumed that the schools were instruments of achieving the nation's ideals. Rules for conduct were seldom written down. No one thought they needed to be: it was assumed everyone knew them as if by birthright.

These understandings were radically transformed in the next two decades. Community standards were challenged, often overturned. Teachers became confused about the basis of their moral authority in classroom and hallway. Some resigned, and many more withdrew psychologically from the exercise of the moral oversight previously taken for granted. By looking closely at what happened in one urban school, this is the story I attempted to tell in my 1987 analysis of *The World We Created at Hamilton High*.

Bureaucracy Replaces Morality

Hamilton High analyzes the effects of a transformation in authority relations. We can see this transformation as an implosion of regulation, a dramatic consolidation of the centralization underway since the end of the nineteenth century. This dramatic recentering of the system rapidly completed the shift from traditional to legal-bureaucratic controls. It went beyond the dictates of administrative efficiency and coordination. Real power shifted as state and federal governments came to supply more than half the funds to run local districts.

The schools' special role in moral education and cultural change make this shift more than a subplot in the story of the rise of the modern bureaucratic state. The schools had been pivotal in the attempt first to make a certain kind of republic possible, then to find a common ground on which the democratic faith could prosper.

By the 1960s, however, it was clear to some that while the nation had prospered, the democratic faith was imperiled. The society turned most powerfully to the schools as a means of writing a new social compact. The schools were seen as the primary means to remedy unacceptable inequalities of status, income, access, treatment, or participation, whether owed to race, ethnicity, sex, emotional or physical disability, or (to some extent) age. Precisely how much inequality was acceptable and exactly what constituted the remedy were never settled (and probably never will be). But the balance usually lay on the side of equality of opportunity rather than of result, and the society looked to the school as the principal engine of opportunity.

School as Bastille

What happened inside Hamilton High was conceptualized as a series of social revolutions—the first and most powerful a racial one. More than any other institution, schools experienced the anger born of generations of racism. In many (including Hamilton High), the dammed-up emotions spilled over into violence. As the civil rights leaders in the North exposed the complicity of schools in maintaining gerrymandered boundary lines, Black parents showed in boycotts that they no longer gave their assent to the moral authority of teachers or school officials. White teachers were no more guilty than the rest of white America for growing up in a society that accepted widespread racial inequality, but their consciousness was raised in face-to-face encounters in ways few other experienced. For many, self-abnegation and doubt were more disabling than rejection by Black parents. They no longer trusted their own moral compasses.

In the short term, ironies abounded. Blacks were brought together with whites only to discover how far apart they really were. Tracking systems were abolished overnight—and replaced by widespread increases of elective options in which the students tracked themselves. The early years of "integration" increased racial animosities as the racism of Black militants and white ethnics resulted in severe segregation within the schools. In some schools, officials attempted to meet racial "quotas" of equal expulsion rates for Blacks and whites and meted out unjust discipline. Achievement scores and real estate values fell. Whites fled.

Twenty years later, things were very different. Scores had risen, neighborhoods had stabilized. But in the short term, integration meant chaos.

The racial revolution was just one—perhaps the most powerful in its immediate effects—of an interlocking set of egalitarian movements: for mainstreaming, children's rights, sexual equality. These were occurring almost simultaneously against the backdrop of a cultural revolution and America's "loss of innocence" over its role in the Vietnam War. Each of them challenged and partly undid the moral authority of the school.

Within this set of movements, the interaction of the children's rights movement with the struggle to desegregate schools deserves notice. Desegregation involved massive, often involuntary, transfers of pupils, radically changing the mix of families in each school and rupturing the informal bonds and understandings that schools build with their clienteles. Although desegregation had high moral aims, it was often designed and implemented by courts, lawyers, and central office experts as a matter of meeting quotas and guidelines. The message to schools seldom came with any appeal to the heart. Almost always, it implied, "We don't trust you to do this right and doubt you know how even if you wanted to."

Outside experts would design the workshops for teachers; lawyers would develop the plans and write the guidelines. There was an absence of moral glue, vision, emotional bonds, and social ties. Relations with students became much more legalistic as school officials feared being overruled.

At the same time, the children's rights movement was pressing a whole new set of due process guidelines on principal and teachers. The traditional individualism of the American child ("Nobody can tell me what to do") became "Don't you dare touch me, or I'll have you arrested."

In many schools, the psychological climate deteriorated markedly. Teachers grew more reluctant to enforce norms against cheating, stealing, or verbal or physical abuse unless they felt they had evidence that would stand up in court, so to speak. In most schools, the staff of specialists and technicians, each ministering to different needs of pupils, grew rapidly. So did the number of new teachers: the student body was expanding, while teachers unable to cope were resigning in large numbers.

The moral order of the typical public school became increasingly legalistic and bureaucratic in its reliance on written rules within a centralized administrative hierarchy and in its formalism, impersonality, and emphasis on legal due process. It was individualistic in its accent on freedom of choice in intellectual and moral realms and in its avoidance of imposing any but minimal ideals guiding conduct or character development. It was technicist in its assumption that there were technical solutions to most problems—sex education, drug education—and that these could be pursued without reference to transcendent values or priorities.

A New Consensus

Our alternative now is not the repeal of the modern world. Certainly, individuals must be protected against the abuse of authority, including at times their own parents or teachers. The privileged frame of the therapeutic relationship can be a helpful means of evaluating distortions of traditional moral discourse. And both values clarification and moral reasoning are valuable and necessary activities in the proper context.

The real alternative is an educational community in which all are bound by some transcendent ideals and common commitments to an articulated sense of the public good for which public education exists. This community is one in which the responsible adults honor individual rights and procedural guarantees but do not believe these are adequate to express the ideals toward which the community strives. It is a community in which therapeutic contracts cannot override some kinds of common expectations and in which some values are not endlessly open.

This alternative is a school with a strong positive ethos. It affirms the ideals and imparts the intellectual and moral virtues proper to the functioning of an educational community in a democracy. It attempts to commit its members to those ideals and virtues, in at least a provisional way, through the espousal of goals, exemplary actions and practices, ritual celebrations, and observance of norms.

The most serious objection to this ideal school is that many parents and teachers not only believe it impossible to attain, but prefer the world they have. Whether reluctantly (because they believe that the moral world of the contemporary public school is the best compromise we are likely to obtain) or willingly (perhaps because they are strong relativists), they embrace a nonjudgmental educational world of individual rights and contractual exchange in which impersonal bureaucratic rules guarantee free access to market choices. They are satisfied with or actively prefer a public school culture based primarily on procedural guarantees and individual choices unbounded by (or at least only minimally connected with) any overarching ideals.

These parents and teachers are keenly aware of the other kinds of reductions that take place when the heavy hand of moralism, bigotry, and class prejudice is laid on public schools in the name of character ideals. Talk of the public good has too often been a screen behind which schools have been made to serve the interests of a privileged few.

No one who has read history can fail to be impressed by the force of this objection. On the other hand, what choice is left to those of us who fear the corruption of education in its contemporary drift toward an impersonal, technicist, rule-bound bureaucratic model? Is private education our only refuge? Must those who wish to pursue the creation of what I have called a strong positive ethos abandon the public sector?

I am not ready to conclude that. Nor do I believe that those who sincerely raise strong objections can be overridden or ignored. Hence I presume that there will be some real choice among models of public schooling. I do not think it either desirable or practical to attempt to shut down the minimalist bureaucratic model. But I hope it will not remain the only, or even the dominant, model.

Three problems or objections lie in the way of the development within the public sector of schools with a strong positive ethos. The first is to show how teachers can take responsibility for addressing moral issues (to show, in fact, that they cannot avoid doing so) while respecting First Amendment guarantees. The second is to demonstrate that teachers need not—in fact must not address all moral issues, but only those virtues and ideals that are proper to the functioning of an educational community. They need not agree on capital punishment, for example, but they ought to be clear about honesty.

Indoctrination: Imposing Whose Values?

The third objection is the fear that this emphasis on virtues will lead to indoctrination. In many school systems, school boards have adopted policies forbidding teachers to "impose their personal values" on students. School board lawyers are inclined to cite the language of the Supreme Court in declaring unconstitutional a compulsory Pledge of Allegiance to the flag: "If there is any fixed star in our constellation," Justice Robert H. Jackson wrote on behalf of the majority, "it is that no official, high or petty, can prescribe what shall be orthodox in politics, nationalism, religion, or other matters of opinion or force citizens to confess by word or act their faith therein." But the Court in this case was arguing for freedom of religion, freedom for children of Jehovah's Witnesses not to be compelled to make a pledge of loyalty to an earthly government that they felt violated the tenets of their faith. The Court has also ruled that schools may not restrict the free-speech rights of students even when they wish to oppose government policy, as when it upheld the right of students in Des Moines public schools to protest the Vietnam War.

But protection of free exercise of religion and of freedom to criticize government or school should not be interpreted to mean that all moral practices are a matter of personal opinion. It is possible to define the moral practices that are necessary underpinnings of educational activity in such a way as to respect differences of opinion on other moral questions such as abortion or gambling. These necessary practices then become not personal values but the justifiable practices and virtues of an educational community.

Yet the skeptic may press:

> Doesn't this involve the imposition of some values on the young? You are telling students what to think and feel about certain basic moral matters. Educators should aim at developing critical intel-

lect and personal autonomy. What is being suggested here would short-circuit true inquiry and amount to a form of indoctrination.

The skeptic has a point. It is true that educators must impose some standards even before children have reached an age to reason about them. After all, even a small child might strike a hammer blow at the temple of a sleeping adult. But we are also suggesting that in high schools, when students can think for themselves in good measure, adults will, by example and conviction growing out of their responsibilities as educators, be teaching students to uphold certain moral standards and ideals.

What can save this activity from degenerating into indoctrination is the manner in which these standards and ideals are taught. If adults teach them in an authoritarian manner as a fixed and unvarying code that must be stamped into the consciousness of children, they can be charged with indoctrination. They will be saved from such an indictment, however, if they give the reasons for the standards, based on universal principles undergirding the educational endeavor, and if they present them as provisional.

By provisional, I do not mean that the standards are so tentative as to be made up anew each week, but that moral standards are always in some sense in the process of development. As R. J. Peters has written, it means that teachers initiate students to such beliefs in a nonbehavioristic way, not fixing a particular moral content for life, but showing students that as adults they will have the responsibility and freedom to reevaluate those beliefs.

This means, for example, that while teachers will uphold the ideal of equality, they will also take pains to show how the ideal of equality of educational opportunity was felt to be satisfied in the nineteenth century by providing common schools open to all, while today equality embodies the concept that compensatory or additional educational services must be provided to some in order to meet everyone's needs.

Further, it means that teachers, while insisting on respect for the dignity of others within the classroom, will also show that respect is partly a cultural concept, subject to change and revision. They may note, for example, that while the Supreme Court ruled in favor of the Jehovah's Witnesses in 1943, it had earlier supported a school board's contention that "the act of saluting the flag is only one of many ways that a citizen may evidence his respect for the government" and thus requiring the salute "did not violate any constitutional rights." In overruling this opinion, the Court held that Jehovah's Witnesses and other children who feel in conscience that they cannot recite the pledge are exercising their democratic rights and are guilty of no disrespect.

These examples can only illustrate the responsibility that teachers have to convey the organic nature of ideals without surrendering to a meaningless relativism. It is not possible to go beyond examples, to be exhaustive, for each faculty will have to come to its own understanding of these questions. The state cannot perform this task, for that would reduce the teacher's role to inert reception of a fixed code.

There will be abundant overlap in the kinds of ideals and virtues that schools affirm, but there will also be differences in their breadth and emphasis from school to school, depending upon local traditions and the state of moral development of the faculty itself. The adults primarily responsible for a given educational community should be continually in the process of reflecting upon and renewing their world. There are no shortcuts. Stimulating and guiding such reflection is a crucial aspect of school leadership.

Grant, Gerald. "Bringing the 'Moral' Back In." National Education Association, January, 1989, 7: #6.

For Further Reading

Bellah, Robert, et al. *Habits of the Heart: Individualism and Commitment in American Life*. University of California Press, 1985. Drawing on extended interviews with a cross-section of middle class Americans, the authors of this study ask questions about the loss of a sense of community and how it might be reconstituted.

Grant, Gerald. *The World We Created at Hamilton High*. Harvard University Press, 1988. The story of what happened inside a real urban high school in the period 1953–1987 chronicles how teachers attempted to transform their school to create a strong positive ethos. The author, who taught in the school for two years, draws on both his research and that of students whom he trained to gather data about the moral life of their own school. Given these data, 12 teachers elected by their peers then made their own diagnosis of what changes should be made.

Jencks, Christopher. "Deadly Neighborhoods: How the Underclass Has Been Misunderstood." *The New Republic,* June 13, 1988. Here Jencks offers the analysis needed for moral standards described at the opening of this essay.

Kaestle, Carl. "Moral Education and Common Schools in America: A Historian's View." *Journal of Moral Education,* May 1984. In this excellent account, Kaestle traces the historical development of the problem of moral education in American public schools.

Lightfoot, Sara Lawrence. *The Good High School*. Basic Books, 1983. This classic study portrays the character and culture of half a dozen exemplary public and private schools.

Rutter, Michael, et al. *Fifteen Thousand Hours: Secondary Schools and Their Effects on Children*. Harvard University Press, 1979. The authors examine 12 London schools with similar student bodies but very different climates and markedly different outcomes. They relate these outcomes to the ethos within the school and the degree of consensus achieved by the faculty about their cognitive and moral expectations for pupils.

CHAPTER 27

The Full Day Kindergarten
Is It Here? Is It Now?

Historical Development of the Kindergarten Movement

In 1837 Friedrich Froebel opened a school for young children and called it kindergarten. "The kindergarten provided a child-centered preschool curriculum for three to seven year old children that aimed at unfolding the child's physical, intellectual, and moral nature with balanced emphasis on each of them (Ross, 1976)." The underlying philosophy as espoused by Froebel was that young children required an environment where like "unfolding plants," children could blossom through the use of play, games and song. This first kindergarten with special emphasis on play was established by Froebel near Keilhau, Germany.

In this country, Margethe Meyer Schurz opened the first German-speaking kindergarten at Watertown, Wisconsin in 1855. Elizabeth Peabody, an exponent of child centered education, learned of this kindergarten system and undertook the private sponsorship of an English-speaking kindergarten in Boston. The year was 1860.

Peabody became so convinced of the validity of Froebel's philosophy that she embarked on a vigorous campaign for the establishment of kindergartens throughout America. She initiated a regular correspondence with Dr. William T. Harris, Superintendent of Schools in St. Louis, urging him to institute kindergartens in the public school system in his district. Dr. Harris, though not easily convinced that early childhood programs based on child's play belonged in the public school system, did finally consent. In 1873, St. Louis became the first city in the United States to adopt this radical educational concept in its public schools. The successful outcomes of the kindergarten system in St. Louis fostered the growth and acceptance of early-childhood classrooms on a nation-wide basis.

These early kindergarten programs focused on the basic concept that child's play was significant and that when it was intelligently directed gave impetus to cognitive development. The schools therefore provided an atmosphere of unrestraint where young children were permitted to associate freely with others. The interaction in a peer group provided a fertile field for the unfolding of maturational development in social, ethical, and cognitive behavior.

In the kindergarten classroom young children were provided with opportunities for self-expression through the use of directed play, singing, story telling, nature study and movement activities. Learning by doing was the underlying principle which guided the kindergaraten programs of the day. Wooden blocks, clay, construction paper, sandboxes, cardboard and color projects were the materials made available to children for their use in their experiential self-expression activities. Free use of these materials together with directed and supervised developmental activities fostered the growth of cognitive and motor skills appropriate to this age group.

Kindergarten Practices Prevalent at Present

Public school kindergarten, finally accepted, were established widely throughout the United States on a half-day attendance basis. Up until the last decade or so this attendance pattern was the norm of kindergarten school experiences. At the present time many school districts have replaced the half-day kindergarten with some version of an extended day kindergarten program.

At present there are several variations of the extended day kindergarten which have been put into practice. Three designs currently in use are the full day program, kindergarteners attend school five days a week in conformance with the established school day. Kindergarten children who attend an extended day program are in school for four hours each day, five days a week and are assigned an additional hour of school time each week. The call back program is a plan whereby all kindergarten children attend a morning session of three hours each day, five days a week, but are called back to school, in small groups, twice a week after lunch. Every student is included in the call back session (Syosset, 1984). And in school districts where the half day kindergarten still prevails, some form of an extended day is made available to accommodate the needs of special education children. Where the IEP (Individual Education Plan) warrants it, a full day kindergarten program is scheduled for the child.

At issue is not a full day versus a half day kindergarten; the reality is that an extended kindergarten day program exists in many school communities across the nation and continues to expand. The New York State Education Department, Information Center on Education, reports that

> in New York State alone 117,211 students were in attendance in a full day kindergarten program as opposed to 68,560 who were enrolled in a half day session. These statistics are for the academic school year of 1988–89.

The question then is how can teachers and school systems best utilize this additional time for the development of appropriate learning experiences for young children? Schools must now cope with the educational and developmental needs of students with and without day care or formal preschool experience, states the ERS Spectrum report of Spring 1986.

Impact of Project Head Start on Kindergarten Education

Children who are at a high risk, i.e. the poor, the homeless, those from minority groups or dysfunctional families are most likely to suffer academic failure. Considerable research has shown that these students can be identified as early as kindergarten, so states Jones, Pollock, and Marockie (1988). Without early and comprehensive intervention they (the disadvantaged) enter the educational system at tremendous disadvantages, reports Morris (1989). In the mid 1960's Project Head Start, aware of the needs of the children of the poor, set out to offer enhancement programs in the critical aspects of the lives of the deprived. The original planning committee of Project Head Start recognized the necessity of comprehensive intervention in the lives of disadvantaged children. George B. Brian, one of the original members of the committee states, "Project Head Start was designed to be something more than a preschool readiness program. It was planned as a comprehensive intervention into many aspects of early childhood development (Zigler, Edward and Jeanette, 1979)." The Planning Committee's report for Project Head Start articulated all-inclusive guidelines permeating several important aspects of child development. Among them were the areas of early childhood education, health, social services, parent involvement, and volunteer effort. It was the belief of the Committee that a comprehensive, multi-dimensional approach would be effective in implementing change in the lives of impoverished children.

The need for Project Head Start in the mid 1960's becomes more relevant when one is apprised of the fact that public kindergartens were non-existent in Albuquerque, New Mexico at the time. Nor were many private nursery schools or kindergartens available, reports James L. Hymes, Jr., another Planning Committee member (Zigler, Edward and Jeanette, 1979). At the present time Albuquerque's elementary schools all have public kindergartens and more than three quarters of five year-olds in the state of New Mexico are enrolled in the school system. Project Head Start undoubtedly precipitated this development.

In the ensuing years Project Head Start has enhanced the lives of many of its participants. It has increased their potential for both academic and social success. Several recent studies, Crittenden (1985) informs us, report that children who take preschool programs such as Head Start do better academically and socially in later life than those who do not.

The important lessons learned from Project Head Start have resulted in some present-day practices prevalent in many kindergarten classrooms throughout the country. For one, the use of aids in the school-room has gained wide acceptance and their number has increased markedly. Public kindergartens, too, have increased in number since the inception of Project Head Start. The involvement of parents in early childhood education has become an important and viable factor. Writes Dr. Morris (1989)

> One of the most cogent aspect of Head Start and programs built on this model is the effectiveness of parent education and involvement.

Entrance Age

Children entering Kindergarten in the fall of the academic school year are generally five years of age. The cutoff date in many school district is December 1, at which time the youngest child in the class will have attained the age of 4.9 years. Age of enrollment may vary according to school districts and parents' preferences. Recent data indicate that school districts are raising the legal age at which children are entitled to enter Kindergarten. In 1958, most districts in the nation require kindergarten children to be 5 years old by December 1 or January 1 (Educational Research Servcice, 1958). Current trends in admissions policy reflect the philosophy that children be required to be older than 4.9 years upon enrolling in kindergarten.

Increasingly school districts are replacing the December 1 or January 1 deadline with earlier cut-off dates such as September 1 or October 1 while Missouri has now raised its school entrance age to July 1 (Shepard and Smith, 1988). Many parents concur with these practices, especially those parents whose children were born late in the calendar year. Parents choose to delay kindergarten enrollment until the following year when they believe that the child's maturity and development level will be best met. The question is—how does this affect the child's performance? The more affluent and better educated parents appear to be more preoccupied with the concept of delayed enrollment. Parents from lower socio-economic groups, who are both in the work force, seem to feel less pressure about holding children back from entering kindergarten. A working mother needs to have her child in school at whatever the cutoff date.

Raising the age of admission to kindergarten is thought to ensure "kindergarten readiness" of the incoming child. Kindergarten curriculum has become more academic and what was once considered first grade material is now found in kindergarten. Kindergartens of today look very much like first grades of only a few years ago (Uphoff and Gilmore, 1986). While raising the entrance age gives the incoming student an advantage in dealing with the requirements of a full day attendance program, it also puts pressure on the school to accelerate the kindergarten curriculum to accommodate older children.

Research continues to document the effect of early childhood education on achievement in the later years. Preschool and early primary years are an optimal time in which to instill appropriate behaviors for subsequent academic success. How effective, then, are full or extended day programs? Several areas impacting on the child's kindergarten experience require examination. These areas are:

1. class size
2. entrance age of children in kindergarten
3. curriculum
4. use of aides/paraprofessionals in kindergarten classroom
5. use of support staff; i.e., art, music, physical education
6. parent/community involvement in kindergarten program

Class Size

An ERS Spectrum report of 1986 informs us that class size in full day kindergartens ran about 24 pupils per class while half day classes averaged 23 pupils in the morning sessions and 22 in the afternoon classes. A more current finding in one Long Island, N.Y. school district revealed a class size of 20 to 21 pupils in its full day kindergarten session.

Some school districts faced with a demographic problem of declining enrollment are experiencing financial difficulties. Full day kindergarten programs may increase enrollment figures in the public schools to accommodate the needs of working mothers. Longer kindergarten sessions may provide working mothers with surrogate care and training as a solution to their problem of inadequate child care and the rising costs of care providers. A review of research literature on full day kindergarten indicates that full day programs encourage the return of pupils currently enrolled in full day private schools, to the public schools (Puelo, 1988).

Kindergarten Curriculum

Full day or extended kindergarten has as many proponents as opponents. At issue is the curriculum—should it reflect academic achievment or should it focus on creative and social maturation as well as cognitive development? The additional allotted time available in a longer kindergarten session implies that the curriculum needs to be augmented with additional learning experiences. What appropriate developmental activities should the curriculum include?

A curriculum program which utilizes the extended time period to allow for individualized instruction, small group activities and a learning center approach appears to be preferable and gaining acceptance. Other areas of consideration involve a child's ability to observe, discover, generalize, experiment, and solve problems (Harding and Safer, 1988).

A latent problem in the lengthened school day is the tendency for some educators to lay greater stress on an academically oriented program. The trend in some quarters to introduce more traditional curriculum in the extended school day only creates greater difficulties for young children. A program which accentuates academic learning or tries to hasten cognitive development before "readiness" is indicated contributes to stress and frustration among the young. Research has shown that unless children are developmentally ready, true learning does not occur.

A proper learning environment provides individualized programs based on the developmental stage of readiness. Harding and Safer (1988) report that in an investigation of the pedagogical implications of Piaget's theory, the necessity for activity and exploration in children's learning is emphasized. When children manifest signs of "learning readiness," appropriate instructional material can be taught efficaciously.

Piaget's theory of the growth of human intelligence is a stage theory (Braun and Edwards, 1972). Individuals assimilate knowledge at each developmental stage. Readiness is a hierarchical learning pattern of skills development where the student learns step by step. In a full day program skills such as reading and math can be developed in stages to suit the cognitive framework of the individual child, without the constraints of time limits. In a heterogeneous kindergarten where the range of intellectual ability is from learning impaired to gifted, skills learning is adapted to the students' needs. A balanced program of formal skills development together with an informal program of self-expression can occur as the students continue to show progress.

A traditional academic program utilizing paper and pencil exercises together with rote learning runs contrary to theories on child development. Exploration and hands-on activities produce more positive results. Children are engaged in their learning when they are permitted to experiment within their own environment. They need to interact with each other as well as with their teachers.

Reading and math materials need not be limited to rote learning and memorization. Fred M. Hechinger (1990) quotes Dr. Bruno Bettleheim as having said,

> a child who is made to read: 'Nan had a pad. Nan had a tan pad. Dan ran. Dan ran to the pad . . ." does not receive the impression that he is being guided toward becoming literate. . . .

Other techniques are possible in the skill subjects of reading and mathematics which would render these curriculum areas challenging and meaningful.

Use of Support Staff in Extended Day Kindergarten

The longer school day allows schools to offer children a wide range of experiences. Enhancement activities in many school systems include art, music, library, physical education, and rhythm and movement. Staff members who are specialists in the field replace the classroom teacher for the instructional period. A specific amount of time each week is allotted to the instruction of each of these added activities. Art, music, and physical education instructors teach all students within a given school as well as kindergarten students. This is true of the library as well, where all pupils in the school utilize the facility. Kindergarten students sense a feeling of belonging when they know what they are sharing "specials" with the rest of the school.

Physical education classes, traditionally, are given twice a week but more time is added through rhythm and movement exercises. The program in physical education provides the kindergarten child the opportunity to develop small muscle control as well as large muscle coordination.

In rhythm and movement education, children engage in multiple creative activities involving space and rhythm. They enjoy the sense that rhythm provides, the patterned recurrence of a beat; allowing them to give way to freedom of expression. This activity nurtures a child's self imagery and when carefully developed expands the possibilities of creativity and self-expression. Children are encouraged to move their entire bodies as well as specific parts only, i.e. the head, the shoulders, the arms, the legs, the fingers, etc. As children are challenged to engage in a variety of movements, they experience their bodies and themselves in a positive and self-affirming ways.

A longer school day permits kindergarten teachers to develop and integrate an arts program in all program areas (Fromberg, 1987). Some school districts employ a specialist teacher of the arts to stimulate and extend a child's aesthetic experiences. Art education provides children with the opportunity to explore, experiment and create with art materials on their own developmental level. Under the skilled guidance of an art specialist, children are encouraged to exhibit independence as they acheive creativity and self-expression. Art activities have been a major component in the kindergarten program so that the use of an art specialist should include more nontraditional approaches in the teaching of art. Leading children to dare make unconventional observations of their surrounding environment and record these perceptions is one technique for heightened awareness. The task of the art specialist is to bring the skills and tools of the profession into play so that the students can articulate the wonder that engulfs the child.

Music education teaches children to create music, appreciate music, and engage in musical activities. A music teacher specialist leads children to create music through the use of instruments such as drums, triangles, shakers, sticks and other found objects. The students perform rhythmic patterns by banding together and interacting with their bodies and voices.

Children can be taught to appreciate music as well. By creating a favorable climate for listening, a music teacher helps to build a child's perception of the music genre. Young children react to musical experiences with unfixed notions. The responsibility of a music teacher is to encourage children to verbalize their feeling and emotions and to foster diversity of opinions.

In music education, children engage in musical activities by raising their voices in song and learning to read music. Holidays scattered throughout the school year as well as the annual seasons serve as the basis for many songs taught to young children. Folk songs too, have special meaning in the musical repertoire of the kindergarten program. Whole class singing, choral singing, solos, performances for school assemblies are all modes for engaging kindergarteners in musical expression. Children derive a sense of belonging and togetherness when they participate in singing experiences.

Schools which fortunately have a library facility, schedule library time for kindergarten students. Here children enter a room unlike their own classroom; a room filled with books. The librarian makes their visit welcome and rewards them with stories and books. School libraries try to replicate public libraries with similar rules and regulations governing the use of libraries by the general public. Children are free to browse, read, look at pictures, and borrow books for home consumption. Many children entering kindergartren have undertaken library visits prior to their school experiences and some are even the proud possessors of library cards. School libraries enhance the child's exposure to the world of books and augment the relationship of books to literature.

The computer is rapidly becoming a part of the kindergarten curriculum. On a space available basis, resource centers are established where computers are housed. Or the library centers may become the focus for the storage and use of classroom computers. Librarians and teachers all share in providing computer education.

Parent/Community Involvement

An important component of the full day kindergarten is parent/community involvement. Parent involvement is critical with regard to a child's education while community support is necessary for fiscal maintenance. In an era of tax-revolt, declining educational revenues are a reality which school boards must acknowledge. Local school districts are obliged to arouse community interest and participation in educational issues which are beneficial to the entire community.

Full day kindergartens entail higher costs. Current research varies on the financial implications of full and half day kindergartens. A number of reports indicate that costs for transportation are unaffected or even reduced while added staffing and space demands necessitate greater funding. Proponents of full day kindergartens argue that additional costs for maintaining an innovative early childhood program are mitigated by long term benefits, especially for those children who enter the educational system greatly disadvantaged. Children who pose no problem and those who have experienced preschool training benefit from a full day program by enhanced cognitive development and social growth.

Project Head Start is mandated by law to involve parents in formulating curriculum and operating the program. Public Schools do not function under this edict and are reluctant to admit external intervention into their professional arena. A successful full day program for kindergarten requires parent services as well as professional educators. Puelo (1988) found that "parents not directly involved in programs are much less supportive of them."

Parent education in the philosophy of the full day program is an initial step in gaining parental support and commitment. School administrators who would seek parental approval arrange pre-registration meetings where parents are apprised of the operation and anticipated goals of the longer kindergarten day. Inquiries arising from these sessions are addressed and an amplification of the agenda of the total school day is presented.

Parent/teacher conferences are a useful tool in the education of the young. An oral exchange between teacher and parent is more meaningful than written notations on a report card. This dialogue makes the parent more cognizant of the child's strengths and weakensses. Meeting such as these provide parents the opportunity to gain a deeper understanding of their children's progress and establish a better rapport between parent and teacher. Parental involvement in the school's kindergarten program is fostered when parent and teacher join in a discussion of an educational plan for the kindergarten student.

Parent/teacher associations have long been an accepted sector of the public school community. The role of the association has been to aid and abet the public school in most non-academic areas such as fund-raising, supervision of the lunchrooms, and assistance in library facilities. Parents who are active in the association participate within the school building and gain access to school personnel on a more informal basis. Members of the association who are committed to seeking quality education for their children work hard on affairs affecting their local school. As they become more involved in school functions, they become greater activists for broader school programs.

It is significant that families of school age children vary from single parent, step-parents, extended groups and nuclear family. And with greater numbers of mothers in the work force, the only direct contact the school has with these parents is in some form of school related events and a weekly or monthly, informative publication would create a positive climate for parental support. Additionally, community interest could be generated by direct mailing of a school newsletter to all taxpayers residing in the school district. Establishing sound communication links with school, home, and the community, results in a better informed citizenry.

The number of activities useful for eliciting an involved parental response is limited only by the imagination of those responsible for school-community relations. Back-to-school night, classroom visits, curriculum night, afternoon coffee hours, and people-as-resource are some specific means for stimulating and generating participation by parents and other adult community members in school affairs. Outreach recruitment programs which attract local business people and other community leaders to the school increase the public's awareness of innovative kindergarten reforms. Local schools and communities need to interact with each other for mutually beneficial results.

Use of Aides/Paraprofessionals in the Kindergarten Classroom

Kindergarten teachers faced with the myriad responsibilities attendant upon young children require services of additional classroom personnel. When asked about factors that kept them from teaching as they would like to, kindergarten teachers cited "lack of time for individual instruction and guidance" as a major problem with "too many students per class" as a close second (ERS, 1986).

Where feasible, the use of aides or paraprofessionals in the school can mitigate the burdens of high pupil/teacher ratio and provide the teacher with additional time for effective teaching. Aides can be efficiently employed in a number of ways. The lunchroom program is clearly one area where teachers can be replaced by paraprofessionals. Here the aides can prepare the children for lunch routines, escort the class to the lunchroom, supervise the lunch hour, handle minor crisis, and finally return the pupils to the classroom. Other areas for the services of classroom aides are within the activities of a normal school day. Paraprofessionals may be engaged in story time, supervision of play time or recess, distribution of work and play materials, and preparation of teacher-made curriculum materials.

School districts with limited financial resources for hiring paraprofessional staff recruit parents to assist in the kindergarten classrooms. Kindergarten teachers seek parent volunteers to participate in non-professional areas of the full day kindergarten program. Parent volunteerism serves a two-fold purpose; it frees the classroom teacher of petty everyday routines and intensifies parent involvement in the operation of a full day kindergarten session.

The use of a competent and committed adjunct staff provides another dimension for the development of a sound early childhood program. Young children need to be accepted and respected by loving and caring individuals. Adequately trained paraprofessionals and parent volunteers can inspire self-confidence and self-worth in kindergarten students.

Conclusion

With the school reform movement gaining momentum in the 1980's educators looked for ways to improve education in the coming decade. The longer school day for kindergarten children such as full day, extended day or staggered day, is an innovative program allied with the school reform process. The challenge to educators, parents and the community alike is to make a commitment to the concept and resolve to make the program functional.

Many questions present themselves on the efficacy of a full day kindergarten program. Areas of the program which are under constant scrutiny and evaluation are:

1. pedagogical practices;
2. educational gains;
3. fiscal outlays.

Research in this fledgling program has not been extensive enough to produce meaningful statistics and results, but some significant outcomes for educators and society-at-large are emerging.

In any discussion of pedagogical practices, theories abound on what constitutes suitable instructional methods for kindergarten children. Is academic achievement in the kindergarten grade a primary consideration to the exclusion of the developmental and maturation needs of early childhood? While it is true that a more academic kindergarten has evolved over the past decade, what distinguishes an exemplary full day program is the attention given to individual differences in the kindergarten classroom population. Educators, charged with the responsibility of designing curriculum guides for use in the full day kindergarten, must take into account the need for individualized instruction based on the developmental stages of growth.

The general consensus is that educational benefits are positive in a full day kindergarten program. Research studies show that a high percentage of students of kindergarten age have attended some type of preschool before entering kindergarten. Students with preschool experience are psychologically prepared for a full day kindergarten and can benefit from a program focusing on beginning academic skills. Because of higher entrance age, incoming kindergarten students of today are older than their predecessors of a generation ago and are thus better able to cope with greater academic expectations.

Of special significance are the gains made by the at-risk school population. Children coming from lower socio-economic backgrounds and slower learning pupils benefit from the additional time in the kindergarten day. There is ample time in the full day kindergarten to enhance the learning and acculturation experiences of disadvantaged children and those with potential learning problems.

The fiscal implications of a full day kindergarten program is a major consideration which must be addressed. Various studies show that greater costs may be anticipated in implementing a full day session for kindergarten children. A suitably staffed program, proper instructional materials, and transportation facilities require increased funding. Transportation costs appear to be the least affected and in some cases are actually reduced since bus service is scheduled to be consistent with that of the general school population. In many areas, state aid doubles when full day kindergarten is adopted. Each child in half day kindergarten is only allotted half day funding by the state but when that same child attends school full day, then funding on a full day basis is granted.

While cost factors are higher initially, economic benefits are reflected over the years through fewer retentions and a reduction of special education placements. Decreased costs in per pupil education are especially evident in communities with substantial numbers of at-risk students. With greater numbers of working mothers, savings are accrued as full day kindergarten students are provided with professional care and preparation for a lifetime school experience. The full day kindergarten gives both student and teacher a broader scope for developing and enriching early childhood education.

Dr. Irene S. Pyszkowski is an Associate Professor of the Division of Education, Notre Dame College, St. John's University, Staten Island, N.Y.

References

Braun, S. J.; and Edwards, E. P. *History and Theory of Early Childhood Education*. Worthington, Ohio: Charles A. Jones Publishing Co., 1972.

Crittenden, A. "Early Education Thrives Outside Public Schools." *N.Y. Times,* Education Section, April 14, 1984, 12: 45.

Educational Research Service. "Administration Policies for Kindergarten and First Grade." Circular No. 3. Arlington, VA, 1958.

ERS Staff Report. "Kindergarten Programs and Practices." *ERS Spectrum,* Spring, 1986, Vol. 4, No. 2: 22–25.

Fromberg, D. P. *The Full Day Kindergarten*. New York: Teachers College Press, 1987.

Harding, C.; and Safer, A. "Keeping our Priorities Straight: The Real Issue in the Full-Day Kindergarten question." *Planning and Changing,* Spring, 1988, Vol. 19, No. 1: 58–62.

Hechinger, F. M. "About Education." *New York Times,* March 28, 1990, Vol. 139, No. 48: 188, Sec. B: 8.

Jones L. H.; Pollack B.; and Marockie, H. "Full Day Kindergarten as a Treatment for At-Risk Students: Ohio County Schools." *ERS Spectrum,* Winter 1988, Vol. 6, No. 1: 3–7.

Morris, J. B. "Early Childhood Education in Urban Settings: the 1990's." *The Delta Kappa Gamma Bulletin,* Fall, 1989, 56-1: 15–20.

Puleo, V. T. "A Review and Critique of Research on Full-Day Kindergarten." *The Elementary School Journal,* March 1988, Vol. 88, No. 4: 427–438.

Ross, E. D. *The Kindergarten Crusade*. Athens, Ohio: Ohio University Press, 1976.

Shepard, L. A.: and Smith Mary Lee. "Escalating Academic Demand in Kindergarten: Counter Productive Policies." *The Elementary School Journal,* November, 1988, Vol. 89, No. 2: 135–144.

Syosset Central School District. "A Proposal for Full Day Kindergarten." Oct. 22, 1984, Syosset, N.Y.

Uphoff, J. K.; and Gilmore, J. "Pupil Age at School Entrance: How Many are Ready for Success?" *Young Children,* January, 1986, 11–16.

Zigler, Edward; and Zigler, Jeanette. *Project Head Start*. New York: The Free Press, 1979.

SECTION 4

Exceptional Children

Introduction

As we move through the 1990's, we will be faced with many difficult decisions in regard to the funding and programming of pre-school and early childhood services. Expanded services for the young began in the 1970's when the federal government passed legislation (Head Start, WIC Programs, Title XX/Social Services Block Grant, Chapter I and Education for the Handicapped) mandating the states to offer pre-school and early childhood programs at public expense. Included in this legislative initiative were two amendments to Public Law 94-142, The Education for All Handicapped Children Act of 1975, which further expanded the availability of special education services to children of pre-school age. These amendments, Public Law 98-199 (1983) and Public Law 99-457 (1986) extended services by the states to handicapped children 3–6 years of age and also established new discretionary programs to children with special needs, starting at birth.

However, since 1985, the number of pre-school children identified as needing special education services has doubled. Costs in education, health and family-foster care has skyrocketed. The federal government estimates that approximately 325,000 children are born each year with post-natel drug or alcohol addiction ($\frac{1}{3}$ from crack alone). By the mid 1990's, approximately 40–60% of these children will require social, health and special education services. The price tag: $200,000 per child by the age of 5.

Today, the cost of special education services (5–21 years of age) is almost triple the amount of a regular education. As we strive to meet the educational, physical and social needs of all our children, the 1990's shape up to be a decade of pre-school and early childhood program initiatives. Throughout the country, new and innovative programs are presently underway: early intervention, teacher training, curriculum enhancement and family counseling. The costs for these services will be staggering, but necessary if we are to help all our children realize their potential as members of society.

Article written by M. MICHAEL LEVINE, Supervisor of Special Education-New York City Board of Education, June 5, 1990. *Education:* Stony Brook-B.A. (1973), Fordham University-M.S. (1978), Brooklyn College-Advanced Certificate Program in Educational Administration and Supervision (1988).

CHAPTER 25

Education of Young Handicapped and At-Risk Children

During the past decade special schooling for children with handicaps has increased substantially. The number of children identified as handicapped and served through special education programs in the schools in the United States expanded from 3.7 million in 1977 to over 4.4 million in 1987. The category of learning disabilities, which accounts for a major portion of the increase, grew from 797,200 in 1977 to 1,926,000 in 1987 (U.S. Department of Education, 1988). About 68 percent of all handicapped children receive most or all of the education in regular classes (with or without part-time resource room instruction); 24 percent are in self-contained classes; only 7 percent are in special schools or other facilities (U.S. Department of Education, 1988).

Of particular interest to early childhood specialists is that the number of handicapped preschool children receiving special education services has also increased substantially over the past ten years. Because of the growing attention to young at-risk and handicapped children, 2.4 percent of the total population of three-through-five year old children in the nation received special education services in 1987 (U.S. Department of Education, 1988). Further, this age group comprised 6 percent of the handicapped children served in the schools (U.S. Department of Education, 1988; Hume, 1988). School services for preschoolers include finding and diagnosing at-risk preschoolers and providing early intervention programs for them (Lerner Mardell-Czudnowski, & Goldenberg, 1987).

Legislation and Its Impact

The growth of special education is closely linked to the civil rights movement and the goal of making equal educational opportunities available for all children. While the Supreme Court decision in 1954, *Brown v. Board of Education* addressed the problem of the segregation of black children in separate schools, it also served as a precedent for establishing the rights of children with handicaps to be provided with equal educational opportunity. This right was officially affirmed in 1974 when a U.S. District Court ruled in *Pennsylvania Association for Retarded Children.*

Nancy Beth Bowman et al. v. Commonwealth of Pennsylvania, David H. Hurtzman:

> It is the commonwealth's obligation to place each mentally re-
> tarded child in a free, public program of education and training
> appropriate to the child's capacity.

This case and other similar judicial decisions that followed reflect federal laws that extend the right of treatment and access to educational services for handicapped children under the Fifth and Fourteenth Amendments to the Constitution. These amendments state that no person can be deprived of liberty and of equal protection of the laws without due process. Federal legislation focusing on the rights of persons with handicaps and governing much of the subsequent activity and improvements in the education of handicapped children was spelled out in three major laws: the Rehabilitation of Act of 1973; Public Law 933-380 in 1974: and Public Law 94-142 (the Education for all Handicapped Children Act of 1975), which was reauthorized in 1986.

(1) The Rehabilitation Act provided that no "program" or "activity" receiving federal assistance can exclude or discriminate against persons solely because of their handicaps. (2) PL 93-380 authorized increased levels of aid to states for the implementation of special education services and set forth due process requirements to protect the rights of affected children and their families. (3) PL 94-142 set forth as national policy the goal that "free appropriate public education . . . must be extended to handicapped children as their fundamental right."

Some of the important basic tenets and subsequent judicial interpretations of these laws include:

1. Children with handicaps, however severe their disability, must be provided with free appropriate public education.
2. Testing and assessment services must be fair and comprehensive (decisions cannot be based on a single criterion such as an IQ score).
3. Parents or guardians must have access to all information used in the assessment and may request a hearing on decisions made by school officials concerning placement.
4. Individualized educational programs (IEPs) must be developed for each child and include both long-range goals and short-term objectives. Periodic review of the IEP goals is required.
5. Educational services are to be provided in the "least restrictive" environment. That is, to the extent appropriate, handicapped children are to be educated with non-handicapped children. A local education agency receiving federal funds must either provide appro-

priate services within the school or provide this instruction elsewhere at public expense.

Preschool handicapped children also have protections under another recent federal law, Public Law 99-457. Passed by Congress in 1986, PL 99-457 is an amendment to the Education of the Handicapped Act (PL 94-142). PL 99-457 affects preschool children who are handicapped or at-risk for handicapping conditions in several ways (Lerner, 1987):

1. It extends the full rights and protections of the law to handicapped children ages 3 through 5. This law is to be implemented by the school year 1990–91.
2. It permits the noncategorical reporting of children ages 3 through 5. Schools may identify young children as "developmentally delayed" rather than by category of handicap.
3. It authorizes an increase in federal contribution for children in this age group.

To summarize the special education legislation for young children, PL 94-142 mandates special education services for children and youth ages 5–21, and PL 99-457 extends the law for children 3 through 5. PL 99-457 also provides additional features for children ages birth to three, although intervention services are not mandated for this age group.

Head Start legislation created another early intervention program for young at-risk children. First launched in 1964, Head Start provided preschool education to four and five year old disadvantaged children. An amendment to Head Start legislation in 1972 requires that ten percent of the total enrollment in Head Start be reserved for handicapped children. Follow-up studies of children who were enrolled in Head Start show that some fifteen or twenty years later these individuals displayed impressive positive long-term effects. Individuals who were enrolled in Head Start were significantly better in cognitive skills, behavior, attitude toward school, and academic achievement in relation to comparison groups (Berrueta-Clement, Schweinhart, Barnett, Epstein, & Weikert, 1984; Lazar & Darlington, 1979).

In terms of costs, special education expenditures rose steadily in the 1970s and 1980s. The average cost of educating a child with handicaps is much higher than the national average for nonhandicapped children, about double the national average of $3,500 (Digest of Education Statistics, 1987). Although federal law requires local school districts to provide free appropriate education, the federal government has contributed relatively few dollars to this effort. Federal expenditures for special education increased from $75 million in 1969 to little more than $1 billion in 1985 (U.S.

Department of Education, 1987), but this amount represents only a few hundred extra dollars per child. Thus, the special education mandates place a heavy financial burden on the states and local educational agencies.

Although children receiving special education services now constitute almost 11 percent of the public school enrollment in some school districts, particularly in major metropolitan areas, large numbers of children with handicaps are on waiting lists for placement into special education programs. It appears that PL 94-142 has been implemented much more successfully in some locations than others (Singer & Butler, 1987; Viadero, 1987).

Classification and Labeling

Classification is used to determine eligiblity for services under the law. However, planning instruction for an individual child depends upon many factors other than the categorical label.

PL 94-142 designates specific categories of handicapping condition, such as learning disabilities, behavior disorders, mental retardation, visual impairments, hearing impairments, speech impairments, etc. For a child to be eligible to receive special services under the law, the category of handicap or label must be identified in the child's written indiviualized education program (IEP) document. The law places the responsibility for classifying the child's category of handicap on the members of the child's IEP team. However, determining the category of handicap is often difficult. For example, the team must decide if the child is mentally retarded and in need for special education services or a slow learner who only requires more time and guidance. Or does a child who is working below capacity have a learning disability or is the low achievement due to poor motivation or inadequate education. Differentiating borderline cases or distinguishing between mild and severe problems are also difficult decisions. For example, is the child deaf or hard of hearing?

Making a differential diagnosis for young children is especially troublesome. This is why the classification requirement has been modified under PL 99-457 for three-through-five year old children. Team members may elect to use the noncategorical classification of "developmentally delayed." This offers more time to observe and work with the child before deciding upon a categorical classification of handicap.

Classifying children with learning disabilities has been especially controversial. The special education category of learning disabilities has undergone the largest increase since PL 94-142 was first implemented in 1977. Several reasons are offered to explain the growing number of children identified as learning disabled. They include more awareness of the problem on the part of parents and teachers, liberal eligibility criteria for learning disabilities, social acceptance and preference for the learning disabled classification, cutbacks in other programs and lack of general education alternatives for children who experience problems in the regular class, and court orders to reclassify minority mentally retarded children (Lerner, 1989). Some studies suggest that many children classified as learning disabled do not meet the criteria for learning disabilities (Reynolds, 1984).

Critics are concerned that a label or classification may generate a self-fulfilling prophecy. For example, if a child is labeled as emotionally disturbed, the child may be inclined to act in a disturbed manner because the label makes this behavior expected and acceptable (Hechinger, 1987; Macmillan and Meyers, 1979; National Coalition of Advocates for Students, 1987).

Another concern is that labeling and placement in a special class or program has detrimental effect on the child. Research on the effects of labeling have investigated the impact on self-concept, peer acceptance, and postschool outcomes. However, this type of research is difficult to conduct because of problems involving definition of terms, the measurement of program effects, and the fact that different children have different reactions to a given program or placement. Moreover, the likelihood that labeling may have a negative effect does not mean that placement in a regular class or setting necessarily will be more beneficial. A basic question is whether the detrimental stigma effects are caused by the label or by the child's failure to learn.

One review of studies on the effects of labeling concluded that the research has not conclusively demonstrated that there are overall negative effects of special or separate classes or programs for handicapped children. Nor have the studies clearly shown that separate classes or programs are more beneficial than placement in regular classes (Macmillan & Meyers, 1979). Another review of research concludes that for children with mild learning problems, restrictive educational settings need not detract from achievement provided that effective practices are used to overcome problems such as stigmatization and slow pacing of instruction. However, the authors emphasize that less restrictive settings are generally preferable on ethical grounds (Leinhardt and Pallay, 1982; Leinhardt & Bickel, 1987).

Mainstreaming

Mainstreaming is the process of integrating children with handicaps into regular schools and classrooms, providing maximum opportunities not only to join in usual school activities but also to be "counted in" among their nonhandicapped peers.

Providing a mainstream preschool setting for at-risk or handicapped preschool children is especially challenging. Finding an integrated setting is difficult because public schools typically do not offer schooling for normally developing three-and-four-year old preschool children. McLean and Odom (1988) suggest that administrators of preschool programs for handicapped children seek other options such as private preschool programs to provide integrated experiences.

The term, "mainstreaming" is not mentioned in PL 94-142 and not synonymous with the *least restrictive environment*. The intent of the law is to provide educational experiences for handicapped children in a setting within a nonhandicapped society wherever possible. It is not to place all handicapped children into regular classes (Hume, 1987). When children are mainstreamed, they usually need extra professional support from specialists skilled in working with a particular handicap and in some cases special equipment. Even for children with severe disabilities where children need to spend most of their time away from the regular classroom, the child can still be encouraged to take part in activities such as art, music, or shop with the other children.

Researchers who have examined the literature on mainstreaming conclude that the data regarding effects on self-esteem are inconclusive. Mainstreaming can improve the social acceptance of students with handicaps provided that direct interventions are made to achieve this goal. However, there is little evidence that mainstreaming practices result in superior performance among handicapped students (Reynolds & Birch, 1988; Semmel, Gottlieb, and Robinson, 1979). This general finding probably is related to difficulties in defining and measuring various mainstreaming approaches, as well as to the special placement settings with which they then are compared. Available evidence indicates that the amount of time in regular classes, without considering the quality of instruction or the criterion employed to determine who gets mainstreamed and for how long, has little impact on social or academic outcomes (Semmel, Gottlieb, and Robinson, 1979).

In summary, researchers seem to agree that the studies have not provided conclusive support for either special class placement or for integrated mainstreaming. In part, this is because research efforts on both approaches have not been carried out very well in a large number of settings. Research does indicate, however, that regular classroom teachers have not been well-prepared to work with handicapped children in their classes.

These pessimistic observations should not be viewed as justification for despair concerning the future of mainstreaming. Mainstreaming may prove to be a positive answer to the long tradition of isolating handicapped children, but by itself it is not a panacea. To be effective, mainstreaming requires a variety of special resources and educators who are skilled in and dedicated to creating an effective learning environment and acceptance for children with handicaps. Thus, one important educational goal is to make the mainstreaming approach more successful than it is at present.

An Optimal Learning Environment

Requirements of PL 94-142 and related legislation specify that school officials must prepare an individualized education program (IEP) for children with handicaps, including special services to help achieve education goals specified in the IEP. These requirements have frequently been interpreted as implying that as part of an "appropriate" free education handicapped children require whatever services are necessary to help them derive as much benefit from education as do other students—perhaps an optimal learning environment for the handicapped.

However, providing an optimal learning environment for handicapped students, particularly those with severe handicaps, can be extremely expensive. In some cases, there have been disagreements between school officials, who claim the school cannot afford to provide maximally effective education to certain handicapped children and parents or advocates who claim that children with handicaps have a constitutional right to whatever service are needed to ensure maximum educational gain (Viadero, 1987b).

A test case on this issue went to U.S. Supreme Court in 1982, when the parents of a deaf first grader demanded that she be provided with a sign-language interpreter in academic classes. Local educators argued that they have provided an FM hearing aid, a tutor of the deaf, and a speech therapist but could not provide an interpreter. In the case *Board of Education of Hudson, Central School District v. Rowely,* the Court ruled that although the law requires the provision of such "supportive services [as] may be required to assist a handicapped child to benefit from public education," it does not require a particular level of benefit above the "basic floor of opportunity . . . [which] consists of access to specialized services individually designed" for a child.

Future Curriculum and Instruction

Even though research has not yet identified or documented the most effective approaches to providing instruction to handicapped students, much has been learned concerning the types of practices that are most likely to enhance their learning. For example, instructional strategies that appear to be the most promising include (Levine & Ornstein, 1981; Weatherby and Lipsky, 1977):

1. General teacher-training programs should provide increased understanding and competency in working with the handicapped.
2. Greater emphasis should be placed on meeting the social and emotional needs to all students.
3. Careful, regular evaluation based on individual performance criteria should be used to ascertain student progress.
4. Teachers should realized that their professional commitment is to all students, including those with special needs.
5. Class placement should be based on careful preassessment of each child's problems and capacity.
6. Better assessment procedures should be developed and used only by professionals skilled in their interpretation.
7. A team approach including the classroom teacher should be utilized in determining if a child is in need of special services, and how best to provide such services.
8. Class size should be limited to a realistic number so that individual needs can be satisfied.

"Education of Young Handicapped and At-Risk Children" was written by: Allan Ornstein, Daniel U. Levine, and Janet W. Lerner. *Illinois School Research and Development,* (imprint 1989).

References

Berrueta-Clement, J., Schweinhart, L., Barnett, S., Epstein A., & Weikart, D. *Changed Lives.* Ypsilanti, MI: High Scope Educational Foundation, 1984.

Digest of Education Statistics. Washington DC: U.S. Government Printing Office, 1987.

Hechinger, F. "Risks of the 'learning disabled', label." *New York Times,* November 24, 1987, C13.

Hume, M. "States dive into programs for disabled students." *Education Daily,* March 25, 1988, 3–4.

Lazar, I. & Darlington, R. "Lasting effects after preschool." *Washington DC: Government Printing Office,* OHDD 80-30179, 1979.

Leinhardt, G. & Pallay. A. "Restrictive educational settings: Exile or haven?" *Review of Educational Research,* 1982, 52: 557–558.

Leinhardt, G. & Bickel, W. "Instruction's the thing wherein to catch the mind that falls behind." *Educational Psychologist,* 1987, Spring: 177–207.

Lerner, J.W. *Learning Disabilities: Theories, Diagnosis, and Teaching Strategies.* Boston, MA: Houghton Mifflin, 1989.

Lerner, J.W. "Legislative update: Reauthorization of the Education of the Handicapped Act and EHA Amendments." *Learning Disabilities Focus,* 1987, 2: 78–79.

Lerner, J.W., Mardell-Czdanowski, C., & Goldberg, D. *Special Education for the Early Childhood Years.* Englewood Cliffs, NJ: Prentice Hall, 1987.

Levine, D.U. & Ornstein, A.C. "Some trends in educating handicapped children." *Journal of Curriculum Studies,* 1981, 13: 261–266.

Macmillan, D.L. & Meyers, C.E. "Educational labeling of handicapped learners." In D.C. Berliner (ed.) *Review of Research in Education,* Washington DC: American Educational Research Association, 1979, Vol. 7: 121–194.

McLean M. & Odom, S. *Least restrictive environment and social integration.* Council of Exceptional Children. Division for Early Childhood. Unpublished White Paper. June, 1988.

National Coalition of Advocates for Students. "Rights without labels." *Education Week,* May 17, 1987, 22.

Reynolds, M.C. "Classification of students with handicaps." In E.W. Gordon (ed.) *Review of Research in Education,* Washington DC: American Educational Research Association, 1984, Vol. 2: 77–94.

Reynolds, M.C. & Birch, J.W. *Adaptive Mainstreaming.* New York: Longman, 1988.

Semmel, M. Gottlieb, J. & Robinson, N. "Mainstreaming: Perspectives on educating handicapped children in public schools." In D.C. Berliner (Ed.) Review of Research in Education, Washington DC: Educational Research Association, 1979, 223–279.

Semmel, M., Gottlieb, J. & Robinson, N. "Mainstreaming." In R.B. Baum. Educating the exceptional child in the regular classroom. *Journal of Teacher Education,* 1979, 30: 20–22.

Singer, J.D. and Butler, J.A. "The Education for All Handicapped Children Act: Schools as agents of social reform." *Harvard Educational Review,* 1987, 57: 125–152.

U.S. Department of Education. "To assure the free and appropriate public education of all handicapped children." *Tenth Annual Report to Congress on the Implementation of the Education the Handicapped Act.* Washington DC: Government Printing Office, 1988.

Viadero, D. "Many state programs for the handicapped are found deficient." *Education Week,* April 19, 1987a, 1–21.

Viadero, D. "Medically fragile: students pose major dilemma for school officials." *Education Week,* March 11, 1987ba, 1–14.

Weatherby, R. & Lipsky, M." Street-level bureaucrats and institutional innovation: Implementing special-educating reform." *Harvard Educational Review,* May, 1977, 185–196.

CHAPTER 26

Language Intervention at the Preschool Level—Language Delay Category: Nonverbal Behavior (Sociolinguistic Reference)

When we read in the literature that; Eighty-five (85%) percent of all children have a language disorder. Wilson (1988), that langue handicaps affect a greater number of children entering school than is generally known. . . Eisenson and Ogilivie (1963), that based on Kindergarten screenings conducted in Freeport, New York 1973–1975, that approximately twenty-five (25%) of the children showed language deficits that required special attention and remediation, Summers (1976), and that children have experienced the consequence of school failures mainly because their language deficiencies were not detected at the preschool level, Bang (1968), then we know that we have a strong documented rationale for Language Development Programs, in addition to the Speech Program at the preschool level.

The purposes of this chapter are to inform and to influence. To inform student teachers, teachers, and administrators about the nonverbal child in the public school classroom and to influence the approach(es) to working with these children. The primary concern is with motivating, stimulating, and facilitating talk in nonverbal preschool children.

Talk may seem unnecessary to a young child when others talk for him or her. When the child is asked a question by the teacher, by the physician, or others and the mother answers; when brothers and sisters answer for the child before he or she has a chance; when teachers seem to prefer the child to speak only when he or she asks a question; and when adults leave the child "alone" by not including him or her, it is very easy to get the impression that talk isn't necessary. This is my opinion based on reflections about my early years in school. I wonder what feelings nonverbal children have about talk for them in the classroom.

Children's knowledge about language is often revealed through conversations with them and from listening to their conversations with others.

I wanted to know what "verbal" children thought about the reasons and necessity for talk. We asked fifty-eight (58) children "WHY DO WE NEED TO TALK?" We received answers from Pre-kindergarten and Kindergarten children in the following categories, except for Jeanne's answer:

> "My daddy knows how to talk in all ways, English, American, Spanish, Whisper, say quack, quack, hop, hop, ribit, ribit, bark like a dog, and use sign language." Jeanne (Pre-K, 1989)

Answer categories:

—"Because we want to hear" (talk goes with hearing)
—"So we won't get hurt" (talk keeps us safe)
—"To tell something" (information sharing)
—"For work" (communication)
—"To know something" (gain information)
—"We have teeth" (teeth help us talk)
—"To read books" (silent reading)

Some children seem to know that language is functional. Perhaps nonverbal children know this also, but require extensive attention with focus on stimulation, motivation, and facilitation of talk.

Rationale for Langugae Intervention

Language development intervention at the preschool level (Pre-K and Kindergarten) is concerned with children who are langugae delayed/disordered. The child's language competence is below age level expectation, with involvement in one or more of the categories of the linguistic system (phonology, semantics, syntax, morphology.)

Linguistic competence of the preschool child is considered, assessed, and developed based on the results from several research studies. One such study by Danwitz (1974) provides the frame of reference for age level expectation. She wrote that:

> A five-year-old child's typical verbal output is between ten thousand (10,000) to fifteen thousand (15,000) words per day of

grammatically correct language. Drawing on a vocabulary of approximately five thousand (5,000) words. The child's comprehension of spoken language may include a vocabulary three times this size. A two-year-old is expected to use two-word phrases and to follow a simple command; a three-year-old is expected to use three or four word sentences; and a four-year-old is expected to use four or five word sentences and to be understood by persons outside the family. (p. 87)

Children who do not follow this linguistic progression require special attention. The lag may be an indication of sensory, neurological, intellectual, emotional or sociolinguistic deficits. The children in the public school classroom who do not approximate these guidelines are usually in the sociolinguistic category.

The focus of this chapter is one category of language delay that does not fit into the pre-linguistic or linguistic system heading. It could, however, come between the two. The confusing characteristics of nonverbal behavior does not provide for a specific label because language must be audible for it to be assessed for form and content. The child's language may or may not be age appropriate. The task is to motivate and facilitate talk so that it can be recorded, developed, and followed.

Bierwirth's (1987) introductory remarks for a language development discussion at a New York State Cultural Diversity Conference offers a rationale for early intervention:

> While the importance of language development in the growth of a student has long been recognized, just how and when to intervene to help a student with a lag in this area has not. A child who does not have sufficient language development is not likely to develop into a good reader. The child is therefore likely to be referred to a remedial reading teacher and/or a learning disabilities specialist. This student is not speech impaired and does not need the assistance of a special education certified Speech Teacher. What we feel that this student needs is a highly focused language development program tailored to the student's specific needs, taught by a specialist with extensive early childhood training and experience, and additional training in Speech and Language Development.

Children who are nonverbal at school are a special concern for language and learning acquisition, for social development, and for some forms of teacher assessment. The children are at risk linguistically, academically, and socially. The teacher is at risk for knowing student's progress, achievement, needs, feelings, and language competence.

Nature and Description of Nonverbal Behavior

Several descriptive terms and phrases are used in research literature, non-research based writings, and in conversations to refer to children who choose not to talk. Some of the labels are: nonverbal, nonvocal, selectively mute, non-languaged, reticent, shy, etc. All of these labels are about children who may or may not be language delayed or disordered, however, when the child begins to talk an assessment can be made to determine if the child is language delayed in addition to being nonverbal.

Eight (8) specific cases of nonverbal behavior for the Early Childhood Center, Freeport, New York are described below; variations and combinations are seen each year:

1. Flat affect—absence of clues of communicative desire or intent; absence of any sign that the child could hear. Totally unresponsive at school.
2. Pleasantly nonverbal—smiled often, laughed, used gesture. Favorite activity—classroom store.
3. Limited English Proficient—smiled often, used gestures and signs, nodded in response to questions and statements. Favorite activity— matching card game. (Research literature discusses the "silent period" that LEP students experience which can last from one week to two years).
4. Limited English Proficient—nonvocal at school for two years (Pre-K and Kgn.) Talked during the third year in the Bridge class. Favorite activities—drawing, coloring and listening to stories.
5. Gesture use—(pointed and nodded). At the end of the Kindergarten year the child whispered answers and requests. Favorite activity— Art.
6. One word responses—(yes, no)
7. Nonverbal for two years at school—At the end of the second year, the child used two to three word utterances with puppets. Favorite activities—puppets and classroom store.
8. Nonverbal with adults—Smiled and talked with children only. Talked briefly with teacher when the teacher telephoned the child at home.

General Observations Made Over the Course of Several Years

—Nonverbal children show interest in using play and authentic telephones when they are a part of the classroom equipment. Interest is usually shown immediately, while for some children it is eventual. Interest is shown by moving toward the instrument, by picking it up, smiling, listening, and standing beside it. Miller (1981)

—The nonverbal child in the classroom is treated by peers as an infant during playtime. The child is almost always considered the baby and is therefore physically carried about and always talked for. Peers often tell others that the child cannot talk. This information is shared throughout the school as the children attend Art, Music and Movement classes.

—Some nonverbal children focus attention on the speaker's mouth, which gives the impression that the child is lip reading.

Halliday's (1973) Functional language categories are listed with the nonverbal equivalent categories that were observed at the Early Childhood Center in Freeport, New York.*

Instrunmental: "I want" (language as a means of getting things, satisfying material needs — frowning, pointing, weeping, grabbing, leading person to object

Regulatory: as I tell you" (controlling the behavior, feelings, or attitudes or others). — pushing and pulling others around, modeling behavior for others to copy.

Interactional: "Me and you" (getting along with others, establishing relative status. Also "Me against you" establishing separateness.) — smiling, holding hands, joining, another, standing close, leaning/-touching others

Personal: "Here I came (expressing individuality, awareness of self, pride) — showing work completed

Heuristic: "Tell me Why?" (seeking and testing knowledge). — repetition of activity, close scrutiny, and observation

Imaginative: "Let's pretend" (creating new worlds, making up stories, poems. — manipulating toys, blocks, etc.

Representational: "I've got to tell you." (communicating information, descriptions, expressing propositions.) — showing/presenting/-pointing to activity and art work

*Early Childhood Center, Freeport, New York District-Wide Center for Pre-kindergarten and Kindergarten children. Population approximately eight hundred (800) children.

Some Suggested Reasons for Nonverbal Behavior

Reasons considered for nonverbal behavior at school are based on research and developing theory that are grouped under such headings as:

Biological, Environmental (home), and Environmental (classroom climate and culture.)

Biological Basis

Nonverbal children who are a part of the public school classroom are without etiological configuration. The speech physiology is fully functional and these children are known to talk in settings other than the school. According to Whitehurst (1987):

> We do not know why these children do not speak. They have five (5) times more middle ear infections than children who speak at age appropriate levels. Such infection may impair a child's ability to hear at critical periods in his or her development. Eight-five (85%) percent of the language delayed toddlers are males which suggests that the condition may have a biological basis. There is evidence that children with delays in language are at risk for later academic difficulties. These children also score below average on I.Q. examinations, even though tests at younger ages revealed that they were within normal ranges. We believe that children with expressive language delay should be thought of as normal children. The problem is readily treatable by varying the child's social stimulation.

Wilson (1988) found that "eight-five (85%) percent of all youngsters have a language disorder, and that eighty (80%) percent of the children with language disabilities or motor disabilities are boys." p. 2.

Environmental Conditions—Home

It is my observation that when young children enter school for the first time they come with many confusing messages from family members. One such message is "be quiet" in school and "be good". Some children seem to interpret these messages as "do not talk for any reason."

One example of a mixed message that I experienced as a Kindergarten Teacher several years ago seems to support my theory. While waiting in the hallway on the first day of school to receive the children for my class, one youngster came to me crying and said, "If you give the teacher ten (10) cents you won't get in trouble and be sent to the Principal." He gave me ten cents. As I tried to console him I asked, "Who told you that this would happen?" He replied, "Mommy". My comment was, "Oh, you know, I think she meant that if you pay attention to the teacher that you will not get into any trouble and need to see that Principal. He quickly smiled and said, "Yeah, that's what she said". Over the years, many children have said "I have to be quiet in school".

The socioeconomic status of the family impacts on the child's language acquisition and use. Several research studies support this theory. One study was conducted by Heath (1983) in North Carolina during the late 60's and early 70's. Teachers were concerned with the wide and varied discrepancy in learning styles and language abilities of socioeconomic groups. Three groups were studied: a White group of low socioeconomic status, a Black group of low socioeconomic status, and a combined Black and White group of middle-class status. A comparison of the groups approach(es) to helping their children acquire language and the success of their children in school indicated that: the White low socioeconomic group used basically a teaching approach to develop language, an approximation of what the school does. This approach involved the teaching of isolated skills followed by questioning. The Black group used a language immersion approach primarily, in which the children were surrounded by and on the fringe of much adult talk and interrogation about their involvement. The middle-class Black and White group used the running narrative/commentary approach. The mother talked and explained constantly to the child about her activities and asked the child about information that she already knew, so that she was able to expand and extend the child's information. It was found that the children in this group experienced success throughout their school years. Children from both low socioeconomic groups experienced some difficulty in school due to language deficits.

Parents of language delayed children seem to be concerned about their children's language form: the errors made and their minimal use of language. Therefore, they tend to spend a great deal of time urging the children to talk more by interrogating them. (McDade and Varnedoe 1987) According to Marshall, Hegrenes, and Goldstein (1973) "parents of language impaired children use more interrogation and directives to get children to talk than parents of normal language learners." (p. 415)

Environmental Conditions
(School Climate/Culture)

Klein (1977) wrote about the school setting and its effect on children's talk. He noted that the nature of our school concept imposes constraints on spontaneous talk: for example, the form of audience that is available to the child. Cazden (1970) found that children's talk is greatly influenced by the topic talked about and by who the listener is. Klein further noted that the school setting eliminates the intimate setting which is so important for inter-personal exchange. Therefore, the school climate itself perpetuates language delay in some children, especially those who are at risk for language use and development.

Classroom talk as well as nonverbal behavior is directly related to the following variables: Classroom atmosphere, teacher attitude and messages, and constraints. A brief clarification of each follows: the atmosphere of the classroom refers to the feeling that the child receives from such influences as the teacher's receptiveness, warmth, and total acceptance, room arrangement, class size, organization of time frame, and goal direction. Teacher attitude and messages refer to the teacher's feeling about talk. This feeling is articulated verbally and nonverbally through expectation, encouragement, attention, and conversation and commentary with the child. Bayless (1974) defines constraints as instruction(s), direction(s), physical limitation of play space and interference from adults and peers. (p. 218)

When language is used freely in settings that encourage it, the opportunity is there for the teacher to listen to and attend to both the form and function that children use, put together, and express. Two means that are used for this purpose are observation accompanied with anecdotal recordings (written or taped) and conversations with the child. With nonverbal children alternative communicative behaviors are observed and written anecdotes are made. The purposes of these notes are to attend to a pattern of behaviors and activity preferences to determine the communicative desire and intent, and to select the most effective activities to use with the child.

Intervention Guidelines and Suggestions

Intervention with nonverbal children is primarily a school focused program for the purposes of this chapter, because this is the setting where the nonverbal behavior occurs.

Frank Smith (1973) wrote that "one difficult way to make learning to read easy is to respond to what the child is trying to do." (p. 195) This concept seems just as applicable for oral language motivation as to reading. We must learn to recognize the nonverbal child's clues to communicative desire and intent (gestures, facial expressions, sustained eye focus, signs, span of activity observation, etc.) and supply the language for the task(s). We must become astute at observation of these clues in order to anticipate the needs, feelings, and desires of the child and be available and/or nearby to offer assistance.

Motivating talk at the early childhood level is accomplished through teacher attitude, practices, approach, and type and use of materials. The overall goal is to create an atmosphere in which the child will feel comfortable enough to take the risk to talk: to feel that talk is accepted, encouraged, valued, necessary, important, and expected. Language delayed children need opportunities for spontaneous speech in the context of genuine conversational relationships: sustained turn-taking talk about a specific subject of interest to the child. Genuine interpersonal relationships Scofield (1978) and Conversations Warren (1985). Scofield wrote that much of classroom talk is teacher talk in the form of questions and commands which function as constraints for child speech. She summarizes that:

> facilitating spontaneous talk requires a "state of mind" that appreciates and values children both as they are and as they might be. With language delayed children an attitude is required that values communication experience as a genuine part of learning to talk. Just as children need intervention focused on linguistic and cognitive aspects of their development, language delayed children need interpersonal experiences with significant adults. p. 719.

Several studies have been conducted with regard to language intervention approaches for language delayed preschool children. However, there is an absence of research that offers approaches, theories, and materials for working with the nonverbal child in the public school setting. An adaptation of some of the general approaches are effective at the Early Childhood Center in Freeport, New York. A summary of research studies that have implications for facilitating oral language are: Hart and Risley's (1975) report on the Incidental approach and its relationship to oral language. In this approach the child initiates interaction by requesting assistance from the adult, either by verbal or nonverbal means. Cazden (1970) emphasized the importance of the context in which a child talks—the environmental effects. The way children talk will be determined by the subject of the discussion and who the listener is. Conditions of constraint (questions and directions) from the teacher, result in children using fewer words in their answers. Bayles (1974) suggests that there are two basic steps to consider in facilitation: first the adult becomes less constraining, and second, the adult follow the child's lead. This approach provides for maintaining and extending the subject of the child's interest. Hubbell (1974) reviewed clinical approaches to facilitating spontaneous talk in young children which has implications for the classroom setting. He summarized that the facilitative approach has been demonstrated to be effective with children who are functionally language delayed in talking. The context for spontaneous talk appears to be related to the presence of various stimulus events such as specific referents and to the structure of the interpersonal relationships involved.

The Teacher's Role

Klein (1977) suggests that the most important role of the teacher is one of facilitator—"tone setter". The classroom atmosphere is central to all learning in school, but is even more important in a talk situation. The teacher is the structure: one who gives careful consideration to the kinds of activities and categories that have the greatest effect for developmental growth. Several ranges must be involved in the planning of activities: the setting range, the audience range, the subject range, the depth of talk range, and cognitive range.

The teacher must know and understand how children acquire, use, and learn language. Three researchers from different fields of child study provide significant information for us: Bruner (1978) wrote about "scaffolding"; Halliday (1982) about "tracking; and Vygotsky (1962) about the "zone of proximal development". Their ideas tell of the importance of communicative interactions between adults and children which are necessary for language development and intervention. Parents play a significant part in their children's language acquisition and these authors suggest that teachers use these concepts to support the child in the classroom:

> "scaffolding"—effective communication on one level is always the beginning point for attempts to communicate on a more adult level. (take the lead from the child): Use clues gained from observation of the nonverbal child.

> "tracking"—adults and older siblings who live with the child share in the language acquisition process with the child (a side-by-side approach). With nonverbal children tracking will take the form of talking about and describing the child's activities, supply the language to accompany the task(s).

> "zone of proximal development"—Educators can make use of work/activity time between the adult and the child and move the child along to a level that he or she cannot attain alone at that time.

Teachers must be aware of and attend to the culturally diverse background of their students. Keifer and DeStefano (1985) suggest that we must be sensitive to experiential background, language behaviors and customs, and customs within and across groups. We must observe the children and follow their lead, and we must use the information to "build bridges rather than walls." (p. 167) Teachers who use children's preferences for relating to adults in groups, met with greater success when they asked questions of the group rather than of individuals or when they permitted voluntary responses to flow freely, Boggs (1972). Some teachers do not single out children to give reports or to answer questions. One approach, highly recommended, is that the teacher make himself/herself available for individual students to approach him or her alone to ask their questions. Phillips (1972.)

Other teachers have effectively used peer tutoring or children from upper grades to work with younger children in order to free them to work with individuals. Similar observations and research will provide us with needed information for facilitating oral language with children of diverse cultures.

Suggestions for Working with Nonverbal Children

1. When children are involved in exploratory activities, the teacher might ask questions such as "I wonder why this is so?" This question and others may help children to reflect on their own thinking and see contradictions in their hypotheses. Goodman (1985). With nonverbal children the teacher might ask and answer the question(s) rather than interrogate the child. This way, the child will hear question forms and answers to the question(s).

2. When a child achieves success in some communicative setting (including reading and writing) the teacher may find a number of ways to extend this to a new and different setting. Goodman (1985). This approach is applicable with nonverbal children when we follow their clues (gestures, facial expressions, signs, etc.) and extend and expand on their activity.

3. When children are observed to be troubled with an experience, the teacher can approach and talk about the situation with them and lead the child to what cannot yet be accomplished alone. Vygotsky (1962).

4. Teachers need to learn with and from children; to be aware of and capitalize on the "side-by-side" concept of learning.

5. Eliciting language by direct prodding and questioning has undesirable results: talking becomes an unpleasant experience for the child who is constantly urged to talk. The child is less likely to talk when pressured by adults. With regard to the questioning process, it becomes a one-way scenario that progresses in this manner: the adult asks a quesiton, a period of silence follows, the adult asks another question or the same one, this time followed by silence, the adult usually supplies the answer and demands imitation. As long as the adult continues to send messages the child remains the receiver. Interrogation and insisting that a child talk at school is ineffective for the purpose of facilitating oral language. Language delayed children, also, cannot be forced, cajoled, tricked, persuaded, reprimanded, or shamed into talking. Nor, is a show of anger and impatience effective. All of these techniques, and others, are used daily in schools. This approach does not work; as a matter of fact it seems to delay the desired behavior. It shows rejections of the child and his/her behavior.

6. Limited English Proficient children and language delayed English speaking children have many of the same needs linguistically and socially. Therefore, some of the same techniques, materials, and approaches are used with great success.

Some Materials That Have Been Used Successfully at the Early Childhood Center in Freeport, New York

1. Authentic telephones used in a Kindergarten classroom, 1976–1985. (Telezonia from Bell Telephone Company). Telezonia used as part of research study conducted at the Early Childhood Center—1979–80. Instruments were effective in motivating nonverbal children to begin talking.
2. Sesame Street English as a Second Language Program (Stage I). Familiar characters from Sesame Street has high motivational effect in addition to the chants, songs, poems, conversations, etc. Nonverbal children usually "join in" group oral language activities before speaking individually.
3. Toy books—classroom made toy books from "Toys R Us" advertising circular found in weekly newspaper. Children are eventually motivated to name the toys that they have and want.
4. Memory card game (concentration) commercial and classroom made. The children enjoy winning and looking at the pictures. The subject areas are unlimited. (animals, toys, colors, shapes, words, numbers, various concepts) Children also experience turntaking, risk taking, hear language of the game, and labels for the pictures, provided by the teacher.
5. Peabody Language Development Kits—puppets, pictures, and story recording are especially effective.

Summary

Functional language-delayed children require oral language intervention in addition to what is currently available in preschool classrooms. When these children's interest is sufficiently piqued, spontaneous oral language is facilitated. Therefore, provision should be made by the teacher for the classroom atmosphere to incidentally suggest that talking is permitted, that it is desired, that it is useful, and that is necessary for social and academic success. She or he should foster this atmosphere in such a way that the child makes use of it for his/her own benefit on a spontaneous basis. To accomplish this goal an atmosphere of nonconstraint must prevail. During playtime there should be no effort on the part of the teacher to direct the children's activities by interference, instruction(s) questioning, or modeling. The classroom teacher's role is to be constantly available and adaptable to following the child's lead to talk and play.

The classroom should be organized in such a way that it provides for several activities that are self-directing. An adaptation of the open classroom type approach, in addition to technological intervention which provokes talk, is the most effective strategy for facilitating spontaneous oral language in functional language-delayed children. The establishment of such classroom centers as a housekeeping area, store area, block corner, etc., are recommended since this is the type of setting in which children seem to feel secure and comfortable enough to talk. This arrangement, whereby there is less formal teacher/pupil and pupil/pupil communication, provides a more optimal environment for oral language, growth, and development.

When children are encouraged, through incidental means, to use their oral communicative competence, there is an increase in language use, and language growth and development indicated by use of longer sentences, an increase in total language use, and an increase in the variety of language used.

Extended use of technological intervention for oral language development beyond the preschool level is recommended both in a facilitating and teaching capacity. At the preschool level the effectiveness of telephone use is in the provocative nature of the instrument and by the fact that it tends to make restricted code inadequate. In the early grades the approach might be both facilitative and teaching to move children toward elaborated code and toward developmental growth in oral language.

The influence of parental intervention in the home might well contribute to the spontaneous participation in oral language in the classroom by functional language delayed preschool children. School personnel could assist parents in fostering oral interaction between themselves and their children and between their children and other children, through the set up of workshops, a periodic newsletter or handbook, and awareness workshops to replace such established school nights as back-to-school night and exhibit night.

Finally, surrounding children with a classroom environment that initiates talk by its appearance, atmosphere, organization, equipment, and procedures seems to be a simple first step in a process that will foster academic and social success at school.

Bettye Glover Miller, Ed.D., Language Development Specialist, Early Childhood Center Freeport, New York

Footnotes

Bayles K. A. "The Effects of Constraint and Non-constraint on the Verbal Behavior of Preschool Children". Masters Thesis (Arizona State University, 1974), cited by Robert Hubbell, "On Facilitaing Spontaneous Talking in Young Children", Journal of Speech and Hearing disorders. XLII (1977). P. 219.

Bierwirth, John. Superintendent of Schools, Freeport, New York. Introductory Statement for Round Table Discussion on Early Language Development. Cultural Diversity Conference—sponsored by the New York State Education Department at White Plains, New York, 1987.

Danwitz, Sister M. Winifred. "Early Speech and Language Problems". *Bulletin of the Orton Society—An Interdisciplinary Journal of Specific Language Disability.* Paper presented at the World Congress on Dyslexia, Rochester, Minnesota: (November, 1974, pp. 86–90).

Marshall, N. J., Hegrenes, and S. Goldstein. "Verbal Interactions: Mothers and their Retarded Children vs Mother and their non-retarded Children." *American Journal of Mental Deficiency.* 77 (1973), pp. 415–419.

Scofield, Sandra. "The Language Delayed Child in the Mainstreamed Primary Classroom." *Language Arts.* September, 1978, p. 719.

Smith, Frank. "Twelve Ways to Make Learning to Read Difficult." In Frank Smith (Ed.) *Psycholinguistics and Reading.* New York: Holt, Rinehart and Winston, 1973. p. 195.

Whitehurst, Grover. "When Speech is Delayed." Long Island: New York. *Newsday* Newspaper, Behavior Section. April 21, 1986.

Wilson, Barbara C. "Why Can't Johnny Talk? A Preschool Answer." New York: *New York Times* Newspaper. Education Section. December 18, 1988.

Bibliography

Bang, Tina. *Language and Learning Disorders of the Pre Academic Child.* Englewood Cliff, New Jersey 1968.

Bruner, J. S., "The Role of Dialogue in Language Learning" in A. Sinclair, R. J. Jarvella, and W. J. M. Levelt (Eds.), *The Child's Conception of Language.* Springer-Verlag, 1978.

Boggs, S. T. "The Meaning of Questions and Narratives to Hawaiian Children", in C. Cazden, V. John and D. Hymes (Eds.), *Functions of Language in the Classroom.* New York: Teachers College Press, 1972.

Cazden, C. and Dell Hymes. *Functions of Language in the Classroom.* New York: Teachers College Press, 1972.

Halliday, M. A. R., *Explorations in the Function of Language.* London: Edward Arnold Publishers, 1973.

Hart, Betty and Todd Risley. *"Incidental Teaching in the Preschool." Journal of Applied Behavior Analysis. Winter, 1975. 414–419.*

Health, Shirley B. *Research Currents: A Lot of Talk About Nothing."* Language Arts. November/December, 1983. 999–1007.

Hubbell, Robert D., "On Facilitating Spontaneous Talking in Young Children." *Journal of Speech and Hearing Disorders.* XLII, 1977. 216–231.

Klein, Marvin. *Talk in the Language Arts Classroom.* Urbana, Illinois: ERIC Clearinghouse on Reading and Communication Skills and National Council of Teachers of English. 1977.

Keifer, B. and J. S. DeStefano. "Cultures Together in the Classroom: What You Saying?" in Angela Jaggar and M. Trika Smith-Burke (Eds.), *Observing the Language Learner.* Newark, Delaware: International Reading Association and National Council of Teachers of English, 1985. 167–168.

McDade, H. L. and Danielle Varnedoe. "Training Parents to be Language Facilitators." in K. Butler and Hiram McDade (Eds.) *Topics in Language Disorders* Vol. 7 #3, June, 24.

Miller, Betty G., "Facilitating Spontaneous Oral Language with Functional Language Delayed Kindergarten Children Using Telephone Technology." Paper presented at the International Reading Association Conference, Anaheim, California. May, 1983. Urbana, Illinois: ERIC.

Phillips, S. *The Invisible Culture: Communication in the Classroom on the Warm Springs Indian Reversation,* New York: Longman Press, 1982.

Sharp, Carrie. Lets Talk: First Steps to Conversation", *Facilitator's Guide,* in Good Talking with You: Language Acquisition Through Conversation. Video Training Program. Portland Oregon: Educational Productions, 1987. 11.

Summers, Marc. D. "Project R.A.I.S.E." Freeport, New York: Freeport School District, 1977. 227.

Warren, Steven and Ann Rogers-Warrn. *Teaching Functional Language—Language Intervention Series.* Baltimore: University Park Press, 1985. 98–100.

Materials Reference

Memory—"The Classic Card Matching Game of Visual Recall", Springfield, Massachusetts: Milton Bradley Company.

Peabody Language Development Kits (levels #P and I) Circle Pines, Minnesota: American Guidance Services, Inc., 1965.

Telezonia: Communicating by Telephone. American Telephone and Telegraph Company,1975.
>   Note: The program was received on loan from the local Bell Telephone Company.

Zion, Jane S. "Open Sesame." State A, English as a Second Language Series. Big Bird's Yellow Book and Tape. Oxford University Press: Children's Television Workshop.

CHAPTER 27

Early Childhood Education and Cross-Cultural Counseling

Early childhood education and cross-cultural counseling are the linkage between personal development and the larger processes of human behavioral changes. Knowledge of human development is essential for personality development, especially during childhood and adolescent years.

I. Comparing the Two Theoretical Views of Personality Development Emphasizing Childhood and Adolescent Years

A. Childhood

A picture of the child and adolescent of each specific developmental stage is presented to gain a deeper and more meaningful perspective of the world of children and youth. During the second and third years of life, the child masters major developmental tasks. Such tasks include walking and running, the recognition of objects and the theory of object permanency, the development of symbolic language, the internalization of the maternal image in the form of object constancy, and the establishment of gender identity. These developmental events prepare the child for peer interaction, relative independence, and socialization. The ability to use symbols in the early preoperational period of intelligence is a prerequisite for language and personality development. The child has the innate ability to use basic grammar to construct infinite sentences. According to Piaget, these stages of development are collectively called *decalage*. By this, Piaget means that this is the ability of a child is to perceive reversibility in action and conservation of matter of transformation of reality.

Moral feelings appear in a child at age eight or ten and older. The child has developed an internal sense of cultural values and does not need to rely on the morality of obedience. This stage of development is referred to as autonomous morality or the morality of reciprocity. The child often complains and projects more troubles or unhappiness onto others. By clinging, blaming, and acting aggressively, the child invites parental punishment. Group affiliations and values influence the child's life either in the conformity, anti-assimilation, or adjustment stage. At these stages, he or she has reached the stage of concrete operation.

In all cultures, the child at this stage receives a form of systematic instruction. The child learns the fundamentals of the technology of that culture. The sense of industry, originality versus inferiority predominates. The child experiences the feelings of accomplishment, achievement, and productivity. At the same time, when he or she compares himself or herself with adults or people in the dominant cultures, he or she feels less productive and inferior, and realizes the need for guidance. The healthy balance between the sense of industry or superiority versus inferiority helps the child to commit himself or herself to hardwork, to learn methods of productivity and higher levels of acquiring languge to gain competence in communication with both groups of bilingual or monolingual members in the community.

B. Adolescence

Between the ages of twelve and eighteen years, the adolescent experiences dramatic physical and psychological growth. A young person becomes capable of abstract thinking. The individual has formed definite ethical, religious, and cultural values, ideals, and adjustment. Between ages fourteen and eighteen, Oriental adolescents experience a relatively quiet revolution or a revolutionary turmoil in establishing and integrating their sense of identity.

By late adolescence, ages sixteen to eighteen, the integrative forces of individuation, along with the establishment of the sense of identity, facilitates the individual's psychological emancipation from the parents. Affective intimacy between young men and women begins to develop outside of the family in a new form of dyadic relationship. The young person begins to think about the future and explores his or her own ability of cultural adjustment. By the end of adolescence, the child of yesterday becomes the adult of tomorrow, ready to assume economic and social responsibilities and the joy of possibilities in a new environoment. The personality development in adolescents in this stage includes cognitive development, psychosexual development, identity and individuation, narcissism, adolescent turmoil and rebellion, and emancipation.

Intelligence quotidient reaches its peak in late adolescence between ages sixteen and nineteen. From a psychodynamic point of view, the young person has begun to develop the ability of self-observation and cultural adjustment. He or she seriously compares the two cultures at-large, and compares his or her opinions to those of peers and dominant cultural adults. Then, with relative objectively, the adolescent makes thoughtful decisions. The minority adolescents, likewise, all decide where they are—in the conformity group, the resistance group, or the synergetic group—while adapting to the dominant cultural social life. During late adolescence, the exaggerated psychological investment in self transfers to some extent to involvement in social, political, religious, and cultural causes.

Peterson (1979) in *Life Long Learning in America* found in the longitudinal studies that adolescents usually develop into one of four possible groups: 1) continuous growth, 2) surgent growth, 3) tumultuous growth, and 4) the remaining group.

The continuous growth group, or the synergetic group in cultural adjustment perspective, consists of young people who are able to cope with internal and external changes with a balance between reasonable and emotional expressions. On the whole, these adolescents are content, happy and have many of the qualities attributed to ideal mental health.

Members of the surgent growth group go through developmental spurts. They experience cycles of progression and regression instead of continuous growth. They are less action oriented than the continuous growth group because they are more prone to temporary depression or anxiety. Their self-esteem fluctuates more profoundly and thus they rely more on the approval and encourgement of peers and parents. Adolescents in this group experience open conflict with their parents. This group, which may also be called the conformity group, prefers to adopt every aspect of the dominant culture, especially the language, and the concept of life. They refuse their own traditions. Although members of this group adapt successfully to the dominant culture, they are more slightly inhibited, able to suppress emotion more easily, and are less introspective than the first and the third group.

Experiences of the members in the tumultuous growth group is quite similar to that of adolescent rebellion and turmoil reflected in psychoanalytic and psychological literature. In a cultural perspective, they are called the resistance or immersion group. Members of this group have ideas opposite those of the conformity and synergetic groups, and they have no sympathy for the dominant cultural concept of life. Their personality development has considerable internal turmoil, and they experience difficulty at home and in school. They have considerable conflicts with parents and show inconsistencies in responding to social and academic demands. A large number of this group consists of students who dropped-out of schools. These adolescents are prone to anxiety and depression, and are more dependent on the peer groups for modulation of their self-esteem. The individuation process in these individuals is accompanied by considerble emotional turmoil, with wide mood swings. However, a strong family bond exists within the group. These adolescents, in spite of experiencing intense pain, suffering, and turmoil, do attain success socially, although they are less happy with themselves and more critical of the dominant social environment.

The remaining group is comprised of the rest of the adolescents who can not be classified. They have characteristics similar to those of the continuous growth group and the surgent growth group; they are either in a transitional phase between the previously mentioned group, or they have not yet developed distinct enough characteristics to be considered a member of a particular group.

II. Examination of Cross-Cultural Influences on Childhood Socialization and Adaptation

Based on the above boundary conditions, the present use of the term cross-cultural adaptation refers to the process of change over time that takes place within individuals from childhood to adulthood. They have completed their primary socialization process in one culture and then come into continuous, prolonged first hand contact with a new and unfamiliar culture. In this new cultural context the individuals are, at least to some extent, dependent on the host society and experience some uncertainty and unfamiliarity in carrying out their daily activities. Cross-cultural adaptation takes place regardless of the circumstances or the specific time and space in which individuals move from one society to another. In all cases, they are strangers who willingly or unwillingly undergo some degree of change in their original cultural patterns (Kim, 1988).

In each culture, individuals are connected to each other through a common system of encoding and decoding. The process in which individuals adapt to the surrounding cultural forces throughout the years of socialization is commonly called enculturation.

Difficulties in cross-cultural adjustment are normal and should be respected; however, individuals use a variety of methods, some requiring more coping mechanisms than others (Diaz and Griffith, 1988). These methods include: nonacceptance (behaving as if they were in the old culture), substitution (behaving like people in the host culture), and addition (behaving one way with fellow nationals and behaving like people in the host culture outside, therefore adopting two modes of behavior). In the observation of first-generation ethnic families, similar conclusions were reached and three modes of adaptation were identified: (1) denigration of the old culture; (2) denigration of the new culture; and (3) integration of the old and new culture (Diaz and Griffith, 1988).

Sue et al. (1983) in *Counseling American Minorities* describes the five-stages of cross-cultural adaptation: conformity, dissonance, resistance and immersion, introspection, and synergetic articulation and awareness. Using these stages one can generate the following examples of how Vietnamese children experience each stage.

The great majority of the Vietnamese parents and children of the first generation refugees did not speak English, which resulted in serious communication problems between them and social organizations, including public and private schools. Besides the comprehension barrier, the other cause of cultural conflict and unhappiness was due to the period of cross-cultural and social adjustment of the Vietnamese and American cultures. Although Vietnamese students have a reputation of being good learners and are able to make good progress at schools, some of them still face problems of academic and social achievement. Students who perform well at schools were the ones who knew how to integrate two different cultures: the American and the Vietnamese. They knew how to adjust to the two different lifstyles and to balance them in order to pursue their own personal interests and benefits. A problem exists with about twenty percent of the Vietnamese students who do not have the opportunity to achieve the same social and academic learning processes experienced by their counterparts. They either fail, drop out, or have disciplinary problems at schools. Results show that students who do poorly at school were the ones who do not adjust to the American way of life. Among the ones who did adjust to the American culture, some adjust too quickly, thus forgetting their Vietnamese culture, identity and values. Students who under-adjust or over-adjust to the American culture perform so poorly at school and have low standardized test scores.

Generally, the individual who knows how to adjust will survive easily in the new society. Those who do not adjust and those who change completely by accepting fully the new culture will generally experience problems.

Stonequist (1937) in the *Marginal Man* viewed the process of cross-cultural adaptation of individual immigrants as following one of three major directions: 1) assimilation into the dominant culture group, 2) assimilation into the subordinate group, or 3) some form of accommodation between the two societies.

There are three main groups of cultural adaptation of the Vietnamese students in America: 1) Americanization, 2) resistance, and 3) adjustment. The Americanization group consists of students who have selected to be self-assimilated into the American culture by totally refusing their own culture. This group feels that to be Americanized is the best solution to live happily and successfully. In contrast, the resistance group consists of students who refuse to assimilate into the American culture. They prefer to live with the traditions of Vietnam, preserving their language and culture. They do not see how the American culture can even depict their way of life because Americans are so liberal, independent, and individualistic. Finally members of the adjustment group are students who have drawn a medium between the Americanization group and the resistance group. They develop their own lifestyles by blending the Vietnamese and American cultures to form a moderate solution. The degree of decoding and encoding is carefully balanced within this group. This third group feels that being too assimilated is nonbeneficial, and on the other hand, being left out by not assimilating into the dominant society is even worse. A student who knows how to adjust and fit into the two cultures moderately will achieve more socially and emotionally. Students in this group achieve higher standardized test scores at schools. The Orientation Resource Center of the United States (1981) stated that the Vietnamese adjustment group progressed better socially and educationally.

III. Cross-Cultural Counseling and Multicultural Education

In comparing two theoretical views of personality deveolopment while emphasizing childhood and adolescent years, we see that the social and cultural development is limited in young age, but it gradually changes when a child becomes adolescent. The id, the ego, and the superego in childhood are the fundamental principles for human growth and personality development in adolescence.

One of the major differences between a native and an immigrant child is the level of adjustment. An American individual does not really have to compare two cultures or to consider living in an adjusted environment because he or she was born and has lived in America. However, an immigrant or a refugee like a Vietnamese individual was born and has lived in a different environment, with characteristics and cultural concepts almost opposite to that of those in America. An individual who was born in one place and moved to another, naturally, must have different aspects of values and moral development.

Cross-cultural and cross-social-strata studies have shown that the sensorimotor, preoperational, and concrete operational forms of thought are apparently displayed by children everywhere, and it seems to be more relative and dependent upon certain forms of educational and social experiences.

Cross-cultural counseling helps maladjusted individuals gain better performance. Cross-cultural counseling would motivate, challenge and reward students for self-esteem, self-motivation, and personal accomplishments. The students' awarenes of their growth in interest and knowledge of cultural adjustment, coupled with an understanding of the amount and difficulty of the work involved, along with positive reactions would have a positive influence on the students' self adjustment and later, academic achievement.

How may we expect individuals to change through cross-cultural counseling? The individual sees himself or herself as entering counseling in distress, decidedly maladjusted, very unlike the person he or she wants to be. During cross-cultural counseling, foreign-born individuals move significantly in the direction of adjustment and integration, becoming inwardly more comfortable and less tense, see others as more like themselves, and relate more comfortably to others around them. They understand themselves and are more confident and self-directing. They alter their personal goals in a realistic and more achievable direction. Individuals move toward a personal exploration and an experince of their reactions to situations. As he or she permits more of these actual experiences to enter his or her awareness, his or her image of himself or herself keep changing and enlarging to include these newly discovered facets of self. When this process occurs the degree of reorganization of personality and behavior is likely to be considerable. When people really want to grow, they may well bring themselves under the discipline of the intensive and continuous experience of personal improvement and learning. If the clients achieve this experience, they may come forth the new person. They will see their life goals more clearly and find themselves more confidently able to move toward these set goals.

Cross-cultural counseling and multicultural education can be viewed as a process through which individuals are exposed to diversity existing in the United States and to the relationships of this diversity to the world. Cross-cultural counseling and multicultural education generate respect, not only for the individual, but for the group as a whole. It encourages insight and sensitivity. It promotes social harmony between races because it fosters understanding and awareness. Educators advocate cross-cultural/multicultural education not because it is the right thing to do, but because it is the appropriate approach of education to make our country a true democracy and develop a more humane and equitable society.

It seems likely that the current trend toward multicultural awareness among educators will have as great an impact on the helping professions in the next decade as Roger's "third force" of humanism had on the prevailing psychodynamic and behavioral systems starting from early childhood.

Joseph T. Vuong is Guidance Counselor at John Ehret High School Marrero, Louisiana.

Biliography

Atkinson, D.R., Morten, G., Sue, D. 1983. *Counseling American Minorities.* Dubuque, Iowa: William C. Brown Company Publisher.
Bates, P.B. et al. 1973. *Life Span Developmental Psychology Personality and*

Socialization. New York: NY: Academic Press.

Clark, H.H., Clark, E.V. 1977. *Psychology and Language.* New York, NY: Harvard University.

Diaz, L.C., Griffith, E.H. 1988. *Cross-Cultural Mental Health.* New York: NY: John Wiley & Sons.

Douvan, E., Adelson, J.B. 1966. *The Adolescence Experience.* New York, NY: John Wiley and Sons.

Erikson, E. 1964. *Childhood and Society (2nd. Edition).* New York, NY: New Norton.

Flavell, J. 1973. *The Developmental Psychology of Jean Piaget.* New York, NY: Van Nostrand Reinhold.

Gould, R. 1978. *Transformation.* New York, NY: Simon and Schuster.

Greene, R.G., Yankey, T.D. 1982. *Early and Middle Childhood: Growth, Abuse and Delinquency.* Lancaster. PA: Technomic Publishing Co.

Kagan, J. 1984. *The Nature of the Child.* New York, NY: Basic Book.

Kim, Y.Y. 1988. *Communication and Cross-Cultural Adaptation.* Clevedon, Philadelphia: Multilingual Matters Ltd.

Levine, R.A. (ed) 1979. *Culture, Behavior and Personality 2nd edition.* New York, NY: Aldine.

Mosher, R. (ed.) 1979. *Adolescents' Development and Education a Janis Knot.* Berkely, CA: Mc Cutham Publishing.

Nesslroade, J.R. and Von Eye, A. 1985. *Individual Development and Social Change: Explanatory Analysis. New York, NY: Academic Press.*

Orientation Resource. 1981. Sach Huong Dan Nguoi Ti Nan Hao Ky. (Vietnamese). Washington: Center Applied Linguistics.

Pederson, R. 1988. *A Handbook for Developing Multicultural Awareness.* Alexandria, VA: American Association for Counseling and Development.

Peterson, R.E. et al. 1979. *Lifelong Learning in America.* San Francisco, CA: Jossey-Bass.

Spodek, B. Saracho, N.O., Peters, D.L. 1988. *Professionalism and the Early Childhood Practitioner.* New York, NY: Teachers College Press.

Steelye, H.N. 1984. *Teaching Culture.* Lincolnwood. IL: National Textbook Company.

Stendler, C.B. 1958. *Teaching in Elementary School.* New York, NY: Teachers College Press.

Vuong, G.T. 1976. *Getting to Know the Vietnamese and Their Culture.* New York, NY: Fredrick Ungar Publishing Company.

Zandon, J. 1987. *Human Development, 3rd edition.* New York, NY: Alfred A. Kenopt.

Periodical and Journal Article

Berdiansky, H., Brownlee, R.F. "Community and School Cooperation." Elementary School Guidance and Counseling. December, 1988.

Berry, J. "They Call It Little Vietnam." New Orleans Magazine, May 1988.

Fernandez, M.S. "Issues in Counseling Southeast Asian Students." Journal of Multicultural Counseling and Development. October, 1988.

Gucione J. "Viet Counselor Works to Bridge the Cultural Gap." WestBank Guide. February, 1985.

Heath, A.E., Neimeyer, Peterson, P.B. "The Future of Cross-Cultural Counseling: A Delphi Pole." Journal of Counseling and Development." October, 1988.

Morris, R. "Viet Student Strike for Success." West Bank Guide. October, 1988.

Nuiry, O.E. "School Counselor Eases Vietnamese Transition." Times Picayune. March, 1988.

Siegel, S. "Jeff's Bilingual Teachings Help Bridge Cultural Gap." West Bank Guide. May, 1985.

"Understanding Group Identity in Group Cross-Cultural Counseling and Psychotherapy." Teacher's College. February. 1989.

CHAPTER 28

Psychotherapy with Young Children

Research has established that temperament and adaptive styles evident in infancy can affect the reactions a child evokes from others as well as the conflicts and resolutions that follow (Thomas and Chess, 1977, 1980; Thomas, Chess, and Birch, 1968). Temperament may be perceived as the behavioral style of the individual child, and its nature can be significantly affected by environmental circumstances. Parental reactions significantly influence the development of behavior disorders in children. This is true even in cases where parental behavior was not to blame for the difficult child pattern (Achenbach, 1982). Research indicates that parental influence is significant even in infancy. Researchers studying attachment theory have studied patterns of attachment and their effects upon later life. They have been able to infer "working models" of specific attachment relationships (Bretherton, 1985). These working models internalized by the child provide rules and rule systems for the direction of behavior and the felt appraisal of experience (Main et al, 1981). Even more important may be the finding that there is a similarity in the rules or working models used by parents and their children in organizing both behavior and representations relevant to attachment. Thus, personality and pathological patterns that characterize family history over generations may be based less on genetic predisposition and more on relearning and reexperiencing basic attachment patterns that create an affect regulation (Koback, 1988; Sroufe and Waters, 1977).

For example, secure attachment would be organized by rules that allow acknowledgement of distress and the turning to others for support. Avoidant attachment would be organized by rules that restrict acknowledgement of distress and the attempts to seek comfort and support. Ambivalent attachment would be organized by rules that direct attention toward distress and attachment figures in a hypervigilant manner that inhibits the development of autonomy and self-confidence. Kobak (1988) has traced the regulation of distress related affect from infancy attachment to late adolescence.

Schere (1987) argued for a positive approach to mental health. He characterized the diagnostic classifications in DSM III as varying behavioral forms that emotional distress takes in different individuals at different stages in life. He pointed out that in many cases an individual seeking therapeutic help has been, since early childhood, classified under a variety of DSM III diagnostic categories. He suggested that it might prove more effective if emotional distress were viewed as the result of developmental deficits in the achieving of (1) personal power, (2) connection to others, and (3) a cognitive problem-solving perspective that relates to perceiving priorities and steps needed to obtain goals. Developmental deficits relate to patterns of interaction within the family dynamic and begin in infancy. Sophisticated use of genograms can help identify family interactive patterns that would profit from intervention. They can also contribute significantly to the prevention of mental ill-health in children if such screening would become a routine of health procedure in the mainstream. In order for this to happen, the mainstream would have to be better educated about the work of psychiatry and psychology. In this manner the many myths that still exist in our culture concerning those individuals who see mental health professionals could be altered and replaced by an enthusiasm for developing the insight and skills to facilitate a higher quality of life.

In working with young children in psychotherapy, a number of principles should be emphasized:

1. *It is imperative to work with the child's family.* The difficulties confronting a young child are directly related to the psychodynamic patterns of the family system. To help the child, the family must become aware of these patterns and work to modify them so that they enhance, not impede, healthy development. In doing so, parents will find they are helping themselves and all the other members of the family.

2. *Words are not the best mode for working with young children.*
   Unlike adults, who possess the capacity to retrieve from memory emotional events that are relevant to the issues revealed in verbal interaction with a therapist, young children are at the cognitive stage of development where emotional issues may be directly experienced. For this reason *play therapy* is the best mode of working with young children. The children will project into their play essential elements of the dynamic problems with which they and their family are confronted. The therapist can intervene directly through the play and help the child experience alternative behaviors, feelings, and attributions that reduce distress. Modeling, role play, and the direct infusion of feelings that counter-condition feelings of distress (such as optimism with a depressed child) can be helpful techniques in play therapy.

3. *Young children tend to be dependent, to lack empathy, and to have difficulty dealing with more than one thing at a time.*

For these reasons, children may be told things directly. They expect authorities to know what is right or wrong, and often sense that thinking for themselves means guessing what the authority wishes them to say or do. Many children need time to establish the ability to feel as others do and to think differently from an adult authority.

4. *As children grow older, strategies that are more cognitive and verbal become increasingly important.*

   Older children profit from such techniques as problem solving training Sarason and Sarason, 1981), verbal self-instructive training (Merchanbaum, 1979 and Craighead, 1982), and attribution retraining (Braswell, Koehler, and Kendall, 1985). In addition, older children profit from appropriate metaphoric strategies (such as "the kid is not the king" or "putting on the brakes") which help to focus important issues in a way that matches an experience to which the child can relate.

Richard A. Schere is Professor of Special Education and School Psychology at Brooklyn College and is the Director of Kennedy Professional Associates. Jennifer J. Schere is a counselor at Kennedy.

Bibliography

Achenbach, T. M. *Developmental Psychotherapy, 2nd Ed.* New York: John Wiley & Sons, Inc., 1982.

Achenbach, T. M. and Edelbrock, C. S. *Manuel for the Child Behavior Checklist and Child Behavior Profile.* Burlington, VT: Child Psychiatry, University of Vermont, 1982.

Barker, P. *Basic Family Therapy, 2nd Ed.* New York: Oxford University Press, 1986.

Braswell, L. and Kendall, P. C. "Cognitive-Behavioral Methods with Children." In K. S. Dobson (Ed.), *Handbook of Congitive-Behavioral Therapies.* New York: The Guilford Press, 1988.

Braswell, L., Koehler, C., and Kendall, P. C. (1985), "Attributions and Outcomes in Child Psychotherapy". *Journal of Social and Clinical Psychotherapy,* 3, 458–465.

Bretherton, T. "Attachment Theory: Retrospect and Prospect". *Monographs of the Society for Research in Child Development,* Volume 5, 3–35, 1985.

Craighead, W. E. (1983) "A Brief Clinical History of Cognitive-Behavioral Therapy with Children." *School Psychology Review,* 11, 5–13.

Kobak, R. "Attachment in Late Adolescence: Working Models, Affect Regulation, and Representations of Self and Others". *Child Development,* Vol 59(1), 135–146, 1988.

Main, M. and Weston, D. "The Quality of the Toddler's Relationship to Mother and Father". *Child Development,* Vol. 52(3), 932–940, 1981.

Merchenbaum, D. (1979). "Teaching Children Self-Control". In B. B. Tahay and A. E. Kazden (Eds.) *Advances in Clinical Child Psychology* (Vol. 2, pp 1–33). New York: Plenum.

Schere, R. A. "Toward A Positive Approach to Mental Health". Invited Address: Annual Convention of Catholic Counselors, St. Francis College, April, 1987.

Sarason, T. G. and Sarason, B. R. "Teaching Cognitive and Social Skills to High School Students". *Journal of Consulting and Clinical Psychology,* 49, 908–918, 1981.

Sroufe, T. and Wates, E. "Heart Rate as Convergent Measure in Clinical and Developmental Research." *Merrill-Palmer Quarterly,* Vol. 23(1), 3–27, 1977.

Thomas, A., Chess, S., and Birch, H. G. *Temperament and Behavior Disorders in Children.* New York: New York University Press, 1968.

Thomas, A. and Chess, S. *Temperament and Development.* New York: Brunner-Mazel, 1977.

CHAPTER 29

How Does the Behavior of Young Children Affect Teacher Behavior?

Waller (1932) asked "What does teaching do to teachers?" The answer to this question has been sought by many researchers in a variety of ways. One group of reseachers believes that a teacher's behavior is influenced and shaped by interaction with an important person or persons in the environment. Therefore, the behavior of the teacher can be affected by the children he/she works with. This branch of research looks at teacher socialization. Haller (1967), Klein (1971), Yarrow, Waxler and Scott (1971) support the idea that students shape teacher behavior.

Haller (1967) found that the language patterns of the teachers in his study were affected by the young children they worked with. The teacher's language became simpler and more childlike even outside of the classroom. The longer teachers worked with young children the greater the changes in their language.

Klein (1971) studied the ways in which the behavior of college students affect the behavior of professors and found that negative student behavior caused negative teacher behavior. Yarrow, Waxler, and Scott (1971) studied the effects of the behavior of nursery school children on the behavior of nurturing and non-nurturing caretakers and found that the behavior of the adult was affected by the behavior of the children.

Other studies by Lortie (1966) and Sarason (1971) described the isolation of the teacher from other adults during the performance of daily duties in the classroom. This isolation leads to the speculation that children play a major role in shaping teacher behavior. It is not only the time spent alone with young children, but the intensity of the interaction with children that makes the difference. Research by Lortie (1966) and Jackson (1968) indicates that pupil-teacher interaction means more to the teacher than interaction with other teachers or supervisors. The "joys of teacher" according to Jackson (1968) happen in the classroom.

All the studies mentioned here discuss the possibility that young children may affect teacher behavior. Research done by Peltzman (1975) looked at the interaction between teachers and young children to find out if teacher behavior is affected by student behavior as a result of the quality and quantity of classroom interaction. The findings of this study provide insight and raise interesting questions in an attempt to find out what teaching does to teachers.

Teachers and children in kindergarten and first grade were observed in September and again in January to find out if there were changes in teacher behavior. The changes found were:

1. There was a change in the type of questions teachers asked. In January, teachers appeared to be trying to help children more toward an understanding of the processes involved in finding an answer to a problem or a question. This indicates an attempt by teachers to help children go through the steps involved in building concepts as Piaget (1960, 1963) suggests.

   Teachers also gave more choices in an attempt to help children become more independent. This resulted in more self-directed activities for the children because they have several alternatives from which they can choose what they would like to do. This helps lay the foundation in the independence, responsibility and decision-making power necessary for future learning.

2. In January, teachers placed more emphasis on academic work. Less time was spent on informal discussion and non-academic matters. Habit formation and routine building which was done in September moved more and more into the background in January allowing for a shift toward more sustained academic activities.

3. In January, there was an increase in negative comments and behavior by the teacher. This may indicate that several things happened:
   a) perhaps over time teachers become more negative by their responses to young children, or
   b) perhaps as teachers encourage children to become more independent and children get more differentiated so that group control gets more difficult, more behavior problems develop requiring more frequent negative comments by the teacher.

This finding suggests that the impulsive, impatient, active young child described by Rudolph and Cohen (1964) and Lewis (1954) continues to act this way and an increase in academic activities may come too soon when most children are not yet ready creating behavior problems. Wright (1923) suggested that children need time to mature before activities become too formalized. If these activities start too soon children become more impatient and impulsive creating more negative teacher behavior.

A pattern is established giving the teacher two ways of dealing with behavior problems—a warning or a negative comment. Over time, teachers learn the effects of both alternatives. It may become easier to respond with a negative comment for both major and minor problems.

Studies by Morrison (1965), Cody (1966), Bookout (1967) and Lahadrene (1967) indicate that there is a connection between positive teacher behavior and positive student behavior and negative teacher behavior and negative pupil behavior. It may also be true that there is a connection between negative student behavior and negative teacher behavior.

Brophy and Good (1974) provide a picture of what goes on in the classroom, clearly showing that children's behavior affects the teacher's behavior. Brophy and Good (1974) state that

> Students shape teacher behavior at the same time that their own behavior is being influenced by the teacher. The complexity of the job demands that the teacher continually focus attention on at least one thing while at the same time attempting to monitor events going on all over the classroom. As a result, few teachers are able to consciously monitor each individual child on a continuing basis and treat him (her) in a deliberate pro-active manner. Instead, most teachers are primiarily reactive in their responses to students, often showing evidence that students have shaped their behavior rather than vice versa. (p. viii).

Thus, the teacher is so busy trying to keep an eye on everyone and everything at once that his/her behavior is a reaction to student behavior as a group rather than each individual's behavior. Teachers become more negative because more activity causes more problems and more things to look at. The teacher's behavior is a reaction to the total classroom activity. In kindergarten and the first grade, children work in small groups with several activities going on at once.

Turner (1967) believes that activities which occur daily in the classroom have power to exert strong controls over the teacher's behavior. Turner (1967) studied pupil characteristics and states that in classroom interaction between the teacher and a pupil that

> . . . each participant depends on the other for reinforcement . . . the pupil cannot maintain his (her) role, nor the teacher his (hers), unless . . . reinforcement occurs . . . It should also be the case that pupils exercise substantial influence over the behavior of the teacher . . . (p. 5).

A dynamic situation exists in every early childhood classroom in which the teacher needs the pupils and the pupils need the teacher to support each other. Each needs the other to strengthen his/her part in the interaction. By supporting the other each influences the behavior of the other. Spodek (1972) comes right to the point and states positively that children influence teacher behavior. He says

> . . . the teacher is to a greater extent reacting to the children in her class. The children control the behavior of the teacher by forcing certain responses which are necessitated by their initial action . . . The teacher is responding to rapid occurances all . . . day . . . (p.2)

Waller (1932) provides more evidence to support the findings that children's behavior affects teacher behavior. Waller (1932) believed that teaching leaves its mark on the teacher because

> . . . the 'inner man (person)' feels a profound effect. The social situation in which teaching takes place along with the nature of the job; the constant contact with children, serve to inflict upon the individual teacher certain shocks, or trauma, which shape behavior. (p. 3)

Waller's suggestion that the job of teaching, which involves constant monitoring of children's behavior, changes the teacher's behavior makes sense. When a teacher must pay attention to what children do right and wrong and try to change the children's behavior, the teacher's behavior is affected. In interviews and during observations of teachers, Pletzman (1975) found that the longer a teacher worked with young children the more likely it was that he/she would talk to another adult in the same way he/she talked to children. For example, a teacher who taught kindergarten for more than 35 years gave instructions to the deli clerk in Waldbaumks in the same slow, one thing at a time way that she did for her children. If a teacher must speak slowly for the pupils to understand and must speak this way for six hours everyday there is going to be a change in the way the teacher talks outside of school.

Lieberman and Miller (1984) provide support for this change in language due to daily work with children. They list ten universal tensions faced by teachers. Number six deals with language and states that

> given the dailiness of teaching and the age of elementary students, teachers are forced to say things in a very simple fashion. The problem then becomes how to maintain one's integrity as an adult, while always translating into elementary language. Being with young children all day has its effects on the teacher. (p. 22)

The pressure to develop concepts for children and yet present them in clear language causes problems. However, Langer (1942) believed these problems were necessary because the development of young children's language and concepts is

> . . . perhaps the most important area of learning in the education of young children . . . while reading is vital to all other areas of school learning, listening and speaking are the basis for learning to read. (p. 26)

If the teacher spends most of his/her teaching time helping children learn to listen by reading and talking to them in simple language, then the teacher's way of talking will change. The teacher needs to explain concepts in words young children understand and in so doing changes his/her everyday speech. The teacher is also in danger of losing her/his place in the adult world because of the way a teacher must behave to help children learn.

Freud (1952) believed that there are dangers which threaten the teacher of young children. She states that

> . . . Working too closely with children fosters a loss of perspective between the children's world and the adult world. The teacher who works with young children only sees them out of proportion. She gets caught up with the children's lives, loses her adult values and begins to live in a child's world . . . (p. 234)

In a 1973 letter Freud stated

> . . . I still believe that teachers in their work with children are affected by the different values, forms of expression, etc., which by necessity they have to adapt to. If they could not do that, they would be out of touch with the child as so many adults are . . .

Thus, in order to teach young children, the teacher must live in their world. It is necessary to explain complex ideas in childlike language and in order to talk like a child one must learn to think like a child. If teachers could not make this "leap backwards" they would never see growth and learning take place. However, these rewards that teachers get come at a high price because as Peltzman (1975) states

> In a way, the teacher gets shut out of both worlds. She is clearly not a member of the child's culture, but who else spends their time currying favor with young children as a major source of rewards?

The research discussed here shows that teacher behavior is affected by the behavior of young children. Peltzman (1975) found that changes do take place in the early childhood classroom. These changes take place because of the pattern of interaction which takes place between the teacher and the children. As a shift in emphasis occurs from helping young children become adjusted to school to more sustained teaching and learning, the interaction between the teacher and the children also changes. The interaction becomes less the tool for building routines and more the tool for developing and challenging young minds.

We have gained insight and found some ways in which to answer Waller's question "What does teaching do to teachers" by looking at the ways in which children's behavior affects teacher behavior in the early childhood classroom.

We have discovered that, as Ruskin says, "Teaching is painful, continual, and difficult work to be done by kindness, by watching, by warning, by precept, and by praise, but above all by example." (Lieberman and Miller (1984), p. vii).

Barbara Ruth Peltzman, Ed.D., Assistant Professor of Education, Notre Dame College, St. John's University, Staten Island, New York.

Bibliography

Brophy, J. E. and Good, T. L. *Teacher Student Relationships: Causes and Consequences.* New York: Holt, Reinhart, and Winston, 1974.

Bookout, E. "Teacher Behavior in Relation to the Social-Emotional Climate of Physical Education Classes," *Research Quarterly,* 1967, 39, 336–347.

Cody, W. "Control and Resistance in Slum Schools." *Elementary School Journal,* 1966, 67, 1–7.

Freud, Anna. "The Role of the Teacher." *Harvard Educational Review,* 1952, 22, 229–234.

Freud, Anna. Personal correspondence with researcher, November 27, 1973.

Haller, E. J. "Pupil Influence in Teacher Socialization: A Sociolinguistic Study." *Sociology of Education,* 1967, 60, 316–333.

Jackson, P. W. *Life in Classrooms.* New York: Holt, Rinehart and Winston, 1968.

Klein, S. S. "Student Influence on Teacher Behavior." *American Educational Research Journal,* 1971, 8, 403–421.

Lahadrene, H. M. *Adaptation to School Settings: A Study of Children's Attitudes and Classroom Behaviors.* U.S. Office of Education Final Report. ERIC Document ED 012 943, 1967.

Langer, S. *Philosophy in a New Key.* Cambridge: Harvard University Press, 1942.

Lewis C. "Prologue." *Know Your Child in School,* Ed. L. S. Mitchell. New York: MacMillan, 1954.

Lieberman, Ann; and Miller, Lynne. *Teachers, Their World and Their Work: Implications for School Improvement.* Washington, D.C.: Association for Supervision and Curriculum Development, 1984.

Lortie, D. C. "Teacher Socialization: The Robinson Crusoe Model." *The Real World of the Beginning Teacher.* NEA, 19th National (T.E.P.S. Conference, Washington, D.C.: NEA, 1966.

Morrison, V. B. *Teacher-Pupil Interaction in Elementary Urban Schools.* Office of Education Final Report. ERIC Document ED 003385, 1965.

Morrison, I. and Perry, J. F. *Kindergarten-Primary Education Teaching Procedures.* New York: The Ronald Press Co., 1961.

Peltzman, Barbara R. "Dyadic Interaction in the Primary School Classroom: An Examination of the Effects of Young Children on the Behavior of Teachers." Unpublished Doctoral dissertation, Teachers College, Columbia University, 1975.

Piaget, J. *Children's Concept of the World.* New Jersey: Littlefield and Adams, 1960.

Piaget, J. *Origins of Intelligence in Children.* New York: Norton, 1963.

Rudolph, M. and Cohen, D. H. *Kindergarten: A Year of Learning.* New York: Appleton-Century-Crofts, 1964.

Sarason, S. B. *The Culture of the School and the Problem of Change.* Boston: Allyn and Bacon, 1971.

Sears, R. R. "A Theoretical Framework for Personality and Social Behavior." *American Psychologist,* 1951, 6, 476–483.

Turner, R. L. "Pupil Influence on Teacher Behavior." *Classroom Interaction Newsletter,* 1967, 3, 5–8.

Waller, W. *The Sociology of Teaching.* New York: John Wiley and Sons, 1932.

Wright, L. *A Non-Reading First Grade Curriculum.* New York: Columbia University Bureau of Publication, 1923.

Yarrow, M. R., Waxler, C. Z. and Scott, P. M. "Child Effects on Adult Behavior." *Developmental Psychology,* 1971, 5, 300–311.

Suggested Reading

Bellack, Arno; Kliebard, Herbert; Hyman, Ronald; and Smith, Frank. *The Language of the Classroom.* New York: Teachers College Press, 1966.

Brenton, Myron. *What's Happened to Teacher?* New York: Coward McCann, 1970.

Chase, Virginia. The End of the Week. New York: MacMillan, 1953.

Dewey, John. *Democracy and Education.* New York: MacMillan, 1916.

Dewey, John. *Experience and Education.* New York: Macmillan 1938.

Highet, Gilbert. *The Art of Teaching.* New York: Knopf, 1950.

Kaufman, Bel. *Up the Down Staircase.* New Jersey: Prentice-Hall, 1964.

Kidder, Tracy. *Among School Children.* Boston: Houghton-Mifflin, 1989.

Ober, Richard; Bentley, Ernest; and Miller, Edith. *Systematic Observation of Teaching.* New Jersey: Prentice-Hall, 1971.

Rosenthal, Robert; and Jacobson, Lenore. *Pygmalion in the Classroom: Teacher Expectation and Pupils' Intellectual Development.* New York: Holt, Rinehart & Winston, 1968.

Zumwalt, Karen, K., ed. *Improving Teaching.* Washington, D.C.: Association for Supervision and Curriculum Development, 1986.

SECTION 5

Curriculum

Introduction

The challenge in early childhood curriculum development for the next century rests heavily on our ability to integrate the social, intellectual, and technological needs of our emerging global society with the developmental needs of our youngest students. As we move away from the familiar concepts of child-rearing of the 20 C., we look towards our educational system to develop curriculums that will include those developmental activities of the past and address the new demands of technological and informational growth.

When we think about curriculum, we generally focus on that aspect of curriculum which is content—information that is to be passed on to students. According to Allan A. Glatthorn, curriculum refers to:

> . . . the plans made for guiding learning in schools, usually repre-
> sented in retrievable documents of several levels of generality, and
> the implementation of those plans in the classroom; those experi-
> ences take place in a learning environment that also influences
> what is learned.

Therefore, curriculum may be viewed as a philosophy of education that is defined in both the content of instruction and the implementation of instructional strategies designed to enable students to master the content; it is both form and process.

The form that early childhood curriculum is taking will reflect the changes in family structure and economics that necessitate increased parental time out of the home. Young children spend less time engaged in "free play" activities in the home and community and more time in adult-supervised, structured environments. The children growing up in today's world are less active participants in activities long associated with "growing up," but are acted upon by electronic games and television; creativity is diminished by the realistic quality of the toys and games presented to them. With the focus on schools being kept open longer each day and extending the school year, the early childhood curriculum will reflect aspects of the young child's life that have only tangentially been considered in the past. Along with intellectual development, issues of physical and social development need to be included in the curriculum plan.

The process contained within early childhood curriculum is the identification of those educational strategies that will balance new technology and vast amounts of information with opportunities for student involvement in process through direct experience, peer interaction, and collaborative learning. A major priority for early childhood curriculum development is to facilitate the development of problem-solving skills so that our children can function both independently and collaboratively in school, home, and in the community at large.

An early childhood curriculum like early childhood itself, provides the foundation for all future intellectual, social, and vocational development of the child; it must be flexible enough to change as our knowledge base grows and society changes, and it must reflect the form of our society and the processes that best meet individual and collective needs.

Jill Levy, is Vice President, Council of Supervisors and Administrators.

References

Glatthorn, A. A. *Curriculum Renewal*. Alexandria, VA: ASCD, 1987.

CHAPTER 30

Reading and Early Childhood Education: The Critical Issues

Here are some thoughtful answers to the first most important questions about the teaching of reading.

The evidence keeps growing on the critical importance of the early years in the development of literacy. Indeed, the recent National Assessment of Educational Progress[1] confirms earlier research that if we wish to have junior and senior high school students read better, we must see to it that they do better in preschool and in the early school years. But there are still a number of controversial issues concerning the teaching of reading—particularly early reading. Some of these issues are relatively new while others have been debated and researched in the past. I believe that a discussion of new and classic issues in the teaching of reading will assist principals and teachers of young children in making reasoned judgments about policy and instruction. I have selected five issues that seem to most concern teachers and administrators, and that are of often the themes of journal articles and conference presentations:

Is reading always the same or does it undergo developmental changes?

This is a classic issue that has been discussed and debated for generations. Some scholars have viewed reading as essentially the same from its beginnings to its most mature forms. Others have viewed it as a process that changes as it develops.[2]

Each viewpoint leans on theory to support its view. However, from my study of the issue, there is more evidence from research and successful practice for a developmental view. What recommends a developmental view most is its usefulness. It provides help in what and when to teach, for developing reading materials and tests, and for ways to find and diagnose those with reading difficulties.

In *Stage and Reading Development,*[3] which is being used in planning schoolwide reading curricula, instructional materials, the construction of reading tests, and research, I have proposed a developmental scheme that includes six stages, from 0 to 5, covering prereading to highly skilled reading. Although I am concerned here with reading in the early childhood years, I present all of the reading stages to give insight into what precedes and follows the early school years.

Stage 0, Prereading, from birth to about age six, is characterized by growing control over language. Current estimates are that average six-year-olds can speak or understand about 5,000 words. During the prereading stage, most children living in a literate society acquire some knowledge and insight into print, and learn to recognize letters, common signs, and common words. Many can write their names and pretend they can read a story that has been read to them several times.

Stage 1, Initial Reading or Decoding (Grades 1–2), involves the alphabetic principle—developing skills and insight into sound-letter relations and into the decoding of words not recognized immediately. Children learn to recognize the words in their books, and to "understand" the material they read. But what they can read at this stage is considerably below what they can understand in speech. Their ability to decode and recognize printed words is limited but growing rapidly.

Stage 2, Confirmation, Fluency, and Ungluing from Print (Grades 2–3), consolidates what students have learned earlier in the recognition of words and in the use of decoding skills to help them gain further insight into the reading and comprehending of familiar texts. By the end of this stage, they have developed fluency and ease in recognizing words, in "sounding" others they do not recognize immediately, and in "predicting" still others from context. The material that they can read fluently is basically within their knowledge linguistically and cognitively.

Stage 3, Learning the New (Grades 4–8), marks the beginning of reading as a tool for acquiring knowledge, feelings, values, insights, and attitudes. It is at this stage that the books students read go beyond their everyday vocabularies, beyond their background knowledge, and beyond simple narrative presentation.

Stage 4, Multiple Viewpoints (High School), requires more complex language and cognitive abilities, since the reading tasks involve more complex texts in many more advanced content areas. Students are also required to comprehend varying viewpoints at ever greater depth.

Stage 5, Construction and Reconstruction (College Level), the most mature stage, is characterized by a world view. Students read books and articles in the detail and depth that they need for their own purposes. Readers in Stage 5 know what not to read as well as what to read. Reading here is basically constructive. From reading what others say, students construct knowledge for their own use.

From these very brief characterizations one can see qualitative changes from stage to stage, with a major qualitative change at Stage 3, which marks the end of the primary grades (the early childhood years) and beginning of the intermediate grades. Stage 0, 1, and 2 can be said to represent the oral tradition, in that text read at these stages rarely goes beyond the language and knowledge that the reader has previously acquired through listening and direct experience. Stages 3, 4, and 5 (Grades 4 and beyond) may be viewed as comprising the literary tradition—when the reading content, as well as the language read, goes beyond what is already known.

Thus, reading at Stage 3 can be seen as the beginning of a long progression in the reading of texts that become ever more complex, literary, abstract, and technical, and that require more worldly knowledge and ever more sophisticated language and cognitive abilities. The materials that are typically read at Grade 4 and beyond show distinctive changes in content, in linguistic complexities, and in the cognitive demands on the reader when compared to those generally read in Grades 1 to 3.

It is important to note that teachers and other school personnel have long been aware of this distinction. They have often considered the primary grades as the time for "learning to read" and the intermediate and upper elementary grades as a time of "reading to learn." In the early grades, the main task is to bring students' word recognition and decoding up to their more advanced linguistic and cognitive levels. From Grade 4 on, the main task is to raise students' language and cognitive abilities to meet the demands of their texts—a more difficult task, indeed.

Reading stages can contribute to a better understanding of how reading is acquired and how the total environment, as well as the school environment and instruction, may be made optimal for pupils at the different stages. For example, most children who enter first grade (beginning of Stage 1) need to acquire a knowledge of the alphabetic principle—how the letters relate to the sounds of the language, or how to "sound out" words. While some children may discover this principle by themselves, the research evidence over the past 70 years is overwhelming that direct instruction is needed and contributes to better development of decoding, word recognition, and comprehension, and provides a better transition to later reading stages.[4] This is because the relations between sounds and letters are usually not discovered without instruction by most children, particularly those at high risk. Toward the end of the decoding stage, the knowledge and skills acquired can become self-generative. That is, some growth can be achieved with practice on one's own.

Stage 2 (Grades 2 and 3), the development of fluency, requires a great deal of reading and practice. This would suggest the necessity for providing many books to be read in addition to texts and workbooks.

With the skills and abilities acquired in Stages 1 and 2, the focus of reading instruction in the middle grades should be on literature and on reading in the various subject areas—textbooks, reference works, and other sources.

While a developmental theory does not prescribe methods, it does suggest the need for certain practices in order for more advanced levels of achievement to take place. Thus, it would appear that a global and playful approach, while suitable for developing "readiness" and "emergent" skills in preschool and kindergarten, would be less effective in Grades 1 and 2, when children need to acquire decoding and word recognition skills, and should be reading many books to gain fluency.

For the immediate grades (Stage 3), or earlier if children are more advanced, instruction in reading should go beyond the familiar in content, in language, and in thought. Therefore, reading instruction needs to be given not only from basal readers, which contain mainly narrative fiction, but from texts and books in social studies, science, health, and literature. For most children, a greater focus on word meanings is needed since their reading materials contain a greater proportion of abstract, technical, and literary words not known to them.

Should we teach reading skills or let children learn by "just reading"?

Each generation asks this question in a somewhat different way, and tends to have answers that vary.

At the present time, the question to be decided is whether to provide reading instruction with basal readers and workbooks, or children's story books. Two decades ago, the question was: Which is better, individualized reading (self-selection of trade books) or group instruction? Another related question that has been debated for more than a century, concerns the use of phonics. Is it necessary to teach phonics? Don't children learn better without sounding or decoding words?

All of these questions have one essential point in common: Do children learn to read better, and love it more, if they are taught how to read, or if they figure it out by themselves by "just reading"?

The evidence from research would seem to indicate that both are needed for optimal reading development. Knowing how (reading skills) is necessary, but not sufficient; and learning from "just reading" bogs down when the student's skills are deficient. The mass of the research on reading indicates that better results are achieved when young children are taught skills systematically and directly, and use these in reading. It also shows that being read to and reading and writing stories, poems, and informational selections—to which they apply their newly gained skills—are also important for reading development.

At each of the reading stages, a balance of "learning how-to" with "practicing and doing" is needed. Too great an emphasis on skills may deprive children of time to read. Similarly, a diet of "just reading" without instruction in the skills may slow down development. The research does not support the claims of some that skills and know-how develop naturally from "just reading." Indeed, it shows that development is enhanced by skills, particularly among those making slower progress—children from low-income homes and those at high risk for learning disability.[5]

Ironically, although the strongest argument proposed for the "just reading" view is a love of reading, there seems to be no evidence to back it up. Indeed, negative evidence can be found from the fact that some of the greatest writers and readers have been educated in schools that taught reading mainly as skill development.

How easy or hard should instructional reading materials be?

Research and theory during the past decade have found that books that are challenging—at or somewhat above the student's reading level—produce higher reading achievement than easier books, particularly when the teacher provides instruction. Research in the Harvard Reading Laboratory which related the difficulty of school textbooks, used from Grade 1 to Grade 12, to SAT verbal scores found that when harder textbooks were used, the students achieved higher SAT scores. Easier books produced lower scores. Further, the difficulty of the first-grade books seemed to exert the greatest effect.[6] Why should first grade be so important? We suggest that it is probably because it is when the child is introduced to the alphabetic/writing system of our language. It is difficult for most children to discover the system for themselves. Hence a stronger, more difficult program in the first grade prepares the child for later stages, which can be practiced even if less direct instruction is provided.

These findings are backed up by the Russian psychologist Vygotsky, whose theory of proximal development proposes that the optimal level of instruction is one above the student's current development, but at which the student can learn when instructed by a teacher.

Thus, the teachers should take pains to see that the books used for instruction are not too easy. In our study of the reading, writing, and language of low SES children in grades 2 to 7, we found that the greatest reading gains were made by students who were learning from basal readers at or above their reading level—but not below.[7] And yet children continue to receive instruction from basal readers below their level. Since most instructional time for reading involves the use of basal readers, it is essential that these readers contain materials that challenge all students— including those who read above level.

Additional evidence for the value of challenging instructional materials come from recent research on classroom grouping. Several studies have found that when children in the lowest reading group were placed in a group that used more difficult materials, they actually did better.

This concept needs to be considered by all of us, for it goes counter to the conventional wisdom of book selection for the past 50 years—the easier, the better.

To test or not to test?

Attitudes toward reading tests have been quite conflicting. We give more and more tests, and we seem increasingly dissatisfied with them, even to the point of rejecting them and research results that are based on them. There is also a fear that the increasing use of tests will lead to teaching for the tests. And yet, when test scores rise, we are happy to accept the results as evidence of hard work by teachers, administrators, and students.

It is easy to overlook the benefits of tests—for evaluating programs, for assessing children's reading development, for noting their strengths and weaknesses. Tests also help us find those children who are falling behind and need extra help.

And yet, I have found that few schools make full use of the tests that they give. Many do not seem to use the results to evaluate a child's reading development from year to year, to make sure that progress is being made as expected. Although standardized tests leave much to be desired, combined with teacher judgment they can be used constructively for this purpose since they are highly predictive of later achievement. Thus, Grade 2 reading scores predict Grade 6 scores, and the Grade 6 scores predict whether students will graduate high school or will drop out—if no special help is given to those who need it.8

The school reform movement has led to greater pressures to give more tests—readiness, standardized, competency, mastery, as well as criterion-referenced tests. In response to these pressures, many teachers would like to stop testing altogether. And yet considerable research indicates that frequent testing characterizes schools that have improved reading achievement, particularly in the early grades.9

What about research? Does it improve practice?

The mass of research on reading, and the highly technical way in which it is written, often intimidate school administrators, policymakers, and teachers. I think sometimes that this growing mass of research has tended to produce an attitude that, while it is well and good, it has little to do with practice. One can well understand this view, for it is difficult, if not impossible, to keep up with all the research published.

And yet, my long years in both research and practice have not lessened my confidence in the value of research for informing practice. Knowing is always better than not knowing.

While research can help administrators make teaching and policy decisions, it is wise to realize that one study on an issue, by itself, is usually not sufficient to inform successful practice. It is recommended, therefore, that teachers and school administrators rely on syntheses of research—reports that sift through and interpret related studies on specific topics.

I hope that this brief discussion of major issues in reading will be of some assistance to principals and administrators who must devise and direct early childhood reading programs. It's an enormous responsibility.

Jeanne S. Chall is professor of education and director of the reading laboratory at the Harvard University Graduate School of Education.

Notes

1. National Assessment of Educational Progress. The Reading Report Card: Progress Toward Excellence in Our Schools; Trends in Reading over Four National Assessments, 1971–1984 (Princeton, NJ: Educational Testing Service, 1985).

2. For an overview of the two views, see J.S. Chall and S.A. Stahl, "Initial Reading Methods," in *The Encyclopedia of Education,* eds. T. Husen and T.N. Postlethwaite (Oxford: Pergamon, 1985). For views of reading as "unchanging," see K. Goodman and Y. Goodman, "Learning to Read Is Natural," in *Theory and Practice of Early Reading,* eds. L. Resnick and P. Weaver, vol. 1 (Hillsdale, NJ: Lawrence Erlbaumk Associates, 1979), and F. Smith, *Reading Without Nonsense,* 2nd ed. (New York: Teachers College Press, 1985). For developmental views, see J.S. Chall, *Stages of Reading Development* (New York: McGraw-Hill, 1983); D. LaBerge and S.J. Samuels, eds., *Basic Processes in Reading: Perception and Comprehension* (Hillsdale, NJ: Lawrence Erlbaum Associates, 1977); C. Perfetti, *Reading Ability* (New York: Oxford University press, 1985); and R.C. Anderson et al., *Becoming a Nation of Readers: The Report of the Commission on Reading* (Champaign, Ill.: The National Academy of Education and The Center for the Study of Reading, 1985).

3. Chall, *Stages of Reading Development.*

4. J.S. Chall, *Learning to Read: The Great Debate* (New York: McGraw-Hill, 1967; updated ed., 1983); Perfetti, Reading Ability; Anderson et al., *Becoming a Nation of Readers;* and What Works (Washington, D.C.: U.S. Department of Education, 1986).

5. See in this connection B. Bettelheim and K. Zelan, *On Learning to Read: The Child's Fascination with Meaning* (New York: Knopf, 1982), and J.S. Chall, "Reading and the Unconscious" (review of Bettelheim and Zelan), Contemporary Education Review 2 (Spring 1983): 7–11.

6. J.S. Chall, S. Conrad, and S. Harris, *An Analysis of Textbooks in Relation to Declining S.A.T. Scores* (Princeton, NJ.: College Entrance Examination Board, 1977).

7. J.S. Chall and C. Snow, *Families and Literacy: The Contribution of Out-of-School Experiences to Children's Acquisition of Literacy,* Final Report to the National Institute of Education, December 1982.

8. B. Bloom, *Human Characteristics and School Learning* (New York: McGraw-Hill, 1976).

9. J.S. Chall, School and Teacher Factors and the NAEP Reading Assessments, position paper prepared for the Committee on the Evaluation of the National Assessment of Educational Progress in Reading, August 1986 (available from ERIC).

CHAPTER 31

Emergent Literacy:
How Young Children Learn
to Read and Write

New insights into how children learn to read and write are changing—dramatically—the teaching of literacy.

> Judy, aged 4, and Mikey, aged 5, are huddled close together looking at a picture storybook. Mikey begins to "read" to Judy. He is self-assured as he turns each page, his face displaying the knowledge of someone very familiar with the text. Although the words he utters are not always exactly those appearing in the written text, his rendering is an extraordinarily close approximation. Moreover, the meanings conveyed by Mikey are consistently appropriate, as are his intonation and style of storybook reading.
>
> Judy notices that Mikey's attention seems rooted to the pictures and asks, "Mikey, what are all those black marks at the bottom of the page for?"
>
> With unwavering confidence, Mikey answers, "Oh, those are for people who can't read the story from the pictures."

Anecdotes such as this one have been told many times, most often as cute vignettes describing a child's view of the world. However, recent research on young children's literacy development has shed new meaning on these stories. Researchers investigating children's explorations into reading and writing now regard stories like this one of reading "imitation" as highly significant demonstrations of literacy learning. Although early childhood educators have always been aware that young children enter school with a remarkable knowledge of oral language, it is only recently that awareness of their written language has received serious attention.

Current investigations build on the work of John and Evelyn Dewey (1915–1962), who contrasted the functional, meaning-driven learning that children engage in before they enter school with "the practices of the schools where it is largely an adornment, a superfluity (and even an unwelcome imposition (p. 2)." More recently, the work of Marie Clay (1982) has provided the foundation for new ways of studying and thinking about early literacy. Teale and Sulzby (1989) outlined the distinctive

337

dimensions of the new research. Among its chief characteristics, they found:

- The age range studied has been extended to include children 14 months and younger;
- Literacy is no longer regarded as simply a cognitive skill but as a complex activity with social, linguistic, and psychological aspects;
- Literacy learning is perceived as multidimensional and tied to the child's natural surroundings, so it is studied in both home and school environments.

New Perspectives

The study of literacy learning from the child's point of view has given us new insights into how young children learn to read and write. Learning to read and write begins early in life and is ongoing. When two-year old Josh rushed to his Mom with the newspaper in his hands and shouted, "Peanut, peanut," she was puzzled at first. After noticing the advertisement for his favorite brand of peanut butter, she was both surprised and pleased at the connections he was making. Young children who live in a "print-rich" environment are constantly observing and learning about written language. Most of their learning occurs as a natural part of their daily lives, not as something rare or mysterious.

Learning to read and write are interrelated processes that develop in concert with oral language. The old belief that children must be orally fluent before being introduced to reading and writing as been replaced with the view that the language processes—listening, speaking, reading, and writing—develop in an interdependent manner. Each informs and supports the other. Recognizing the value of informal activities with books and other print materials, one teacher in an urban program for four-year-olds sets aside a short period of time each day especially for "book browsing." Children are encouraged to find a book they like and a comfortable place to read. They may read alone or with a friend. Book browsing usually follows a read-aloud session. The teacher uses this time to observe children as they recreate renderings of stories read to them. Children discuss and argue about their favorite pictures and characters. The teacher is amazed at how these children, most of whom have rarely been read to at home, have become so absorbed with literature. They constantly make connections between the content in books and related discoveries inside and outside the classroom. And, not surprisingly, the books that have been read to them are also their favorites for independent browsing.

Learning to read and write requires active participation in activities that have meaning in the child's daily life. Participating in listing all of the items needed to prepare a particular recipe, for example, can be an important literacy event for a young child. Helping to check off each item as it is purchased and then used in the recipe makes oral and written language come together through an activity that has current meaning for the child. This immediacy makes the activity much more meaningful than one that serves merely as preparation for something to be learned in the future.

Learning to read and write involves interaction with responsive others. As parents, caregivers, and teachers become increasingly aware of the importance of young children's attempts to write, they take time to listen to the stories and messages evoked by scribbling, which may be intelligible only to the writer. One kindergarten teacher shared her amusement as she recalled how an eager writer confidently began to share a story elicited from an entire page of scribbling. After a few minutes of reading, the youngster stopped abruptly and in an apologetic tone exclaimed, "Oops, I wrote that twice!"

Learning to read and write is particularly enhanced by shared book experiences. Family storybook reading plays a special role in young children's literacy development, and researchers have learned much through observations of this familiar ritual. Sharing books with young children has long been recognized as a crucial aid to their language and literacy development and as a socializing process within families. Teachers and caregivers can further support this process when they use "big books" to encourage children to participate in reading. These allow children to see the print as the story is being read to them at school in much the same way they do when being read to at home. The highly predictable language and storylines of these picture storybooks permit groups of youngsters to "read along." Saying aloud the repeated refrains and rhymes with the reader helps give them a sense of what it means to be a reader.

Traditional Perspectives

Traditionally held views about reading and writing differ fundamentally from the concept of emergent literacy. Although learning to speak is accepted as a natural part of the maturation process that doesn't require formal instruction, the mastery of reading and writing has been considered an arduous learning task, requiring a period of intense readiness. Only after children were thoroughly primed with the necessary prereading skills was "real" reading instruction begun. "Getting them ready" consisted largely of direct instruction in learning letter names, letter-sound relationships, and a variety of visual-perceptual tasks. The task of learning to write waited until reading was well underway. Children were considered literate only after their reading and writing began to approximate adult models.

In contrast, an emergent literacy curriculum emphasizes the ongoing development of skill in reading and writing and stressed participation in literacy activities that are meaningful and functional from the child's point of view. In operation, here is how the two viewpoints might look in a kindergarten classroom.

Old Ways Versus New

Teacher A has spent considerable time planning a program that will ensure her students are ready for the 1st grade curriculum. Preparing them for the reading program is of particular interest to her, since that is a high priority of the parents and of the 1st grade teachers. The entire year has been blocked out so that each letter of the alphabet is given equal time for in-depth study.

Using a workbook as her guide, she teaches the children the names of the letters of the alphabet, their corresponding sounds, and how to trace them in upper and lower case. The children play numerous games and engage in a variety of activities based on each letter. All of the children go through all of the activities in the order prescribed by the workbook, regardless of their previous knowledge. Reading instruction takes place during a specified time each day, and except for occasionally reading a story aloud, the teacher does very little to make literacy connections beyond that time.

Since kindergarten children are thought to be incapable of and uninterested in writing, the teacher makes no provision for it in the curriculum. She gives workbook unit tests periodically. These closely resemble the nationally normed readiness test that will be given at the end of the year. The tests help Teacher A to identify those children who may be falling behind. Although she tries to give these children extra help, the very nature of the program allows little differentiation of instruction.

Thus, children who fail to catch on early keep falling farther and farther behind. By the end of the year, they either repeat kindergarten or are assigned to transition classes. Even those children who do well on the standardized test must often repeat the phonics program in 1st grade—this is a consequence that has baffled both Teacher A and the 1st grade teachers.

Teacher B relied heavily on the classroom environment to prompt student involvement with literacy. There is an inviting reading center filled with books within reach of the children. Most of the titles are familiar, since the books have already been read aloud. A writing center is also available with plenty of writing tools, paper, magnetic letters, and an alphabet chart at the eye level of the children. Children are encouraged to use these centers daily. Printed materials are everywhere. There is a message board where they record important news and reminders each day, and personal mailboxes made of milk cartons encourage note writing. Teacher B values scribbles, pictures, and beginning attempts at spelling as engagement in the writing process.

Adorning the walls are numerous charts depicting graphs, poems, lists, and other important information related to the theme currently under study. Read-aloud time occurs at least twice each day. Stories, poems, and informational books are shared. Books with highly predictable language and storylines are stressed, since they encourage group participation and independent rereading in the reading center.

Although Teacher B has definite goals regarding the concepts and skills she wishes to foster, she sees no need to organize them hierarchically or to introduce them in isolation. Rather, the print environment and related activities are carefully orchestrated to allow children to build on what they already know about literacy, refine it, and use it for further learning. Although a unit of study about bugs might lead to a poem about a busy buzzy bumblebee and an opportunity to discuss the letter b, the emphasis is not placed on merely matching letter to sound but on helping children gain an understanding of a pattern in their language—that certain letters and sounds are often related.

Teacher B looks for evidence of these understandings and assesses learning through observation and analysis of children's independent reading and writing and through their participation during storytime. She is distressed when what she has documented about a child's knowledge is not always revealed on a standardized test.

In this classroom, literacy learning is not relegated to a specific time of day. Rather, it is integrated into everything that occurs throughout the day. Most important, content of interest and importance to children is the basis for learning language, learning through language, and learning about language.

It is important to recognize that both Teacher A and Teacher B are caring, concerned professionals. Each is a fine example of the theoretical framework from which she operates. Teacher A operates from a traditional readiness framework, in which the teacher is both keeper and dispenser of knowledge. Her lesson plans are segmented and preorganized into what are thought to be manageable bits and pieces, dispensed in small increments over a specified time. All children receive the same instruction, and little use is made of the knowledge about language that children bring with them to school.

Teacher B sees her role as that of facilitator of children's learnings. The classroom environment is structured so that certain events are very likely to occur. Learning stems as much from these incidental literary events that occur by virtue of living within a print-rich environment as from the numerous daily activities planned to involve children in oral and written language. Teacher B expects differences in the way children respond to the activities she plans. She carefully monitors their responses and plans accordingly. She emphasizes helping children build on what they already know in order to make connections to new learning.

Issues for Instruction

The move toward full-day kindergartens and programs for four-year-olds has prompted increased concern for developmentally appropriate instruction. Many schools are addressing this concern by implementing programs reflecting an emergent literacy perspective.

Not surprisingly, interest in emergent literacy has brought with it a host of issues. The issues reflect the problems schools face as they attempt to serve a younger population and, at the same time, change perspective on a host of long-held beliefs. Issues that predominate are those related to the place of writing and invented spelling, the development of skills, assessment, and continuity.

Writing and invented spelling. Because the importance of paying attention to young children's writing is a relatively recent concern, teachers and parents often feel uneasy about how they should respond to children's scribbles, strings of letters, and one-letter words. Traditional writing lessons have been associated with neatness, correct spelling, and proper letter formation. Teachers need to learn as much as they can about the early spellings that children produce independently. Encouraging children to scribble and invent their own spellings does not lead them to think that phonetic spelling is systematically being taught; they are aware that their inventions may not conform to adult norms. The children know that, as with other areas of their development, they are simply functioning as young learners moving gradually toward adult standards. Child, teacher, and parent should celebrate each new learning by focusing on what is known rather than what is lacking. Providing daily opportunities for varied experiences with literacy is the best assurance that children will begin to demonstrate what they know about writing and spelling as they compose stories and messages. Spelling errors should never be allowed to interfere with the composing process.

The development of skills. As educators, we must be careful not to give parents the impression that we are anti-skills; we are not. Rather, we need to help them see the differing ways that skills are developed through and emergent literacy perspective: not as an accumulation of information about a task but embedded within the child's growing ability to actually do the task. For example, children learn letter names and the sounds they represent as a part of the purposeful reading and writing they do, not as a set of meaningless fragments of information. Stress is placed on helping children think with text and helping them to become independent learners. Unfortunately, poor and minority children—who would benefit most from holistic approaches that require them to think with text and encourage them to become independent learners—are often the least likely to get this type of instruction.

Appropriate assessment. Although standardized tests have undergone severe criticism as screening devices and evaluative measure of young children's literacy, they unfortunately continue to be highly regarded by some policy makers as definitive evidence of young children's learning (Chittendon, 1989). Challenges regarding the assumptions underlying such tests, particularly the narrowness with which literacy is defined, raise serious questions about their use (Valencia & Pearson, 1987). Children's initial explorations with literacy involve a variety of experiences with books and print, which may be used for assessment. Among these are their knowledge of print conventions, their understandings about the relationships between letters and sounds (invented spellings), and their growing interest in listening to and making sense of stories. Standardized tests tap but a few of these. Yet, even as early as kindergarten, standardized test results are used to make important decisions about placement, retention, and promotion.

The integration of assessment and instruction is fundamental to an emergent literacy perspective. Increased reliance on systematic observation, record keeping, and analysis of children's classroom participation and work products and less reliance on standardized tests are the hallmarks of student evaluation and teacher planning.

The need for continuity. Continuity in the early grades critical. Children who are supported by an emergent literacy curriculum in the prekindergarten and kindergarten years, only to be faced with a subskills approach in 1st grade, will not only be confused, they will be unable to demonstrate what they do know about literacy. Collaborative curriculum decision making with teachers and administrators within a particular school and with those in the early childhood centers that feed into them is essential. In addition to supporting articulation between schools and grades within a school, educators must help parents understand new approaches to literacy that may be outside their experience. Children benefit from consistency in their lives. They function best when the adults they care about most reflect a comfortable harmony in their expectations and beliefs.

Dorothy S. Strickland is State of New Jersey Professor of Reading, Rutgers University, Graduate School of Education, 10 Seminary Place, New Brunswick, NJ 08903

References

Chittendon, E. "Assessment of Young Children's Reading: Documentation as an Alternative to Testing." In *Emerging Literacy: Young Children Learn to Read and Write,* edited by D. S. Strickland & L. M. Morrow. Newark, Del: International Reading Association, 1989.

Clay, M. *Observing Young Readers.* London: Heinemann, 1982.

Dewey, J.; & Dewey, E. *Schools of Tomorrow.* New York: Dutton, 1915/1962.

Teale, W.; & Sulzby, E. "Emergent Literacy: New Perspectives." In *Emerging Literacy: Young Children Learn to Read and Write,* edited by D. S. Strickland and L. M. Morrow. Newark, Del: International Reading Association, 1989.

Valencia, S.; & Pearson, P. D. "Reading Assessment: Time For a Change." *The Reading Teacher,* 1987, 40: 726–733.

Resources on Emergent Literacy

Bissex, G. *GNYS AT WRK: A Child Learns to Write and Read.* Cambridge, Mass: Harvard University Press, 1980.

Clay, M. *What Did I Write?* Portsmouth, N.H.: Heinemann, 1975.

Genishi, C.; & Dyson, A. H. *Language Assessment in the Early Years.* Norwood, J. J.: Ablex, 1984.

Hall, N. *The Emergence of Literacy.* Portsmouth, N.H.: Heinemann, 1987.

Harste, J.; Woodward, V.; & Burke, C. *Language Stories and Literacy Lessons.* Portsmouth, N.H.: Heinemann, 1984.

Holdaway, D. *The Foundations of Literacy.* New York: Ashton Scholastic, 1979.

Schickedanz, J. A. *More Than the ABC's: The Early Stages of Reading and Writing.* Washington, D.C.: NAEYC, 1986.

Strickland, D. S.; & Morrow, L. M. (Eds.). *Emerging Literacy: Young Children Learn to Read and Write.* Newark, Del.: International Reading Association, 1989.

Taylor, D.; & Strickland, D. *Family Storybook Reading.* Portsmouth, N.H.: Heinemann, 1986.

Teale, W.; & Sulzby, E. (Eds.). *Emergent Literacy: Writing and Reading.* Norwood, N.J.: Ablex, 1986.

Temple, C. A.; Nathan, R. G.; Burris, N. A.; & Temple, F. *The Beginnings of Writing.* Boston, Mass: Allyn and Bacon, 1988.

CHAPTER 32

Coming to Literacy Through the Shared Book Experience in Kindergarten

Picture a kindergarten classroom. Large sheets of manila drawing paper covered with children's paintings of billy goats are displayed. Green grass, planted in pans by the children, is growing in the shape of an upper case "G" and a lower case "g." Several children are using puppets depicting three billy goats and a troll for a dramatization of the story. A trio of children are grouped closely around an adult who is reading the classic children's book to them. A small boy is standing in front of an enlarged copy of *The Three Billy Goats Gruff,* pointing with a ruler to each word as he reads to his classmates with expression and accuracy. He grins broadly as he reads to his classmates with expression and accuracy. He grins broadly as he explains to the adult visitors, "I can read. I can read this book, and I can read *Brown Bear,* too."

The classroom described above is fairly typical of developmental kindergarten classes in many ways. A multi-sensory approach to learning, "hands-on" experiences, exposure to good literature, close contact with caring adults, and activities to enhance self-concept are important elements of a developmental early childhood program.

The two noticeable differences are the teacher (or teacher aide) reading to a trio of children rather than to the entire class, and the young boy reading to his peers. Having an adult read to a small group was a specific part of an experimental program designed to improve children's literacy. Having a five-year old reading well was actually an unexpected by-product of the program.

Parent education literature, magazines and workshops abound with the recommendation that parents read to their children and frequently. Children who have been read to at home generally learn to read earlier and with more ease at school (Hymes, 1958; Durkin, 1978; Sutton-Smith, 1964; Gardner, 1970; Briggs & Elkind, 1977; Clay, 1979; Smith, 1978; Doake, 1981; Hoffman, 1982; Wells, 1982; Teal, 1985). The child's development of a "literacy set" (Holdaway, 1979) has been cited as a benefit of home reading and includes such information as familiarity with handling a book, orienting the book in an upright position, and turning pages (Ilg & Ames, 1965; Heath, 1983; Taylor, 1983; Teal, 1985, Goodman, 1986).

Home story reading by parents appears to be more effective than the traditional large group story reading time found in preschools and primary classes. Reading to large groups of children at school does not appear to produce the same ease of learning to read that individual or home reading does. This would suggest that not only is reading to children important, but that the setting in which the reading occurs may well be significant. There would appear to be a qualitative difference in story reading at school and at home. The experience of a child being read to as a class member, seated some distance away from the teacher-reader and seeing the cover of the book and pictures only, and experience of a child sitting in physical contact with the parent-reader, observing the print as well as the pictures, and participating by turning pages and co-telling familiar lines in the relaxed atmosphere of the home, are very different indeed. Both the large group story setting and the individual story setting are valuable experiences for children, however, the individual setting provides experiences not available from the large group setting. Schickendanz (1978) has suggested that in the home story reading experience, (1) the child selects the book of greatest interest and has the parent read it until the child has learned the story by memorization; (2) the child sits so that he/she can see the print; (3) the child participates in the reading by turning the pages and co-telling the repetitive passages; (4) the child is free to interrupt the story with comments and questions such as "Why did Goldilocks go in the bears' house?" or "What does this word say?"; and, (5) that the child associates positive emotional feelings with the reading experience.

These qualitative differences in the typical home and school story reading episodes have lead theorists to suggest that teachers and other group care givers provide children with "home-style" reading episodes (Holdaway, 1979; Cazden, 1981; Smith, 1983, Teale, 1986). Home-style reading at school provides the child with contextual support by more closely resembling the natural learning processes with which the child is familiar (Hiebert, 1981; Ferreiro & Teberosky, 1982; Heath, 1982; Scallon & Scallon, 1982). The recommendation that school provide home-style literacy experiences for young children is based on insight, theory, and some experience, but not on quantitative data. Heath (1982) suggests that children who have been read to understand what literacy is prior to any formal instruction. When their first grade teacher begins formal reading instruction, they have a context in which to apply the newly-taught skills. Children with little or no prior experiences with books apparently do not know how to apply the skills being taught. Children fail to learn to read, not because the first grade teacher presented too much information, but because they don't get enough information to form a context in which to place the skills being taught (Schickendanz, 1978).

Incorporating the Shared Book Experience into a developmental kindergarten program is appropriate, and can be accomplished with little difficulty. However, as with any classroom activity, enthusiasm, careful planning and organization of ideas on the part of the teacher are essential.

Implementation begins with the selection of quality literature for children. In the selection process, several points need to be remembered. The books should (1) be of high interest to children; (2) deal with familiar events; (3) incorporate sequenced story lines; (4) be repetitious; (5) employ predictable outcomes; and (6) be enjoyable for the teacher.

Books of high interest to children include those classics which have been read to children for generations and new books about topics children exhibit interest in. Children's preferences may vary from locale to locale and the teacher will sense whether a specific book interests children.

Closely related to assessment of high interest for children is the factor of dealing with familiar events. Smith (1983) identifies books as "potentially meaningful" when they are on subjects familiar to the everyday world of children. Holdaway (1980) emphasizes the need for reading materials to be close to a child's previous experiences. When the story being read relates to prior experiences of children, they move quickly into understanding the text.

Sequenced story lines are a staple in the classics of children's literature, and are found in many recent publications which are of high interest to children. Logically sequenced events make sense to children, and are easier for them to "read" as they develop skills.

Repetitions, which may seem redundant to an adult, are fun for children. These repetitions quickly generate feelings of ownership for the child as a familiar refrain is repeated.

Predictable outcomes in story books are of great benefit to emergent readers. Holdaway (1980) describes prediction as a basis of the problem-solving process in learning to read, and he encourages teaching prediction as a skill. Predicting is more sophisticated than guessing, because the prediction has a basis in prior experience.

Teacher enjoyment adds a new dimension to stories being read aloud to children. Pleasure in the reading process is modeled by a teacher every time a book is read aloud enthusiastically, and both the enjoyment and enthusiasm are contagious. Learning that reading is fun can increase the pace at which children master the literacy process.

After selecting the literature, the teacher gathers all available information and materials about the book: Big Book, small books, tapes, and other resource material. A Big Book is an enlarged (usually 24″ by 36″) exact copy of a regular child-size book. Big Books may be teacher made or purchased commercially. The teacher is now ready to plan an intense one-week teaching unit around the particular book, including preparation of daily lesson plans which weave the theme of the teaching unit into each classroom center.

The design used in the Shared Book Experience is dynamic and spirals back to earlier experiences. The "steps" listed here describe the sequence of events used to implement this program in early childhood classes.

To further illustrate each step, lesson plans based on THE VERY HUNGRY CATERPILLAR by Eric Carle are included.

I. Whet the Appetite.

    A. Mention the name of the Big Book for several days prior to presentation.

    B. Display a commercially produced stuffed caterpillar during the week before presenting THE VERY HUNGRY CATERPILLAR.

    C. Share a copy of a student-made book about THE VERY HUNGRY CATERPILLAR from the previous year.

    D. Mention activities which are planned for the class in connection with the Big Book.

II. Present the Story.

    A. Discuss the cover of the Big Book, the author, the illustrator, the publisher, place of publication, and date.

    B. Read the story to the whole group, using much expression.

    C. Point to the words as they are being read, with a pointer and/or hand, using a sliding motion.

    D. Read the story a second time, encouraging the children to supply the words to complete phrases.

III. Read the Story Again and Again.

    A. "Mama reads" are begun. An adult reads to individuals or groups of no more than three or four children from a small book which is a replica of the Big Book.

    B. Be sure each child is sitting close enough to maintain physical contact with the adult and to see the print.

    C. Point to the words as they are being read, using a sliding hand motion.

    D. Read the book as often as the child requests, if possible.

    E. Encourage parents or other adult volunteers to help with small group readings.

F. Peer readers, from grades 1, 2, and 3, can read to the kindergarten children.

IV. Implement Multi-Sensory Activities In Learning Centers.

  A. LANGUAGE ARTS CENTER
1. Objective: THE LEARNER WILL BE ABLE TO (TLWBAT) name and supply two descriptive words to tell about an object.
2. South Carolina Basic Skills (SCBS): #7 The student communicates with others by using expressive language. #8 The student is receptive of language in communicating with others.
3. Teacher Preparation (TP): Secure one large tray (14″ × 20″ or larger) and display the following items: apple, pear, plum, strawberry, orange, chocolate cake slice, ice cream cone, pickle, swiss cheese slice, salami slice, lollipop, cherry pie slice, sausage, cupcake, and watermelon slice. Placing items in clean plastic bags to facilitate handling. After the introduction and demonstration of the activity by the teacher, each student is given the opportunity to participate.
4. Activity: Each student will select one item from the tray containing food items like those in THE VERY HUNGRY CATERPILLAR and tell two things about it. An example of a student response is, "This is a slice of watermelon. It is red and has seeds in it."

  B. SCIENCE CENTER
1. Objective: TLWBAT compare and order caterpillars according to size from the smallest to the largest, and left to right.
2. SCBS: #1 The student compares stimuli on the basis of one or more attribute(s). #12 The student sequences stimuli on the basis of one or more attribute(s).
3. TP: Make a set of eight to twelve caterpillars of various sizes and a tree branch from construction paper. After laminating the caterpillars and the tree branch, mark the tree branch with a green star on the left and a red star on the right, to insure the left to right progression when the caterpillars are being sequenced. Store items in appropriate container.
4. Activity: Each student will arrange caterpillars from the smallest to the largest, and from left to right.

C. BLOCK CENTER
1. Objective: TLWBAT develop structures to aid in his/her creative expression.
2. SCBS: #2 The student performs tasks involving fine motor skills.
3. TP: Make a variety of caterpillars from scrap materials and cotton using the illustrations in THE VERY HUNGRY CATERPILLAR as an example and provide a set of Unit Blocks.
4. Activity: Each student will have an opportunity to create structures, using homemade stuffed caterpillars and unit blocks to aid in his/her creative expression.

D. HOUSEKEEPING CENTER
1. Objective: TLWBAT classify clothing and accessories according to when they are worn, night or day.
2. SCBS: #10 The student classifies stimuli on the basis of one or more attribute(s).
3. TP: Secure clothing (various sizes and gender) and accessories that are worn at night or during the day and place in an appropriate container. Suggested items are: gowns, pajamas, bedroom shoes, dresses, slacks, sweaters, coats, bathing suits, belts, shoes, scarves, shirts, mittens, socks, gloves, bath robes, jewelry, ties, hats. Prepare a "night box" and a "day box" with appropriate visual clues painted on each. The "night box" may be painted dark blue with stars and a moon while the "day box" could be painted light blue with fluffy white clouds and the sun.
4. Activity: Each student will classify clothing and accessories into two categories, night or day, by placing items into appropriate boxes.

E. GAME CENTER
1. Objective: TLWBAT match different colored butterflies.
2. SCBS: #4 The student determines likenesses and differences in visual stimuli.
3. TP: Secure a commercially-produced game such as "The Butterfly Match" from Child Craft Education Corporation, or create your own matching game sheet using construction paper/poster board and commercially-produced stickers of butterflies.
4. Activity: Each student will match identical butterflies according to design and color.

F. LIBRARY CENTER
1. Objective: TLWBAT select a copy (small book) of THE VERY HUNGRY CATERPILLAR or a related book and "read" at his/her leisure.
2. SCBS: #9 The student expresses an interest in language.
3. TP: Secure multiple copies of THE VERY HUNGRY CATERPILLAR and related books from the school library and display in the center. Related books may include: SALLY'S CATERPILLAR by Anne and Harlow Rockwell, THE CATERPILLAR AND THE POLLIWOG by Jack Kent, CREEPY CATERPILLAR by Garry and Vesta Smith, IT"S EASY TO HAVE A CATERPILLAR VISIT YOU by Caroline O'Hagan, FROM EGG TO BUTTERFLY by Marlene Reidel, CATERPILLARS AND HOW THEY LIVE by Robert M. McClung, and I LIKE CATERPILLARS by Gladys Conklin.
4. Activity: Each student will select a copy (small book) of THE VERY HUNGRY CATERPILLAR or a related book and "read" silently or aloud.

G. MATHEMATICS CENTER
1. Objective: TLWBAT write numerals on individual circles and arrange the circles in numerical order, which will form a Number Caterpillar.
2. SCBS: #2 The student performs tasks involving fine motor skills. #12 The student sequences stimuli on the basis of one more attribute(s).
3. TP: Prepare thirty-eight (38) circles, approximately five (5) inches in diameter and three (3) caterpillar heads from construction paper and laminate. This will provide three sets of circles to be used by students on three different levels (0-5 or 0-10 or 0-20). Secure three black crayons for writing, three paper towels for erasers and three storage containers, one for each of the three levels.
4. Activity: Each student will write on individual circles numerals (0-5 or 0-10 or 0-20) and arrange the circles in numerical order, which will form a Number Caterpillar.

H. LISTENING CENTER
1. Objective: TLWBAT follow along in a read-along book.
2. SCBS: #2 The student performs tasks involving fine motor skills. #9 The student expresses an interest in language.
3. TP: Make an audio tape and secure multiple small ($3\frac{3}{4}'' \times 5''$)

copies of THE VERY HUNGRY CATERPILLAR. These small books, as well as the regular sized books, published by Philomel Books, a division of The Putnam Publishing Group, 51 Madison Avenue, New York, NY 10010, are available in selected bookstores.

4. Activity: Each student will listen and follow in a read-along book as the taped copy of THE VERY HUNGRY CATER-PILLAR is played.

I. ART CENTER

1. Objective: TLWBAT illustrate a personal copy of THE VERY HUNGRY CATERPILLAR.

2. SCBS: #2 The student performs tasks involving fine motor skills. #16 The student displays a positive attitude toward self.

3. TP: Provide prepared pages (teacher printed text on 8½″ × 11½″ paper) and a variety of art mediums (tempera paint, crayons, finger paints, watercolors and collage materials) for students to use in illustrating each page. One page is done each day until the personal copy of the book is completed.

4. Activity: Each student will illustrate prepared pages for a personal copy of THE VERY HUNGRY CATERPILLAR which will be carried home.

V. Expand The Experience.

A. Have copies of the Big Book and small books available for children to read.

B. Have tapes and copies of small book available for children to hear the story.

C. Have books and pictures in the library center which correlate with the subject of the story.

D. Display pictures to correlate with THE VERY HUNGRY CAT-ERPILLAR.

E. Tape students as they "read" the story, and play back with student's permission.

F. Read a story on a related subject.

G. Return to one of the activities suggested earlier whenever children express an interest.

VI. Begin The Process of Writing.

    A. Children dictate sentences to the teacher who writes them on a large chart in front of the group.

    B. At the end of dictation children "read" what they have dictated.

    C. Focus on certain things in a systematic way, such as a particular letter, a particular high frequency word, color words, or punctuation.

    D. Daily entries may be on a specified subject, such as the foods which appear in THE VERY HUNGRY CATERPILLAR.

    E. Daily entries are dated and kept together to form a classroom journal. Share journal entries with another class.

    F. In the spring of the year, following extensive experience with group journal keeping, children begin individual journals. On Monday, each child is given five sheets of plain white paper which have been stapled together, so that they may write individual journals daily. ANYTHING the child "writes," from squiggles through illustrations, is acceptable. The child may select an entry to share with the class. Individual journals are taken home AFTER a letter of explanation has been sent to parents.

    G. Teachers write in their journals while students are writing in their journals. The children need to see teachers writing.

    H. Children create a new story using the format of the Big Book and changing nouns, verbs, or adjectives. An example would be a story about THE VERY BUSY CATERPILLAR which would detail the many daily activities the caterpillar could perform.

After the intense one-week period the Big Book is not shelved and forgotten, but is added to the classroom classics. The children ask, virtually demand, that it be read and reread frequently because, as in the bedtime story situation, the children have discovered that the Big Book means fun.

An important advantage of using the Shared Book Experience in kindergarten is the fact that it can be woven into any developmental program. It is not something done instead of the present program; it becomes an integral part of what is already going on.

The Shared Book Experience demonstrates the power of an idea. The idea in this instance is a simple one, accepted intuitively by people who care about children, that reading to and with a child is an important element in helping the child learn to read. What is different in this program is the attempt to translate the story reading experience into the school kindergarten program.

The use of the Shared Book Experience within the context of a developmental kindergarten appears to be a powerful tool for producing an increase in children's literacy awareness and competence. It is strongly recommended for schools and teachers who recognize that children are active participants in their own education and who would like to create holistic learning environments within which children can come to be literate.

Dr. Mac H. Brown is Associate Professor of Early Childhood Education at the University of South Carolina, Dr. Sylvia H. Weinberg is superintendent of Clarendon Country School District Two, Manning, S.C., and Ms. Nell B. Price, Kindergarten Teacher, Manning Primary School, Manning, S.C.

References

Asbjornsen, P. C. & Moe, J. E. (1957). *The Three Billy Goats Gruff.* New York: Harcourt, Brace & World, Inc. (Taken from the translation of G. W. Dasant; illustrated by Marcia Brown.)

Briggs, C. & Elkind, D. (1977). Characteristic of Early Readers. *Perceptual and Motor Skills, 44,* 1231–1237.

Busching, B., & Schwartz, J. (9183). *Intergrating the Language Arts in the Elementary School.* Urbana, IL: National Council of Teachers of English.

Cazden, C. B. (1981). *Language in Early Childhood Education.* Washington, DC: National Association for the Education of Young Children.

Clay, M. M. (1972). *Reading: The Patterning of Complex Behavior,* Auckland, New Zealand: Heinemann Educational Books.

Clay, M. M. (1979). *Reading: The Patterning of Complex Behavior.* (2nd ed.) Auckland: Heinemann Educational Books.

Doake, D. (1981). *Book Experiences and Emergent Reading in Preschool Children.* Ph.D. Dissertation, University of Alberta.

Durkin, D. (1978). *Teaching Young Children To Read.* Boston: Allyn and Bacon.

Ferreiro, E. & Teberosky, A. (1982). *Literacy Before Schooling.* Exeter, NH: Heinemann Educational Books.

Gardner, K. (1970). Early Reading Skills. In *Reading Skills: Theory and Practice.* London: Ward Lock Educational.

The Gingerbread Man. (1975). San Fernando, CA: The Superscope Story Teller. (Designed and Illustrated by Rex Irvine and John Strejan.)

Goodman, Y. (1984). *The Development of Initial Literacy.* In Goelman, H. (et.al.) *Awakening to Literacy.* Exeter, NH: Heinemann Educational Books.

Goodman, Y. (1986). Children Coming To Know Literacy. In W. H. Teale & E. Sutsby (eds.) *Emergent Literacy: Reading and Writing.* Norwood, NJ: Ablex.

Harste, J., Woodward, J. & Burke, C. (1984). *Language Stories & Literacy Lessons.* Portsmouth, NH: Heinemann Educational Books.

Heath, S. B. (1982). What No Bedtime Story Means: Narrative Skills at Home and School. *Language and Society, 11,* 49–76.

Heath, S. B. (1983). *Ways With Words.* Cambridge, United Kingdom: Cambridge University Press.

Hiebert, E. H. (1981). Developmental Patterns and Interrelationships of Pre-School Children's Print Awareness. *Reading Research Quarterly, 16,* 236–260.

Hilbert, M. (1963). *The Three Little Pigs.* Chicago: Folbet Publishing Company. (Illustrated by Irma Wilde.)

Hoffman, S. J. (1982). Preschool Reading Related Behaviors: A Parent Diary. Paper presented at the Third Ethnography in Education Forum, Philadelphia.

Holdaway, D. (1979). *The Foundations of Literacy.* Sidney: Ashton Scholastic.

Holdaway, D. (1980). *Independence in Reading.* 2nd ed. Gosford, NSW: Ashton Scholastic.

Holdaway, D. (1984). *Stability and Change in Literacy Learning.* London, Ontario, Canada: The University of Western Ontario.

Hymes, J. L., Jr. (1958). *Before the Child Reads.* Evanston, IL: Row, Peterson, and Company.

Ilg, F. L. & Ames, L. B. (1965). *School Readiness.* New York: Harper & Row Publishers.

Schickendanz, J. A. (1978). Please Read that Story Again. *Young Children, 33,* (5), 48–54.

Scollon, R. & Scollon, S. B. K. (1982). Face In Interethnic Communication. In Richards, J. & Schmidt, R. (eds.), *Communicative Competence.* London: Longman.

Smith, F. (1978). *Understanding Reading.* New York: Holt, Rinehart & Winston.

Smith, F. (1983). A Metaphor for Literacy: Creating Words or Shunting Information? In Smith, F. *Essays Into Literacy.* Exter, NH: Heinemann Educational Books.

Sutton-Smith, B. & Sutton-Smith, S. (1964). *How To Play With Your Children: And When Not To.* New York: Hawthorne Books, Inc.

Taylor, D. (1983). *Family Literacy: Young Children Learning to Read and Write.* Exeter, NH: Heinemann Educational Books.

Teale, W. H. (1981). Parents Reading to Their Children: What We Know and Need to Know. *Language Arts, 58,* 902–912.

Teale, W. H. (1985). The Beginnings of Literacy. *Dimensions, 13*(3),5–8.

Teale, W. H. (1986). Home Background and Young Children's Literacy Development. In W. H. Teale and E. Sutsby (Eds.) *Emergent Literacy: Reading and Writing.* Norwood, NJ: Ablex.

Vygotsky, L. S. (1981). The Genesis of Higher Mental Functions. In Wertsch, J. V. (ed.), *The Concept of Activity in Soviet Psychology,* White Plains, NY: Sharpe.

Wells, G. (1982). Story Reading and Development of Symbolic Skills. *Australian Journal of Reading, 5,* 142–152.

Wells, G. (1986). *The Meaning Makers: Children Learning Language and Using Language To Learn.* Portsmouth, NH: Heinemann Educational Books, Inc.

without beginning to wish for something a bit more interesting. One consequence was that students often responded to the early programs with intentionally incorrect answers because the feedback given to the wrong answer (often a branch to a more elaborate subject) was more inviting. Today, that early form of computer-assisted instruction has been replaced by far more exciting presentations which use graphics and which create stories through which material can be learned.

The array of available programs at all levels makes the computer a more and more useful tool for simple and complex learning. Advances have been made far beyond the simple computer assisted instruction of earlier years and now software can retain student interest and can capture the complexity of subjects.

Computer and Child Work Together

A computer is an amplifying device which enhances the natural and learned ability of a child and permits the accomplishment of more advanced learning tasks in a more efficient and effective manner. Early research on the use of computers to assist students in their learning assignments gave stark evidence of the differences in accomplishment possible with and without computer assistance. Kemeny, an early pioneer in the use of computers to help students learn, has shown persuasively that students can accomplish far more in a given period of time when working with a computer than they can when working with older methods. (1972, p.33) Students at Dartmouth, where one of the first interactive computing systems for students was established, were routinely expected to accomplish problems which would have been impossible before. In a physics course, for instance, students who would have demonstrated Newton's Law by doing manual calculations of what happens when one billiard ball hits another, now write computer programs to plan a rocket trip to the moon. Engineering students can do serious engineering problems as undergraduates.

Kemeny was prophetic in describing the way computers could gain widespread use in education and in the home, but even he did not foresee the gains which would come from the invention of the microcomputer (1972, p.82). His expectation that terminals connected to large time-sharing systems would make computing widely available has been vastly surpassed as, in one short decade, small and inexpensive home computers have achieved far more capability than he or any one else envisioned. Today, the home computer is the child's homework tool and companion, vastly amplifying the ability to write, to calculate, and to organize information in preparation for lessons in school. Today, the number of children who write term papers and class projects by hand is decreasing rapidly as memory. The button can be changed in size and shape or can be moved around on the screen. It can even be copied to new programs, but it does not lose its learned ability to carry out its proper function and that function can be applied to many different situations without reprogramming. It's a bit like a child's learning the concept of multiplication. Once the concept is learned, it can be used on many different numbers and can even be used in higher operations such as in solving equations. The act of multiplying is an "object" which does not always need to be relearned.

Programming with objects enormously extends the ability of the average computer user to make the computer perform useful functions. Children learn to program more quickly and can create highly complex applications in a fraction of the time it formerly took. Perhaps the best example of a program which uses the object-oriented approach is HYPER-CARD, a program which comes with every Macintosh computer. Programs, or "stacks" as they are called, consist of a series of "cards" which contain information and buttons. The buttons are programmed to manipulate the information in a variety of useful ways to accomplish useful purposes. Such stacks as diaries, telephone books, maps, and demonstrations have been produced in such quantity and quality by relatively inexperienced programmers that a whole new industry has sprung up to market them. Young programmers are showing clearly that teaching the computer how to carry out a complex task requires the programmer to learn how the task is structured first, and then to find new creative ways to do it better. Such learning is perhaps the greatest benefit.

Available Software for Children

An extensive array of software is available for children of different ages. This selection is from a recent edition of *The Family Guide to Educational Software* published by Haven Laboratories (1989). There are five different types of software available for children from pre-school through high school.

Practice and Drill

These programs are similar to classroom activities such as flash cards, but with the advantage of individual levels and endless repetition. Many can be customized with problems from school. Rewards such as praise or pleasing sound and visual effects are given for correct answers and generally are set to give the right answer after a number of tries to inhibit frustration.

ALF's World of Words (Ages 6 and up) — three reading and vocabulary lessons featuring the TV character teach children to alphabetize, create compound words, and use prefixes and suffixes.

Math and Me (Preschool–1st) — twelve activities are included which help children develop skills in shapes, numbers, patterns, and beginning addition. Rewards are graphic in the form of colored pop-up monkeys.

Tic Tac Show (Preschool–adult) — designed with a trivia or game show format, this package presents questions and answers in between 14 and 22 different subjects at all learning levels.

Learning Games

Games motivate students by combining school content with the kinds of challenge children find in arcades. Their forte is high motivation through graphics and sound effects. They operate on a principle that increased learning provides increased reward. Game programs, which can be used to teach some of the same things as can. Drill programs (such subjects as spelling, typing, and math) work well because they make learning enjoyable.

Ten Little Robots (Preschool–2nd) — five different games a child can play with robots to learn letter recognition, counting, addition, and subtraction. Program also allows doodling on the screen and dipping the robot in paint.

Designasaurus (Preschool to Adult) — game of survival as one of 12 different kinds of dinosaurs. Program allows player to design a prehistoric beast from various body parts, which can be named, and then printed out as a picture.

Think Quick (2nd–8th) — six adventure games of increasing difficulty involving a dragon which must be dealt with through logical and problem-solving skills. Children learn to interpret maps, decipher codes, and make quick decisions.

Creative Discovery

Useful for more advanced subjects such as geometry or physics, these programs allow exploration and experimentation as a means of learning. They allow a student to feel the excitement of working with real events without all the tedium of careful preparation or the problems of messy experimental preparation. The freedom to play and to learn at the same time make creative discovery programs among the most effective.

Where in the World is Carmen Sandiego? (5th and up) — an adventure game designed to teach world geography through a detective story. The game changes each time it is played.

Audubon Wild Life Adventures — Whales (3rd to adult) — interactive stories which allow the user, as a marine biologist, to learn about the life and habits of whales. Also develops awareness of problems affecting the environment.

Chem Lab (4th to 7th) — an exploration of chemistry experimentation using a fully equipped "lab" with lots of "dangerous" chemicals, all without the worry of blowing up the house.

Tutorials

A step beyond practice and drill programs, tutorials teach a subject in its entirely from the basics to advanced levels. They enable a student to proceed at an individual speed and present their material in an interesting way, one step at a time, and with frequent quizzes to check progress. Tutorials are useful for academic subjects, for professional and job-training activities, and for learning new software. They supplement and even replace the initial orientation often needed by students using a new program.

Typing Tutor III (4th to adult) — program to teach the skill of touch typing through organized drill with focused practice on those letters most in need of it. On-screen help at every level makes the program easier to use.

Success with Math Series (1st and up) — self-paced tutorial for learning math concepts from the most basic through those needed for algebra. Random problems are generated to test skill and errors are noted with instructions on how to correct them.

Computer Preparation for the SAT — an integrated self-paced tutorial that claims to increase SAT scores by over 100 points. It combines diagnostic tests, plans for improvement, and special exercises to create a test-like atmosphere.

Simulations

Simulations put the child in imaginary situations which have many of the same characteristics as real life situations. They require of the child that choices be made using increasing skills and judgment. The learner can play the role of another person, in a situation which because of complexity or danger, may not fall within the student's normal experience. Simulation programs are most useful for helping students with complex, high-level learning with many variables and many factors which play a part in judgment.

Three-Mile Island (7th to adult) — a simulation of the management of a nuclear power plant. The player controls the maintenance cycles and power levels of a nuclear electric plant in accord with principles of cost-effectiveness. Benefits of the simulation include knowledge of complex decision-making and the structure of complex technology.

Car Builder (8th and up) — simulation of the role of car designer lets the user design, construct, test, and refine any kind of car. Decisions must be made about style, aerodynamics, power and handling, and fuel economy, all in the context of life-like marketing.

Millionaire II (high-school and up) — simulation of stock market strategies which teaches buying on margin, puts and calls, commissions, and tax consequences. Choices of buying and selling are made under realistic conditions based on actual market trends.

Summary

This chapter has shown how computers have changed the face of childhood education and even of the way children interact in our society. It suggests that the younger generations have several distinct advantages over earlier ones by virtue of the technological advances that seem to increase in power and speed as time goes by. Children are exposed to more knowledge and to the means to assimilate and manipulate it. They are introduced to higher skills by machines which make learning fun and which teach them those skills while at the same time showing them how to expand and enhance them.

Perhaps the greatest obstacle to the use of computers by children is the sense that some adults have that children have to be "taught" how to use technology. Adults, parents and teachers alike, bring attitudes to the learning situation which may inhibit the child's free exposure to computers. These attitudes were born in a time when there were no computers and when they were seen as new and even scary devices. Teachers and parents who are themselves afraid of new technology can often instill in their children an aversion which is both necessary and damaging. The best approach is to provide the computer and the software and then get out of the way. Children who have been born into a world where computers are commonplace will learn to use them as we use a stove or a telephone, and will even after a time (an incredibly short time) be able to teach their parents or teachers a thing or two.

Parents and teachers have a major role to play in helping their children become computer literate and ready for the next century, but it is not a direct teaching role. Rather it is a supporting role of making computers and software available at home and of encouraging their use in the schools. Parents who use a computer in their home should make the machine freely available to children for games and for doing their schoolwork. As early as is economically feasible, parents should invest in a computer for their children, and then in a computer for each child. The key is to engender an attitude that the computer is a technological assistant to the child, to help the child learn, to accomplish useful work, and most importantly to have fun.

J. Bruce Francis, Ph.D., Walden University

References

Bowman, Sally. "Preparing Our Children for the 21st Century" *Shareware,* Vol. IV No. 4 Sep–Oct, 1989 p. 6

Puskas, P. (ed.) *Family Guide to Educational Software.* Fall 1989. Rockville Centre, New York: Haven Laboratories.

Kemeny, John G. *Man and the Computer.* New York: Charles Scribner's Sons, 1972.

Papert, S. *Mindstorms: Children, Computers and Powerful Ideas.* New York: Basic Books, 1980.

CHAPTER 33

Theoretical Framework for Preschool Science Experiences

Children construct physical knowledge by acting on objects—feeling, tasting, smelling, seeing, and hearing them.

Recently I received an advertisement announcing a newsletter for early childhood educators. The brochure contained a sample science lesson you could eat—"Sink and Float: Jello." Intrigued, I read through the instructions provided. The lesson involved first graders making Jello and then adding some or all of the following ingredients: blueberries, sliced bananas, sliced peaches or strawberries, grated coconut, and crushed pineapple. Children were to observe which of these items floated and which sank. Up to this point, everything seemed pedagogically sound, but then I read further: "Some of these things will float. Some will sink. Talk about *why* things float or sink" (italics mine).

Obviously, experienced teachers will expect answers in terms of what the child can see, such as which objects float and which object sink. Children may enjoy classifying objects into these two groups. Teachers should encourage children to experiment with floating and sinking and accept simple answers that refer to the object's weight, size, or shape.

Yet beginning teachers with a strong science background, using the instructions in the advertisement as a guide, might be misled by the direction, "Talk about why" and expect a more sophisticated explanation from the children. The cause-effect relationships, however, that cause some objects to sink and others to float (buoyancy and displacement concepts) are beyond the intellectual capabilities of preschoolers and most primary grade students (Ward, 1978; Wolfinger, 1982).

Another example of inappropriate science for 3-, 4-, and 5-year-olds would be to expect them to understand concepts such as air is almost everywhere; air is real—it takes up space; or air presses on everything from all sides (Harlan, 1984). Because air is invisible, such concepts are not understood by the young child (Kamii & DeVries, 1978). Iatridis (1981), in designing a science curriculum for 4s and 5s, eliminated air as a topic at the suggestion of both science and early childhood educators.

Some experiences with air are appropriate for preschoolers. They can feel air as they try to blow up a balloon; they can feel air on their faces as they release it from the balloon; they can feel air (wind) on their faces on a windy day. They can also observe the effects of wind, for example: papers or leaves blowing, or sailboats moving across water.

Many new and inexperienced teachers depend on the literature (journals, magazines, curriculum guides, newsletters) for appropriate science activities. Some teachers take it for granted that what they find in these resources is developmentally or pedagogically sound. This is not always the case, as the examples I have cited demonstrate.

A theoretical framework for a preschool science curriculum, with illustrative experiences, can help preschool teachers develop their ability to let—or make—appropriate science experiences happen in their classrooms. In addition, such a framework can help teachers evaluate activities or experiences suggested in the literature in terms of developmental appropriateness for 3-, 4-, and 5-year olds.

A Theoretical Framework

A theoretical framework can be developed by integrating research that examines how children construct knowledge and how appropriate science experiences contribute to children's ability to construct knowledge or learn about their world.

The most significant research about the construction of knowledge was done by Piaet (1929; 1954; 1973), Kamii and DeVries (1978) and Forman and Kuschner (1983) discuss the theoretical significance of Piagetian constructivism and its implications for early childhood education. More specifically, Howe (1975) and Smith (1981) discuss the implication of Piagetian theory for early childhood science education.

For Piaget,

> the foundation upon which all intellectual development takes place is physical knowledge, knowledge that comes from objects. This includes information about the properties of objects (their shape, size, textures, color, odor), as well as knowledge about how objects react to different actions on them (they roll, bounce, sink, slide, dry up). Children construct physical knowledge by acting on objects—feeling, tasting, smelling, seeing, and hearing them. They cause objects to move—throwing, banging, blowing, pushing, and pulling them, and they observe changes that take place in objects when they are heated, cooled, mixed together, or changed in some other way. As physical knowledge develops, children become better able to establish relationships (comparing, classifying, ordering) between and among the objects they act upon. Such relationships (logicomathematical knowledge according to Piaget) are essential for the emergence of logical, flexible thought processes.

Table 1. Criteria for developmentally appropriate science experiences (ages 3 to 5)

Are the materials selected those that
- children will naturally gravitate to for play?
- provide opportunities for the development of perceptual abilities through total involvement of the senses (perception of color, size, shape, texture, hardness, sound, etc.)?
- encourage self-directed problem solving and experimentation?
- children can act upon-cause to move-or that encourage children's observations of changes?

Do the experiences that evolve from children's play with the materials
- provide opportunities for the teacher to "extend the child's learning by asking questions or making suggestions that stimulate children's thinking (NAEYC, 1986, p. 10)?"
- allow for additional materials to be introduced gradually to extend children's explorations and discoveries?
- allow for differences in ability, development, and learning style?
- allow children to freely interact with other children and adults?
- encourage children to observe, compare, classify, predict, communicate?
- allow for the integration of other curriculum areas?

Informal experiences (for example, at the water table, or in the animal center, sandbox, or block corner) allow children to explore objects freely and discover their properties, what they are made of, and how they react when acted on in various ways. Iatridis (1981) found that children exposed to specific science experiences using carefully selected materials

> increased their self-directed discovery (active, child-initiated exploration rather than aimless handling of materials and verbalized curiosity) (p.26).

Such behaviors, that is, active active exploration initiated by children themselves and increased verbalization, contribute to the child's construction of knowledge. Educators and researchers have long advocated the importance of experiences in preschool science education that promote the development of these behaviors (Flavell, 1963; Greenberg, 1975; Hawkins, 1965; Hockman & Greenwald, 1963).

A theoretical framework for a preschool science curriculum integrates the child's construction of knowledge with science-related experiences and promotes active, child-initiated action on objects and observations of changes.

Using such a framework, criteria have been developed (see Table 1) that can be used to determine whether the science experiences suggested for preschoolers are developmentally appropriate. They can also be used by teachers to develop their own preschool science curriculum.

The teacher's role in implementing such a curriculum is a challenging one:

1. Teachers should be aware of daily experiences that might involve science, for example, painting (Lasky & Mukerji, 1980), cooking (Wanamaker, Hearn, & Richarz, 1979), or playing with musical instruments (McDonald, 1979). Such an awareness enables the teacher to capitalize on the children's involvement with a science experience, either by leaving them alone to pursue their own curiosities or initiatives (Kamii & DeVries, 1978), or by encouraging them to observe more closely, ask questions, and compare and classify what they are acting on, or to make their own discoveries (Iatridis, 1981).

2. To encourage and facilitate children's explorations with science-related phenomena, a variety of equipment and materials should be made available (Holt, 1977). Kamii and DeVries (1978) suggest principles for planning physical knowledge activities that are applicable and that involve children with materials related to science experiences. The way in which materials are introduced to young children can maximize their initiative. The teacher can put out materials that children will naturally gravitate toward. For example, a variety of musical instruments can be displayed to encourage children's explorations with sound. Or the teacher can present specific materials and ask children to think of different things they could do with these materials. One set of such material might initially include an inclined plane and different-sized balls or other round objects. Objects that are not round or toy trucks and cars of different sizes can gradually be added to the collection when the teacher feels it is the right moment "to enter the child's world (Forman & Kuschner, 1983)."

3. In guiding children's experiences in science, teachers should remember that "meaningful learning is an active, self-regulated process (Forman & Kuschner, 1983, p.123)." Any attempt to shape the child's behavior according to predetermined objectives may interfere with this self-regulation. Forman and Kuschner (1983) clearly describe when and how teachers can begin appropriate learning encounters with young children and set for the following special requirements: skillful techniques for observing children's behavior, a broad child development knowledge base with which to interpret observed behaviors, good entry techniques, and sensitive timing.

Illustrative Experiences for 3- and 4-Year-Olds

Developmentally appropriate experiences that illustrate how teachers can let or make science happen in the preschool include the following:

Paints

Young children love to paint; they enjoy experimenting with color and can be quite creative in their artistic expression. Teachers can use experiences with painting to heighten children's awareness of colors and color changes. As children become familiar with the primary and secondary colors through painting activities (naming or labeling colors is not necessary at this time), color matching and sorting on the basis of visual comparisons can gradually be introduced. "Visual comparisons remain the principal concept for young children to master (McIntyre, 1981a, p.40)." As the children use different colors in their paintings, the teacher can encourage them to match the colors of their paints to the clothes they are wearing or to other objects in the room. Further opportunities for developing color perception can be made available through additional materials or experiences (Lasky & Mukerji, 1980; McIntyre 1981a; Neuman, 1978; Schools Council, 1973b).

During their painting activities, children may mix paints together and produce a new or different color. Teachers should help children focus on this color change; the observation that a change has taken place, however, is more important at this stage than what combination of colors produced the change. Children can even be encouraged, through the teacher's example, to experiment by mixing different paints together to discover what happens. An activity that allows children to combine colors (mixing food colors in water or mixing paints), is an excellent example of observing changes in objects, a type of physical knowledge activity described by Kamii and DeVries (1978) in which observation is primary and the child's action is secondary.

Tactile experiences can also evolve from children's painting. Their dried, finished products may be lumpy or bumpy in some spots and smooth in others. Having children carefully feel their dried paintings enhances their sense of touch and begins to focus their attention on different kinds of surfaces. Appropriate language—smooth, rough, bumpy, scratchy—can be introduced by the teacher. Thus, an added dimension of an object's properties, that of roughness or smoothness, begins to become part of the child's developing knowledge. Zeitler (1972) found that a small sample of 3-year-olds did not mention texture (roughness or smoothness) of an object as one of its properties. More informal experiences, similar to those described here, can encourage 3- and 4-year-olds to focus on texture.

Test science activities by criteria included here.

Sounds

"Listening to, making, and sharing sounds with others are enjoyable activities for young children and provide a base for simple generalizations and understandings related to the science of sound (McIntyre, 1981b, p. 34)." Thus, classrooms for preschoolers should include a sound corner where a variety of musical instruments are available for the children to play with. At first, only a few instruments should be displayed for exploration. As children become familiar with the sounds these instruments make, others can be added. As children freely explore each instrument, they rely on their sense of hearing—they begin to discriminate between the sounds each different instrument makes. They are also actively involved in producing their own sounds; they experiment by plucking, banging, tapping, striking, or shaking. Children as young as 3-years-old begin to see that action or movement is necessary in order to have sound.

When children become familiar with each of the different instruments, games can be introduced to help them develop their perception of sound. The teacher can select one instrument at a time, hide it from the children's view, and make a sound with it; the children can guess which instrument the teacher is playing. To help children make discriminations, the teacher can make sounds with two instruments simultaneously; the children have to guess what both instruments are. Children can also play these guessing games with each other, and tape recordings can be made of the instrument sounds for children to identify. To learn, a child does not always need teaching.

Children should have greater opportunity to listen to and identify ordinary sounds in the classroom, for example, voices, moving chairs, splashing water, footsteps, tumbling blocks, and cars or trucks rolling across the floor. They can also listen for sounds outside the classroom. The teacher plays a key role in helping children focus their listening on specific sounds and in introducing appropriate vocabulary: "the chirp of a bird, the thump of a heartbeat, the crunch of footsteps on gravel (Schools Council, 1972a, p.31)." Children can be asked to talk about the sounds they like and dislike, they can imitate sounds of familiar objects and show that they have associated specific sounds with specific objects, and everyday events in the classroom can be used to help children identify loud and soft sounds.

Foods

Cooking activities are an integral part of the preschool curriculum and provide a unique opportunity to engage children in developing sight, touch, taste, and smell. Foods, fruits and vegetables in particular, vary in color, texture, taste, smell, size, and shape. All these properties can be explored by the children during snack time or a special cooking activity (Christenberry & Stevens, 1984; Parent Nursery School, 1974; Wanamaker et al., 1979). Three- and 4-year-olds tend to focus on taste because this is the most desirable property of a particular food. The teacher's role, however, is not only to provide the children with enjoyable tasting experiences; she or he can also intervene by helping the children focus on other properties of a food. Appropriate questions might include: "How does it feel?"; "Can you find something on the table the same shape as your orange?"; or "Which smell do you like the best?" The shape of a particular fruit can be used to explore the movement of round objects. Children can roll an apple or orange across various surfaces; they can compare the action of the apple with that of a pear or banana ("Which fruit rolls best?" "Can you find other objects in the room that roll like your apple?")

In addition to offering children opportunities to act on individual foods—to feel, taste, and smell—experiences with cooking also give children chances to observe changes taking place: corn seeds changing to popcorn, cream turning to butter, apples changing into applesauce. Making applesauce in two different ways enables children not only to observe changes taking place, but also to observe and compare different textures and tastes. Children can first cook apples to make applesauce; they can also grind raw apples, with the teacher's assistance, with a small food mill. They then can compare textures and tastes of cooked and raw applesauce.

Constructing Logical Relationships

These examples of science experiences suitable for 3- and 4-year-olds are only a small sampling of what can be incorporated into a science curriculum for them. Other experiences could include: waterplay (Kamii & DeVries, 1978); discoveries with sand (Hill, 1977); science using toys (Hirsch, 1984; Schools Council, 1972b); investigating themselves (Holt, 1977; Schools Council, 1973a); and investigating animals (McIntyre, 1984). Only selected specialists are referenced here, but many fine nursery educators have been encouraging activities like these for years.

As preschoolers construct physical knowledge, they will be better equipped to begin constructing logical relationships between and among the objects they have already encountered. Such relationships include classifying objects on the basis of a common property (size, shape, color, texture, taste); ordering objects according to a common property (size, weight, length); and comparing objects (shorter-longer, darker-lighter, smoother-rougher, thicker-thinner).

An activity that involves the movement of objects (Kamii & DeVries, 1978) clearly illustrates how these relationships begin to emerge.

The teacher presents each child with a straw and shows them a box containing several of each of the following items: tissues, popsicle sticks, straws, empty cans (frozen orange juice, coffee), marbles, and small blocks. She or he then asks, "Can you find something that you can blow across the floor?" (p.6).

As the children look at each object in terms of its blow-ability, they begin to think, "at some vague, intuitive level" (p.7), about each object's weight, shape, or both. Consideration of these objects' properties at this time depends on previous knowledge constructed through action and observation. As children experiment to find an answer to the question, they begin to construct logicomathematical relationships. For example, children might group the objects according to the "things that never move (a block)" and "things that always move (a tissue, marble, straw, and popsicle stick)" (p.7).

The same objects could also be categorized according to whether they slide or roll.

Conclusion

A theoretical framework, then, that evolves both from research and experiences with young children, enables preschool teachers to provide the appropriate environment and science experiences to help children learn about their world. New and inexperienced teachers can use this framework as a guide for developing their own science curriculum and also as a criterion for evaluating those activities suggested in the literature. In fact, such a framework serves to heighten teachers' awareness that science is not necessarily a separate curriculum area: "Science in the infant [early childhood] classroom is very much interwoven into the activities that normally go on there, it is indistinguishable as a separate entity . . . (Schools Council, 1972a, p.2)."

Robert F. Smith, Ph.D., is Associate Professor of Early Childhood Education at Brooklyn College, Brooklyn, New York.

References

Christenberry, M.; and Stevens, B. *Can Piaget Cook?* Atlanta: Humanics Limited, 1984.

Flavell, J. H. *Developmental Psychology of Jean Piaget.* New York: Van Nostrand, 1963.

Forman, G. E.; and Kuschner, D. S. *The Child's Construction of Knowledge: Piaget for Teaching Children.* Washington, DC: NAEYC, 1983.

Greenberg, P. *Bridge-to-Reading Comprehensive Preschool Curriculum: Discovery Science.* Washington, DC: Acropolis, 1975.

Harlan, J. *Science Experiences for the Early Childhood Years.* Columbus, OH: Merrill, 1984.

Hawkins, D. "Messing about in science." *Science and Children,* 1965, 2: 5–9.

Hill, D. *Mud, Sand, and Water.* Washington, DC: NAEYC, 1977.

Hirsch, E. S. *The Block Book.* (rev. ed.). Washington, DC: NAEYC, 1984.

Hochman, V.; and Greenwald, M. *Science Experiences in Early Childhood*. New York: Bank Street College of Education, 1963.

Holt, B-G. *Science With Young Children*. Washington, DC: NAEYC, 1977.

Howe, A. "A rationale for science in early childhood education." *Science Education*, 1975, 59: 95–101.

Iatridis, M. "Teaching science to preschoolers." *Science and Children*, 1981, 19: (2), 25–27.

Kamii, C.; and DeVries, R. *Physical Knowledge in Preschool Education: Implications of Piaget's Theory*. Englewood Cliffs, NJ: Prentice-Hall, 1978.

Lasky, L.; and Mukerji, R. *Art: Basic for Young Children*. Washington, DC: NAEYC, 1980.

McIntyre, M. "Color Awareness." *Science and Children*, 1981a, 18: (7), 40–41.

McIntyre, M. "The sounds of music." *Science and Children*, 1981b, 18: (5), 34–35.

McIntyre, M. *Early Childhood and Science*. Washington, DC: National Science Teachers' Association, 1984.

National Association for the Education of Young Children. "NAEYC position statement on developmentally appropriate practice in early childhood programs serving children from birth, through age 8." *Young Children*, 1986, 41: (6), 3–19.

Neuman, D. B. *Experiences in Science for Young Children*. Albany, NY: Delmar, 1978.

Parents Nursery School. *Kids are Natural Cooks*. Boston: Houghton Mifflin, 1974.

Piaget, J. *The Child's Conception of the World*. New York: Harcourt & Brace, 1929.

Piaget, J. *The Construction of Reality in the Child*. New York: Basic, 1954.

Piaget, J. *To Understand is to Invent: The Future of Education*. New York: Grossman, 1973.

Schools Council. *Early Experiences*. London: Macdonald Educational Ltd., 1972a.

Schools Council. *Science from Toys*. London: Macdonald Educational Ltd., 1972b.

Schools Council. *Ourselves*. Milwaukee, WI Macdonald-Raintree, 1973a.

Schools Council: *Coloured Things*. London: Macdonald Educational Ltd., 1973b.

Smith, R. F. "Early childhood science education: A Piagetian perspective." *Young Children*, 1981, 36: (2), 3–10.

Wanamaker, N.; Hearn, K.; and Richarz, S. *More than Graham Crackers: Nutrition Education and Food Preparation with Young Children*. Washington, DC: NAEYC, 1979.

Ward, A. "The clay boat project: Floating and sinking studies with infants." *School Science Review*, 1978, 29: 626–633.

Wolfinger, D. M. "Effect of science teaching on the young child's concept of Piagetian physical causality: Animism and dynamism." *Journal of Research in Science Teaching*, 1982, 19: 595–602.

Zeitler, W. R. "A study of observational skill development in children of age three." *Science Education*, 1972, 56: 79–84.

CHAPTER 35

Accommodating for Individual Differences in Early Childhood Mathematics Education

Our technological world is changing at an ever-increasing rate. New demands are being made on the populace. There are new expectations and new employment patterns. Mathematics is affected by both this new technology and the subsequent rapid sociological change it produces. As the demands of society have been changing, the essential competencies needed by individuals to live productively in society have been changing as well. All students, including those of all races and both sexes, now need competence and confidence in essential areas of mathematics, yet devastatingly few have been able to obtain either. Mathematics education today is a debacle.

Today's students can expect to change jobs many times during their lifetime. The jobs that they will hold will develop and change around them. A thorough understanding of mathematical concepts and principles is a critical filter in this dynamic environment, but mathematics education in the United States today has yet to come close to meeting this challenge. In the report by the National government on The *Conditions of Education* (1985), we find that fewer than 240,000 United States high school students take any level of calculus compared to the Soviet Union where every teenager studies the subject (in greater depth) for at least two years. American youngsters take between seven and nine years of basic arithmetic; whereas in most European countries the same material is covered, more thoroughly, in two-thirds of the time. One third of the math teachers in American high schools did not graduate with even a college minor in the subject, a problem not shared by other technological societies.

The truth is that a large segment of the population dislikes mathematics and that this dislike leads to the avoidance of mathematics and anything mathematical. Mathematics avoidance is very closely linked to mathematics anxiety and is actually a natural consequence of a set of attitudes that develop as a result of a student's early educational experiences. Students experience mathematics avoidance when they take only the required amount of mathematics required by a particular institution although they are aware that further study in mathematics could benefit them in the future (Tobias, 1978). This situation used to be tolerable when there were sufficient jobs requiring little or no mathematics. Today, however, mathematics avoiders are cut off from full participation in a technological society.

Although developmental theorists claim that human beings are alike in more ways than they are different, the fact is that humans *do* differ in important and significant ways. Considerable interest has been given to the quandary of how knowledge about individual differences in learning can be used to provide appropriate differentiated instruction and thus enhance mathematics education. In the following fable we find pressing reasons for considering individual differences in the design of any instructional program:

> One time the animals had a school. The curriculum consisted of running, climbing, flying and swimming, and all the animals took all the subjects.
>
> The duck was good in swimming, better in fact than his instructor, and he made passing grades in flying, but he was practically hopeless in running. Because he was low in this subject he was made to stay after school and drop his swimming class in order to practice running. He kept up until he was only average in swimming. But average is acceptable, so nobody worried about the duck anymore.
>
> The rabbit started out at the top of the class in running, but then had a nervous breakdown and had to drop out of school on account of so much make up work in swimming.
>
> The squirrel led the climbing class, but his flying teacher made him start his flying lesson from the ground up instead of from the top of the tree down, He developed Charley horses from overexertion at the takeoff and began getting C's in climbing and D's in running.
>
> The practical prairie dogs apprenticed their offspring to a badger when the school authorities refused to add digging to the curriculum.
>
> At the end of the year, an abnormal eel who could swim fairly well, climb O.K. and fly a little bit was made valedictorian. (Author Unknown)

One of the first attempts to deal with individual differences in the mathematics curriculum was the *Individualized Mathematics Instruction Programs* that arose in the late 1960's. The underling philosophy of this movement was that in a class containing students with diverse skills and backgrounds, a teacher using one pace of instruction would either be "wasting" the time of those who already grasped the material or teaching to students who do not have the conceptual background to grasp the information. Individualized instruction was supposed to be a way out of this dilemma; offering instruction, via individual packets or units, that each student could complete at his/her own pace. In the late 1960's Individualization was seen as a wave of the future. The 1970's, however, saw the rise and fall of this wave and today *Individualized Mathematics Instruction Programs* are mostly a memory. (Rothrock, 1982) There are many factors contributing to its demise. This movement, according to Thomas Romberg, (1984), was coupled with an existing environment of anti-professionalism. Teachers were mandated to carry out the orders from above. Their tasks were distilled. They were not the decision makers but instead the implementors and the technicians. Socialization in the classroom was virtually non-existent and students, even very young students, were basically left on their own to find the answers to questions and to find the motivation to continue.

One of the major problems of the *Individualized Mathematics Instruction Programs* was the complexity of managing all the paperwork created by this individualization. One study of individualized instruction (Broussard 1976) evaluated a program for 344 fourth-grade students that involved, in addition to the students regular teachers, a mathematics coordinator, five instructional specialists, three instructional aides, five materials clerks and special mathematics supplies, materials and equipment.

Because of the great need to check the students papers, teachers were turned into clerks. The students themselves received practically no teacher instruction. All the material was presented through programmed booklets. A basic assumption of the *Individualized Mathematics Program* was that mathematics learning is a totally linear experience that one could approach in a step-by-step programmable manner. As a result of research in cognition that has been done in recent years, we now know that is quite far from reality. It is not surprising that research on Individualized programs failed to find consistent benefits for students' achievement (Hartley, 1977; Horack, 1981; Schoen, 1986).

Albeit, Individualization was not the mecca in mathematics education hoped for, the problems that it was created to solve still exists. Students are, if anything, becoming more diverse; mathematics competency and confidence have not improved; and teachers still experience frustration in teaching heterogeneous groups.

A shift from studying performance to studying process is a major redefinition of the study of individual differences today. Instead of using overt responses as indicators of aptitudes and categorizing each student by their "levels of intelligence," researchers are increasingly turning to the study of internal mental processes. In psychological literature, scholars are attempting to describe *intelligent behavior* instead of measuring the conundrum *intelligence.* In mathematics education this shift is demonstrated by the present attempt to study problem solving aptitude instead of just the production of correct solutions. More and more researchers are asking students to solve problems and then observing the solving of these problems through a variety of vantage points.

Related to this qualitative change from product (the correct answer) to cognitive process (the method of problem solving) is the concern about the long standing separation between the psychometric tradition and cognitive psychology. The emphasis on the former has been the identification, measurement and classification of an individuals performance so that a student may be "tracked" into an ability group. Tracking is based on the assumption that a student's ability is static and one-dimensional and, further, that we are able to assess it. Research on cognition suggests that the complex multidimensional qualities that constitute a student's ability defy simplistic attempts at classification. The result of tracking has been to create vast differences in children's opportunities. Mounting evidence indicates that tracking produces detrimental effects on those labeled as "low" ability and suggests, contrary to popular belief, that it does not benefit those identified as "high" ability students either.

It should be emphasized that mere identification of different individual traits that effect learning is not a particularly profitable area for research unless it is related to the implementation of instruction to benefit these differences. In addition to interindividual differences, intraindividual differences should be explored. Tyler (1974) speaks to the issue of a pluralistic approach to individuality claiming that each person is several potential individuals. This suggests that the successful problem solver might be able to apply different techniques depending on the problem being solved. Thus, we find the necessity of teaching information using a variety of techniques.

We will now examine how individual differences that affect learning support the demand for presenting information in a multitude of ways. We will look at how individuals differ: cognition, environment, attitudes, and beliefs. This list is by no means an exhaustive list of individual differences that affect learning, nor are the categories totally independent, but they will provide us with an overview of the complexities that educators need to consider when designing curriculum and instruction.

Cognitive Differences

Exploring the dimensions of cognitive style holds great promise for understanding behavior. A cognitive style, as defined by Witkin (1976), is a characteristic mode of functioning that is revealed throughout perceptual and intellectual activities in a highly consistent and pervasive way. It is theorized that cognitive styles permeate all of an individual's behavior and serves as heuristics of a high level that organize lower-level strategies, operations and inclinations. It is often quite pronounced when teachers observe complex cognitive processes such as problem solving. Witkin believes the particular cognitive style of the individual affects academic choices, vocational preferences and academic development. He thus believes that knowing the particular type of cognitive style an individual possess should be of paramount importance to those wishing to educate the individual.

Perhaps the best way to begin analyzing individual differences in cognition is to start with an understanding of the brain itself. The human brain is asymmetrical, and no two human brains are identical. This is true even in fetal life. This asymmetry, generally favors the left hemisphere, particularly the temporal lobe. Each hemisphere is generally superior in certain functions. For example, the left hemisphere is generally dominant for language and manual skills and the right for spatial and musical abilities. Dominance is reflected in both cortical and subcortical structures. The left hemisphere develops later than the right in the fetus and is at a greater risk from prenatal influences for a longer time.

One of the prenatal influences is testosterone which can slow cortical growth and impair neuronal migration, enlarge the right hemisphere and cause a shift of dominance to the right brain. The shift in dominance to the right brain is higher in males and accounts for the higher incidence of left handedness in males in general and a dominance favoring talents associated with right brain skills. However, findings from neurological research have demonstrated that intelligence and personality are not fixed and that the physical environment, as well as the biological environment, can create measurable changes in the physiology of the brain. (Treffert, 1989)

It is believed that there is a tendency among individuals to show a preference and a dominance for either visual learning, verbal learning, or tactile learning. When puzzled over the direction to take on a particular task, the visual learner needs to "see" the situation clearer, while the more verbal learner seeks a concrete model to feel ownership of the information. Being aware of these different preferences suggests a need to insure that information in a classroom be presented in visual, verbal, and tactile modes. It is also important that all students be provided with tasks to strengthen their visual, verbal and tactile skills to facilitate the learning of mathematics.

Professors Renner and Rosenzweig (1987) of the University of California, Berkely, conducted experiments with animals in controlled environments in which they provided different degrees of stimulation. Those animals, especially rats, brought up in larger cages with a more enriched environment manifest considerable changes, chemical and anatomical, in their brains than the group of rats raised in smaller cages with little stimulation. The former had heavier and thicker cerebral cortices, larger neuronal cell bodies and neuronal nuclei. They were also found to have more ribonucleic acid (RNA) per cell and more dendritic spines with a more intricate pattern of neuroma: branching. The enriched rats were able to perform better on all tests put before them.

The research of Frostig and Maslow (1980) support Renner and Rosenzweig's findings in humans. According to their research, x-rays of the brain indicate that the structure and functions can change to accommodate different environments. They thus concluded that in a classroom it is the teacher who is ultimately responsible for providing an environment so that positive changes in the brain can occur in children. According to Buzan (1978), the nervous system functions best when used and challenged, implying that educational interventions can, indeed, improve brain functions.

Sometimes seemingly unrelated problems originate in the same basic brain function. For example, difficulties in verbal logical behavior and spatial orientation may be overcome if the perception of spatial relationships is improved. Spatial visualization is an aptitude related to mental manipulation of rigid figures. The aptitude emerges as a component of mathematics ability in most factor analytic studies (Schonberg, 1976). Smith (1964) believes that elementary programs could enhance this aptitude if they would incorporate multiple activities with the presentation of each new skill and concept. For example, to introduce addition the teacher should not limit the presentation to one method, but should instead use multiple means of presentation such as manipulatives, a number line or chart, a calculator, money, play acting accompanied with symbolic representation and algorithmic procedures.

Research findings from psychology indicate that learning does not occur by passive absorption alone. By allowing and encouraging students to use calculators, manipulatives, charts, and play acting in the classroom, teachers can help students to become more active learners (Resnick (1987). Frostig and Maslow also found that movement is intimately involved in the brain's cognitive functions. Their findings indicate that not only is active learning beneficial, but that in fact, passive learning may be detrimental for any extended period of time during the learning process.

Further studies indicate that learning and emotion cannot be separated. The pathways between the cortex [higher brain] and the limbic system [emotional brain] and the reticular formation in the upper brainstem [primitive brain] always function simultaneously, even in the person who believes that his/her actions are solely directed by the intellect. Animal research indicates that cortical (higher brain) impulses are amplified two or three ties by motivation, suggesting a strong tie between more primitive attentional functions and higher cognitive activity. Thus, educators must consider motivation as a major part of their presentation of ideas.

Environmental Difference

Environmental variables offers us another dimension to explain individual differences in learning. Since development comes about through interaction with the environment, as one might imagine, studies of children with very different environmental histories yield significantly different achievement. (Tyler, 1974). Educational sociologists have attempted to explain differential achievement on the basis of environmental variables of the learner's home, neighborhood, community, school and classroom.

Most of our knowledge of environmental effects on intelligence comes from studies of infrahuman species, although many studies have indicated that the effects of such programs as Head Start can positively effect the cognitive process. It is possible, and perhaps desirable, to consider education as a process of giving the child an intelligent environment. The teacher is responsible for the control of this environment both intellectually and emotionally. Teachers and students bring very different expectations and perspectives to the classroom. Theodore Sizzler (1984) noted that a successful classroom is one where the teacher and student agree on what is to be taught and how this is to be implemented. In addition, an ideal learning environment is one that encourages risk taking, breaking of limits, cooperation rather than competition, the security to ask questions and the mutual support and respect of each students individuality and the ability and the right to succeed.

Mathematics educators have begun to look at new ideas and approaches to improve the environment of learning mathematics. The National Council of Teachers of Mathematics (NCTM) has addressed many of these ideas in the new Curriculum and Evaluation Standards for School Mathematics (1989). According to *Standards:*

> The major emphasis should be on establishing a climate that places critical thinking at the heart of instruction. A spirit of investigation and exploration should permeate instruction . . . Teachers need to provide a caring environment in which students can feel free to explore mathematical ideas, to ask questions, to discuss their ideas and make mistakes (p.12)

The role of the teacher should shift from one of dispensing information to facilitating learning. In order for students to internalize the view of mathematics as a process, a body of knowledge and a human creation, they need many opportunities to experiment with ideas, develop strategies, formulate and communicate conclusions, apply fundamental skills and interact in groups. Instruction in mathematics should be based on problem situations that are amenable to individuals, small groups and large groups of instruction and involve a variety of conceptual domains and be open as to the methods to be used to solve these problems. The benefits of cooperative small group learning has been to help establish a positive environment to learn mathematics. John Holt in his book *How Children Learn,* (1986) finds that one reason why children learn so well from other children is that not only do they speak the same language, but because they are within reach, other students are more helpful confidence models. Holt observed that most of us do not like to be confronted, constantly, by someone who knows a great deal more about something then we do. Cooperative education takes advantage of children learning from other children.

One of the pioneers in cooperative learning is Robert Slavin (1984, 1987). At the center for Research on Elementary and Middle Schools, Slavin was experimenting with a method of instruction by which students cooperate in small teams to learn material initially presented by the teacher. Slavin's research established that if students were properly organized and motivated they could take a great deal of responsibility for their own learning, for their teammates' learning and for classroom management. Slavin's studies have shown that students in cooperative learning groups develop more problem solving strategies and do significantly better on standardized tests than students in traditional programs.

Differences in Attitudes and Beliefs

Much attention has been given to the interrelationship between attitudinal variables and learning. Studies have shown that there is a positive relationship between attitude and mathematical achievement (Fennema, 1974). It seems that grades six to eight are the most critical in the development of attitudes about education, which seem to be fairly stable once developed. All of us enjoy doing that which we do well. Aside from any personal satisfaction our skills bring, the approval we get from others is important and acts as reinforcement and motivation to do even better and meet our needs for self-esteem.

Work within the confidence/anxiety attitudinal dimensions has produced some interesting results. Callahan and Glennon (1975) concluded that anxiety and mathematics learning are related and in general high anxiety is associated with lower achievements in mathematics.

A great many factors in the learning environment have the potential to overshadow, either temporarily or permanently, the effect of a given attitude towards mathematics. Of these factors, the teacher is probably the most obvious one although the effects of home, school, and other social factors have varying strengths and each changes as the child matures. What is noted is a steady decrease in positive attitudes regarding mathematics from elementary through high school. Often mediating factors impinge on the judged utility or enjoyment of mathematics especially for subgroups such as females, minorities, the non-college bound, and the economically disadvantaged.

In the most basic sense, a belief is any guiding principle, dictum, faith, or passion that can provide meaning and direction in life. Unlimited stimuli are available to us. Beliefs dictate many of the commands in our brain. Beliefs could be the most powerful force creating positive effects in an individual or can be devastating and limiting. Beliefs help one see what one wants and how to get it.

Perhaps the biggest misconception that people often have of beliefs is that they are static, intellectual concepts, understandings that are divorced form action results. Beliefs come from a person's environment, events, knowledge, past results, and through visions or dreams and are always subject to change.

If all one sees is failure and despair it becomes difficult to form positive internal beliefs. According to Albert Einstein, "few people are capable of expressing with equanimity opinions which differ significantly from the prejudices of their social environment." A teacher has the power to help create positive beliefs in his/her students. NCTM has stated definitively in the *Standards* that the teacher must share the belief that all students have abilities to explore, conjecture and reason logically as well as the ability to use a variety of mathematical methods effectively to solve routine and non-routine mathematical problems. This vision is supported with another belief that mathematical power aids in the development of personal self-confidence.

What Can Be Done to Improve Mathematics Learning

An individual is more than the sum of all the labels and categories attributed to him/her. In the study of human development we are often confronted by those that seek so intensely to have us all the same shape and size. Our quest should be to study and admire the different shapes and sizes and appreciate the contribution to knowledge that these differences offer.

If a child in school is experiencing particular difficulty with a mathematics skill or concept, he/she should never be considered as unintelligent. Instead, the reason a child is experiencing this difficulty needs to be thoroughly examined. Environmental, nutritional, and attitudinal deficiencies should be looked for and dealt with. If the reasons are not to be found in these aspects of the child, then a minor malfunction in the brain's general system may be the culprit and other ways of teaching a particular concept should be employed. In this way all children can be assisted to develop more completely. The categorizing by hierarchical ability (tracking) is no longer an appropriate yardstick by which children can be measured. Research on cognition suggests that the complex multidimensional qualities that constitute a students abilities in any area defy simplistic attempts at classification.

The mass of evidence about the human brain, about the potential of the very young, about the inadequacy of our previous teaching and testing methods leads to a need for a total re-examination of the responsibilities of the teacher. We must begin to teach how to learn and not just what to learn. We must concentrate on retention and recall, new approaches to study, an examination of the way in which information itself is structured and how information is received, stored and used by the human brain. It is essential that we teach every child all that we currently know about what his/her mind actually is, and that his/her mind has the unlimited potential to achieve. Motivation and teacher expectation have long been known to be prime factors in mental functioning. It is critical that these factors work to enhance the learning process. Children need to know why they are studying mathematics, how it relates to their lives and that the teacher expects every child to succeed in mathematics learning.

The commitment to improve mathematics education also necessitates a re-examination of the teachers role in the learning process. By helping individuals to learn, the teacher needs to assume the role of facilitator, partner, salesperson, cheerleader, orchestrator, communicator, ambassador, assessor, trainer, investigator, instructor, demonstrator, informer, liberator and more.

Teaching is not like programming a computer. It is not just a matter of sliding a floppy disk into someone else's brain. It is promoting and encouraging learning by helping to create associations between simultaneous or consecutively active bits of information and stimuli. Improving mathematics education is one of the greatest challenges that has ever been put to elementary school teachers, and one that can reap the greatest of rewards to our society as well as our planet.

Marilyn K. Simon, doctoral candidate, Walden University; President of Math Power, Del Mar California; Instructor of Mathematics, University of California, San Diego.

Selected Bibliography

Broussard, Vernon "A Personalized-Individualized Approach to Achievement in Mathematics," *California Journal of Educational Research* 1976, 26:233–37.

Buzan, Tony, *The Evolving Brain*. New York: Holt Rinehart & Winston, 1978.

Callahan, L. G. & Glennon, V. J. *Elementary School Mathematics: A Guide to Current Research. (4th ed.)*. Washington, DC.: Association for Supervision and Curriculum Development, 1975.

Cooney, Thomas, "The issue of Reform: What Have We Learned from Yesteryear?" *Mathematics Teacher.* 1981 81:352–363.

Cooney, Thomas J. "A Beginning Teacher's View of Problem Solving." *Journal for Research in Mathematics Education.* 1985, 16: 324–36.

Fenemma, Elizabeth, "Mathematics Learning and the Sexes: A review" *Journal for Research in Mathematics Education.* 1974, 5: 126–39.

Frostig, Marianne and Phyllis Maslow, "Neuropsychology in Educational Techniques."
Journal of Learning Disabilities. 1980, 8: 40–53.

Hartley, Susan, "Meta-analysis of the Effects of Individually-paced Instruction in Mathematics." Unpublished doctoral dissertation, University of Colorado, 1977.

Horak, Virginia, "A Meta-analysis of Research Findings on Individualized Instruction in Mathematics," *Journal of Educational Research.* 1981, 74: 249–253.

Holt, John. *How Children Learn*. New York: Dell. 1986.

National Council of Teacher of Mathematics. *Curriculum and Evaluation Standards for School Mathematics.* Reston, Va,: The Council, 1989.

National Council for Educational Statistics. "The Conditions of Education: Statistical Report." Washington, D.C.: U.S. *Government Printing Office,* 1985.

Renner, Michael and Rosenzweig, Thomas. *Enriched and impoverished environments, effects of brain and behavior.* New York: Springer-Verlay, 1987.

Resnick, Lauren B. *Education and Learning to Think.* Washington, D.C.: National Academy Press, 1987.

Romberg, Thomas A. "School Mathematics: Options for the 1990s. Chairmans Report of a Conference." Washington, D.C.: U.S. *Government Printing Office,* 1984.

Rothrock, Dayton. "The Rise and Decline of Individualized Instruction." *Arithmetic Teacher.* 1982 33: 528–31.

Schoen, Harold. "Research Report: Individualizing Mathematics Instruction." *Arithmetic Teacher.* 1986 38: 44–45.

Schonberger, A. K. "The Interrelationship of sex, visual spatial abilities and mathematical problem solving ability in grade seven." Unpublished doctoral dissertation, University of Wisconsin, 1976.

Sizzler, Theodore. *Horace's Compromise: The Dilemma of the American High School.* Boston: Houghton Mifflin Co., 1984.

Slavin, Robert. *Cooperative Learning.* New York: Longman, 1984.

Slavin, Robert "Cooperative Learning and Individualized Instruction." *Arithmetic Teacher.* 1987, 35: 14–17.

Smith, I. M. *Spatial Ability.* San Diego: Knapp, 1964.

Tobias, Sheila. *Overcoming Mathematics Anxiety.* Boston: Houghton Mifflin Co, 1978.

Tyler, L. E. *Individual Differences: Abilities and Motivational Directions.* Englewood Cliffs, N.J.: Prentice-Hall, 1974.

Treffert, Darold, *Extraordinary People, Understanding "Idiot Savants".* New York: Harper & Row, 1989.

Witkin, H. A. "Cognitive Style in Academic Performance and in Teacher-Student Relations." In S. Messick & Associates (Eds), *Individuality in Learning.* San Francisco: Josey-Bass, 1976.

CHAPTER 36

Sing a Song of Mathematics

What is music to the adult ear can be a multisensory learning experience to the young child. Music has long been considered an important ingredient of the curriculum areas presented to young children. It makes a contribution to their developing brain and creates favorable attitudes and feelings. Theresa Denman (1988) acknowledging the importance of brain behavior in learning mathematics, cites music as a means of improving brain function. Music is an active mode of learning and when accompanied by movement further benefits are anticipated. A program of multisensory learning is one of the several areas which may help students improve their levels of mathematics performance (Wheatley, Frankland, Mitchell, and Kraft, 1978). Music with movement can include hearing, seeing, and possibly touching (as touching the shoe in "One, Two, Buckle My Shoe").

Brain function in early life has been described. Asymmetry of the newborn infant's brain has been established and it is important to consider in teaching mathematics. These detectable asymmetries may account for the left hemisphere dominance for speech in most people. On the basis of medical studies it was concluded that the male brain matures later than the female brain and the left hemisphere matures later than the right. Right hemisphere function is important in spatial function, emotion and attention. In some individuals it may contribute significantly to speech and handedness. It is important to remember that since the right hemisphere develops earlier than the left hemisphere and over a shorter period of time, there is less chance of impairment. The standard dominance patterns of left/right hemisphere for other functions is found in in most people (Geshwind and Galaburda, 1985). Early learning activities which use right brain capabilities can capitalize on what has been felt to be the dominant form of early thinking, particularly for sensory information processing and spatial concepts (Kraft and Languis, 1978).

Environmental influences on lateralization have been shown. Handling of newborn rats, for example, influenced emotionality and right hemisphere lateralization of spatial performance. Variations from certain countries or nationalities also point to differences. The Chinese and Japanese ideographic scripts are examples offered as reasons for lowered rates of dyslexia in these countries. Research on memory suggests the possibility that it can be changed through environmental factors because newly grown synapses to the brain were observed in a controlled experiment (Johnson, 1987) and calcium was also found to be a trigger for this reaction.

Music is one curriculum area that has both educational and psychological benefits for children. It is an uplifting experience which enhances brain function. One illustration is where music therapy has been used to rejuvenate people who have not moved for a long period of time. With music therapy they were observed to walk, dance, talk or sing at the sound of music (*The New York Times,* 1966).

The National Council for Teachers of Mathematics (1989) has set standards for mathematics in grades K–4. New goals for students are listed: (1) valuing mathematics; (2) confidence in the child's ability; (3) solving mathematics problems; and (4) communicating and reasoning in mathematics. Numerous and varied experiences are advocated for students to become confident in their own ability to do mathematics. The National Council for Teachers of Mathematics emphasizes the use of other curriculum areas for integration with mathematics, but somehow music is not included in their list of science, social studies, language arts, physical education and art (1989, p.35). Certainly music can be added to the various areas they list. Singing songs is an active learning process that will enhance the learning of mathematics concepts and skills. It is a joyful method of drill and practice and should be tension free.

Mathematics Curriculum and Music Number sense can be achieved through a combination of music and movement. Start with the music and words of "Ten Little Indians" and rephrase with "Ten Little Children." With older children when singing reaches ten, continue to twenty. Then count backwards from twenty. Liven up the song and increase the children's number sense by having one child stand as each number is reached, and then have one child sit down as the singing continues in the last verse (and numbers greater than twenty can easily be added to include the whole class).

Another song children can develop a concrete association of number sense from is "One, Two, Buckle My Shoe" by using movement and pantomime to accompany the counting to twenty. "This Old Man" and "Five Chartreuse Buzzards" are other counting songs which are fun to sing. Foreign counting songs for cultural enrichment include a "Counting Song" from Japan (White and Akiyama, 1960) and the "Mexican Counting Song" (Hart, 1982). On a more sophisticated level, "Green Grow the Rushes-o" is believed to have been rewritten from the words of the Passover service beginning with "Who knoweth thirteen? 'I,' saith Israel, 'knoweth thirteen.'" (Brand, 1957). Other holiday songs include "Jack-o'-lanterns" and "The Twelve Days of Christmas" (Quackenbush, 1977).

Patterns and relationships can be approached through musical selections which are described in songs. "The Noble Duke of York" (Hart, 1982) has ten thousand men marching up and down. A game is also suggested for this English traditional singing game. "Three Little Kittens" (Margaretten, 1975) tells a story that children can use to surmise a cause and effect relationship. An old folk song, "The Months of the Year" (Kennedy, 1975) relates patterns of nature during the year. "Era Una Vez" (Rockwell, 1971) describes the relationship of sailors on a tiny boat which was overloaded and could not sail until their supplies were exhausted. In seven weeks they finally sailed to go fishing. The "Left-Right Song" (Joyner, 1988) can use movement with patterns of up and down, in and out, and left and right.

Whole number operations are also described in songs. "Adding Sets," "Jumping," "Tap out the Answer," (Palmer, 1971) can be sung. "I Can't do That Sum" (Winn, 1966) is a humorous approach to math problems. Dr. Seuss (1967) lists "I Can Figure Figures."

A favorite subtraction song is "Roll Over" (Nelson, 1981). Another song, "Teddy Bear Subtraction" (Joyner, 1988) allows for many variations in numbers to be subtracted and the use of concrete materials such as counters.

Geometry and spatial sense can be dealt with through simple songs like the "Number March" (Palmer, 1971) where words convey that one, two or more students are to march around a circle. "Triangle, Circle and Square," and "How Many Ways" are also included in Palmer's collections (1981). Dr. Seuss (1967) can be used to take a humorous look at measurement in "Cry a Pint."

Using music to reinforce and review in mathematics is a pleasant way to add zest to the lesson. As a positive emotional experience, it fits well with the early right hemisphere development. Successful early childhood mathematics can be only a song away.

Margaret Godfrey, Math Teacher, District 8, Bronx, J.H.S. 123.

References

Commission on Standards for School Mathematics of the National Council for Teachers of Mathematics. *Curriculum and Evaluation Standards for School Mathematics*. Reston: NCTM, 1989.

Denman, Theresa I. "Building Brain Power: Mathematics and the Neurosciences." Session at NCTM 66th Annual Meeting. Chicago: National Council of Teachers of Mathematics, 1988.

Geschwind, Norman and Galaburda, Albert M. "Cerebral Lateralization Biological Mechanisms, Associations, and Pathology: II. A Hypotheses and a Program for Research." *Archives of Neurology*, June 1985, 42: 527–536.

Johnson, George. "Memory Learning How It Works." *The New York Times Magazine,* August 9, 1987, 16–21.

Kraft, Rosemarie Harter and Languis, Martin L. "Dimensions of Right and Left Brain Learning in Early Childhood." In *Early Childhood,* edited by Barry Persky and Leonard Golubchick. Wayne: Avery Publishing Company, Inc., 1978.

"Music Helps Reach the 'Unreachables'." *The New York Times,* June 6, 1988, 37.

Wheatley, Grayson H., Frankland, Robert L., Mitchell, Robert and Kraft, Rosemarie. "Hemispheric Specialization and Cognitive Development: Implications for Mathematics Education." *Journal for Research in Mathematics Education,* January 1978, 9: 20–38.

Selected Song List Bibliography

Brand, Oscar. *Singing Holidays The Calendar in Folk Songs.* New York: Alfred A. Knopf, 1957.

    Green Grow the Rushes-O

Hart, Jane. *Singing Bee.* New York: Lothrop, Lee & Shepard Books, 1982.

    Mexican Counting Song, p. 137

    Noble Duke of York, p. 88

    Five Little Chicadees, p. 77

Joyner, Jeane. "Math, Music, Movement and Motivation." Presented in Chicago: National Council of Teachers of Mathematics, April 8, 1988.

    Cricket Song (Counting on a number line)

    Left-Right Song

    Teddy Bear Subtraction

Kennedy, Peter (ed.). *Folksongs of Britain and Ireland.* London: Oak Publications, 1975.

    The Months of the Year, p. 565

Margaretten, Bill (ed.). *Old King Cole and 49 other Best-Loved Songs.* Levittown, N.Y.: SLM Distributing Company, 1975.

    Old John Braddleum, p. 68

    Three Little Kittens, p. 88

    Ten Little Indians, p. 93

Mitchell, D.; Carey, B.; and Howard, A. *Every Child's Book of Nursery Songs.* New York: Crown Publishers, Inc., 1986.

    O Dear Sixpence, p.97

    One, Two, Buckle My Shoe, p.38

    One, two, three, four, five, p. 114

    This Old Man, p. 70

Nelson, E. L. *The Silly Song Book.* New York: Sterling Publishing Company, 1981.

    Five Chartreuse Buzzards, p. 88

    Five Little Monkeys, p. 31

    Roll Over, p. 95

    This Old Man, p. 64

Palmer, Hap. *Hap Palmer Songbook —Learning Basic Skills Through Music.* Freeport: Educational Activities, Inc., 1971.

Number March, p. 8

Palmer, Hap. *Hap Palmer Favorites. Songs for Learning Through Music and Movement.* Sherman Oaks, CA: Alfred Publishing Co., 1981.

    Adding Sets, p. 88

    Can You Catch a Set? p. 83

    Clap and Rest, p. 120

    Countdown, p. 84

    How Many Ways, p. 72

    Jumping, p. 90

    Numbers Tell a Lot About You, p. 56

    Paper Clock, p. 100

    Tap Out the Answer, p. 92

    Triangle, Circle and Square, p. 68

Quackenbush, Robert. *The Holiday Song Book.* New York: Lothrop, Lee and Sheperd, 1977.

    Jack-O-Lanterns, p. 96

    The Twelve Days of Christmas, p. 120

Rockwell, A. *El Toro Pinto.* New York: The Macmillan Co., 1971.

    Era Una Vex, p. 34

Seuss, Dr. *The Cat in the Hat Song Book.* New York: Random House, 1967.

    Cry a Pint

    I Can Figure Figures

Winn, Marie (ed.). *The Fireside Book of Children's Songs.* New York: Simon and Schuster, 1966.

    I Can't do That Sum, p. 130

    Three Little Piggies, p. 50

White, Florence and Akiyama, Kazuo. *Children's Songs from Japan.* New York: Edward B. Marks Music Corporation, 1960.

    Counting Song, p. 86

CHAPTER 37

History Is for Children

Returning History to the elementary school curriculum is one of the decade's major movements for school reform. This movement is not, of course, without its critics. Certain school folk, wedded to assumptions that have dominated the elementary school curriculum for over fifty years, strongly protest the change. Children, they argue, cannot attain the perspectives of historical time and therefore are incapable of understanding the past. The immediate surroundings and present-day world that children daily experience are rich enough, these critics maintain, to serve as the subject matter of their curriculum. Forays into distant times they cannot understand, or studying about people they cannot place in historical perspective, are a poor and irrelevant curriculum alternative for the young.

Such objectious to the teaching of history must be addressed by those who speak for history in the education of school-age children. Fortunately, these objections yield in the face of what we know from contemporary studies of childhood learning and development and from tested practices in a good number of forward-looking schools, public and private. This article will explore such evidence and consider its implications for building an appropriate curriculum in history for the elementary school years.

At issue is the long-lived and sacrosanct "near to far" or "expanding environments" curriculum mode. This is the curriculum adopted over the past half-century by virtually all school systems in the nation and strongly sustained by the nation's textbook industry. Up to grade five, this curriculum has little or no historical content; instead, it emphasizes the sociological and economic aspects of children's lives in the family, the school, the neighborhood, and the community.

The most comprehensive and so far successful challenge to the constraining assumptions of the near-to-far curriculum model is the recently adopted *History-Social Science Framework for California Public Schools, Kindergarten through Grade Twelve (1987)*.

The framework committee that drafted this document included classroom teachers and curriculum leaders from the schools, and historians, social scientists, and learning and curriculum specialists from universities and from research and development centers. Every issue that arises when considering change in the elementary school curriculum was soundly debated by this group. One by one the arguments barring history from childhood education fell, and the curriculum that emerged reflects the accord achieved within the committee for a history-enriched and, in four years out of the seven from kindergarten through grade six, a history-centered program of studies. The most enthusiastic proponents for this change were, in the end, those best qualified to judge: the experienced elementary school classroom teachers on the framework committee.

What arguments rallied the forces for change? First among them was the evidence that the monolithic march from near to far in the customary expanding environments curriculum model is supported neither by developmental psychology nor by research in children's learning. Through circulation of correspondence received by committee member Diane Ravitch from four eminent educators, each a seminal thinker in his field, the committee was provided searching appraisals of the validity of the expanding environments model.

Philip Phenix, philosopher and Arthur I. Gates Professor Emeritus of Teachers College, Columbia University, wrote on May 24, 1986:

> The self/family/community/region progression is presumable based on the notion that learning must proceed within the context of the known and familiar and only gradually move out into the larger domains of the unknown and unfamiliar, as the child expands his or her experience. But such a view seems to me a recipe for boredom and sterility, doing poor justice to the expansive capacities of the human mind. Although teaching must obviously take account of where the student is, the whole purpose of education is to enlarge experience by introducing new experiences far beyond where the child starts.
>
> The curious, cautious, timid presumption that the limits of expansion are defined in any one grade year by the spatial boundaries defining the expanding boundaries dogma is whole universe of space and time and even far beyond that into the worlds of the imaginary. And all this from kindergarten years or even before! The concentric circles of the expansion dogma appear nothing more than a very adult conceit designed for administrative control through neat curriculum packages unrelated to the realities of human learning.

Joseph Adelson, director of the Psychological Clinic at the University of Michigan, wrote on June 2, 1986:

> I have never understood the logic presumably informing the "expanding environments" approach, since it did not seem to me to be based on anything we knew about cognitive development in that period. . . . Let me assure you that there is nothing in cognitive science, or in developmental research, which supports the present way of doing things. In fact, I'm quite convinced you could turn

the sequence on its head, going from the community to "myself," without its making much of a difference. Furthermore the current curriculum is quite vapid and seems to induce a considerable degree of boredom.

Bruno Bettelheim, the distinguished psychoanalyst and professor of education who for twenty-six years directed the University of Chicago's residential school for highly disturbed children, wrote on May 7, 1986:

> . . . the presently taught curriculum in the social sciences in the early grades is a disservice to the students and a shame for the educational system. Children of this age are sufficiently surrounded by the realities of their lives. The texts I have seen do not explain [their] sources or meaning to the child, and only repeat in tritest form a reality with which they are all too well familiar . . What children of this age need is rich food for their imagination, or a sense of history, how the present situation came about . . What formed the culture of the past, such as myths, is of interest and value to them, because these myths reflect how people tried to make sense of the world.

Jerome Bruner, a cognitive psychologist long recognized for his distinguished contributions to the field of instructional psychology and to the study of thinking, included in his correspondence of May 12, 1986, the following analysis along with references to his recent book, *Actual Minds, Possible Worlds,* for its treatment in depth of the reasons behind his comments.

> There is little beyond ideology to commend the Hanna [i.e., expanding environments] program and its endlessly bland versions. Whatever we know about memory, thought, passion, or any other worthy human process tell us that it is not the known and the settled but the unknown and the unsettled that provokes the use of mind, the awakening of consciousness . . Starting kids off with the familiar and then going out to the unfamiliar is altogether in violation of this deep principle of thought and of narrative.

These are stinging comments from four of education's most erudite and respected scholars. With one accord, all judge the expanding environments model to be the offspring of unsupported dogma and in violation of known principles of learning. Phenix, in a final passage, concludes his indictment of the model with the judgment that it is both "irrelevant to the child's growth and unduly limiting of normal development of thought and feeling," strong words indeed.

By contrast, three of these four scholars address the question of alternatives, and specifically propose history and literature as developmentally appropriate studies for the young child. "History and literature," Phenix wrote, ". . . are essentially concretizing presentations of human experience and are therefore best suited as a basis for social studies. These forms of symbolizing enlarge the child's experience as interesting unanalyzed wholes, from which as he grows older abstractions can be developed." Among the virtues of history for children, Phenix noted its ability vicariously to provide "a sense of personal involvement in exemplary lives and significant events, and to supply an appreciation of values and vision of greatness, all this within the context of moving narrative and dramatic appeal."

Parents, children's librarians, and teachers of the young have long known the power of superbly written biographies, myths, legends, folktales, and historical narratives to capture children's imagination and to hold their interest. Incorporating enduring themes of conflict and personal choice; of sacrifice and responsibility; of power and oppression; of struggle, failure, and achievement, sometimes against overwhelming odds, these stories connect in powerful ways with these same impulses and conflicts in children's own lives. They engage children vicariously in the experiences and perspectives of others, expand their ability to see the world through other's eyes, and enlarge their vision of lives well lived and of their own human potential.

Whether these biographies, stories, and narrative histories are drawn from the recent past or from some long-ago reaches of human history is not the critical factor in their accessibility to children. Rather, it is the nature of the story told, its power to capture children's imagination, to draw them into the historical event or human dilemma, and to speak to children on matters of enduring worth that should determine its selection for inclusion in the curriculum.

The continuing appeal of Aesop's fables, the tales of Robin Hood, or the frontier adventures of Wilder's *Little House* series speaks to this point. So, too, does the extraordinary success of the Odyssey and Aeneid programs for elementary schools that are sponsored by the American Philological Association through teacher institutes supported by the National Endowment for the Humanities and operating today in individual schools throughout the United States.

Reporting on the success of these programs in their schools, one group of teachers commented that the *Aeneid* addressed universal questions as it recounted particular events. Students who are so frequently uprooted themselves can identify with the Trojans in their wandering. Those who have lost a parent or a friend can mourn with Aeneas as he returns to Sicily for the funeral games. When students discuss the merits of the Trojan journey—asking whether Aeneas should remain with Dido, whether the Trojan women were justified in burning the ships—they participate as actors in the past. They come to understand circumstances and character, to begin to grasp their own part in the spiritual civilization that continues into the present moment.

Observing how children's involvement in the adventures of Aeneas had spread throughout all levels of one elementary school, one observer from the National Endowment for the Humanities asked why children found these programs interesting. "They're so exciting," came one child's eager answer, immediately echoed by the rest. One is reminded of Paul Hanna's 1935 indictment of the history-centered programs he was seeking to displace. He objected to them, he said, because they provided children a "happy life for the few hours they spend in school"! Given the terrible strains of the Depression years, children should, he argued, be engaged instead in community studies of the great social and economic ills then facing the nation. But can these programs really be historical if children have not yet grasped the structure of time and chronology necessary for placing long-ago events in their proper historical context and relationship to each other? The answer, of course, lies in understanding and working with the developmental sequence through which children achieve such higher powers of historical thinking. Recent studies by Levstik and Pappas (1987) support these observations by demonstrating that second-grade students can think, and that continuing growth in their historical understanding proceeds developmentally over the elementary school years.

It matters not that young children have no well-developed mental maps of time for placing people's adventures in temporal relationship according to years, decades, centuries, or eras. For young children it is enough to know that they happened "long ago." Before "I was born?" younger children may ask. "Oh, yes." "Before my mother was a little girl?" they may continue. "Yes, even before that. Long before that." "Oh, long ago," they may solemnly conclude. And soon, more refined time concepts take shape, as teachers help children to differentiate today, yesterday, long ago, long, long ago. The concept of time, children quickly learn, is a spatial one, involving the mental construction of a continuum of time along which events can be arranged. Historical dates are irrelevant in these early stages and do not belong in the primary classroom, for the mathematical understandings that make their relationships meaningful are not yet formed. But the spatial learnings that allow these critical insights to develop are under way.

Within their first five years of life, young children, we now know, develop ordered sets of causal, spatial, and temporal relationships that render their world not a "buzzing, booming confusion," but a causally ordered, comprehensible, and meaningful environment. This process starts in early infancy. Infant cognitive development is now found to be surprisingly abstract, with infants even in their first year of life using rules for dealing with time, space, and causal relationships. "Well-mothered" infants, interacting with a caring adult, repeatedly play out motion-time-and-space patterns that test their environment and disclose its regularities. Interacting with their environment in this manner, and then "turning over in their minds" what they have discovered, infants develop their sense of order and their rules for operating within the regularities of their world.

As infants gain mobility, their exploratory world widens, and with it the complexity of their temporal, spatial, and causal understandings. Depending upon the richness of experiences available to children and the nurturing they receive from supportive and interested adults, the years of later infancy can be a time of increasing problem solving, creative play, and abstract symbolization. By ages three and four, well-nurtured children regularly produce "mental maps" or cognitive patterns of time and spatial relationships that they have abstracted and detached from the specific activities that brought them forth.

So important are the growing networks of spatial understandings developed during these early years, that psychologists who have studied their development suggest that "spatial knowing" may in fact be paradigmatic for the ways children come to know. Spatializing the non-spatial, their findings suggest, may in important ways facilitate learning even in non-spatial fields.

This notion is intriguing and brings to mind two down-to-earth examples of teachers who have had good success developing in young children some early understandings of historical time. One, an inner-city supervising teacher, constructs with them a temporal sequence of events using a clothesline and clothespins that together create a visual representation of the passage of time. The children first tie a knot near one end of the clothesline to represent "today" and then clip at that place a recent photo of themselves. They then move back a little distance along the clothesline to attach a baby picture brought from home. After the teacher read a biography of Martin Luther King, Jr. to the class, the children made drawings illustrating the Reverend King's life and clipped them to the line farther back in time. The Reverend King, they then understood, lived earlier, a contemporary of their grandparents. A "long, long ago" story is similarly illustrated and attached to the time line still farther back, a process repeated as each new historical story is read to the children. Inevitable, dinosaurs are brought up, and children decide that these precursors of the human story should occupy a place on the time line long, long, long, long ago.

Spatially displayed on this clothesline's representation of time, these historical moments become easily accessible to children in terms of their "before" and "after" relationships and establish a sense of historical analysis in coming years. Another teacher, this one of somewhat older children, lacking bulletin board space, converts the classroom windows along one side of her room into a time line. Then, as her third graders' study of their local history unfolds, they paint pictures to illustrate specific historic events and tape them to the windows, in succession, to represent each succeeding period of their study, from prehistoric to modern times.

By the middle elementary years, mathematical understandings are sufficiently developed to allow children's meaningful identification of years, decades, and centuries on the basic time line, and their accurate placing of events according to the date of their occurrence. By this age, children's intellectual development also permits some kinds of historical analysis that link events in terms of their antecedents and consequences and support early stages of causal analyses.

One should not, of course, overreach the limitations of children's thinking in this regard. Analyzing the multiple causes of an event (the Revolutionary War, for example, in a fifth-grade study of American history) is a developmental achievement in preadolescence and requires strong instructional support. It is important to remember that in history, as in mathematics, science, or any other field of learning, the process is developmental. Children will not approach all at once the intellectual complexity demanded by historical analysis. It is folly, however, to suggest for that reason that history should not be taught in elementary schools. Leaving all such instruction to later secondary years, when the adolescent mind has emerged "recognizably adult," would be incomprehensible in other fields of school learning. We do not defer all instruction in mathematics to the senior high school and then rush students through textbooks of a thousand pages or more in a forced march to "cover" the material for which no prior foundations or deep personal interests have been established. Only in history are such approaches seriously contemplated and applied. The unhappy results are widely evident in the displeasure high school students take when a meaningless parade of facts, dates, and hurried events is imposed upon them.

Historical thinking, including causal analysis, takes many years to acquire, but its foundation is rightly laid in the elementary school. One approach being developed for older children in our work with experienced Teacher Associates in the National Center for History in the Schools incorporates striking a balance between (1) rich narrative history that moves the chronology of events along a compelling and interesting manner and (2) specific "dramatic moments" in the narrative that the students plumb, looking for deeper meanings of the selected landmark events and turning points in the historical narrative. The dramatic moments chosen are those that best bring the period vividly alive for students out of the problems and actions of real men, women, and children who were caught up in the forces of their time.

In developing the "dramatic moments," we use history as the great integrative and synthesizing discipline of the social studies, since understanding historical events involves geographic and economic analysis and the study of political institutions, to mention several of the social sciences that are embraced by thick historical narrative. Take geography as an example. Studying why societies developed when and where they did reveals the critical geographic relationships among site, resources, people's technological skills, and settlement patterns. Studying human movement, a dominant theme throughout all of history, must include the motivations that drove such migrations as the European conquest and colonization of the Americas, the enforced transport of millions of Africans to these regions, the westward movement of American settlers into the trans-Appalachia and trans-Mississippi territories, and the northward movements of Mexican settlers into their vast territories in present-day western and southwestern United States.

A history-centered curriculum for elementary school children can be a rich curriculum indeed, drawing widely upon learning in the social sciences and the humanities and deeply involving children through activities that are developmentally appropriate. It remains, then, to consider how such a curriculum might best be organized for learning across the elementary school years. The California curriculum framework offers one approach by beginning each year of instruction from kindergarten through grade two in the child's immediate present and then moving outward in space and back in time to enrich children's geographical and historical understandings. The model is sometimes termed the "here-there-then" approach to widening children's horizons and expanding their universe into realms far beyond their immediate surroundings. With the middle grades the curriculum becomes history centered and adopts a rich narrative approach in grade-three studies of local history, grade-four studies of state history, grade-five studies of American history through 1850 (and of the immigrant experience 1850 through the present day), and grade-six studies of the ancient world, in which children will have developed interests, through the lively literary selections in mythology, folktales, narrative histories, and literature provided throughout the preceding grades.

A second approach, also recommended by the Bradley Commission's 1988 guidelines for history in schools, follows the conventional "expanding environments" curriculum but includes yearly historical and literary studies that connect with that year's topics of family, neighborhood, or community, thus wrenching them free from the narrow presentation from which they now suffer. By incorporating literary selections and historical studies of children, families, communities, peoples, and nations throughout the grades, this modification opens for children far richer and more engaging materials than most now enjoy.

A third pattern recommended by the Bradley Commission centers around yearly instruction in literature and primary documents that are then studied in relation to the historical times they bring to life. The pattern is, essentially, a child's version of the "Great Books" approach to curriculum making, with literature used to take children into adventurous excursions through historical periods.

Are teachers ready for such changes? Our wide experiences with teachers in the field strongly suggest that this is the case. The elementary curriculum has become so thin, so skills driven, so intellectually sterile and boring to teachers and students alike that teachers are reaching out with enthusiasm for a curriculum that returns to classrooms the pleasures of stories worth telling, of ideas worth pursuing, of adventures that capture and hold children's attention and lead them into the historical perspectives that help each find his or her place in the long sweep of human history.

Charlotte Crabtree is a professor in the Graduate School of Education at the University of California, Los Angeles, where she specializes in curriculum theory. She was principal co-writer, with Diane Ravitch, of the California History-Social Science Framework, 1987, and is director of the National Center for History in the Schools, a cooperative research program of UCLA and the National Endowment for the Humanities.

This article is adapted with permission of Macmillan Publishing Company from *Historical Literacy: The Case For History in the Schools.* © 1989, Educational Excellence Network.

References

Crabtree, Charlotte. "History Is For Children." *American Educator,* 34–39.

CHAPTER 38

The Magic of Music Across the Curriculum

Music is part of our every day lives. Music motivates us to respond in many ways. It stimulates us to sing, drives us to dance, taps our imagination, and encourages us to participate in social function. All of these highly motivating forces work hand in hand with children's natural abilities. Young children's talents and abilities become apparent as they are exposed to appropriate music.

While there are those who consider music and the arts superfluous frills when it comes to budgeting, the people in the schools are the first to cry for its return after every fiscal crisis. In his article, in the *New York Times* (Sept., 10, 1989) "The Arts are Basic," Albert Shanker talks about how the arts encourage diverse thinking, problem solving, respect for our multi-cultural society, and most of all reach children's untapped talents and hidden abilities. Music permeates the curriculum as it crosses over into all the other arts including drama, dance, literature, and poetry as well as the Basic 3 "R's."

Reading, Rhythm, and Rhyme

Tradition tells us that children love the classical nursery rhymes. They love to respond to their jingling sounds, rhythmic patterns, and love to dramatize the actions of the characters. The rhyming words and sounds enhance ear training, extend vocabulary, and enrich language skills. Singing rhymes and songs further provide experiences with sequencing. The rhythmic patterns, the rhyming sounds, and the events of the story within the nursery rhyme all provide these reading skills. Ultimately, children are able to read these rhymes from the printed page along with their illustrations. Once these basic skills have been developed, creative activities can be encouraged. Original poetry and parodies are challenging activities that these children can aspire to.

Music, Motion, and Mathematics

We walk in rhythm. We march in rhythm. We dance in rhythm. When we listen to music our bodies respond intuitively to its rhythmic patterns.

The hands of the clock move in rhythm. The earth rotates in rhythm as it revolves around the sun with the other planets within our solar system. Time, rhythm, and mathematics strive for perfection. When we convey to our children the precision and order of mathematics, we find that songs about counting and counting games have inherent self-motivating qualities that promote success as children sing and move to music. Songs about the three kittens, the three pigs, the big bad wolf, the seven dwarfs, and the ten little Indians further enhance counting experiences. In addition, circle games provide children with invaluable knowledge about their own bodies, laterality and directionality.

Music, Social Studies, and Drama

The beauty of America lies in its cultural diversity. This cultural diversity continues to grow as a broader spectrum of immigrants continue to come to our shores further enriching our culture. A school's social studies program should include music from countries around the world, along with their customs, ceremonies, songs, and dances. All of us share the universal language of music, which allows our similarities and feelings to surface, while our differences fade.

As children learn about famous historical figures along with fictional giants of literature, there are many opportunities to write class plays enhanced by songs and music. The integrative link between Social Studies and English can by musical plays and puppet productions starting in the early years. Certainly, Mark Russell has shown that musical parodies about politics and current events in not just a favorite amusement vehicle for children.

The Science of Sound

At a very early age young children enjoy experimenting with sounds produced by striking rhythm band percussion instruments. They love the tooting, jingling, clanging, strumming, and drumming of these instruments. Finding out which sounds are produced by forced air, sound waves produced by striking percussion instruments, or sounds produced by strumming string instruments opens the door to stimulating children's curiosities about the mysteries of sounds.

Sounds of the Synthesizer

The most recent significant contribution, through advanced technology, has been the mass production of the electric keyboards and synthesizers for the home. The home keyboards now make it possible for very young children to learn how to play, experiment with sounds and rhythms, and imitate playing the instruments of the orchestra. This new style of learning music now makes it possible for every child to have a full music education. This can only come about with the schools upgrading their music and art programs.

Regina Persky is an Early Childhood Teacher, P.S. 272, Brooklyn, New York City Schools.

References

Cocks, Jay. "Keys to the Kingdom." *Time Magazine,* March 6, 1989, 64.
Shanker, Albert. "The Arts Are Basic." *New York Times,* September 10, 1989, 10.

CHAPTER 39

Designing the Environment of a Quality Childhood Center

Robert Sommer, a psychologist, has studied the effects of environment on behavior apart from environment, even in utero" (Sommer, 1974). Recent studies have begun to explore the implications of this statement for the neonate in areas as varied as alcohol, tobacco, drugs, and AIDS, to avoidance of intrusive instruments in procedures such as amniocentesis, to the effects of music played for the embryo in the womb. Philosophers, educators and psychologists have been aware of the influence of the environment on the child for centuries.

Jean Jacques Rousseau in his classic *Emile* physically removed this fictional child from his family to the seclusion of the countryside where he would not be contaminated by the evil ways of the society. G. Stanley Hall, who coined the term "paidocentric," or child-centered, conducted one of the first major investigations of the influences of environment on the child, in the manuscript "The Contents of Children's Minds." Based on a rather unscientific survey, Hall concluded that children's concepts vary widely with all changes in their environment. He urged parents and teachers to familiarize children with "natural objects" which he thought would increase the conceptual range of children's minds (Hall, 1883). This recognition of the value of studying the child was one of the factors responsible for the nursery school movement from the end of the nineteenth century to the beginning of the twentieth century.

Maria Montessori, the first woman doctor in Italy (1896), and later the founder of the Montessori Method of Education, drew heavily upon her medical background using what she called the "union of pedagogy and medicine" in the development of a prepared environment. Much of this highly didactic, individualized, self-chosen, self-correcting system can be found in today's accepted definition of quality early childhood education as espoused in the National Association for Early Childhood Education's "Guidelines for Appropriate Curriculum Content and Assessment in Programs Serving Children 3 through 8 Years of Age."

The Swiss psychologist, Jean Piaget, who was a student in Maria Montessori's teacher training program, extended the importance of the environment beyond the traditional definition which includes physical space, furnishings and equipment, materials, and scheduling. He took the position which has come to be known as the "constructivist theory" which asserts that children build their own learning by interacting with their environments. The importance of play as a vehicle of learning cannot be overemphasized. It is through this medium that the total child is developed. Many early childhood programs stress a single facet of development such as cognitive skills or socialization to the exclusion of all others. Total development encompasses the physical, intellectual, sensual, creative, emotional, social, and spiritual needs and interests of the child. The mnemonic aid PISCES(S) is helpful in planning learning experiences in the early childhood classroom. Early childhood teachers who are concerned with the development of the whole child have learned it is necessary to teach "children" not "lessons." Their daily preparation requires that they focus on seven aforementioned areas for growth and change.

This brief outline may appear artificial in that many of these areas can overlap, rightfully so, because it is difficult to compartmentalize the whole child. However, it will serve to demonstrate the multifaceted nature of the youngster in an early childhood classroom.

Research has clearly demonstrated that play is the main avenue of a child's development. Play enables children to develop fine and gross motor skills, enhance language development, practice problem solving, use their senses to acquire new ideas and organize old knowledge, to explore different media, role play, work out emotional needs and to develop prosocial behaviors and a conscience, to name just a few benefits.

Decisions on how best to set up the early childhood environment for the needs and interests of the child inevitably derive from a particular perspective or theoretical framework. In keeping with the idea of the development of the whole child, David Elkind has said:

> Young children's learning is permeable. Children do not organize their thinking and knowledge in subject matter areas such as reading, math, science, and art. Rather their thinking is organized around projects, activities and frames. Each project, activity, or frame includes skills and information which at a later age might be grouped under one or another subject matter category, but which for young children are part of a global whole (Bredekamp, 1989).

The following six developmental assumptions will be utilized as the basis for designing a quality early childhood environment that will meet the developmental levels and learning styles of young children:

1. Children construct knowledge
2. Children learn through experimentation and manipulation
3. Children learn through constructive error
4. Children learn through play

5. Children learn through social interaction
6. Children's interests and "need to know" motivate learning (Bredekamp, 1989).

If, indeed, children construct their own knowledge then the learning environment must provide the physical space and materials children need for exploration. Between 30 and 50 square feet of indoor free floor space per child and 75 square feet of outdoor space per child has been recommended as ideal for preschool and primary classrooms. Space for storage of their clothing and belongings is essential, too. Montessori was also the first person to realize that low open shelves for storing materials was necessary so that children can make independent choices of materials and also be responsible for replacing them after they have finished using them. She also developed the concept of self-space defined by a rug on the floor or mat at a table. This private space enables a child to work on his or her own project without interruption or if the child so chooses s(he) may invite another child to share the space. Montessori provided only one piece of each type of didactic equipment per classroom. More current research (Rohe and Patterson, 1974; Smith and Connolly, 1980) has shown when there are few toys and many children in a play environment, they tend to congregate in larger groups, and the combination of confined space and paucity of materials tends to result in more aggression amongst the children, Weinstein (1979), in a review of the research on the physical environment of the school, suggests that learning centers which have been set up in early childhood classrooms have "coercive power" over the children which curbs certain behaviors and inspires others. She states that different educational activities require different environments, as do different children and that sensitivity to the environment may differ with development age. Altman and Wohlwill suggest that young children may be particularly sensitive to modification in their environment, while Phyfe-Perkins (1979) contends the "skill of arranging the early childhood environment to support the maximum involvement of children with materials and with each other is a skill that can and should be taught (Day, 1988).

Provision for children to learn through experience and manipulation requires the teacher to arrange the room so that it facilitates learning. The arrangement will change as children grow and mature or as their interests require a different organization. Children should be involved in the re-arrangement of the classroom. Young children can derive much pleasure and learning experiences from clearly delineated work and play areas planned around different themes called interest centers. Interest centers are designed to meet the broad goals of a program, and to meet children's need for activities, decision making and interaction. Interest centers differ from learning centers in that the latter are much more specific and are designed to teach, reinforce, clarify and extend learning objectives, with specific objectives for each center usually identified. Rosenthal (1974) found that the length of stay in a center was attributable to the center's ability to hold the child's interest rather than to the child's attention span (Day, 1988). Centers which are commonly found in early childhood settings are blocks, dramatic play, library, manipulative play, music, art, writing, and science. In these centers children will have the opportunity to manipulate and experience a wide variety of media.

Children's active involvement and experimentation is their method of research. Montessori has described the process of constructive error as auto-education. This process is divided into two separate phases. The first she calls the unconscious absorbent mind. In this stage, the child between the ages of birth and three years old takes in all of the knowledge from his/her environment. In the second stage, the conscious absorbent mind, between the ages of three and six years old, the child organizes this knowledge into distinct categories and classifications. This latter period requires a prepared environment which is developmentally arranged and child-sized so that the child can have a hands-on experience with the materials. These materials are self-correcting so that there is little input from the teacher. The child is able to draw his/her own conclusions and construct his/her own knowledge. Piaget terms all of the knowledge that a person has as his/her scheme or schema. He contends that when no learning is taking place the child is in a state of equilibration. For construction of knowledge to occur there must be a state of disequilibration. Through a process of assimilation the child attempts to compare and contrast the new knowledge to what is already in his/her schema and eventually through a series of trial and error accommodates the new ideas into an expanded schema.

Play, as noted, serves a variety of functions in a child's world. According to Rogers (1985), the major function of play is active mastery. With this in mind, David Weikart, one of the principal investigators in the High/Scope Foundation's Perry Preschool study, a twenty year longitudinal study, set out to answer the question "Can high quality early childhood education help to improve the lives of low-income children and their families and the quality of life of the community as a whole?" (Berrueta-Clement, et. al., 1982). In phase one he focused mainly on setting up a high quality early childhood program which had cognitive development as its primary goal. The focus of this program was play and child-initiated activities as contrasted with a direct-instruction program and a traditional nursery school program. As this study progressed through the years it began to look at school achievement patterns and family attitudes. "Real world measures grew in importance and included examinations of scholastic placement, delinquent behavior, after school employment, and cost benefit analysis" (Berrueta-Clement et. al., 1982). They followed these initial children until the age of nineteen. The curriculum became more developed but always included play and self-chosen activities by children. The results indicate lasting effects of pre-school education by those groups which were child-centered rather than teacher-directed; i.e. the High/ Scope Model where children and teachers set up the environment to include interest centers to encourage active learning and the traditional nursery school where the children initiated their own companions. As children get to know one another better, they interact more frequently, intensely and competently" (Berk, 1989). Additional research on class size has demonstrated that smaller group size contributes to more intense and cooperative social interaction amongst children. Studying the development of peer interaction amongst toddlers, Vandell and Mueller (1977) reported that the number and complexity of interchange increased when the youngsters played in twos rather than in a group situation (Berk, 1989).

In addition to the research on the scarcity of materials encouraging aggressiveness, studies have focused on the types of toys in the environment. It has been shown that giving children toys with specific purposes such as dolls or trucks as opposed to materials with ambiguous functions such as pipe cleaners, cylinders or paper bags influences peer sociability. The former led to realistic role playing amongst the children while the latter led to greater fantasy play and increased social interaction with greater planning for the play (McLoyd, Warren and Thomas, 1984).

Another area of the environment which researchers (Lougee, Grueneich, and Hartup, 1977; Graziano, et. al, 1976; Graziano and Musser, 1983) have assessed is the interaction of different age groups in the same classroom. It was determined that under mixed-age conditions there was more inter-age interaction from younger children while older children made special accommodations for the younger ones by reducing their rate of social communication and assuming greater responsibility for task performance. However, for both preschool and elementary age children it has been reported (Day and Hunt, 1975; Lederberg, et. al, 1986, Roopnarine and Johnson, 1984) that same-age interaction is more positive, more verbal, and more likely to bring on more cooperative play (Berk, 1989).

Children also interact with same sex peers more frequently. This tendency is apparent by two years of age, extremely young considering they are just beginning to move out of the stage of solitary play. Research has shown that mixed-sex play can be promoted if the environment of the classroom is changed. One study demonstrated that boys and girls played together more after a wall of shelves separating the housekeeping and block areas was taken down permitting greater interchange between the two (Kinsman and Berk, 1979). Contrary findings were reported by Feld who studied the relationship between teacher/child ratios and partitioned play areas yielded "optimal" behaviors including interactions with peers, verbal interactions, fantasy play, and associative-cooperative play (Feld, 1980). Much current literature deals with the ways in which both of these areas of the classroom can be changed to encourage use by both sexes, concurrently. Classroom research has demonstrated that in the block corner, boys generally build up and girls build out. A simple solution for encouraging participation by girls seems to be to enlarge the block area as well as enlisting female teachers to participate in traditionally "male" activities.

Systematic assessment of the classroom environment and how it is responding to children's interests and "need to know" will alert a teacher to those areas of the room that are being under-utilized or improperly utilized. Interest centers that have been free play activities and the teachers played a supporting but noninterfering role. They show increased intellectual performance in early childhood, fewer students who were either retained in a grade or placed in special education settings during their years in school, with greater numbers graduating from high school and enrolling in post-secondary education; decreased self-reported juvenile delinquency or policy arrests; and less usage of welfare assistance and less teenage pregnancy.

The authors conclude:

> These benefits considered in terms of their economic value make the preschool program a worthwhile investment for society . . . The positive implications of these findings for improved quality of life for participating individuals, their families, and the community at large are of enormous importance (Berrueta-Clement, et. al., 1982).

Other research has found that "on the whole, children in highly structured classes displayed more self-regulatory behaviors" (Huston-Stein, et. al., 1977) which at first glance appears to contradict the data on juvenile delinquency and police arrests, but the authors caution that the "results cannot be interpreted with certainty as indicating that the classroom structure influenced the children's behavior," because it must be taken into consideration that the highly structured classrooms correlated with large class size that was made up of white ethnic children. These same children were found to engage in less imaginative play than those in lower structured classrooms. It is clear that play is a major component needed in a high quality early childhood education environment for children of all socio-economic backgrounds to meet a broad range of developmental goals.

Dr. Phyllis Povell, Chairperson, Dept. of Curriculum and Instruction, Long Island University/C. W. Post Campus

References

Berk, L. E. *Child Development.* Boston: Allyn and Bacon, 1989.

Berrueta-Clement, J., Schweinhart, L. J., & et. al. *Changed Lives: The Effects of the Perry Preschool Project on Youths Through Age 19.* Ypsilanti, Michigan: The High/Scope Press, 1982.

Bredekamp, S. *Guidelines for Appropriate Curriculum Content and Assessment in Programs Serving Children 3 through 8 Years of Age. Draft.* Washington, D.C.: National Association for the Education of Young Children, 1989.

Day, B. *Early Childhood Education: Creative Learning Activities.* Third Edition. New York: Macmillan Publishing Co., 1988.

Feld, T. M. "Preschool Play: Effects of Teacher/Child Ratios and Organization of Classroom Space." *Child Study Journal,* 1980, 10: 3, 191–205.

Hall, G. S. "The Contents of Children's Minds." *Princeton Review,* 1883, 11, 249–272.

Huston-Stein, A., Friedrich-Cofer, L. & Susman, E. J. "The Relation of Classroom Structure to Social Behavior, Imaginative Play, and Self-Regulation of Economically Disadvantaged Children." *Child Development,* 1977, 48, 907–916.

McLoyd, V. C., Warren, D., & Thomas, E. A. C. Anticipatory and Fantastic Role Enactment in Preschool Triads." *Developmental Psychology,* 1984, 20, 807–814.

Rogers, D. L. "Relationships Between Block Play and Social Relationships of Children." *Early Childhood Development and Care,* 1985, 20, 245–261.

Sommer, R. *Tight Spaces.* Englewood Cliffs, N.J.: Prentice Hall, 1974.